Praise for *MCU*

"These three authors—Ms. [Joanna] Robinson and ~~.~~ ~~~~
zales are pop-culture podcasters, while Mr. [Gavin] Edwards has
written a number of books about Hollywood—weave new details
into their narrative of Marvel's rise. Celebrity-watchers will appreciate the alternate-casting ideas that might have reshaped some of
our era's biggest blockbusters—imagine *True Blood* star Alexander Skarsgård as Thor. There's a remarkable business story here as
well. . . . Success . . . they argue, became possible when Hollywood's
creative franchises learned to adhere to a few significant principles. . . . [W]atching the story of a legendary team coming apart can be
just as fascinating as watching it coming together."

—Julia Alexander, *Wall Street Journal*

"Undoubtedly qualifies as the definitive history of the MCU. . . . Robinson, Gonzales and Edwards combined their powers to create an expan-
sive historical tome with the grandiosity of an Asgardian thunder god,
the guts of a boy-scout super solider and the wit of a genius billionaire
playboy philanthropist. *MCU: The Reign of Marvel Studios* is about as
all-encompassing as one could hope for when it comes to charting the
rise of this modern (and mad) Hollywood titan."

—Joshua Axelrod, *Pittsburgh Post-Gazette*

"A highly entertaining, well-researched, wide-ranging, detailed, and
objective examination of one of the greatest Hollywood success stories. Documenting this specific story illuminates the universal story of
big-budget studio filmmaking in the 21st century. There will never be
another story like the Marvel Studios story, and maybe there shouldn't
be. But those who want to understand this phenomenal story can do no
better than read *MCU: The Reign of Marvel Studios*."

—Michael Curley, *PopMatters*

"Not to skip to the post-credits scene, but the book is necessary reading for anyone who fancies themselves an MCU fan. . . . [H]onest and

unmerciful. . . . *MCU: The Reign of Marvel Studios* delivers a wealth of new context. . . . It's a testament to the authors that the narrative thread remains easy to follow given the growing expanse of Marvel Studios' reach. . . . There is no better document charting Marvel's improbable rise and total disruption of the Hollywood paradigm than [*MCU*]. Readers are sure to learn something new on every page, from which MCU stars first auditioned for roles years earlier to exactly what happened with Edgar Wright's *Ant-Man*. A volume of trivia, drama, and humor, *MCU: The Reign of Marvel Studios* belongs on every Marvel fan's bookshelf."

—Carlos Freytes, *Agents of Fandom*

"Over the course of more than 500 pages and hundreds of interviews, the authors explore how an iconic 20th-century comic-book brand pretty much willed itself into becoming this century's most potent box-office force. The focus is not on a critical dissection of the individual movies; instead, the book concerns itself with the people and decisions that have shaped Marvel Studios from before *Iron Man* through today."

—Josef Adalian, *Vulture*

"*MCU* reveals the real saga behind the Marvel Cinematic Universe. . . . [A] fresh backstage perspective into the successes, failures, and twists that have spanned Marvel's long production history. I thought I knew everything there was to know about the MCU, but the book is filled with revelations I never imagined. . . . [*MCU*] is not only enlightening, but enthralling."

—Vin Aziz, *Cosmic Circus*

"A superb chronicle of how Marvel Studios conquered Hollywood. . . . This definitive account of the Hollywood juggernaut thrills."

—*Publishers Weekly*, starred review

"[A] compulsively readable book. . . . Marvel fans and film aficionados alike will appreciate this highly recommended, smashing insider look at one of entertainment's greatest success stories."

—*Library Journal*, starred review

MCU

The Reign of Marvel Studios

✴

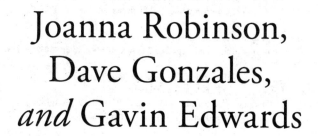

Joanna Robinson,
Dave Gonzales,
and Gavin Edwards

LIVERIGHT PUBLISHING CORPORATION

A Division of W. W. Norton & Company

INDEPENDENT PUBLISHERS SINCE 1923

For information about permission to reproduce selections from this book,
write to Permissions, Liveright Publishing Corporation, a division of
W. W. Norton & Company, Inc., 500 Fifth Avenue, New York, NY 10110

For information about special discounts for bulk purchases, please contact
W. W. Norton Special Sales atspecialsales@wwnorton.com or 800-233-4830

Manufacturing by Lakeside Book Company
Book design by Lovedog Studio
Design graphic (shield): ©focalpoint - Can Stock Photo Inc.
Production manager: Lauren Abbate

Library of Congress Control Number: 2024941151

ISBN 978-1-324-09558-3 pbk.

Liveright Publishing Corporation, 500 Fifth Avenue, New York, N.Y. 10110
www.wwnorton.com

W. W. Norton & Company Ltd., 15 Carlisle Street, London W1D 3BS

10 9 8 7 6 5 4 3 2 1

To Diana, through friendship, failure, and cake.

To Java, for her support through pandemic and publishing.

To Dash, my favorite movie fan.

CONTENTS

Phase Zero

Phase One

Phase Two

Phase Three

Phase Four

MCU TIMELINE

An overview of Marvel Cinematic Universe releases and important moments in Marvel Studios history. Select non–Marvel Studios projects featuring Marvel characters are added for context; they appear in [brackets and dark gray type].

1990s

- April 22, 1993—Marvel puts Avi Arad in charge of film and TV projects
- August 1996—Marvel Studios founded
- June 28, 1998—Toy Biz, run by Ike Perlmutter, acquires Marvel and creates Marvel Enterprises
- [August 21, 1998—*Blade*]

2000

- [July 14, 2000—*X-Men*]
- August 1, 2000—Kevin Feige's first day under contract at Marvel

2002

- [May 3, 2002—*Spider-Man*]

2003

- [February 14, 2003—*Daredevil*]
- [June 20, 2003—*Hulk*]

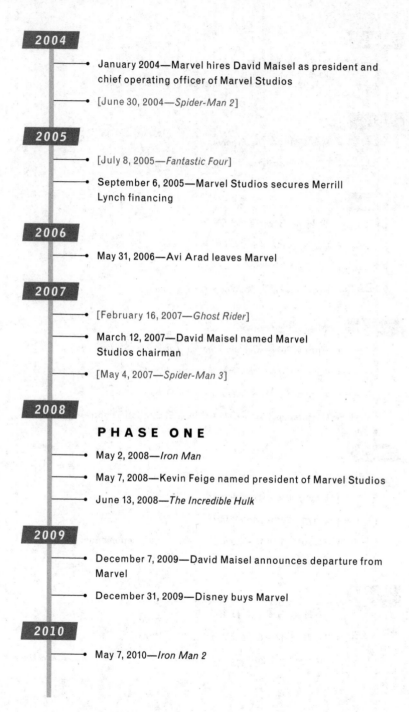

2004

January 2004—Marvel hires David Maisel as president and chief operating officer of Marvel Studios

[June 30, 2004—*Spider-Man 2*]

2005

[July 8, 2005—*Fantastic Four*]

September 6, 2005—Marvel Studios secures Merrill Lynch financing

2006

May 31, 2006—Avi Arad leaves Marvel

2007

[February 16, 2007—*Ghost Rider*]

March 12, 2007—David Maisel named Marvel Studios chairman

[May 4, 2007—*Spider-Man 3*]

2008

PHASE ONE

May 2, 2008—*Iron Man*

May 7, 2008—Kevin Feige named president of Marvel Studios

June 13, 2008—*The Incredible Hulk*

2009

December 7, 2009—David Maisel announces departure from Marvel

December 31, 2009—Disney buys Marvel

2010

May 7, 2010—*Iron Man 2*

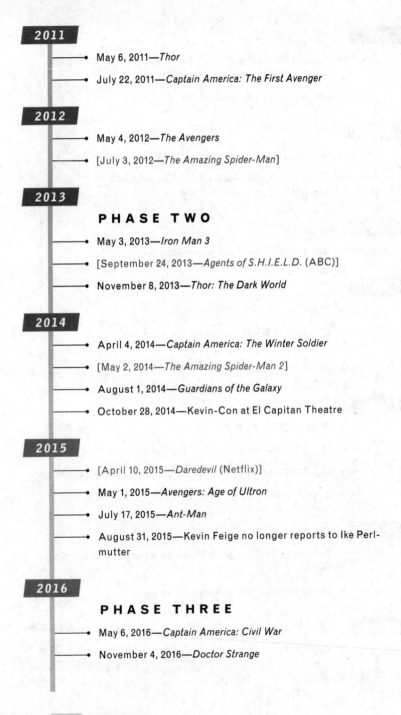

2011

- May 6, 2011—*Thor*
- July 22, 2011—*Captain America: The First Avenger*

2012

- May 4, 2012—*The Avengers*
- [July 3, 2012—*The Amazing Spider-Man*]

2013

PHASE TWO

- May 3, 2013—*Iron Man 3*
- [September 24, 2013—*Agents of S.H.I.E.L.D.* (ABC)]
- November 8, 2013—*Thor: The Dark World*

2014

- April 4, 2014—*Captain America: The Winter Soldier*
- [May 2, 2014—*The Amazing Spider-Man 2*]
- August 1, 2014—*Guardians of the Galaxy*
- October 28, 2014—Kevin-Con at El Capitan Theatre

2015

- [April 10, 2015—*Daredevil* (Netflix)]
- May 1, 2015—*Avengers: Age of Ultron*
- July 17, 2015—*Ant-Man*
- August 31, 2015—Kevin Feige no longer reports to Ike Perlmutter

2016

PHASE THREE

- May 6, 2016—*Captain America: Civil War*
- November 4, 2016—*Doctor Strange*

2017

May 5, 2017—*Guardians of the Galaxy Vol. 2*

July 7, 2017—*Spider-Man: Homecoming*

November 3, 2017—*Thor: Ragnarok*

2018

February 16, 2018—*Black Panther*

April 27, 2018—*Avengers: Infinity War*

July 6, 2018—*Ant-Man and the Wasp*

[December 14, 2018—*Spider-Man: Into the Spider-Verse*]

2019

March 8, 2019—*Captain Marvel*

April 26, 2019—*Avengers: Endgame*

July 2, 2019—*Spider-Man: Far from Home*

October 15, 2019—Kevin Feige named chief creative officer for Marvel Enterprises

November 12, 2019—Disney Plus launches

2020

February 25, 2020—Bob Chapek replaces Bob Iger as Disney CEO

2021

PHASE FOUR

January 15, 2021—*WandaVision* (Disney Plus)

March 19, 2021—*The Falcon and the Winter Soldier* (Disney Plus)

June 9, 2021—*Loki* (Disney Plus)

July 9, 2021—*Black Widow*

August 11, 2021—*What If . . . ?* (Disney Plus)

September 3, 2021—*Shang-Chi and the Legend of the Ten Rings*

November 5, 2021—*Eternals*

November 24, 2021—*Hawkeye* (Disney Plus)

December 17, 2021—*Spider-Man: No Way Home*

2022

March 30, 2022—*Moon Knight* (Disney Plus)

May 6, 2022—*Doctor Strange in the Multiverse of Madness*

June 8, 2022—*Ms. Marvel* (Disney Plus)

July 8, 2022—*Thor: Love and Thunder*

August 18, 2022—*She-Hulk: Attorney at Law* (Disney Plus)

October 7, 2022—*Werewolf by Night* (Disney Plus)

November 11, 2022—*Black Panther: Wakanda Forever*

November 20, 2022—Bob Iger returns, replacing Bob Chapek as Disney CEO

November 25, 2022—*Guardians of the Galaxy Holiday Special* (Disney Plus)

2023

PHASE FIVE

February 17, 2023—*Ant-Man and the Wasp: Quantumania*

March 17, 2023—Victoria Alonso, president of physical and post production, visual effects, and animation, fired

March 29, 2023—Ike Perlmutter, Marvel Entertainment chairman and CEO, fired

May 5, 2023—*Guardians of the Galaxy Vol. 3*

[June 2, 2023—*Spider-Man: Across the Spider-Verse*]

June 21, 2023—*Secret Invasion* (Disney Plus)

October 5, 2023—*Loki* (season two) (Disney Plus)

November 10, 2023—*The Marvels*

December 22, 2023—*What If . . . ?* (season two) (Disney Plus)

2024

January 9, 2024—*Echo* (Disney Plus)

PROLOGUE

Origin Story

★

If you want to do something right, you make a list.

Ant-Man and the Wasp

MARK RUFFALO HAD NO IDEA HOW BIG THE FUTURE could be. But when he became a Marvel superhero, he found out.

In April 2012, Marvel Studios sent a team of its actors and producers to Europe to promote its sixth movie, *The Avengers*. (In Spain, it was called *Los Vengadores*; in the United Kingdom, it was retitled *Avengers Assemble* so it wouldn't be confused with the 1960s British spy TV series.) In London, Robert Downey Jr., louche in a plaid jacket and tinted glasses, charmed a room full of journalists by confessing that he had taken one of his character's Black Sabbath T-shirts from the set. "Do you know where I put it?" he joked. "I've mislocated it."

The expensive road show, financed by the Walt Disney Company, Marvel's brand-new owner, moved on to Rome, where the leading actors were greeted by a screaming crowd outside the Space Cinema Moderno, including some fans who were well-versed in the minutiae of Marvel costumes and props and mythology. One particularly enthusiastic Italian had a gift for Tom Hiddleston, the classically trained British actor who played the movie's villain (Loki, the conniving Norse god of mischief): a plush Kermit the Frog doll, dressed up in a Loki costume.

The Avengers, which brought together the superheroes that Marvel had established across four years of blockbuster movies, already looked like it was going to be a huge worldwide hit. It was the culmination of a decade of work by Marvel's producers and executives, including Kevin Feige, the president of Marvel Studios. It was also a sign that Marvel had placed a winning bet when, emerging from bankruptcy, the company had mortgaged the rights to its own characters to secure a line of credit from a Wall Street bank. The studio had staked its entire future on that loan, which financed the first movies Marvel Studios made.

On the night of April 21, after the Italian premiere, Feige went out to dinner with some of the movie's stars and producers at a family-owned restaurant called Antica Pesa. Scarlett Johansson, who played Natasha Romanoff, the lethal secret agent also called the Black Widow, was wearing a navy dress ornately patterned with flowers and honeycombs. Chris Hemsworth's posture was closer to surfer dude than Norse deity, and he kept his hair pulled back in a ponytail, but he remained, unmistakably, the heroic thunder god Thor. Even in a suit and tie, Ruffalo, who played the scientist Bruce Banner and his alter ego, the gargantuan green Hulk, looked rumpled, like a history professor who had fallen asleep during office hours. Back then, however, he was the only person at the meal with an Oscar nomination, for *The Kids Are Alright*. The Avengers table didn't have actual gods and superheroes seated around it, but it had movie stars—which in the twenty-first century, most people have decided are an acceptable substitute.

Like the other actors at the table, Hemsworth had made a multi-film commitment when he accepted his role in the Marvel movies: six movies, in his case. "I thought, 'Let's just make the first one,'" he remembered. "If I don't screw that up, I thought maybe I might be in the first Avengers movie, but I never thought there'd be a second one." Hemsworth tried to tell Feige that the studio's success stemmed from the talents and foresight of the production head himself. He wasn't sure whether Feige believed that, or even believed that Hemsworth meant it.

The dinner started late and ran even later, and the waitstaff got anxious, even if the restaurant was illuminated by the glow of celebrity. Many bottles of wine were brought to the table. And sometime after the homemade prosciutto and the grilled zucchini with goat cheese, but before the grilled beef with spinach and rosemary potatoes, Feige shared more about his vision for the future of Marvel. Nobody anticipated the breadth of his plans.

Just thirty-eight years old, Feige didn't carry himself like the head of a Hollywood studio, or like a veteran of bloody internal corporate battles who already ranked as one of the most successful movie producers of his generation. He seemed more like a film fan who had won a "Have Dinner with the Avengers" radio contest. But when he explained his ambitions for Marvel, which would span multiple series of interconnected movies, everybody fell silent.

"I would like to take all the comics and start to build the Marvel Universe," he told the table.

"That was the first time I ever heard him say 'Marvel Universe,'" Ruffalo remembered. "And I thought, *Okay, that's ambitious. That would be historical as far as filmmaking goes.*"

Feige's vision for Marvel wasn't linear, limited, or safe. He yearned to explore the weirder nooks and crannies of Marvel's comic-book history, and was excited about movies that would star wizards and African kings and secret enclaves of superpowered beings. (That would be Doctor Strange, Black Panther, and the Inhumans.) "We will have fifteen productions in the next two years," he said.

"That blew my mind," Ruffalo recalled. "I was like, *This guy isn't kidding.*"

"I'm socially awkward and not very good at talking about the weather or talking about the sports scores—I just talk about what I think we can do next," Feige admitted in 2017. "I always presume that people think that I'm full of crap, like many film people. Historically, ninety-nine percent of anything anybody says in Hollywood never actually happens. So I feel sensitive about that whenever I'm pitching anybody something. I'm thinking, 'Well, you probably think that this is just that ninety-nine-percent Hollywood talk, but we're going to work to do it.' "

In fact, Feige and his colleagues would deliver on almost every single promise he made that night. Some of the details would change along the way: the Inhumans would get consigned to a TV show, and although the *Civil War* movie he described as a future Avengers outing would star most of the superteam, it would technically be billed as a Captain America movie. But those were minor aspects of his grand scheme. By February 2024, when we finished writing the new chapter for the paperback edition of this book, Marvel had made thirty-three feature films with a worldwide gross of over $29 billion. Considered as a whole, that output was easily the most successful film series of all time. (In second place was the *Star Wars* series, with twelve movies grossing a total of $10.3 billion.) Connected and complicated by overlapping plotlines and dozens of TV shows, the films have formed a vast tapestry of character and incident and high emotion. Some have been defined by the conventions of the superhero genre, while others have expanded the possibilities of the form. And some have merged older modes of genre filmmaking with fantastical settings, resulting in outer-space swashbuckling and metafictional domestic dramas. No one thought that one movie franchise could contain installments that were variously a war movie, a superhero battle royale, and a paranoid political thriller, until Marvel did it with the Captain America movies.

The Marvel Cinematic Universe, or MCU, as it would quickly come to be known, is synonymous with the dominance, lauded and lamented, of the superhero movie. Yet even as the studio redefined the genre in its own image, and aggressively exercised quality control, it made sure to surprise its audience. Feige and the other producers could see the future and work their way toward it, but they also were able to adjust, to discard ideas that no longer worked, to veer off in unexpected directions. This flexibility, so unlikely with so much money on the line, is one of the central reasons for Marvel Studios' success.

"Phase One" of the MCU, when a nosy Italian waiter could over-hear Marvel's plans while topping off an Avenger's Chianti, is long in the past. Marvel Studios, like any show-business enterprise that becomes massively profitable, has adopted a code of secrecy as well as strict security protocols. Some of the biggest and most powerful stars in the world will look spooked if you ask for a nugget of future Marvel news. The studio has produced plenty of behind-the-scenes features and even a glossy coffee-table book on its own history, but anyone who was (or is) there knows that some of the crucial stories are missing. "Someday," a Marvel insider told us, "we knew all those stories would have to be told."

✱

WHEN WE BEGAN work on this book, Marvel Studios didn't obstruct us—for the first few months. Then we started getting word that Disney was asking people not to talk to us. Despite that stone-walling, we interviewed more than a hundred people who made the Marvel Cinematic Universe what it is, from Kevin Feige to the woman who designed the Stark Industries logo: producers, directors, movie stars, special-effects gurus, stunt doubles, writers, animators, hairstylists, set designers, showrunners, assistants, Oscar winners, personal trainers, and even Doctor Strange's Cloak of Levitation. Our sources told us about secret rooms, epiphanies in the desert, flying cars that never left the ground, a polka-dot horse, a mysteri-ous glut of purple pens, and screaming matches that almost became fistfights. We have also drawn on other books, magazine articles, and podcasts. We are far from the first writers, after all, to cover the MCU. But our ambition with this book is to tell those missing stories as part of the most thorough, authoritative history of Marvel Studios to date.

Although Feige wasn't looking for personal celebrity or conflict, he ended up with plenty of both. Marvel Studios willed itself into existence and then made one hit movie after another. Others in Hollywood tried very hard to mimic its success—and failed. But the story of Marvel Studios isn't one of inevitable ascent, not even in retrospect. The studio had to claw back the rights to characters that had been sold for quick hits of cash. When its parent company, Marvel Entertainment, established a heavy-handed Creative Committee to oversee the Marvel Cinematic Universe, Marvel Studios had to fight for control of its own movies. The Committee, obsessively focused on which characters would sell the most toys, preferred for Marvel's heroes to be played by young white men named Chris; Feige and his fellow producers fought for years to make movies around non-white and female superheroes. Some of the studio's early battles were internal: wrestling matches with stubborn directors and belligerent actors. When Feige became famous as the man behind an unblemished streak of blockbusters, however, he had to adjust to a different scale of conflict. Constructing a leviathan fantasy airship can be extremely challenging, but maintaining it and making sure it remains aloft while competitors try to shoot it out of the sky—or make their own, larger airships—is just as difficult.

The old Hollywood studio system was built around five major conglomerates—Paramount, Warner Bros., RKO, Loews/MGM, and 20th Century Fox—that in the 1930s and 1940s not only made hundreds of movies, treating their soundstages like factories, but controlled their own chains of cinemas that showcased the resulting products. A 1948 Supreme Court decision led to the breakup of those vertical monopolies, although the centralized studio system staggered on until the 1970s, when the movies those studios made started to feel painfully old-fashioned and they began to outsource creative control to a younger generation of filmmakers. In this book, we document how Marvel Studios grew by combining the improvisational bootstrap culture of a Silicon Valley start-up with a modern version of the studio system, signing up actors for long-term contracts, cultivating a coterie of staff writers, and bringing on a small army of visual artists who sometimes determined the look of a movie before a director was even hired. The only thing it lacked when compared to the old behemoths was its own means of distribution. That's where Disney came in. And beginning in 2019, Marvel Studios had access to Disney Plus, a streaming service that provides direct access to a vast number of homes (over 150 million by 2022).

The Marvel method could have ended up as an assembly line, but as with the old studio system, it has resulted in a mix of entertaining diversions and inarguable masterpieces. From the start, the Marvel Studios ethos was "best idea wins," and all of its productions were open to suggestions from anyone working on a movie, or even people who were just standing in the vicinity, like a studio janitor or a kid visiting the set. The studio made it possible for off-kilter geniuses to construct movies like *Guardians of the Galaxy* and *Thor: Ragnarok* and *Black Panther*, which melded big-budget superhero adventures with personal visions.

The triumph of Marvel Studios hasn't merely been financial, although in 2019 it released the most successful movie of all time, *Avengers: Endgame*, as measured by global box office. (It edged out *Avatar*, which has since reclaimed the crown.) The studio exploded conventional ideas about what a superhero is and can be. In the 1960s, Marvel Comics reinvigorated superhero publishing by giving its heroes real-world problems (homework, paying the rent) and by making readers feel like they were part of a club of hip insiders. Marvel Studios replicated that achievement in a new era, finding a fresh tone for its movies and its heroes: sly, conversant in modern pop culture, trusting the audience to be in on the joke. Marvel Studios forged its own style, both with its movies and with its methods of making them.

Not everyone has been a fan, of course. Martin Scorsese famously said in 2019 that superhero movies were "not cinema," adding, "Honestly, the closest I can think of them—as well made as they are, with actors doing the best they can under the circumstances—is theme parks."

Francis Ford Coppola agreed, calling superhero movies "despicable." He spelled out his contempt: "There used to be studio films. Now there are Marvel pictures. And what is a Marvel picture? A Marvel picture is one prototype movie that is made over and over and over and over and over again to look different."

Marvel fans who reacted vehemently to such remarks didn't prove the movies were art; the movies, or at least the best of them, did that themselves, through wit and spectacle and the manifest passion that went into their making. But the business has changed, and largely because of Marvel. Strange and formally ambitious movies still get made at the margins of Hollywood; there are so many of them, in fact, that people can't hope to watch them all, or even keep track of all the proliferating streaming services on which to watch them. But among blockbusters, intellectual property (IP) is king, and no IP is as valuable as Marvel's. And since Marvel's IP draws from thousands of comic-book stories told over many decades, there is no danger of it running dry anytime soon.

Perhaps the most obvious measure of Marvel's dominance has been the appearance of such movies and TV series as *The Boys*, *Invincible*, and *Watchmen*, each deconstructing our omnipresent superhero culture, sometimes with gleeful, bloody rudeness. (All were adaptations of comic books that originally had been intended as commentary on printed superheroes.) Yet the challenge Marvel faces now is not from other shows or studios, but itself: it needs to maintain its benchmarks of quality and, even after dozens of movies and TV shows, make each project feel like essential viewing because it's thrilling, not because it's a homework assignment necessary to understand the next installment. The studio has sailed at full speed into a sea of dilemmas familiar to the writers and illustrators of Marvel comics: how to extend a story with no obvious endpoints, how to keep familiar characters relevant, how to constantly reinvent the formula for success without rebooting the whole enterprise.

At the behest of Disney, Marvel Studios kept accelerating the pace of production, pushing the boundaries to determine how much of a good thing would be too much. Phase One of the MCU movies took roughly five years to roll out, only a slightly shorter span than the schedule for Phases Four, Five, and Six combined. Making three movies and roughly six TV series a year was a pace that fatigued both the audience and the filmmakers themselves. The success of the MCU relied on the hands-on input of some key executives, especially Feige, and it turned out that there were limits to how much that model could be scaled up into mass production. Fans complained that *Ant-Man and the Wasp: Quantumania* was lackluster and overwhelmed by mediocre computer graphics—but that didn't stop it from spending weeks as the top movie in the United States in early 2023, when it grossed hundreds of millions of dollars.

Although Marvel released plenty of sequels and brand extensions of varying quality, it also made oddball gothic black-and-white programs and surreal TV series about the very nature of reality, as if the producers wanted to find out just how much you can get away with when you rule the world. The answer, it turns out, is a lot.

The MCU is inevitable, as Thanos says of himself. Or so it seemed—a decade of dominance made Marvel Studios feel like the only real game in town. And although it may not have engineered show-business failure out of existence, it could easily survive a misstep or three. The Marvel Cinematic Universe had so thoroughly taken over our own universe, it was hard to imagine a timeline in which it didn't run forever. Which makes the chaos of its own origin story all the more surprising.

PHASE
ZERO

★

CHAPTER ONE

Phoenix Saga

Before we get started,
does anyone want to get out?

Captain America: The Winter Soldier

MARVEL STUDIOS BEGAN WITH FAILURE AND RUIN
and bankruptcy.

That's also how Marvel superhero comics had started
decades earlier. The comic-book business was roiled in the 1950s
after the United States Senate held hearings on the lurid contents of
horror comics. Marvel, founded as Timely Comics in 1939 but then
called Atlas, stayed in business by copying whatever genres sold for
other companies, including romance comics like *Millie the Model*
and Western comics like *Rawhide Kid*. In 1957, however, Atlas got
locked into a bad newsstand distribution deal that limited the company to eight comics a month and had to fire most of its staff. The
superhero market was dominated by DC Comics, home to Superman and Batman and Wonder Woman.

In 1961, however, genius writer and huckster Stan Lee, collaborating with genius artist and workhorse Jack Kirby, created a new
superhero team called the Fantastic Four. Their comic book, combining outlandish science-fiction adventures and family squabbles,

had verve and attitude that the DC titles lacked. It was an immediate smash. Marvel soon published dozens of other titles and eventually created a stable of hundreds of other heroes, including Spider-Man and Ant-Man and Iron Man (and even a few women). In the following decades, the Marvel Comics Group grew into a cultural empire that published thousands of stories, with overlapping narratives and cross-title cameos that added up to one mind-bogglingly elaborate modern epic, stretching from the sewers of New York City to the farthest reaches of outer space.

By 1991, Marvel was so popular that an issue relaunching its flagship team of mutants ("feared and hated by a world they have sworn to protect!"), *X-Men* #1, sold 8,186,500 copies that year, still a world record. Those eight million copies (words by Chris Claremont, pencils by Jim Lee) featured five different covers, and many fans bought multiple versions, at $3.95 a pop, to be treated as investments in mylar sleeves rather than to be read and dogeared.

X-Men #1 was the most extreme example of the comic-book mania, but there were plenty of others. Many mainstream magazine articles touted the dark, complex, genre-exploding work of creators such as Alan Moore (*Watchmen*), Frank Miller (*Batman: Year One*), and Art Spiegelman (*Maus*). Their work made it clear that, as many of the articles put it, comics weren't just for kids anymore. The 1989 *Batman* film, starring Michael Keaton and Jack Nicholson, directed by Tim Burton in a pop-gothic style, was not only the most popular movie of the year, it drove viewers to an endless array of tie-in Bat-product, from toys to beach towels to the Prince soundtrack album. In 1991, a copy of *Detective Comics* #27, featuring the first appearance of Batman, sold at auction for $55,000; the *New York Times* article on the sale was headlined "Holy Record Breaker!"

"I think comic books are on the ground floor of an explosive market," said Harold M. Anderson, who bought that copy of *Detective Comics* #27.

Neil Gaiman, later a best-selling author and the showrunner of TV programs such as *Good Omens*, but then best known as the writer of the mythologically minded comic book *Sandman* (published by

DC), disagreed. In 1993, Gaiman gave a speech at a convention for comic-book retailers where he warned that the practice of treating variant covers and other comic-book collectibles as investments was a speculative bubble, and that it would inevitably collapse, just like the seventeenth-century Dutch market in tulip bulbs.

"Too many comic stores are trading in bubbles and tulips," he declared. "I'm not here to play Cassandra: I don't have the figure or the legs. . . . One day the bubble will burst, and tulips will rot in the warehouse. . . . The next time someone tells you about comics as the hot investment item of the '90s, do me a favor and tell them about the tulips." Retailers didn't want to hear it, but he was soon proved right. In the next few years, two-thirds of all comics specialty stores went out of business. And with its distribution network in shambles, Marvel Comics filed for bankruptcy in 1996.

Stan Lee was still the public face of Marvel. He had cocreated many of the company's most iconic characters, including Thor and Doctor Strange and Black Panther and the Incredible Hulk, and had scripted hundreds of comic books. But it was his editorial voice—not just in captions, but in editorials and letters pages, where Lee responded in print to fan mail—that cemented his bond with Marvel readers. He was full of bonhomie and brio and catchphrases ranging from "Face front, true believers" to "Excelsior!" Above all, he flattered readers with the notion that they were sophisticated consumers of comic-book entertainment. The very first appearance of Spider-Man, in *Amazing Fantasy* #15 (written by Lee, drawn by Steve Ditko), began with this pitch: "Like costume heroes? Confidentially, we in the comic mag business refer to them as 'long underwear characters'! And, as you know, they're a dime a dozen! But, we think you may find our Spiderman [*sic*] just a bit . . . different!"

By the time Marvel filed for bankruptcy, Stan Lee no longer supervised the company's day-to-day editorial affairs, although his name still appeared on the title page of every comic book the company published. Lee, who had been dreaming of California for many years, finally moved to Los Angeles full-time after *The Incredible Hulk* TV show became a solid success. (The series, which starred Bill

Bixby as David Banner—incredibly, network executives thought the name "Bruce" made him "sound homosexual"—and Lou Ferrigno as his muscled alter-ego, aired on CBS from 1977 to 1982.) "When Marvel started to get some traction and some media attention in the late sixties," said Sean Howe, author of *Marvel Comics: The Untold Story*, "[Lee] was talking, privately at least, about getting Jack Kirby to go out to California with him and get into movies, rather than stick around in comic books, where you don't make any money and nobody appreciates you."

Lee had moved to LA to take charge of a new, pocket-size studio called Marvel Productions. It launched in 1980 with an ad in *Variety* that declared, "We are looking forward to taking the reins for the development of our own properties as well as sharing our expertise with other suppliers." In the early days of Marvel, Lee routinely ad-libbed concepts for characters or stories, which would quickly be rendered on the page by Kirby, Ditko, and other artists. He was still a font of ideas and storytelling expertise, but in LA he could no longer make things happen just by talking, because nobody in Hollywood wanted to listen to him.

In 1981, CBS executives insisted that Spider-Man wasn't enough of a draw to be the solo star of an animated Saturday-morning cartoon series. Instead, *Spider-Man and His Amazing Friends* teamed up the character with the mutant Iceman and a new female hero called Firestar. Though he wound up doing narration for it, Lee hated the show, even telling a crowd of fans at the 1984 Heroes Con in Charlotte, North Carolina, "Those of you who were careless enough to tune into *Spider-Man* may have seen that he's there with Iceman and a girl named Firestar as a team of three people. . . . I'll give you a little apology about that too. The way that it's run in network television, it's like when I was consultant on a live-action series: you could go to a network and say, 'Hey, we want to do this show, will you buy it?' And the network says, 'Okay, we'll buy it.' But that doesn't mean they'll do it the way that you want."

At Heroes Con, Lee also touted a Doctor Strange movie, made by the *Back to the Future* team of director Robert Zemeckis and screenwriter Bob Gale, and an X-Men movie with a screenplay by the comic-book writers Roy Thomas and Gerry Conway. Neither happened, but Marvel Productions did produce successful animated shows in the 1980s that licensed other companies' intellectual property, such as *G.I. Joe* and *Muppet Babies.*

Lee tried to encourage Hollywood interest in adapting the company's characters for movies and TV shows. For the most part, he failed abjectly. In his Stan's Soapbox column, printed in the back of Marvel comic books, Lee would periodically hyperventilate about an upcoming movie or TV show, which would almost inevitably not materialize. The handful of movies based on Marvel characters were bad enough that viewers wished they had never happened: *The Punisher* (starring Dolph Lundgren as the titular vigilante) in 1989; a straight-to-video American-Yugoslavian production of *Captain America* in 1990; and one of the most notorious Hollywood bombs ever, the George Lucas–produced *Howard the Duck* movie in 1986.

Two years earlier, Margaret Loesch, previously an executive vice president at Hanna-Barbera, became the president and CEO of Marvel Productions, which meant that she and Lee pitched studio executives together. "Stan wasn't rude to people," Loesch remembered, "but he would say to me when they left the room, 'I don't understand why they don't have any imagination. I don't understand why they can't understand what I'm saying.'"

She summed up her years at Marvel Productions: "We were great producers, but not of Marvel property. So I felt like a failure."

★

LEE'S WORK in Los Angeles did not determine the fate of Marvel. The company's future emerged from a convoluted series of corporate changes that ultimately led to the creation, and ascent, of Marvel Studios.

Back in 1968, Marvel Comics publisher Martin Goodman had sold the company to the Perfect Film & Chemical Corporation, which soon renamed itself Cadence Industries. When Cadence was liquidated in 1986, Marvel was acquired by New World Pictures (the low-budget film distribution company founded by Roger Corman, director of dozens of B movies such as *Teenage Caveman*). In 1989, New World sold the Marvel Entertainment Group to Ronald Perelman, the billionaire mogul most famous for his hostile takeover of the cosmetics company Revlon—the Marvel editorial staff promptly nicknamed him "Lipstick Guy." Perelman had made an art of acquiring troubled companies ranging from Technicolor to the supermarket chain Pantry Pride. Sometimes he would strip-mine them; sometimes he would use their assets to secure massive amounts of junk-bond debt that he would use to acquire other companies: either way, a large amount of money ended up in his pocket. Perelman owned an expensive art collection and homes that included a sprawling estate in the Hamptons. In his lavish office suite, huge paintings by Lichtenstein and Warhol hung next to two needlepoint pillows with the messages "Love Me, Love My Cigar" and "Happiness is a Positive Cash Flow."

Perelman increased Stan Lee's salary to approximately a million dollars a year, not out of sentimentality but as compensation for the value "Stan the Man" provided as brand ambassador. Meanwhile, Perelman used Marvel as a vehicle to acquire other businesses, most notably, Fleer and Skybox (both sports trading-card companies) and Panini (an Italian manufacturer of collectible stickers for kids). Marvel's revenue quickly plummeted—not just because the comic-book speculation bubble burst, but because the 1994–1995 baseball strike canceled the World Series and threw a beanball at the trading-card business.

Marvel was saddled with over $700 million in debt from all those acquisitions, far more than it could pay off. In the short run, Perelman had tripled Marvel's stock value, but in 1995, Marvel posted its first annual loss, and more red ink followed. Perelman had Marvel file for Chapter 11 bankruptcy in December 1996. He was hoping to "restructure" its debt, a euphemism for canceling some of it and delaying some of the payments (banks would rather get a smaller percentage of something than a larger percentage of nothing).

Perelman didn't expect any other billionaires to take an interest in

Marvel. But one did: Carl Icahn, famed as an "activist investor" (his preferred term) or a "corporate raider" (what the rest of the world called him). Icahn had taken over the airline TWA and the appliance company Tappan, and also made hostile bids for U.S. Steel and Pan Am; his practice was to sell off a company's assets to cover the debt he incurred acquiring it. Both Perelman and Icahn were sometimes called "greenmailers"—investors who would get paid off by a corporation to go away so the company could go about its business—and each had been cited as an inspiration for the character Gordon Gekko, who advocated for the value of greed in the movie *Wall Street*. Icahn quietly bought a third of the Marvel junk bonds that Perelman had issued and moved to take control of the company.

Icahn, Perelman, and the banks that had loaned Marvel money then spent months engaged in tedious legal wrangling and elaborate financial maneuvers. The proceedings, in and out of bankruptcy court (and an appeals court) in Delaware, were fueled by the egos of two rival billionaires as much as by Marvel's financial realities. In a comic-book idiom, it was Lipstick Guy versus The Raider. While Perelman hadn't invested the vast sums of money in Marvel that he had promised, it seemed likely that Icahn would quickly dismember the company if he were given the chance. Nevertheless, in June 1997, Icahn won, taking control of Marvel.

That didn't stop the legal battle. The bankruptcy was still in progress, so motions and lawsuits and billable hours all mounted up. And then a surprise contender emerged. Despite being less than a quarter the size of Marvel, a toy manufacturer named Toy Biz made a serious play for the company. Toy Biz's chairman of the board was yet another mogul, but somebody who didn't make tabloid headlines like Perelman or Icahn.

Almost nobody wants to talk about Ike Perlmutter on the record. An intensely private man, he went thirty-five years without being photographed—magazines writing about him had to commission speculative illustrations, as if he were a fugitive wanted by the FBI—before somebody snapped a picture of him visiting president-elect Donald Trump at Mar-a-Lago in December 2016.

Yitzhak Perlmutter was born in the British Mandate of Palestine in 1942, before Israel was founded—that happened in 1948, when Perlmutter was five years old. He grew up in Israel and joined the country's military, fighting in the Six-Day War between Israel and the neighboring Arab countries of Egypt, Syria, and Jordan. (Rumors followed Perlmutter for the rest of his life based on that military experience. Some people said he kept a pistol strapped to his ankle, while others claimed that he had been an agent for Mossad, the Israeli intelligence agency.) After the Six-Day War, Perlmutter left the Israeli military, and Israel itself, emigrating to the United States. It was 1967, but he wasn't looking to participate in the Summer of Love: he wanted to make his fortune.

A 24-year-old Perlmutter had just $250 in his pocket when he arrived in New York City. He paid his rent by frequenting Jewish cemeteries in Brooklyn. If he showed up with a prayer book in his hand and a yarmulke on his head, he could make money by reciting kaddish prayers for the dead. He wasn't actually an Orthodox Jew, but since his Hebrew was fluent, grieving families couldn't tell.

Perlmutter Americanized his first name from Yitzhak to Isaac, often going as "Ike." He made enough money hawking wholesale goods on the streets of Brooklyn to go on vacation at a resort in the Catskill Mountains, north of New York City. There he met and wooed a woman named Laura Sparer; a few months later, in 1971, they were married.

Perlmutter impressed his new in-laws enough that they gave him a substantial loan, which he invested in his business, Odd Lot Trading. Perlmutter would buy overstock merchandise for Odd Lot—anything from dolls to bars of soap—that was getting liquidated to clear out space in warehouses. He paid pennies on the dollar and then resold the goods at prices far below market value but far above what he had paid, turning those pennies into dimes and quarters. By the end of the 1970s, he had dozens of Odd Lot stores across New York City, each one a jumbled bazaar of discounted merchandise, with bright orange signs promising "Brand Names for Less."

Sam Osman, who ran the rival company Job Lot Trading, succinctly explained the financial model that he and Perlmutter shared: "Our business is other people's mistakes."

The Perlmutters kept a condo in Palm Beach and a country house in New Jersey, but they didn't live ostentatiously; their greatest indulgence might have been the huge tanks they kept full of exotic tropical fish. A typical dinner for the Perlmutters would be a salad prepared by Ike: a bowl of vegetables diced into tiny cubes, in the Israeli style. Perlmutter woke up early every morning for a game of tennis, spent the day running his companies and making deals, and ignored his phone after 8:00 p.m. He had no formal business training, but he had a keen mind and an intuitive understanding of balance sheets.

Odd Lot Trading became profitable enough that the Revco drugstore chain bought it in 1984 for $109 million in stock. But when Perlmutter tried to convince the Revco board of directors that it should fire the company's top management and put him in charge, they bought the Revco stock back instead, paying him $120 million to go away, with a five-year noncompete clause barring him from the retail and the wholesale trade. A year later, he paid Revco $3 million for the right to get back into the wholesale business, meaning that he (and his then partner, Bernard Marden) had turned an empire built on excess bars of soap into $117 million.

Perlmutter could now afford to buy entire companies, not just their overstock. He had an eye, developed during his time running Odd Lot, for toys and games, and he bought and flipped the failing toy company Coleco, making about $40 million in profit when he sold it to Hasbro. And in 1990, he bought Toy Biz. Previously known as the Charan Toy Company, it had been a small but successful family-owned Canadian firm that did well by acquiring the Canadian license for popular toys like Cabbage Patch Kids. But Toy Biz experienced a windfall in 1989, when the toymaker Kenner let its license to manufacture merchandise based on DC superheroes lapse. Toy Biz acquired the DC toy license just in time for the summer of Batmania.

Perlmutter believed that he could make Toy Biz even more profitable, and he was right. Renting a bare-bones office in New York City, leasing warehouse space in Arizona, and outsourcing manufacturing to China, he established a stunning sales-per-employee ratio, eventually generating $2 million for each person on his payroll.

✳

AS PERLMUTTER GOT MORE involved in Toy Biz (and the toy business more generally) he found the partner he hadn't realized he needed in Avi Arad, one of the most successful toy designers in the world. Like Perlmutter, Arad was also an Israeli immigrant and a veteran of the Six-Day War. They diverged in personal style: while Perlmutter was a lean predator in a business suit, Arad was a bear in black leather.

Arad's parents, refugees from Poland after World War II, had struggled to build a new life in Israel. Arad, who was six years younger than Perlmutter, grew up reading American comic books translated into Hebrew. "Maybe I just wanted to escape that life into something more fantastic," he said. Wounded during the Six-Day War (with injuries he wouldn't detail), Arad spent fifteen months recuperating in the hospital, and in 1970, he emigrated to the United States, speaking no English except for a few phrases he had learned from reading the poetry of Percy Bysshe Shelley and Walt Whitman. He attended Hofstra University on Long Island, studying industrial management, paying for his tuition by driving a truck and teaching Hebrew. After Arad graduated, his first job was at a toy company. He had never thought about the toy business—"When you grow up in Israel, you want to build airplanes, not toys," he said—but that changed when he saw that the company had sold a million copies of a miniature pool table for $15 apiece.

He became a freelance toy designer, a profession he excelled at. In 1993, *The New York Times* profiled him in an article with the headline "A One-Man Thrill Factory for Children." Arad sold hit toys to just about every company in the industry, with a resume that included Troll Warriors, My Pretty Ballerina, and the Zap It disappearing-ink gun. "In baseball, if you bat .300 you are a superstar," he bragged. "I'm batting in the high .800s."

One of the things that set Arad apart from other toy designers was that he approached his job like a marketer, not a tinkerer. He determined what the market was lacking and then came up with a toy that filled the gap. When he presented a prototype to a toy company, it came with an entire marketing and advertising plan. He wasn't just selling a product; he was selling an entire vision.

Arad dressed all in black, from his leather boots to his leather vest, and rode a Harley-Davidson motorcycle. "I don't believe in work hours," Arad said. "Any structured existence never worked for me. I enjoy the lack of structure—chaos." Nevertheless, Perlmutter convinced him (and his twenty-two-person development team) to work for Toy Biz full-time in exchange for 10 percent of the company. Arad was eventually named CEO of Toy Biz (replacing Joseph Ahearn), while Perlmutter served as chairman of the board.

One of Arad's earliest successes at Toy Biz was a line of X-Men toys, based on the Marvel team of mutant superheroes. It came out in 1991 (the same year as *X-Men* #1) and did $30 million of business. Seeing how well Marvel toys could sell, Perlmutter cut an unusual deal with Perelman, who was Marvel CEO at the time: he would give 46 percent of Toy Biz to Marvel in exchange for an "exclusive, perpetual, royalty-free license" to all of Marvel's characters.

"It is a mini-Disney in terms of intellectual property," Perelman said of Marvel. "Disney's got much more highly recognized characters and softer characters, whereas our characters are termed *action heroes*. But at Marvel we are now in the business of the creation and marketing of characters."

Nevertheless, Perelman didn't commit any resources to making Marvel movies. While he recognized that they might increase the value of his characters, he didn't want to encumber Marvel with expensive long-term commitments that might make it harder for him to flip the company at some point. Perelman wanted *rumors* of a movie (raising the value of his intellectual property and spurring sales of ancillary products), but not an *actual* movie that could flop and hurt the brand. (His desires comported well with Marvel's miserable track record of getting movies made.)

When it came to toy sales, a low-budget cartoon series could have a more powerful effect than an expensive movie. By 1992, Margaret Loesch had become the head of the Fox Kids TV programming block. At Fox, she launched an X-Men animated series; she had been unable to set up a single cartoon series during her years at Marvel, but now she could green-light one herself. Stan Lee and Avi Arad were both executive producers on the show, although Lee's involvement was nominal. Rick Hoberg, who wrote for the series, said, "We realized he didn't know the characters we were talking about for the show."

According to Will Meugniot, supervising producer on *X-Men*, the version of the show Lee pitched was "a conventional kids' show about two guys in a van with a dog." He recapped it as "Professor X and Cyclops . . . in a van with Cerebro and an animal sidekick, cruising the country, finding mutants in a mutant-of-the-week show."

Arad didn't remember Lee talking much during meetings about the series: "But he would nod his head when he liked something and go side-to-side if he had some doubts." And for himself? "I did the show from '93 to '97 because I related to being a mutant," Arad said. "The toy company went crazy because everybody was collecting action figures." Arad was much more involved with the show than Lee, frequently pitching storylines that he thought might lead to greater toy sales.

When Perelman and Icahn started battling over Marvel, Perlmutter and Arad supported Perelman. If Icahn won, they feared he might convince the bankruptcy court to cancel their extremely valuable royalty-free toy license on Marvel's characters so he could sell the toy rights elsewhere. When Icahn triumphed over Perelman, he promptly named a new board of directors to Toy Biz (more lawsuits followed over whether this was a valid move). Perlmutter started fighting back in ways both conventional and unusual, even faxing pages from the Torah to Icahn. The four pages of Judges 16 he sent tell the story of the powerful warrior-judge Samson, and how, after his hair is shorn and he's sold into captivity, he commits suicide by pulling the temple of the Philistines down upon himself.

The turning point came on October 1, 1997. The syndicate of banks that held Marvel's debt was deciding on whether to accept Icahn's latest offer to settle their accounts, and Toy Biz wasn't invited to the big meeting. Perlmutter called the office that was hosting the conference, over and over, and each time got swatted away by a bored receptionist. Then Toy Biz lawyer Larry Mittman had an idea: They should just show up. Perlmutter, Arad, Mittman, and Ahearn bolted out of the Toy Biz office in midtown New York City, not waiting for Perlmutter's limousine, because Manhattan traffic was, as usual, at a standstill. They ran down Park Avenue and East 53rd Street, Arad perspiring in his black leather, the wiry Perlmutter leading the pack. (Arad promptly gave Perlmutter a new nickname: "Road Runner.")

The disheveled quartet appeared at the meeting, much to the surprise of the forty bankers in the room, but they were granted an audience. Arad made the pitch, arguing that Icahn's offer, pricing Marvel at $385 million, hugely undervalued the company, and not just because its stock had recently been worth four billion dollars.

"What do *you* believe Spider-Man is worth?" Arad asked. "If you had the right to get Spider-Man forever and ever, I think Spider-Man alone is a billion-dollar entity. It will make numerous amounts of movies, endless licenses, television shows. In spite of bankruptcy, it's always a great license. You know the way little kids learn about Spider-Man? From their pajamas! It was always the leading pajamas. Spider-Man works for all ages, all countries, everywhere around the world. It's maybe the best-known intellectual property character, on a worldwide basis." (As it turned out, Arad was underestimating the value of the Spider-Man license.)

He reminded the bankers of all the other famous Marvel characters and implored them, "Ladies and gentlemen, stick around and share in this. This is big! This is going to be something very, very special. We just have to fix the company. Please give us a chance to do that." Hyperbole and exaggeration were Arad's superpowers—and now he was pushing his abilities to the limit.

In that sweaty, high-stakes moment, the leather-clad toy designer discovered something about himself: He was having the time of his life talking to a room full of bankers. As Arad said later, "It was so much fun trying to convince people that Marvel is worth something."

Toy Biz couldn't offer as much cash up front as Icahn, but its proposal had more potential upside: $130 million in cash plus 40 percent of the company resulting from a merger between Marvel and Toy Biz. It was a better deal—if Perlmutter and Arad could indeed turn Marvel around—and the banks went for it. More months of haggling and hearings followed, but in July 1998, Judge Roderick McKelvie of the United States District Court for the District of Delaware finally approved the deal called the Fourth Amended Plan. Toy Biz now owned Marvel and all the dreams that came with it.

CHAPTER TWO

Gifted Youngsters

You hope for the best and
make do with what you get.

Avengers: Age of Ultron

I N 1993, THREE YEARS BEFORE THE MARVEL BANKRUPTCY
began, Marvel Productions (the company's Hollywood venture) was renamed Marvel Films, and Avi Arad, in addition to
his various duties at Toy Biz, was appointed CEO. Arad had some
Hollywood experience from consulting on the animated *X-Men*
show, and he was a supremely talented salesman, but putting a toy
designer in charge of Marvel Films made clear what Marvel wanted
out of Hollywood: shows and movies that would help them sell more
toys. In industry argot, they wanted to make entertainment that
was "toyetic."

Arad began telling people that he had been a Marvel Comics fan
since he was a boy in Israel, but more fundamentally, he was a man
who had figured out how to maximize the value of superhero intellectual property—and how to tell a good story about it. Arad exuded
enthusiasm for Marvel's entire roster, but he was especially interested
in the two most recognizable properties: the X-Men and Spider-Man.

The fundamental dilemma at Marvel Films was that Arad needed lots of projects green-lit to stoke public excitement for Marvel's superheroes (and the toys) but he had to be careful enough with quality control that there wouldn't be any more embarrassments like *Howard the Duck*. His first major challenge was the *Fantastic Four* movie—a film that Arad didn't know existed until he was on vacation in Puerto Rico, wearing a Fantastic Four T-shirt. He was approached by a comics fan, who struck up a conversation and informed him that there was a Fantastic Four film in the works.

Arad was alarmed: it was his job to be aware of adaptations like that. He made some calls and learned that the movie's producers had shown a trailer at the San Diego Comic-Con in August 1993, promoting a 1994 release. To his surprise, the movie was legitimate. In the early 1980s, German producer Bernd Eichinger had made a deal for the Fantastic Four movie rights. Marvel received a reported $250,000; Eichinger had until the end of 1992 to get a motion picture into production. Eichinger spent years pitching major studios, to no avail. He finally made a deal with Roger Corman, "King of the B-Movies," to produce a Fantastic Four movie budgeted at just one million dollars. The movie, directed by Oley Sassone, went into production on December 28, 1992, just in time for Eichinger to hold on to the rights.

Even in the early '90s, a million dollars was not enough money to make a professional action movie, let alone one starring the stretchy Mr. Fantastic, the flaming and flying Human Torch, and the Thing, a man-monster covered in orange rocks. (At least the special effects for the Invisible Woman were cheap.) The movie deployed the same shot of the Human Torch flaming on multiple times, and at one point, Mr. Fantastic's elongated arm was clearly just a sleeve and a glove covering a long pole.

The movie "was never supposed to be seen by any living human beings," Stan Lee later insisted. He believed that Eichinger had spent a million dollars just so he would retain the Fantastic Four movie rights, hoping that he could still make a big-budget version. "The tragic thing was that the people involved with the film were not aware that the movie was never supposed to be shown to anybody," Lee said.

Corman, at least, insisted he had every intention of releasing the film. "Everybody liked the film," he said. Well, not Arad—the last thing he wanted was a movie that made Marvel superheroes look Grade-Z tacky.

As Eichinger told the story: "Avi's a very fine guy, and he calls me up and says, 'Listen, I think what you did was great, it shows your enthusiasm for the movie and the property, and I tell you what. I understand that you have invested so-and-so much, and Roger has invested so-and-so much. Let's do a deal.'" Arad paid them off, buying all rights to the film and all prints (although fans still pass around bootleg copies). He then announced that he had the negative burned.

Marty Langford, director of the documentary *Doomed! The Untold Story of Roger Corman's* The Fantastic Four, has always been suspicious of that particular claim: "I absolutely believe that the negative exists." Destroying a low-budget superhero movie in a bonfire might seem theatrical and over-the-top, but it was more civil than some of the maneuvers of the Marvel bankruptcy.

Arad decided that the way Marvel had been doing business with Hollywood for the past couple of decades didn't make sense: it was hard to convince studios of the viability of Marvel characters, and impossible to control the development process or the final results. "When you get into business with a big studio, they are developing a hundred or 500 projects; you get totally lost," he said. "That isn't working for us. We're just not going to do it anymore. Period."

When Ron Perelman sold off a big chunk of his ownership stake in Toy Biz in 1996, he cashed in that stock to finance a new entity called Marvel Studios, which replaced Marvel Films (again with Arad as CEO). The plan was that Marvel Studios would package talent, attaching sympathetic directors and stars to superhero properties, and then deliver the whole deal to the studios. It was an end-run around studio executives who didn't believe in the appeal of the Marvel characters—and it was a way for Arad to make himself into a producer, not just a consultant. "If the movies do great, I do great," Arad reasoned. "I'm like a commission salesman."

Some second-tier characters, like Iron Man and the Silver Surfer and Blade, had already been optioned to studios that weren't particularly interested in further input from Marvel Studios. Spider-Man, the character that Arad had touted as being worth a billion dollars, was immobilized in a web of complicated deals and lawsuits, but Fox, intrigued by the success of the *X-Men* cartoon series, had started developing a live-action movie starring the mutants. "There wouldn't have been a movie until we did the series," said Margaret Loesch, head of Fox Kids and former Marvel Productions president. To test the movie's viability, Fox aired the animated *X-Men* in prime-time one night: the ratings were high enough to validate Loesch's belief in the characters' wide appeal.

Before Arad could make his mark in Hollywood, Marvel went into bankruptcy. During Carl Icahn's brief period where he controlled Marvel, he fired Arad as CEO of Marvel Studios. Movie development continued without Arad.

In 1998, when Toy Biz swallowed up Marvel Comics, Perlmutter reorganized the business. The new parent company, called Marvel Enterprises, had four subsidiary groups: Marvel Studios, Toy Biz, Licensing (for products that weren't toys or movies), and Publishing (aka Marvel Comics). Perlmutter fired multiple Marvel staffers, including Joe Calamari, the president Icahn had installed. Whenever an employee in the publishing division was terminated, another employee would inspect his personal belongings. Any comic books would be pulled, because Perlmutter insisted that those belonged to Marvel. Perlmutter instituted austerity measures in ways both large (auctioning off expensive conference-room glass doors etched with images of Spider-Man) and small (insisting that all paper clips be reused). Demoralized employees wondered whether Perlmutter would outsource the production of all Marvel comic books and made morbid jokes about the debt-laden company being downsized to one guy with a telephone, making deals to license the characters.

"Why waste money on anything else?" one said, summarizing the prevailing mood.

The Marvel board of directors insisted that Marvel Enterprises needed a CEO with show-business experience, and so Perlmutter chose Eric Ellenbogen, formerly of Broadway Video and its parent company, Golden Books. Ellenbogen and his free-spending ways clashed with Perlmutter's business philosophy, so Perlmutter fired him after only six months, replacing him with Peter Cuneo (who had previously been the CEO at Remington Products when Perlmutter owned the razor company). Meanwhile, Perlmutter named Arad chief creative officer of Marvel Enterprises and reinstated him as CEO of Marvel Studios.

*

ARAD RETURNED TO the movie business in 1998, just as a Marvel movie was coming out, albeit one starring a then-obscure character. Wesley Snipes had long wanted to star in a Black Panther movie but settled for *Blade*, a vampire hunter based on a character created by Marv Wolfman and Gene Colan to be a supporting player in Marvel's *Tomb of Dracula* comics in the 1970s. Directed by Stephen Norrington from a David S. Goyer screenplay, the movie, with its $45 million budget, was a big gamble for the independent studio New Line.

"Marvel as a movie-making entity was inconsequential, and it was during the course of making *Blade* that the ownership changed," said Peter Frankfurt, *Blade*'s producer. "Avi Arad kind of arrived on the scene. He really had nothing to do with the first *Blade*. I think Marvel was paid $25,000—that was what their upside on *Blade* happening was. That all happened before I even got involved; that was the deal that New Line made with Marvel. They [Marvel] didn't think that it was worth anything."

Snipes initially relished playing Blade, which became a defining role for him, and even gave some press interviews in character. The main challenge during production was the movie's ending: Deacon

Frost, the villainous vampire played by Stephen Dorff, turned into a "blood god," which was just a CGI tornado of bright red blood. Reshoots added a climactic swordfight and saved the movie, which grossed $70 million domestically and was a solid hit for New Line. Marvel was so out of the loop on *Blade*, it didn't even release a line of toys to capitalize on the movie's success.

"*Blade* was a weird oddity," Frankfurt remembered. "It came out the second weekend of *Saving Private Ryan*; it knocked *Saving Private Ryan* out of first place. Everyone was like, 'What is that thing? Is it a horror movie? Is it a superhero movie? Is it a vampire movie? Is it a kung fu movie?' No one could figure it out, which is exactly what we had wanted to do, a total genre-bender."

Even if Marvel didn't make real money from *Blade*—the movie wasn't especially toyetic—the success of one of its properties was good for Arad as he resumed control of Marvel Studios. He turned his attention to Spider-Man, a character that Marvel had signed away in 1985 to producer Menahem Golan and his Cannon Films production company. When Cannon went bankrupt in 1990, the production company Carolco bought the Spider-Man movie rights from Golan.

That same year, as the popularity of the X-Men was exploding, Marvel set up a meeting with Lightstorm Films, owned by James Cameron of *Aliens* and *The Terminator* fame, to pitch Cameron on making a movie starring the mutant team. Marvel sent Stan Lee and the longtime *X-Men* writer Chris Claremont. "So we're chatting," Claremont remembered, "and at one point Stan looks at Cameron and says 'I hear you like Spider-Man.' Cameron's eyes lit up. And they start talking. And talking. And talking. About twenty minutes later, all the Lightstorm guys and I are looking at each other, and we all know the *X-Men* deal has just evaporated."

Carolco, which had produced Cameron's *Terminator 2: Judgment Day*, was thrilled that Cameron was interested in making a Spider-Man movie. The production company signed him to a deal similar to his *Terminator 2* contract, which gave him final say over producing credits. Cameron wrote a "scriptment" (halfway between a screenplay and a treatment, combining dialogue and plot summary) and moved toward production: Leonardo DiCaprio was the top choice to star as Peter Parker, the spectacular Spider-Man, while Arnold Schwarzenegger was expected to play the bad guy, Otto Octavius aka Doctor Octopus.

None of the publicity mentioned Golan, however, and his deal had stipulated that he would get a producer credit. He sued, while Carolco sued Viacom and Columbia Pictures for, respectively, the broadcast and home-video rights to Spider-Man, which Golan had sold separately to each company. Not wanting to miss out on the fun, MGM, which believed it had inherited the Cannon rights, sued everyone in sight for fraud. Carolco went bankrupt in 1995, with litigation still in progress, leaving it unclear who controlled which Spider-rights.

Lightstorm had a production deal with 20th Century Fox, so Cameron hoped Fox would intervene. "I tried to get Fox to buy it, but apparently the rights were a little bit clouded," he said. "Sony had some very questionable attachment to the rights [and former Fox president] Peter Chernin just wouldn't go to bat for it. He didn't want to get into a legal fight. And I'm like, 'Are you kidding? This thing could be worth, I don't know, a billion dollars!'"

Tired of waiting for the lawsuits to resolve, Cameron (and DiCaprio) moved on to *Titanic*, which came out in 1997. The director would later call *Spider-Man* "the greatest movie I never made."

By 1998, the litigation had wound down and most of the Spider-Man movie rights had reverted to Marvel. The exception was Columbia (and its parent company, Sony), which maintained a claim on the home-video rights, which in turn made it hard for Marvel to cut a deal with any other studio. Sony made Marvel an offer for the Spider-Man movie rights: $10 million, plus 5 percent of the gross and half of the toy revenue. Marvel countered by offering the movie rights to every character it still had available. That lineup didn't include the Fantastic Four or the X-Men, but it did cover Captain America,

Black Panther, and Doctor Strange, in addition to Spider-Man. For just $25 million, Sony could have the rights to most of the future stars of the MCU.

This offer contradicted Arad's loud public statements that Marvel wanted to maintain control of its own characters going forward. Were Arad's principles situational? Or did Perlmutter, accustomed to selling off pieces of a corporation for fun and profit, care more about guaranteed infusions of cash than the murky potential of a film division? Or did Marvel need money immediately following its bankruptcy, especially if Perlmutter was to recoup his personal outlays? Yes, yes, and yes. Luckily for Marvel, Sony turned down the offer, with Sony Pictures executive Yair Landau declaring, "Nobody gives a shit about any of the other Marvel characters."

✱

WHILE THE DISCUSSIONS over Spider-Man continued, 20th Century Fox handed off development of *X-Men* to producer Lauren Shuler Donner, who ran Donner/Shuler-Donner Productions with her husband Richard Donner, the director of the first big-screen superhero smash, 1978's *Superman*. Shuler Donner pushed forward with the live-action version of *X-Men*, not waiting for Arad or Marvel. In 1996, Fox approached Bryan Singer, director of *The Usual Suspects*, which had won two Oscars that year, to helm *X-Men*. Singer had never heard of the heroes, but his producing partner Tom DeSanto was a fan; with DeSanto's encouragement, he took the job.

Developing an acceptable *X-Men* script was a tortuous process, as Shuler Donner tried to balance high-stakes adventure with Singer's desire to emphasize the mutants as a metaphor for the gay experience. (The X-Men have long served as stand-ins for marginalized groups.) She brought in a parade of writers, including Christopher McQuarrie and Joss Whedon, to revamp and polish drafts, while DeSanto and Singer's assistant David Hayter ensured that on-screen characters remained recognizable to comic-book fans. (Hayter would end up with the screenplay credit, while DeSanto and Singer got story credit.) As the projected budget drifted north of $75 million, Shuler Donner had to assuage Fox executives' growing concerns.

Among the feedback on Shuler Donner's desk, as the pile of *X-Men* scripts grew, were notes on the scripts from her assistant, who had started four years earlier as an intern. "Because Lauren is an amazing mentor and is so gracious, she would read the notes," said that assistant, Kevin Feige. "Eventually she started saying, 'Hey, come into the office and sit with me.' I would be sitting with Tom DeSanto, who's the producer of *X-Men*, and Bryan Singer, who was the newly hired director, and I just started to become a part of that creative team."

Kevin Feige, born in 1973, grew up in Westfield, New Jersey, obsessed with movies. When he was sixteen years old, he wallpapered his bedroom with posters for blockbusters like *Back to the Future Part II*. He skipped his prom, going to a movie instead. He was familiar with Marvel Comics ("I had the toys, I had the Underoos, I watched the cartoon series"), but he wasn't a superfan and comic book films were hardly popular when he was growing up. "Richard Donner's *Superman*," Feige said. "Back then that really was the biggest example. I was sixteen when Tim Burton's *Batman* came out. But the *Star Wars* movies, the *Star Trek* movies, the *Indiana Jones* movies, the *Back to the Future* movies, the Amblin movies: they all could have been based on comics."

He obsessed over those fictional universes and kept a journal to record every movie he saw, noting the theater where he watched it and what the sound system was like. Even then, he was paying attention to more than plot. "It was all very nerdy," he confessed.

He had a particular fascination with sequels: "I was always excited to see how characters I loved would grow and change. I'd be disappointed sometimes. Every time a movie disappointed me, I'd sit and think about what I'd have done differently. I wouldn't write a screenplay, but I'd tease it out in my head."

Feige's grandfather, Robert E. Short, was a soap-opera producer and got his movie-obsessed grandson an internship at *Guiding Light*.

His senior year of high school, Feige applied to just one college: USC, the alma mater of George Lucas. He was admitted, but not as a student at the School of Cinematic Arts, so he moved to LA, enrolled as an undergraduate at USC, and applied to the film school again in the spring. He was rejected again.

Every semester, Feige applied to the film school—and five times in a row, he was rejected. "My friends and my family started to politely suggest that maybe I look for another major," he said. "They said USC was actually a very large university with a number of wonderful areas of academic study outside of film. I told them I had no idea what they were talking about." The sixth time Feige applied to the USC film program, he got in.

In the fall of 1994, now officially a film student, Feige realized "that the smart kids were getting these internships where you go and work for no money, but you get college credit and feet-on-the-ground experience. I thought, 'Well, if I'm going to work somewhere for free, wouldn't it be fun to do it for somebody that I admire?'"

Characteristically, Feige described the key moment of his life in cinematic terms. Although he was standing in front of a wall in a USC administration building, looking at the internship listings, he remembered it as if he were starring in a Richard Attenborough movie, with the world dimming except for a golden shaft of light that illuminated the card for Donner/Shuler-Donner Productions. Feige didn't know much about Lauren Shuler Donner, but he was a big fan of Richard Donner's movies, including *Lethal Weapon*, *The Goonies*, and "the most perfect superhero movie," *Superman*. For the first time in his life, Feige put together a résumé. A few weeks later, he was interning for the Donners.

Through the rest of his USC career, Feige worked steadily for the Donners, filling in wherever he was needed in their office. Whether he was making copies or picking up lunch orders, his credo was "Don't screw it up." One summer, he even got paid to be the receptionist. "I learned to enjoy the adrenaline rush of phones ringing," he said.

Every time Feige went into Richard Donner's office with coffee or a package, he had to pass under a sign the director had hung over his door that read, in capital letters, "VERISIMILITUDE." "A word that I was never able to pronounce but always understood," Feige said. It had animated Donner's approach to film: famously, the tagline for *Superman* was "You'll Believe a Man Can Fly."

Feige became fast friends with Geoff Johns, one of the other junior staffers at the office. Decades later, they would each be in charge of the direction of a major superhero film franchise—for some years, Johns served as president and chief creative officer of DC Entertainment—but at Donner/Shuler-Donner Productions, they were gofers. "The two of us washed cars together, walked dogs together," Feige said. The first time Feige went to San Diego Comic-Con—an impulsive outing on a slow Thursday afternoon to check out the massive annual festival of comic books and pop culture—he borrowed Johns's car to make the drive down the I-5.

During Feige's final semester at film school, two plum positions at the production company became vacant: Richard Donner and Lauren Shuler Donner each needed an assistant. If Feige had been required to choose between those two jobs on his first day at Donner/Shuler-Donner Productions, when he still dreamed of being a director, he would have wanted to work with Richard. But two years later, he saw that "when Dick wasn't working, he would relax between projects and work from home. Lauren, on the other hand, was in the office every day, developing multiple projects and producing multiple movies." Hoping to be where the action was, Feige opted for Shuler Donner.

He studied his boss even more closely than before, learning how she navigated delicate situations when she had been brought in by the studio to supervise a less-experienced producer, and how she would always volunteer to handle the tricky conversations that nobody else wanted to touch. For example, telling Tom Hanks that the producers thought he had put on too much weight for 1998's classic rom-com *You've Got Mail*. "And she'd achieve the desired goal, and they didn't hate her for it!" Feige said. "I thought, 'Oh, there's an art form to that.'"

Feige worked for Shuler Donner while she produced *You've Got Mail* and the disaster movie *Volcano*. On the former, his responsibilities included going to Meg Ryan's house and teaching the actress how to log onto America Online. "I had probably only learned to use email the summer before that," he confessed. On the first day on the set, months later, Feige heard a voice calling "Hi, Kevin!" and turned around to see Ryan greeting him. Awestruck, he thought, "*She remembered my name.*"

When Shuler Donner started developing *X-Men*, Feige saw an opportunity to dive into making the kind of blockbusters he grew up on. Longtime Marvel producer Craig Kyle said, "He saw Marvel, right from the very beginning when he was working on *X-Men* as an assistant for the Donners, as a chance to be a part of that journey."

Feige had been only casually aware of the mutants' history and lore, but he quickly made himself into an expert, and soon everyone around him assumed he had been a lifelong fan. Feige was so diligent with his notes, and so immersed in the details of the comic books, that Shuler Donner sent him to Toronto when *X-Men* started shooting there in 1999; he was her emissary, keeping an eye on things. "As a walking encyclopedia of Marvel, he was really indispensable," Shuler Donner said. (Pressed for one of Feige's shortcomings, Shuler Donner allowed that "neatness is not his forte.")

The more deeply Feige studied the comics, the more he came to believe in their cinematic potential. "I would hear people, other executives, struggling over a character point, or struggling over how to make a connection, or struggling over how to give even surface-level depth to an action scene or a character," he remembered. "I'd be sitting there reading the comics, going, 'Look at this. *Just do this.* This is incredible.'" Adapting superhero comic books was a challenging process, since not everything on the page had the same impact on the screen, but Feige understood early on that, when in doubt, he could trust the original stories.

He was also smart enough not to meddle: he watched, learned, and intervened only at key moments. He advocated for the casting of Australian musical-theater actor Hugh Jackman as Wolverine (aka Logan), even though he was considered too tall to play a character traditionally rendered as compact. The cast also included Halle Berry,

Ian McKellen, and Patrick Stewart—but not Michael Jackson, who had lobbied the production team for the role of Professor Charles Xavier. When Shuler Donner reminded the pop star that Professor X was an old white guy, Jackson replied, "I can wear makeup."

On the *X-Men* set, Singer banned comic books to keep everyone focused on his own cinematic vision, but Feige would sneak issues to actors hungry to understand their characters. "Kevin was someone who, at that stage, was trying to be the voice of 'We can actually run towards the books. We don't have to run away from the books,'" Kyle said. "He was someone who really helped save the first *X-Men* film from being a disaster, and he did that by working very closely with Avi." Feige kept in regular phone contact with Arad, who was Marvel's official liaison on the production, filling him in on the day-to-day decisions on the set. "Avi, I know you said how important it is that he looks like Logan—well, they're not doing it. They're going to undo it now," Feige told Arad at one point. "Then Avi would have to come back and play heavy because he was the only one that had any other voice besides the producers for Fox," Kyle said.

Feige made a stand on the question of Wolverine's tufty hair. One day on set, Shuler Donner and Arad watched as an exasperated stylist, at Feige's insistence, sprayed and teased Jackman's hair higher and higher to make him look more like the comic-book character. The stylist "eventually went, 'Fine!' and did a ridiculous version," Feige recalled. "If you go back and look at it," he admitted, "he's got big-ass hair in that first movie. But that's Wolverine!" The experience stuck with Feige. "I never liked the idea that people weren't attempting things because of the potential for them to look silly," he said. "Anything in a comic book has the potential to look silly. That doesn't mean you shouldn't try to make it look cool."

✳

RELEASED IN the summer of 2000, *X-Men* was a hit that far surpassed the success of *Blade*, grossing nearly $300 million worldwide. Shuler Donner and Fox were moving to make a sequel as quickly as possible, so when she got a phone call from Avi Arad, she assumed he wanted to discuss *X2*. To her surprise, Arad asked her permission to hire Feige for a full-time job at Marvel.

If Arad was going to realize his cinematic ambitions, he needed a larger production team, and when he had visited the chaotic *X-Men* set, he had been impressed by Feige's focus and composure. "I had been in touch with Avi for two or three years during the course of the production on *X-Men*," Feige said. "I would keep him in the loop and give him my opinions. By that point, I was an expert in all things X-Men and all things Marvel." Shuler Donner gave her blessing. On August 1, 2000, less than three weeks after the release of *X-Men*, Feige started working at Marvel Studios.

Feige was assigned office space at a Toy Biz subsidiary in Los Angeles: Spectra Star, a kite company. While Feige liked the Spectra Star employees, he quickly realized that their schedules weren't compatible with his. On windy days, the kite people would leave early to test prototypes, and they weren't accustomed to keeping the office open past 6:00 p.m. for diligent young production executives.

While Feige toiled, surrounded by kites, Amy Pascal, who ran Columbia Pictures, was trying to find a director for her Spider-Man movie. Believing that Cameron's scriptment was too edgy, she hired David Koepp to rewrite the movie as more of a teenage romance, closer to the tone of the original comics. With a screenwriter in place, she and Arad approached Chris Columbus and David Fincher, among other proven directors. An unenthusiastic Tim Burton told Pascal he was a "DC guy" and didn't even schedule a meeting. Arad said that some directors were very excited about the project, "but they took it from the point of view that they know what to do. 'Just give me all the money, leave me alone, and I'll make a great movie.'" Sam Raimi wasn't as big a name as some of the other options—although he specialized in comedy-horror flicks like *Army of Darkness*, his biggest box-office hit was the off-kilter Western *The Quick and the Dead*—and he had to lobby just to get a meeting. But as a lifelong fan of the character, he made a passionate pitch that got him the job. Arad said, "Sam was unique. Sam didn't come into it for money. Sam was a guy who needed to make it."

Pascal handed off day-to-day production duties on *Spider-Man* to Laura Ziskin, a friend but more importantly the executive producer on *Pretty Woman* and *As Good as It Gets* and, until her resignation in 1999, the president of Fox 2000. She was eager for work as a freelance producer: "I had to leave everything behind at Fox," Ziskin said. "I literally said, 'Just give me the biggest motherfucker you have.' I just wanted to be in production in something big. I had never read a comic book." Ziskin joined Raimi on *Spider-Man* in early 2000 for script development and stayed with the *Spider-Man* franchise until she died from cancer, at age sixty-one, in 2011 (she received a posthumous credit on *Amazing Spider-Man* in 2012).

Looking back, Shuler Donner could see how closely Feige had studied her and Ziskin. "There's a difference between a male producer and a female producer," she said. "Women have a little more empathy and intuition. I think he just picked up that style through osmosis."

The production designer Rick Heinrichs said that Feige also took pains not to overwhelm people with his opinions. "He's an iceberg of an intellect. Not cold at all—he's a very warm person. But you can see just one-tenth of it; there's all this other stuff going on underneath, and you wish you could track his intuitions about things. He's got a grasp of a much bigger picture, but he doesn't want to confuse people beyond what they're specifically doing with their film or their character."

Preproduction on *Spider-Man* lasted through 2000: Raimi and Ziskin hammered out what would make for the most entertaining film while Arad kept advocating for elements that would make the lead character feel more like his comic-book counterpart (and the associated toys). Feige said he learned two important things from working with Sam Raimi. "And when I say 'working with,'" he clarified, "I say that more as 'hanging out and watching.'" One was to exert maximum effort on a movie, so that at the end, you would feel "like a deflated balloon," knowing that you had put everything you had into it. The other was to make decisions based on how you wanted the audience to *feel*, rather than trying to overwhelm them with your artistic vision. "If it's not going to translate, it's literally meaningless," Feige said. "Sam always put everything he had into those movies, from a passionate fan's point of view and from the audience's point of view."

Arad was so excited by how *Spider-Man* was coming together, he wanted to show Stan Lee that Marvel's flagship character was finally getting the big-budget treatment. Arad sat Lee down and played a tape of a pre-visualization sequence: digital artists had blocked out Spider-Man swinging through Manhattan, rendering the thrilling journey with a crude red-and-blue avatar. At the end, the usually jovial Lee sat stone-faced, eyes locked on the screen. Then he whispered, "That's it?"

Horrified, Arad realized that Lee didn't understand what a pre-visualization (or "pre-viz") sequence was, and how different the film would look when it finally appeared in theaters. "He was new to the technology side of things," Arad said. "He was so disappointed! I almost cried!"

When *Spider-Man*, starring Tobey Maguire, Kirsten Dunst, and Willem Dafoe, was released in May 2002, it wasn't just the successful movie Arad and Perlmutter sorely needed, but a hit on a scale that no one involved expected: it was the first film ever to make over $100 million in its opening weekend. "Wow," Raimi said, "they really, really love this character even more than any of us thought." He knew that the movie's immediate success wasn't a reflection of its quality: "How would they know? They're coming in the first weekend."

Arad hired a bus with a bar and took the Marvel Studios staff on a celebratory tour of Los Angeles, stopping at one movie theater after another so they could watch audiences' reactions. The world's response to *Spider-Man* validated Arad's pitch to the banks, in which he had boasted of the character's potentially huge value. The movie's profits allowed Perlmutter to pay off all of Marvel's outstanding loans. And, as Arad pointed out, there was another consequence, one that mattered a great deal to his boss: "The toys sold like crazy."

CHAPTER THREE

Once upon a Time in Mar-a-Lago

I came to realize that I had more to offer this world than just making things that blow up.

Iron Man

LUNCHTIME, EARLY 2003: DONALD TRUMP WAS ONE year away from starring in *The Apprentice* and fourteen years away from being sworn in as the forty-fifth president of the United States. He owned a share of the Miss Universe beauty pageant, some Atlantic City casinos on the verge of bankruptcy, and a luxury beach resort in Palm Beach, Florida, called Mar-a-Lago. Trump had bought the Mar-a-Lago mansion in 1985 and converted it into a private club. Unlike the other upscale clubs in Palm Beach, Mar-a-Lago was willing to accept Black people, Jewish people, and gay people as members, so long as they could afford the $100,000 membership fee.

Trump, circulating through the Mar-a-Lago dining room, glad-handing and schmoozing, came upon an odd couple: Ike Perlmutter and David Maisel. Trump knew Perlmutter well as a friend and a fellow member of the unofficial New York City plutocrats club. Perlmutter would become a major donor to Trump's presidential run and, during Trump's presidency, would be part of a three-person Mar-a-

Lago cabal that unofficially ran the Department of Veteran Affairs. (When news broke of that unusual arrangement, Perlmutter and his associates insisted that "At all times, we offered our help and advice on a voluntary basis, seeking nothing at all in return.") Membership at Mar-a-Lago was the only known luxury for the frugal Perlmutter.

Trump wasn't familiar with Perlmutter's lunch companion. David Maisel wasn't socially adept by anyone's measure, including his own. Tall and lanky, he seemed much younger than his forty years. His mind was always spinning with business plans and financial schemes. Sometimes Maisel came up with ideas faster than he could get words out of his mouth; he spoke quickly and enthusiastically, and with an occasional stammer. Now, in Donald Trump's dining room, he was eagerly trying to talk his way into a dream job.

Perlmutter had taken Maisel to Mar-a-Lago for a meal that would help chip away at the club's annual $2,000 dining minimum. Before the appetizers arrived, Maisel launched into his pitch. What if Perlmutter and Marvel could keep the money from blockbuster superhero movies, instead of most of it going to studios like Fox (for *X-Men*) and Sony (for *Spider-Man*)? What if Marvel Studios was a real studio, not just a glorified production company? And what if he, David Maisel, could make that happen without Perlmutter having to contribute his own money?

Maisel had grown up in Saratoga Springs, a resort town in upstate New York. "My dad would take me to the comic-book store, but my mom would always make me do my homework first," he remembered. "Tony Stark was one of my favorite characters—it seemed like he had such a cool life." Maisel attended Duke University and then Harvard Business School. In a moment of self-reflection, he said, "The best description of me—I got it from my mom—is if you mix Peter Pan with Tony Stark. I don't have Tony's wealth, but I have his love of intellect."

After getting his MBA in 1987 and spending some years working at a Boston consulting firm, Maisel read a 1993 magazine article on Michael Ovitz, then the most powerful of Hollywood agents, and managed to obtain a five-minute job interview with him. "I had to sit there for two or three days waiting for my five minutes with the king," Maisel said.

Before the interview, Maisel bought a watch at his hotel's gift shop, an indulgence he couldn't really afford, but one that he hoped would make him look like more of a player, or at least bring him some luck. Whether it was because of the watch or because of his credentials, he landed a job at Ovitz's agency, Creative Artists Agency (CAA). Two years later, when Ovitz left CAA to be the president of Disney, Maisel followed him; when Disney fired Ovitz in 1997 after just fourteen months on the job, Maisel left too. Maisel had come to Hollywood for the usual reasons—excitement, glamour, love of big-budget storytelling—but he thrived because of his business smarts and his talent for finding loopholes and inconsistencies in dense contracts. He spent a peripatetic decade moving from one show-business job to another, including stints at the Broadway production company Livent and at the Endeavor Talent Agency, before making a deal with himself. Maisel decided to allow himself just two more years to leverage everything he had done in Hollywood and to figure out a way to be the guy making the movies, not just packaging them. That's when Ben Affleck, dressed head to toe in cherry-red leather, changed Maisel's life.

Affleck played the title role in *Daredevil*: Matt Murdock, the blind lawyer with superhuman senses and a secret life as a crime-fighter. The movie also starred Jennifer Garner, Colin Farrell, Michael Clarke Duncan, and, as Murdock's wisecracking lawyer buddy, Jon Favreau. Marvel and Fox hoped the 2003 movie would be their next big superhero franchise, but despite a respectable box office return, it landed with a thud for many critics and comic-book fans—including Maisel.

To his credit, Marvel Studios CEO Avi Arad had made sure that even when a movie underperformed, Marvel made money, from both licensing and merchandise sales. If Ang Lee's *Hulk* (which premiered later in 2003) didn't do as well at the box office as hoped, Universal

Pictures would absorb any losses while Marvel kept selling Hulk underwear. Arad sometimes referred to his approach as "layering": if each of the popular Marvel characters provided income streams (or "layers"), he reasoned, then the key to long-term profitability was having as many overlapping layers as possible.

Daredevil, however, galvanized Maisel. As a lifelong comics fan, he saw the potential for more, and as a minor shareholder in Marvel, he wanted to figure out just how much money Marvel had left on the table. (He had bought some Marvel stock as a lark, indulging his inner comics geek.) Working his Hollywood contacts, Maisel got a meeting with Arad, who passed him on to Perlmutter. Now, at Mar-a-Lago, Maisel made his case to Perlmutter that although Arad's layering approach had provided Marvel with a steady cashflow—and had enabled it to pay off its bankruptcy-related debt of approximately $250 million—Marvel could be doing even better, and it pained him to see how much money the company was squandering. Maisel pointed out that on *Spider-Man*, the top box-office hit of 2002, "Sony made nine figures—$100 million or $200 million—and then they made their share of the merchandise. Marvel only made maybe $20 or $30 million."

While the Spider-Man deal was skewed in Sony's favor—it yielded Marvel just 5 percent of the box-office receipts—the X-Men deal with Fox was even more unbalanced, giving Marvel about 1 percent. "It was so bad," Maisel said.

Maisel asserted that if he were running Marvel, he would not waste the potential of characters like Daredevil and the Hulk. He pointed to another example of neglect: Iron Man. Arad had licensed Tony Stark and his armored alter ego to New Line, where the property had sat unused for eight years. "Your character is in limbo and somebody else controls it," Maisel said. "When you make a movie deal for a license, you're freezing animation, you're freezing a lot of other things. You're handing over your babies to somebody, and nothing happens."

Arad and Kevin Feige were well aware of the limitations of the layering approach. They tried to exert their influence over Marvel movies, but not having the final say rankled them, even on projects where they respected their collaborators. "We suggested but they didn't listen," Feige said years later, diplomatically declining to call out any of the superhero flops of that era by name or to criticize any of the specific studio executives for their misunderstanding of Marvel's characters. "We didn't have the control. I hated that."

"From the moment I touched down in Marvel, Kevin had been telling Avi we have to get the rights back," Craig Kyle recalled. "Avi was in a situation where he represented all of Marvel. He was the face of Marvel Studios. Kevin was in there to make great movies. That could never be a guarantee until we could actually control the process."

Perlmutter cared about profits, not the quality of the films featuring Marvel characters, so Maisel framed his argument in terms that would appeal to him. If Marvel owned its own studio, then it could control which characters appeared in movies—and, importantly, *when*. "As a public company, Marvel was reliant on selling toys," Maisel said. "But they couldn't sell toys unless someone made the movie. They didn't schedule the movies." Fox had released the *X-Men* feature earlier than expected, and Marvel had been unable to saturate the market with merchandise in time. Perlmutter, Maisel guessed correctly, was still frustrated about that lost opportunity.

Maisel also believed that Bryan Singer's take on the X-Men was too adult for what he considered to be the primary market for the team: the kids who had watched *X-Men: The Animated Series* and bought X-Men toys. If Marvel made its own films, Maisel argued, it could keep the on-screen tone toy-friendly and ensure that each movie starred whatever lineup of heroes would move the most action figures.

Best of all, Maisel told Perlmutter, they could transform Marvel from a $250 million company into a multibillion-dollar company, and it would cost Perlmutter nothing. Maisel offered to work in exchange for stock options, meaning that he wouldn't make money unless Perlmutter made money.

Staring at the high-strung man sitting across from him at the table, Perlmutter saw a fellow striver and hired him.

✳

IN LATE 2003, Maisel showed up for his first day of work at the office space Marvel Studios shared with Spectra Star, the building Marvel staffers had nicknamed "the kite factory." Maisel, the new president and COO of Marvel Studios, immediately found himself at odds with Arad, the CEO. When he had first approached Arad hoping to pitch Perlmutter, Maisel hadn't revealed the scope of his ambitions; he had sold Arad on the idea that his time with Michael Ovitz at Disney had qualified him to work on brand management, intellectual-property management, and theme-park rights. Arad was shocked to learn, only after Maisel had been hired, that Maisel wanted to launch a new studio, a move that would likely make Arad irrelevant. And Arad took offense at the implication that any of the film deals he had made were bad ones.

"I love *Daredevil*. I thought it was enjoyable. Okay?" Arad said in 2004 when, bafflingly, Fox went into production with *Elektra*, a disastrous spinoff from *Daredevil* starring Jennifer Garner's assassin character. Arad made excuses for *Daredevil* underperforming: the opening-weekend weather was bad; Ben Affleck's real-life relationship with Jennifer Lopez distracted people; Daredevil wasn't a famous enough character.

Maisel had a simpler explanation. "Really, the movie just wasn't done in the way that it should have been," he said. He intended to do better.

The relationship between Arad and Maisel started tense and quickly got worse, stopping just short of a duel with sai blades in the parking lot. After a full decade with Marvel and Toy Biz, Arad was confident he could outlast Perlmutter's new golden boy and his crackpot schemes. Indeed, he believed that Maisel's long-term plan to turn Marvel Studios into an actual studio was doomed to failure. If Arad was certain of anything, it was that Maisel wouldn't be able to start a studio without a source of funding. He waited for the interloper to run headlong into that harsh reality.

Maisel ignored Arad. Poring over the fine points of the film deals that Arad had brokered, he noticed that for some of the characters, Marvel still retained the direct-to-video animation rights. Maisel promptly negotiated a deal with Lionsgate for four direct-to-DVD animated features based on Marvel characters. A typical Arad-era deal would have sold the license to the character in exchange for some cash and a seat at the creative table. Maisel instead negotiated a contract in which Lionsgate would pay the budget of $300,000 per film. Marvel Studios would make the movies, retaining complete creative control, and deliver them to Lionsgate, which would market and distribute them. After Lionsgate earned back its investment in each movie, it would split the profits evenly with Marvel.

"It was the first time that we fully had producing responsibility," Maisel said. "We had to make these on budget and deliver them to Lionsgate. When I talked to the board and Ike, I explained that we were guaranteed money. So we're making $1.2 million, but we're also producing stuff, so that was really fun." At long last, Maisel was making movies: *Ultimate Avengers: The Movie* and *Ultimate Avengers 2: Rise of the Panther*, both released in 2006, sold a combined 1.5 million copies, with each disc placing in the top ten children's DVDs that year. (The Marvel-Lionsgate partnership would eventually yield eight animated films.)

Maisel also worked his contacts to set up TV deals. Ari Emanuel, his old boss at Endeavor, paid a $1 million advance for the rights to produce a live-action pilot featuring the superpowered detective Jessica Jones for ABC. The show never happened, but that hardly mattered: Maisel had brought in a million dollars on a side deal while Arad's pet project, *Ghost Rider* (about the motorcycle-riding, demon-possessed Johnny Blaze), had been stuck in development for years. Any questions Perlmutter had about betting on Maisel evaporated. Perlmutter was occasionally uncertain about his gut, but he never doubted the bottom line.

After his early success, Maisel went to the Marvel board of directors with his proposal to build a live-action studio. (In recent years, Arad has claimed that, earlier in 2003, he pitched the board a plan in which Marvel would form its own studio, only to get shot down because "Ike's scared of the film business," but nobody else at Marvel seems to remember this happening.) Perlmutter and the board approved the new master plan, siding with Maisel. Arad was no longer allowed to make new deals or license any characters to other studios. All the remaining Marvel superheroes would stay at home while Maisel tried to make his big idea work.

That decision left Arad embittered. The rift between him and Perlmutter would never heal. But Perlmutter hadn't written Maisel a blank check, or a check of any amount whatsoever. As Maisel remembered the pivotal meeting, it ended with the board telling him, "Don't come back and talk about movies unless we have no money at risk."

✷

SINCE MARVEL WASN'T going to provide any money itself, Maisel needed to convince a large financial institution to stake him the hundreds of millions he needed to launch Marvel's studio. He proposed that the new studio would use the borrowed money to make films, earning enough to pay back the loan with interest. The collateral for such a large loan would be significant: The film rights to ten of Marvel's characters. A bank that ended up with those characters could keep them in perpetuity, even if it didn't use them, or it could sell them to any interested studio, with no benefit to Marvel. It was a serious risk, but Maisel needed the money.

Marvel executive John Turitzin, a lawyer who knew his way around a complicated bank deal, was assigned to oversee the ambitious project. He outranked Maisel on the Marvel corporate ladder, but he nevertheless thought of himself as Maisel's "assistant." As Turitzin put it, Maisel did most of the work "in his own head. . . . It was him all by himself, conceptualizing and developing it, thinking it through, pursuing thought pathways."

Arad had been so successful licensing Marvel intellectual property, most of the company's biggest names were already under contract with various Hollywood studios. That left Maisel with a weaker selection of characters to play with. These ten superhero properties, most of them future marquee names for Marvel, were considered B-listers and C-listers at the time: Captain America, the Avengers, Nick Fury, Black Panther, Ant-Man, Cloak and Dagger, Doctor Strange, Hawkeye, Power Pack, and Shang-Chi. Maisel had to tell two contradictory stories: while he persuaded banks that those assets were worth a fortune, he simultaneously needed to convince the Marvel board of directors that, if the deal went bad, losing the American film rights to Captain America and his superfriends would not be a huge loss.

Persuading the board was easier than he expected: no studio was interested in any of the characters in question. As Turitzin remembered it, the comic-book version of Captain America was "this funny-looking red-white-and-blue character, dressed, basically, in a cut-up flag with little white wings on his head, carrying a shield, and just weird." He added, "There's a reason why those characters had not been turned into movies or TV shows."

Also helping Maisel's case was that his offer didn't include all the rights to the characters as collateral, just the American film rights. As with other Marvel characters, including Spider-Man (movie rights controlled by Sony) and the X-Men (permanent residents of the Fox lot), Marvel would retain the rights to merchandising, publishing, videogames, and international film rights. If Marvel had ever wanted to make a Spider-Man movie to be shown exclusively in China, it legally could have done so without Sony's input, although that would have been impractical. The realities of big-budget filmmaking being what they were, Sony and Marvel were forced to work together to make movies that could be released in the US and around the world.

"I had to ask my board for zero money, and they were guaranteed to make money," Maisel recalled, almost giddily. "It was so exciting for everybody."

Turitzin, however, remembered the Marvel board being dubious: "It was a very frightening idea to the company because of the enormous potential downside to making movies. There was a lot of resistance at the board level to doing it."

For more than a year, Maisel pitched banks with his Marvel Studios scheme, and failed again and again. Finally, in the spring of 2005, Perlmutter set up a meeting for him at Merrill Lynch. Knowing that this was probably his last chance, Maisel poured everything into his presentation, drawing on his varied experiences as a comics geek, as a Hollywood player, and as a world-class contract-cruncher. Turitzin, who was in the room, said, "David spun a story about how popular these characters were and the depth of the storylines behind them and what they could support. He clearly had a passion for the source material."

Facing a room full of skeptics, Maisel wore them down, persuading them that a goofy overgrown Boy Scout named Captain America could one day be a cinematic icon. But he couldn't sell his vision for Marvel Studios solely on the name recognition of lesser-known Avengers like the Vision. Arad, however, had unwittingly done Maisel a favor. Because of the hit movies that Arad's deals produced, most notably *Spider-Man* and *X-Men*, Maisel was able to claim truthfully that, despite *Daredevil*'s middling reputation, films based on Marvel characters had an excellent track record at the box office. As Feige, who was operating very much in the background at the time, put it, "We were able to get the financing because almost all the movies worked."

Six months of tough negotiations followed, but Maisel and Merrill Lynch arrived at a deal: the bank would put up $525 million, with the legion of substitute heroes as collateral. Maisel reasoned this would be enough money to cover the budgets of four feature films (with some cash set aside for overhead). The brand-new studio had four chances to make at least one hit—or as Maisel put it, "We were guaranteed four at-bats." Maisel also brokered a deal with Paramount Studios, which would handle the distribution and marketing, taking a modest percentage of the box-office gross in return.

Then, on a September afternoon in 2005, the bankers flinched. "Ike, they're changing the terms," Maisel whispered into the phone, speaking with his boss from a Merrill Lynch conference room. The bank now wanted Marvel to come up with one-third of the money itself. Maisel and Turitzin knew Perlmutter and the board would never approve that outlay. Turitzin leaned back in his chair, put down the pen he had been using to take notes, and took a moment to reflect on the end of Maisel's dream. "This has been a fun project," he thought. "But it's over and done. It's dead."

"I'm in the conference room," Maisel quietly told Perlmutter. "I'm not going to leave." Maisel stubbornly refused to get up from his chair. As he described it: "I just held my breath like a little kid." Maisel knew there was another option for covering the shortfall: Marvel could bring in a third party (likely another studio) as an investor. That move, however, would require giving up on his aim of full creative control, so he didn't even want to mention it.

Before he turned blue, Maisel came up with a solution. Marvel would shoulder some of the production costs by preselling distribution rights in five foreign territories for each of the four films. Maisel persuaded Merrill Lynch to agree on contractual language that said Marvel would *try* to cover a third of the budget. "They changed the word from 'requirement' to 'target' and solved the issue," Maisel said, grinning. If Marvel didn't produce 33 percent of a film's budget with foreign presales, the bank was still on the hook for the remainder, so long as Marvel could demonstrate that it had attempted, in good faith, to raise the money.

In November 2005, Marvel and Merrill Lynch finalized the deal. Two and a half years after his lunch at Mar-a-Lago, David Maisel had his studio. The final contractual hurdle for Merrill Lynch to commit was for Paramount to sign on officially as Marvel's distributor. So it was a big day at the kite factory when the fax arrived confirming Paramount would distribute six movies made by Marvel Studios. The staff gathered around the fax machine, looking at the newly printed document as if it were a holy relic, realizing that they would soon be making movies and contemplating what an amazing opportunity and responsibility that was.

Arad poked his head into the room, witnessing the moment when his rival's dream was coming true. In his baritone voice, he dramatically intoned, "Be afraaaaaaid."

PHASE ONE

★

CHAPTER FOUR

Plausibility

★

> Tony Stark was able to build this in
> a cave with a box of scraps.
>
> *Iron Man*

IKE PERLMUTTER BARKED QUESTIONS AT KEVIN FEIGE, interrogating him from New York via speakerphone—he wanted to make sure the half-billion dollars from David Maisel's Merrill Lynch deal wasn't being frittered away. "I had not talked to Ike much at all at this point, because he just talked to Avi," Feige said. (At Marvel Studios in late 2005, Avi Arad was the CEO, Feige was executive vice president, and Maisel had just been promoted to vice chairman, which meant he reported directly to Perlmutter, who remained the CEO of Marvel Entertainment.) "But he literally was asking 'Are you going to be able to do these two movies in two years?'"

Marvel Studios' leaders had been considering the critical question of which characters to use for their four Merrill Lynch at-bats, knowing that they needed at least one home run to stay in the game. The three strongest contenders were Iron Man (the movie rights had finally reverted to Marvel from New Line), the Incredible Hulk (Universal retained some crucial rights to the character but was willing to cut a deal), and Ant-Man (largely because Edgar Wright had already written a top-notch treatment).

The general public wasn't familiar with Iron Man. In fact, Marvel had done consumer testing that revealed awareness of the character was almost zero. But the Marvel executives had reason to believe the character was a strong choice for a movie: they knew Iron Man made for a good toy. In 2005, Marvel ran a focus group for children. The person leading the focus group described Marvel characters to the kids—origin, personality, powers—and at the end of the presentation, asked which hero they would most want to play with as a toy. John Turitzin remembered, "After describing Iron Man, he jumped from the eighth most popular character to being the first character. Kids thought it was really cool to have, basically, a robot that could fly and could shoot beams out of the palms of his hands. They thought that was great."

Hulk-branded merchandise already sold steadily—so based largely on toy potential, Marvel Studios planned to start with Iron Man and the Hulk.

Standing next to Arad's telephone, Feige listened as Perlmutter asked him outright: "Kevin! Kevin! Can you make these two movies in two years?" Feige swallowed and declared that yes, he could.

To prepare two feature films and then shoot them back-to-back, Marvel Studios needed more space than the kite factory provided. In October 2005, it relocated to a larger office, formerly the Los Angeles headquarters of *Playboy* magazine, an unrenovated but centrally located suite above a Mercedes-Benz dealership in Beverly Hills. There was a warren of cubicles (many empty at first), but Maisel and Feige had offices; Arad claimed the largest office for himself. Among the others working there were Jeremy Latcham (Maisel's assistant), Stephen Broussard (Feige's assistant), Ari Arad (Avi's son, hired by his father as a junior producer) and Craig Kyle (busy with Marvel's animated projects).

By the time Marvel Studios left the kite factory, Avi Arad was planning his own exit. Arad had lost his turf war with Maisel; Arad's method of making Marvel movies had fallen out of favor with Perlmutter, who was unhappy with the financial yields from his licensing deals. But since the two Israeli buddies had been through a war together to win control of Marvel in the 1990s, Perlmutter was generous. In May 2006, Arad's 3.15 million shares of Marvel stock became fully vested, allowing him to sell a chunk of them for $60 million. Having made it in Hollywood, Arad had no interest in returning to toy design. Instead, he planned to create his own production company, Avi Arad Entertainment. He signed a non-compete deal, which meant that he could be an advisor on Marvel characters appearing in movies made by other studios (such as his beloved Ghost Rider), but he could not make any superhero or fantasy movies unless they were based on Marvel properties. Because he was still on staff when the deals were made for *Iron Man* and *The Incredible Hulk*, he received a producer title on each movie; he would also continue to produce Spider-Man movies for Sony, including future spinoffs such as *Venom* and *Morbius*. (Avi's son Ari left Marvel Studios with him.)

Arad publicly insisted that his departure "was only my choice because one day came when I said 'I think I've had enough of this.'" He dismissed the ambitions of the new regime: "The company was growing with the CEO of this, and the CFO of that, but it was basically [a situation in which] we were doing everything but now there's way too many people for me to deal with. And everybody wanted to make movies. Everyone. I mean, you name it, the people who were cleaning the place wanted to read the scripts."

Around the time Arad left, Perlmutter signed a licensing deal with Hasbro for Marvel toys. That made the impact of any particular toy on the Marvel bottom line less direct, but Perlmutter kept making Marvel decisions based on how they would affect toy sales. Meanwhile, in November 2005, Marvel Studios brought in a new chief operating officer: Michael Helfant, who had held the same position at Beacon Pictures. At the time, he was described as second-in-command to Arad, who claimed, "I needed the security and safety of someone who has been doing this forever." Helfant's job would prove short-lived: he was forced out on the day *Iron Man* started principal photography, when Feige was named president of production. (On the same day, Maisel was promoted to chairman.) In retrospect, it seems clear that Helfant was an insurance policy in case Feige couldn't handle the job.

Arad's former office was turned into a conference room, which Marvel Studios sorely needed. The main office space was filling up with concept artists on short-term contracts who adorned their cubicles with illustrations of Iron Man flying and the Hulk fighting tanks. When they ran out of room, they pushed the cubicles up against the edges of their shared multiuse room to make more space for art. Though Marvel hadn't yet hired directors—Feige and Maisel were working on that—the studio was already figuring out what its first two movies would look like. Marvel already had a few cultural reference points to serve as cornerstones for the movies. Given recent world events, Feige was convinced that the world craved superheroes more than ever.

✱

THE FIRST TEASER trailer for 2002's *Spider-Man* had reached theaters in the summer of 2001; it featured a scene shot specially for the trailer. In a New York City bank, a half-dozen robbers breach the vault, grab some cash, and get to the roof (via grappling hook) before escaping by helicopter. Celebrating the completed job, they make their getaway over the streets of downtown Manhattan—until the helicopter is caught in a strand of adhesive webbing and pulled into a giant web spun between the Twin Towers of the World Trade Center.

After the terrorist attacks of September 11, 2001, the entertainment industry, as unprepared for the attack as the government, haltingly cobbled together an emotionally appropriate response. Sony promptly pulled the *Spider-Man* trailer from theaters and took down coming-attractions posters that featured the New York City skyline (including the Twin Towers) reflected in Spidey's eyes.

In November 2001, Karl Rove, a senior advisor to President George W. Bush, and Jack Valenti, chairman of the Motion Picture Association of America, hosted a conference at the Peninsula Hotel in Beverly Hills. In attendance were more than forty executives from all the major studios and broadcast TV networks. In a two-hour meeting, Rove emphasized that the US government needed a unified response to 9/11 from the entertainment industry, outlining six major points:

1. The US campaign in Afghanistan was a war against terrorism, not Islam.
2. People can serve in the war effort and in their communities.
3. US troops and their families need support.
4. 9/11 requires a global response.
5. This is a fight against evil.
6. Children should be reassured that they will be safe.

(Rove also had a seventh point, though it seemed tacked on: he told them that none of these efforts amounted to propaganda.) Rove declared, "It's clear that the leaders of the industry have ideas about how they want to contribute to the war effort."

After that meeting, Sam Raimi did some reshoots for *Spider-Man*, adding a scene to the climax where New Yorkers come together to help the webslinger fight the Green Goblin. "If you mess with one of us, you mess with all of us," says an extra with a heavy New York accent. The movie also added a new CGI sequence: Spider-Man, swinging through Manhattan, lands on top of a flagpole flying the Stars and Stripes. The scene had such resonance in that ultrapatriotic moment, it was shoehorned into the final trailers for the movie.

TV shows like *The X-Files*, built on the premise that there were numerous, massive government conspiracies, were suddenly out of vogue. New series like *24* and *Alias*, in which American agents fought against enemies of the United States, had been in the works before 9/11, but their creators found that they had inadvertently met the moment. "It might have seemed an opportunist move to do a show so patriotic and so much about a young American hero," said *Alias* producer/director J. J. Abrams. "The truth is, I wanted to change the pattern. The idea of doing a show in which the government is an evil conspirator didn't interest me."

Popular storytelling rooted in clear delineation between good and evil seemed to have even greater appeal, evidenced by the success of *Harry Potter* and *The Lord of the Rings* (even if *LOTR* director Peter Jackson had to resist post-9/11 pressure to rename his 2002 installment, *The Two Towers*). It seemed like a moment custom-made for superheroes.

When *Spider-Man* broke box-office records in 2002, it put all Hollywood superhero content on the fast track. Studios that had optioned Marvel properties with Avi Arad hustled to move them into production. After two of its superhero movies bombed in 1997 (*Batman & Robin* and the Shaquille O'Neal vehicle *Steel*), Warner Bros. had gotten out of the superhero business for a while, even cancelling a Tim Burton Superman movie that would have starred Nicolas Cage. Now, as home of the DC superheroes, Warner Bros. wanted back in, but nothing the studio tried seemed to work. It scrapped a somber screenplay by Darren Aronofsky called *Batman: Year One* and a failed Man of Steel reboot called *Superman: Flyby*. In 2002, Warner Bros. chief operating officer Alan Horn tried to reboot both franchises simultaneously with *Batman vs. Superman*, but judged the script he had commissioned from Akiva Goldsman to be too dark. Since *Batman vs. Superman* already had a slot on the 2004 release schedule, Warner Bros. replaced it with a Catwoman movie, resuscitating a script for a spinoff of *Batman Returns* (1992) originally intended to star Michelle Pfeiffer. Rushed into production with Halle Berry as the lead, *Catwoman* made its release date but flopped.

At that point, Warner Bros. went back to basics, turning the Batman franchise over to Christopher Nolan (with massive success) and stealing Bryan Singer away from the X-Men to take on Superman (with middling results). Brett Ratner replaced Singer as director to do a rush job on *X-Men: The Last Stand*, the third movie starring the mutants. The *Blade* series concluded in 2004 with *Blade: Trinity*; also released that year was another Marvel adaptation, the ultra-violent and unpopular *The Punisher*. (That was one of Arad's final licensing deals to make it to the screen, except for *Ghost Rider*, which became a vehicle for Johnny Blaze superfan Nicolas Cage in 2007.) Over at Fox, Tim Story's two Fantastic Four movies weren't disasters, but they (and most other superhero movies of the moment) were overshadowed by a different movie about a superpowered family: Pixar's *The Incredibles* (2004), directed by Brad Bird.

∗

AGAINST THIS BACKDROP, Marvel Studios embarked on the production of its first movie, *Iron Man*. The studio's leadership was confident it could connect with audiences—even if most people weren't familiar with Iron Man's backstory or mythology. The character had been neglected for so long that the only collection of *Iron Man* comics readily available was *Demon in a Bottle*, compiling the 1979 run of issues where Tony Stark succumbed to alcoholism. That confused some of the Hollywood screenwriters who were trying to get up to speed on the character before meeting with Marvel to pitch their takes on the character. Was Marvel really trying to launch a new studio with a superpowered version of *The Lost Weekend*?

Even without addiction issues, the character of Tony Stark was a complicated figure: as a billionaire weapons manufacturer, he was the face of the military-industrial complex. "We're in two wars, Iraq and Afghanistan, and the vice president [Dick Cheney] was formerly the CEO of Halliburton, the weapons manufacturer," pointed out Matt Holloway, one of *Iron Man*'s credited writers. "We're going to take that kind of guy and make him a hero. How do we do that?" (One assumes Karl Rove would have had fewer qualms.)

That was exactly the challenge Stan Lee set himself when he created Iron Man in 1963 (in collaboration with his brother Larry Lieber and the artists Jack Kirby and Don Heck). "I think I gave myself a dare," Lee said years after the fact, trying to retrospectively discern the logic in his improvised decisions. "It was the height of the Cold War. The readers, the young readers, if there was one thing they hated, it was war, it was the military. So I got a hero who represented that to the hundredth degree. He was a weapons manufacturer, he was providing weapons for the Army, he was rich, he was an industrialist. I thought it would be fun to take the kind of character that nobody would like, none of our readers would like, and shove him down their throats and make them like him."

Holloway was excited by the opportunity to make the character relevant in the modern era. "It wasn't even a question of 'Would this be cool?'" he said. "It was like, 'Holy fucking shit, this is amazing, this character. And a character with these huge flaws, but with so much potential, and potentially squandered potential, or potential used in the wrong direction.'" Although Marvel briefly considered making the movie a period piece, Holloway and his writing partner, Art Marcum, updated Iron Man's origin story, moving the location where Tony Stark is captured by foreign soldiers from Vietnam to twenty-first-century Afghanistan: a simple switch that thrust the movie into the politics of the moment. Even if Marvel Studios didn't subscribe to Rove's Peninsula Hotel propaganda plan, it didn't want to make a movie that cut against the hyperpatriotic military mood of the nation. There were a variety of reasons for this choice, but one of them was that half a billion dollars were at stake.

"*X-Men* was proving that you could tell interesting metaphorical stories through superheroes," Marcum said. "But I don't think we were ever self-consciously saying, 'Hey, let's make this the riposte against things that are already out there.'"

Or as Mark Fergus (who joined the *Iron Man* writing team later in the process) put it, "9/11 and terrorism essentially supplanted Russia and the Cold War. That all seemed to be quaint now that we're dealing with terrorism and unknowable forces that were not really tied to one nation. But it also helped to tell the story about what is America's response to that? And how we help create these things by weapon sales, or we've destroyed the stability of their country, so we created our own next foe."

While Holloway and Marcum turned out drafts of the *Iron Man* screenplay, Feige courted the director he wanted, Jon Favreau. While Favreau has since become known for effects-heavy Disney entertainment like *The Jungle Book*, *The Lion King*, and *The Mandalorian*, at the time, he was most famous for the 1996 indie movie *Swingers* (which he wrote and starred in opposite Vince Vaughn, but didn't direct). His biggest hit as a director had been the 2003 Will Ferrell comedy *Elf*, which is not just a modern Christmas classic but a movie that grossed $220 million at the box office against a $33 million budget. That success put Favreau on the shortlist for any studio trying to maximize a modest investment (i.e., all of them).

Favreau had maintained a career as both an actor and director, and by appearing in the disappointing 2003 *Daredevil* as "Foggy" Nelson, he had formed a relationship with Avi Arad. For years, Favreau and Arad had casually kicked around the idea about a comedic take on Captain America, focused on how the innocent 1940s Super Soldier Steve Rogers would grapple with an unfamiliar modern society. Favreau's success with a broadly similar story in *Elf* seemed to make him the obvious choice. But when the darker story of Iron Man was chosen as the first Marvel Studios film, Feige and Maisel decided Favreau was still the right director for the job.

"Going back to my experience watching Sony and Laura Ziskin and Avi hire Sam [Raimi], or Fox hire Bryan Singer, those were not people who had just come out with a big, giant blockbuster and now were doing their next," Feige recalled. "They were filmmakers who'd done super-interesting movies on a lesser scale coming into a bigger platform." From the beginning, Marvel believed in the expansiveness and possibilities of the superhero genre.

Picking Favreau meant Marvel was backing a director who prized smaller character moments over big action sequences—but wall-to-wall action might have been too expensive for the incipient studio, anyway. "That's why Jon Favreau was our top choice," David Maisel said, explaining that Marvel prized his actor-oriented ability "to make a scene around the kitchen table as interesting as a fight at the end of the movie."

On Favreau's first day on the job, as he was beginning the earliest stages of preproduction, he walked into his shabby new Marvel Studios office and wrote one word on a whiteboard: *PLAUSIBILITY*. He was making a movie about a man who could fly, but he wanted to keep the story as earthbound as possible. Hundreds of ideas about the film came and went on that whiteboard, but that one word, *plausibility*, always stayed. (Favreau was echoing the sign over the door to Richard Donner's office—*VERISIMILITUDE*—but at least chose a synonym that was easier for Feige to pronounce.)

For Favreau, the appeal of joining a fledgling independent studio like Marvel was that, so long as he brought in the movie on time and for the expected budget, he would have more freedom than the director of a typical tentpole movie, who needs to manage both the production and a barrage of studio notes. "We were outsiders," Favreau said of those early, heady days when he operated with minimal corporate oversight.

The Marvel executives were happy to leave him alone, both because they trusted him and because they were busy making sure they could pay the bills: every dollar they could get from foreign sales was money that Marvel wouldn't have to borrow from its Merrill Lynch line of credit. "People forget that *Iron Man* was an independent movie," Feige later said. "I pitched that movie dozens of times to foreign buyers because we had to get—I don't remember exactly what the percentage was, but a large percentage of financing it was from pre-selling the foreign. We had a completion bond company. It was an *independent movie*."

Stephen Platt, an *Iron Man* concept artist, remembered something Favreau told him early on: "Look, I'm going to lean on you guys to really pump up and elevate the action, because I'm going to be focusing on character. I'm going to be the character guy, but when it comes to action, just turn it up to 11, and we'll see where it takes us. Then I'll be able to figure out from there how it's supposed to feel."

Favreau brought in two additional screenwriters: Mark Fergus and Hawk Otsby, who had been working with him on an adaptation of the Edgar Rice Burroughs novel *The Princess of Mars* that never got made. While all four writers (plus the director) labored on the script, Favreau and Marvel Studios turned their attention to a crucial issue: which actors would actually speak all this dialogue.

The first actor to join what would become the Marvel Cinematic

Universe was Terrence Howard, who would play Lt. Col. James "Rhodey" Rhodes, the best friend and conscience of Tony Stark. Not yet famous as the leading man of the show *Empire*, Howard was coming off an Oscar-nominated turn in the movie *Hustle & Flow*. "That was a huge get," Marcum recalled. Howard, a Marvel Comics fan, signed a three-picture deal, knowing that his character could become the superhero War Machine later on.

A bigger task was finding the perfect Tony Stark. "Hollywood likes them to be twenty-six and cut, but Tony Stark was not a young kid," Arad said. Ten years earlier, when the *Iron Man* rights were at 20th Century Fox, Tom Cruise, then thirty-four, had flirted with the idea of playing Stark. According to Feige, however, Cruise's asking fee at the time was more than even a profitable studio like Fox was willing to risk on an untested superhero property.

"The big internet rumor was that Tony Stark was going to be played by Johnny Depp," recalled Eric Vespe, who wrote for the site *Ain't It Cool News* under the name "Quint."

Marvel Studios couldn't afford actors at the top of the A-list like Depp, star of the *Pirates of the Caribbean* franchise, or Cruise. Several lesser-known candidates surfaced. One was the thirty-eight-year-old Jim Caviezel, best known for playing the title role in *The Passion of the Christ*, who had declined the role of Cyclops in *X-Men* several years before. But it was thirty-eight-year-old Timothy Olyphant's grimly conflicted turn as Sheriff Seth Bullock on HBO's *Deadwood* that made him "the one everyone was rooting for," according to one Marvel insider. Favreau had one other name in mind: Sam Rockwell, also thirty-eight, a character actor then best known for his leading turn in George Clooney's antic movie *Confessions of a Dangerous Mind*. But that was before Favreau met with Robert Downey Jr.

Despite decades of work in Hollywood and a 1992 Oscar nomination (for *Chaplin*), Downey, then forty-one, had an almost perfect record of commercial failure and a well-publicized reputation as a substance abuser. Most famously, under the influence in 1996, he broke into the house of a neighboring family in Malibu and passed out in an empty bed belonging to an eleven-year-old child. In 2001, after another drug arrest, he was fired from the TV show *Ally McBeal*. But he had cleaned up, married the whip-smart producer Susan Levin, and gradually worked his way back into Hollywood's good graces. Despite his troubles, many people in the movie business liked him and wanted to keep working with him.

Many at Marvel thought that Downey's past problems made him too risky—only two years earlier, he had been on probation. Favreau, however, believed that his troubled public persona made him the perfect actor for the role. Tony Stark is an extremely gifted man whose achievements are undermined by his struggles with personal demons and substance abuse. Downey's face was visual shorthand for that character.

Favreau convinced the leaders of Marvel Studios that Downey was Tony Stark. The Marvel Entertainment executives in New York were, however, less enthusiastic, worrying that Downey didn't just have a general atmosphere of risk, but came with specific financial hazards. Screenwriter Matt Holloway recalled Favreau's advocacy for Downey: "Jon, I know, felt in his bones that it should be Robert and fought for him to the point of saying, 'It's going to be him or it's going to be me.'" With neither Favreau nor the New York executives yielding, the production was at an impasse. Looking for a way forward, the casting director, Sarah Halley Finn, suggested to Favreau that they at least have Downey make an audition tape.

Downey, just as certain as Favreau that he was the right man for the job, had three weeks to get ready. He had three scenes to learn, and he worked on them relentlessly: "The missus says she could have woken me up in the middle of the night and I'd have recited the audition dialogue in double time." The audition happened in a rented room at Raleigh Studios in Hollywood. "Right before the first take, I felt like I almost left my body—a sudden surge of nerves," Downey said. "Then all of a sudden, it was like coasting downhill on an old Schwinn Cruiser, like I could do no wrong."

The scenes included a contentious-but-flirty encounter with a reporter, a confrontation with Rhodes, and badinage with American troops in the back of a Humvee in Afghanistan before it's attacked. Together, they showcased Downey's ability to shift effortlessly between glib humor and quiet intensity. Downey had already figured out how he wanted to play Tony Stark: as a "very broken guy," he said, whose "façade is confident."

"There was a lot of conversation with a lot of great actors," Stephen Platt said of that audition. "Then Tony Stark walked in."

Armed with that screen test, Maisel and Feige had a meeting with Ike Perlmutter, John Turitzin, and some Marvel board members. "We recommended Robert," Maisel said. "Kevin and I gave our reasons why. We were nervous, you know? We were a public company, and we were betting our future on *Iron Man*. At the time, Robert had won many awards but never had a big box-office success and had his own personal issues—that he had overcome."

Nevertheless, the answer from New York, according to Favreau, was "Under no circumstances are we prepared to hire him for any price."

Uncowed, Favreau anonymously leaked the news that Downey was in talks to star as Tony Stark. When movie fans on the internet reacted to that planted story with overwhelming enthusiasm, the New York executives finally acquiesced.

Once Downey had the role, Favreau found that the actor served as a "great beacon" who attracted a "tremendous wealth of talented people" who would make sure the movie didn't play like a cartoon. Favreau's longtime friend Gwyneth Paltrow (they met on the set of *Mrs. Parker and the Vicious Circle* in 1994) had won an Oscar in 1998 for *Shakespeare in Love* but had fallen into a career lull in her thirties (an all-too-common situation for Hollywood actresses). Favreau convinced her that the role of Pepper Potts would go beyond the stereotypical damsel in distress.

David Maisel identified the secret Douglas Sirk heart of *Iron Man*: "It's like a 1950s love story—with ten or fifteen minutes of action—about a man in his forties changing his life and deciding that, while he could have a million different women, the love of his life is Gwyneth Paltrow, Pepper Potts. There's a million so-called friends, but his only true friend is Terrence Howard, Rhodey. And it's almost like a father-son thing with Jeff Bridges."

Rounding out the core cast was Bridges in the role of Obadiah Stane, Stark's mentor and the film's heavy. The original plan was to use Stane as a red herring, setting up a gonzo appearance by a villain called the Mandarin and a climactic sequence in China. At the San Diego Comic-Con in 2006, Favreau even announced that the Mandarin would be the film's villain. "There was a point where Mandarin was going to be Crimson Dynamo, and he was going to pop out of the ground at Stark Enterprises as a surprise," remembered Matt Holloway. (The Crimson Dynamo was a frequent foe in the *Iron Man* comic book, where the name was used by various Russian and Soviet agents wearing their own superpowered suits of armor.)

"We thought we were making only one Iron Man movie," Holloway's partner Art Marcum explained. "We had to pack it all into one."

But during script development, the film's other screenwriting duo, Mark Fergus and Hawk Otsby, were "begging," they said, to leave the Mandarin out. They felt that the villain—built on broad racial stereotypes—undercut, in a fairly spectacular manner, Favreau's plausibility mandate. The higher-ups listened, in part because they were already beginning to think about the long term. In a crucial meeting, Feige said to Fergus, "Why don't we just save the Mandarin for another day?" (A Mandarin imposter appeared in 2013's *Iron Man 3*, and the genuine character finally made his Marvel Studios debut in 2021's *Shang-Chi and the Legend of the Ten Rings*, thirteen years after *Iron Man*.)

It was the right creative choice. The third X-Men movie (in 2006) and the third Spider-Man movie (in 2007) both demonstrated how a superhero movie could become overstuffed with too many villains and too much plot. It was also a sound financial decision, Maisel pointed out: "It saved a ton of money, because we didn't have to shoot all those scenes."

Some of the money that was saved by not filming in China went to shooting the movie in California, a more expensive location than states with film-production subsidies (such as Georgia, North Carolina, and New Mexico, all of which Marvel would use in future years). Favreau insisted on California. He believed in keeping film-industry jobs in LA, and he wanted to stay close to home during the shoot; on an artistic level, he knew that most superhero movies were set in New York City (or fictional variants such as Metropolis and Gotham City) and wanted to distinguish *Iron Man* with an authentic West Coast feel. Marvel wasn't eager to spend the extra money, but Favreau had negotiated a clause in his contract guaranteeing that production would happen in Los Angeles.

While Favreau strove for geographic authenticity, down to the Ferris wheel on the Santa Monica Pier, the movie deliberately blurred the ethnicity of some of its antagonists. The filmmakers attempted to make the terrorist Ten Rings organization vaguely, although not definitively, Middle Eastern.

When designer Dianne Chadwick created the logo for the Ten Rings—visible in an early scene in the background of Tony Stark's hostage video, on the flag behind him—*Iron Man* production designer J. Michael Riva asked her to put extra care into its creation, noting that "this character [meaning the Mandarin] could come back" in future movies. That flag was one of Marvel's earliest Easter eggs: It implied that the Ten Rings had a geographical reach that went beyond Afghanistan. The art department knew, Chadwick said, that the Ten Rings were affiliated with the Mandarin, who in turn claimed to be a descendant of Genghis Khan. Chadwick and Riva sought to design an image that would hint at this lineage.

Chadwick designed the overlapping rings, the swords, and the ornate border, but had to track down translators and calligraphers who could render the characters within the rings in a Mongolian script. "They were actually in Mongolia," Chadwick said. "There aren't that many people who can do this calligraphy anymore." The words within the final logo were the names of real Mongol and Turkic tribes and clans.

Downey Jr., not yet a global superstar, was fond of visiting the modest Marvel offices to see how the production was progressing.

"There was no script, and we were basically writing the movie on the wall," says Stephen Platt. (The screenwriters had generated reams of pages, but nothing had been nailed down.) "There's no action beats, there's nothing. It's literally like 'Iron Man fights an army.'" As the art team showed off their work, Platt said, Downey eagerly posed in fight stances, playing out potential scenarios in front of the sketches taped to the wall. "He was just like a little kid at Christmas," Platt recalled. "He couldn't wait to get going."

CHAPTER FIVE

Proof of Concept

Let's face it, this is not the worst thing
you've caught me doing.

Iron Man

"**T**HEY HAD NO SCRIPT, MAN," JEFF BRIDGES GROUSED. "We would show up every day and we wouldn't know what we were going to say. We would have to call up writers on the phone: 'You got any ideas?' I like to be prepared. I like to know my lines. I made a little adjustment in my head. That adjustment was: *Jeff, just relax, you are in a 200 million dollar student film, have fun, just relax.*"

Before *Iron Man* started shooting, Jon Favreau and his collaborators moved out of the overcrowded Marvel Studios office above the Mercedes-Benz dealership in Beverly Hills, leaving the Marvel Studios executives behind and relocating the movie's production to the old Howard Hughes studios in dusty Playa Vista, California. (As a bonus, that was one step further away from supervision by Marvel's East Coast executives.) "I don't even know how to describe it—it was, like, all dirt," hair designer Nina Paskowitz recalled. "There were a couple of little sheds on the property, a couple of little housing things, and that's it."

By the time various departments—makeup, editing, design— moved to Playa Vista, they were working off outline plot points and concept art. There was still no locked script. The creative staff had plenty of work, but their isolation also fostered a party atmosphere. Art director Dave Klassen and production designer Michael Riva, who had also collaborated with Jon Favreau on his 2005 film *Zathura: A Space Adventure*, hosted cocktail hours that soon became legendary. "Martinis, beer, whatever," Stephen Platt reminisced. "It was great because it's a morale thing, right?"

"I remember Jeff Bridges bringing this game with these little plastic pigs called Porkers," *Iron Man* makeup artist Jamie Kelman said. "They're like dice and you would roll them, and in between takes, we'd sit around and play this game on set. It doesn't seem like you could ever do that on a Marvel movie anymore—play a little dice game with a lead actor sitting there rolling plastic pigs around and saying, 'Hey, they're making bacon,' because one of their noses lands in the other one's hind cheeks. But this was the easy fun of those days. And it wasn't a million takes. It seems like they all became a million takes after that." There was plenty of time for Porkers while the cast waited around for the next pages of their script.

"It was crazy, but the idea that we had no script in preproduction sounds a little more scary than it actually was," Art Marcum said. "We had a lot of good material to build on and an amazing character in Tony Stark."

Shortly before the cameras rolled, Mark Fergus and Hawk Otsby cobbled together a functional screenplay, drawing from years' worth of brainstorming and failed efforts. "We looked at everything, all the drafts from day one, even going back fifteen, twenty years. We just wanted to see what everyone had done," Fergus said. They produced a shooting script in only twelve days—although Favreau didn't stick to it. The director had discovered that Downey was a performer who flourished when allowed to improvise, and he planned to keep his set as spontaneous as possible.

"We continued to rewrite it all through the next five months, on set, nonstop. And it was a blast," Marcum recalled. "A blast" wasn't how everyone viewed it—while Downey thrived and Paltrow soon adapted, Bridges remained uncomfortable.

"Jeff loved to have a script a good three months before he did the scene," Favreau recalled. That wasn't remotely possible on *Iron Man*. "Robert would come in and bounce the script off the wall of the trailer every day."

"They had an outline," Bridges conceded.

Loyd Catlett, Bridges's longtime stand-in (an actor of similar build and complexion who can substitute for a star during lighting tests and other technical rehearsals), expanded on the shooting method: "In the morning, we'd go in and then Jeff and Favreau, a couple of the producers, a writer, and Robert Downey would go sit in the dressing room, and they wouldn't come out for four or five hours. And we were all just hanging out, taking breaks, going to lunch, wondering, 'What are we going to get done today?' But then they'd come out with a pretty good idea of what they were going to do with the scene for the day."

Favreau's method required rapid adjustments from the crew. Sometimes they were relatively minor: Paskowitz remembered having approximately "five seconds" to change the hairstyle on actress Leslie Bibb during a party scene. Sometimes completed sets would be torn down without having been used because an associated scene had been scrapped. "The script changed so much," art director Susan Wexler said. "We started building the cave where Iron Man is really conceived, when Tony Stark is kidnapped. That was the *one* thing we knew that we were going to be doing. It was three-quarters of the way done, and they said, 'Maybe we won't do the cave.'" According to Wexler, Michael Riva then stepped in, saying, "You know, the set is pretty much standing there. It would be really silly to not do the cave."

It's hard to imagine *Iron Man* without that cave scene, the place where Tony Stark stubbornly built a suit of armor, turning himself into Marvel's first superhero. It's a setting so iconic for the Marvel films that over a decade later, the credits of *Avengers: Endgame* concluded with audio of Tony Stark's hammer echoing off the cave's walls.

Favreau found that Downey and Paltrow had genuine chemistry as Tony and Pepper. The director became obsessed with one specific scene where Pepper would, in a moment initially scripted as gross-out comedy, stick her hand into Tony's chest cavity to replace his arc-reactor heart. Jamie Kelman had built a prosthetic device that would attach to Downey's chest and would fill it with KY jelly to simulate the goop surrounding Stark's biomechanical heart. Favreau knew the scene needed emotional weight, so he decided to rewrite it himself.

"He wanted that to be a bonding moment for them," Fergus explained. "He wanted to really revel in it. It's kind of intimate and kind of gross and kind of sexy. He really wanted that moment to land, and he spent a lot of time on that scene." Favreau was highlighting that Tony Stark, the man with a hundred girlfriends, trusted only Pepper Potts with his heart.

To make the romance work, Favreau needed to draw out the intelligence and charm of his leads, making sure they were playing heightened versions of themselves. In the comic books, Tony Stark doesn't have much of a sense of humor, but Downey infused him with his own wit and wrapped the character in a blanket of sarcasm. Although Paltrow wasn't as comfortable with improvisation as Downey, Favreau found a way to inject her personality into the script—he would jot down things Paltrow said during rehearsals and then repurpose them as Pepper's dialogue.

When Favreau was running through a scene in which Pepper advises Tony on his art collection, Paltrow corrected Favreau on a few of the finer points. He then had Pepper do exactly the same thing to Tony in the final version of the script. (The idea that Tony Stark had an art collection at all had roots in the actor's own life: set decorator Lauri Gaffin put the collection together after Downey "plopped down" in her office one day and nattered on about art for an hour.) Paltrow also drew from her own life for an unexpected comedy beat in the big party scene shot at Walt Disney Concert Hall, when Pepper tells Tony she's not wearing deodorant.

That scene, where Pepper in a deep-blue evening gown dazzles

Tony, reverberated through the rest of the franchise. "When they were storyboarding, it was so much fun," costume designer Laura Jean Shannon recalled. "She turns around and it's the moment when Tony Stark realizes he's in love with Pepper. He's a dummy—we all knew that a long time ago—but whatever, that's a man for you."

Favreau's controlled chaos reached its zenith with that scene, which came midway through the shoot. "Jon was really intense about that," Gaffin remembered. She, like the rest of the crew, had no script to work from, no idea where the scene was going. In some takes, Downey and Paltrow kissed. "All of a sudden, they're going to the rooftop of Disney Hall and they're kissing," Gaffin said. "And we're like, what the hell?"

"This is one of those scenes where everyone from the studio is looking at you like you're crazy because it's four in the morning, and you're doing ten takes, and you're running in and telling them to do something completely different from the last time," Favreau said. Ultimately, in the editing room, Favreau spliced together a few different takes to make it look like Pepper and Tony *almost* kissed. Their big romantic moment, like the Mandarin, would have to wait.

✴

TONY STARK IS a playboy and a wiseass and a weapons manufacturer, but only that last quality required the cooperation of the United States military to look right on screen. Hewing to his mantra of plausibility, Favreau wanted to use real military equipment and to give Terrence Howard's Lt. Col. Rhodes the accoutrements of an actual Air Force officer. Any fictional movie that wants to use US military equipment or titles needs the cooperation of the Department of Defense and its public relations branch—which means the military needs to approve the movie and its script, down to the smallest details.

When a studio makes a movie involving the armed forces *without* Pentagon approval, it alters the look of props and costumes to avoid violating any copyrights or trademarks the government holds on its logos, fonts, and materiel. Putting military equipment on-screen without the Pentagon's cooperation requires the filmmakers to find a private collector of multimillion-dollar war machines or to make a deal with another country that buys American weapons.

As journalist Siddhant Adlakha explained, "The US military has made it almost impossible to make an American movie featuring the US military without their help, without their input. And because of that, any company that wants to make that movie, they are incentivized to work with the Pentagon. In exchange for that, the Pentagon gets final say on the script. And they have people on set from the DOD making all these little decisions—'You can say this, you can't say that'—to make the military look good, or to make them not look bad."

After approving the script, the Department of Defense granted *Iron Man* in-depth cooperation, including leasing out Edwards Air Force Base in California for three days of production and providing real service members as extras. Staff Sergeant Joe Gambles, from the 31st Test and Evaluation Squadron, who appears in the backgrounds of *Iron Man* scenes as three different airmen, said that he made sure to be in the movie after he missed a similar chance with Michael Bay's *Transformers*. "I figure that it would be a waste of my time at Edwards if I didn't take advantage of this opportunity," he said.

Captain Christian Hodge, the DOD's project manager for *Iron Man*, said, "This movie is going to be fantastic. The Air Force is going to come off looking like rock stars."

The production's main point of contact with the military was Phil Strub, the entertainment liaison of the Pentagon's Entertainment Media Office. (He was also the person at the Pentagon who had final script approval.) The Pentagon wants to shine a flattering light on the military, but it also wants to ensure that movies properly portray the chain of command, rather than breaking it willy-nilly for dramatic convenience. Later on, this issue would cause a rupture between Marvel and the Department of Defense, because—believe it or not—the military couldn't countenance the all-powerful fictional espionage agency S.H.I.E.L.D. On the *Iron Man* production, however, Strub remembered only one major conflict with Favreau. It was over a single line of dialogue.

"It never got resolved until we were in the middle of filming," Strub said. "We're on the flight lines of Edwards Air Force Base, and there's 200 people, and [Favreau] and I are having an argument about this. He's getting redder and redder in the face and I'm getting just as annoyed."

The line was spoken by a serviceman who says that he would "kill himself" for the opportunities that Tony Stark has. Favreau, who had been spending weeks freestyling dialogue with Downey, didn't see what the big deal was. As he saw it, that phrase was a common idiom. Strub insisted that he didn't want an enlisted man making a joke that he believed made light of suicide. "It was pretty awkward," Strub recalled.

An angry Favreau shot back: "Well, how about they'd walk over hot coals?"

Strub immediately approved the new line. "[Favreau] was so surprised it was that easy," he said.

While the movie contractually wasn't allowed to disparage the military, it also didn't want to look as if it were stereotyping all residents of the Middle East as terrorists working for the fictional organization the Ten Rings. So the casting choice for the little-known character Ho Yinsen—a fellow prisoner and ally of Tony Stark in the cave in Afghanistan—was the Iranian American actor Shaun Toub. Adding to the multicultural blend was the Mongolian script in the Ten Rings logo. And the primary language for the terrorist cell, selected so as not to demonize any of the actual populations of Afghanistan, was, of all things, Hungarian.

Favreau said that in the original screenplay, there was a scene where a Ten Rings member displayed a set of crates to Stark, showing him how recent American presidents had let weapons get out into the world. "Reagan, Clinton, Bush," the character said, indicating which crates were from which era. The scene, deemed too overtly political, was cut.

"[Stark] does get a firsthand look at what weapons do," Adlakha said. "It's strange that he wouldn't know that before, but I think it works for what the film is, and especially with Downey Jr.'s performance. But if you take a step back, he is learning that his weapons hurt people when they fall into the wrong hands—but the wrong hands in this case are these vaguely foreign, nebulous terrorists, not anyone who is American. And these weapons are only bad when they are hurting American soldiers and American interests."

As Matthew Alford wrote in *Reel Power: Hollywood Cinema and American Supremacy*: "The emotional appeal of *Iron Man* rests on the idea that Stark, the self-confessed 'Merchant of Death,' has changed his carefree attitude towards arms manufacturing. . . . These readings of the film ignore the blatant fact that Stark actually continues to build weapons, only they are now more hi-tech and produced covertly as part of his own bodily attack armor."

This ideologically loaded armor was also the shiniest object in the movie (and the basis for an entire line of Marvel toys, naturally). You can't have Iron Man without the suit. Adi Granov designed a flashy suit based on his own comic-book art; the difficult job of molding it precisely to Downey's body and making it wearable on the set fell to Stan Winston Studios, the storied effects house run by Winston, who designed the robotic Terminator skeleton in James Cameron's *The Terminator* and the animatronic *Tyrannosaurus rex* in Steven Spielberg's *Jurassic Park*.

Downey claimed he never felt silly wearing the red-and-gold armor—but a decade later, he vividly remembered Terrence Howard wisecracking that he looked "like a ladybug." Although the actor had gotten into peak physical condition, thanks to a superheroic workout plan, even test-driving the heavy suit left him exhausted. Acting inside the completed suit on the set was so unpleasant, and so restrictive to his movement, that barely any footage of Downey in full gear made it into the film. Most full-body suit shots in *Iron Man* are actually of stuntman Mike Justus.

In the following years, Downey would become more insistent about not being trapped inside a costume, but even on the *Iron Man* shoot, CGI technology was advanced enough to save him the troublesome of the time. Skin, like the gummy green flesh of the Hulk, was still hard to render realistically, but state-of-the-art graphics could make an entirely convincing metal suit. On *Iron Man*, digital effects served as a backstop. Using lighting reference from the set, the digital wizards could fix problems with how the suit looked (and in an emergency, render new scenes that plugged plot holes). One fight scene in the fictional town of Gulmira, for example, involved a physical Iron Man suit that Favreau thought "looked like a Power Ranger" in broad daylight, so he replaced the entire suit with CGI.

Although computer graphics gave Favreau more flexibility with his action sequences, he soon realized that the longer audiences spent watching a digitally rendered Iron Man, the more disconnected they would feel from Tony Stark. Neither Favreau nor Feige wanted to lose sight of their characters; each had seen too many comic-book movies that made that mistake. "The depth of character is amazing in the comics, and a lot of people don't realize that," Feige said. "Including some of the people who used to be in charge of comic-book movies."

To solve the problem of their leading man's face being covered by an inexpressive mask, the filmmakers created a heads-up display, or HUD, for the character: Favreau shot close-ups of Downey's face as if he had a camera inside the helmet of the suit. Marc Chu, the animation supervisor at Industrial Light and Magic (the venerable effects house founded by George Lucas, often called ILM), described the process: "They shot a bunch of B-roll of him looking around or reacting after the fact, and then added the [graphics] on it so you know he's in the suit. It brings the human character into it."

While improvisations kept the shoot loose and energetic, sometimes Favreau's high-speed approach caused serious problems. In the middle of filming, Paltrow wrenched her knee while shooting a scene where Pepper Potts ran away from Ironmonger (Bridges' character, in his own armored suit). When she informed Favreau of her injury, she remembered, "he was rolling his eyes, saying 'you're fine,'" so she acted through the pain during several scenes. Later on, Paltrow, Favreau, and his wife, Joya Tillem, went out for pizza. "I was sitting next to Jon's wife," Paltrow said, "and my knee swelled up. She said I had to go see the doctor. Jon had to say he was sorry for not believing that I hurt my knee."

For the final battle sequence, production supervised a controlled detonation on top of a building, representing the explosion of Tony Stark's giant arc reactor. The proper authorities had been notified and the set had been cleared for safety. As scheduled, the explosion went off promptly at 10:00 p.m.—but it was so massive that it fried all $180,000 worth of lights meant to simulate the glow of the reactor. The spectacle drew the attention of passing helicopters and the Los Angeles Police Department, which dispatched officers to what they assumed was the scene of a horrible disaster.

*

EVEN WITH all the time spent in trailers hashing out scenes on the day of shooting, Favreau finished principal photography in less than four months. The shoot wrapped and raw footage was sent to various post-production companies for digital enhancement. While the filmmakers waited for those shots to come back, editor Dan Lebental cut a rough three-hour version. That was when Favreau and Marvel Studios made an unpleasant discovery: The ending didn't work. At all.

Favreau had hired Jeff Bridges and Robert Downey Jr., who could handle emotionally intricate dialogue, but then he (and the screenwriters) had concocted a story that ended with their characters clobbering each other in giant metal suits. "Act three was basically two robots punching each other," makeup artist Jamie Kelman recalled. "And they didn't know what to do with it. So they just made it really short." That didn't solve the problem; the shortened fight scene was now both emotionally unsatisfying and abruptly anticlimactic.

It was the fall of 2007, and *Iron Man* had an unmovable release date in May 2008. Shooting a new final sequence was a daunting task, given that the movie's sets had been torn down and would need to be rebuilt, and reassembling actors and production staff would be complicated and expensive. On the other hand, there was just enough time to pull something together—and nobody liked the current ending.

After five frantic months of production rewrites, all four of the credited screenwriters had been released from their *Iron Man* duties. Art Marcum and Matt Holloway, the original writing team, had also taken a break during the middle of the shoot because they had to write a TV pilot they had previously sold. But now Marvel Studios rehired Marcum and Holloway, explained the problem, and screened the latest cut of the movie for them. Almost immediately, the writers saw a way out, with a "callback" ending that played off an earlier scene in the movie. Holloway remembered how they presented it to Feige: "What if Iron Man's getting the shit kicked out of him, but he remembers that Obadiah didn't build this suit, he stole it—and he doesn't know its defects. At a certain altitude, it ices up." Feige loved the idea but, at that early point in his career, didn't believe he was the final word. He told the duo: "Pitch it to Jon."

Favreau, desperately trying to bring in *Iron Man* under budget, was hesitant, because the sequence would cost $6 million. But a labor dispute forced him into a decision. The Writers Guild of America had been negotiating a new contract with the Alliance of Motion Picture and Television Producers, and there were many sticking points, including the pay structure on streaming services. With a writers' strike looming, Favreau realized he wasn't going to be offered a better option anytime soon.

"Suddenly it was, 'Guys, you know that sequence you pitched us? *We need you to write it*,'" Holloway said. "We wrote it up against the deadline to the strike." Holloway and Marcum turned in their draft of the new finale just before midnight on November 4, 2007. On November 5, the writers' strike began (and would last more than three months).

ILM then had to make that sequence work, and do it for as little money as possible. "It was a process of pitching what we could do within the amount of time and also what plates were available," Marc Chu of ILM said. (*Plates* is visual-effects jargon for real footage that will get composited with digital effects for a VFX shot.) The ending couldn't be further rewritten because of the strike, and Jeff Bridges wasn't available to shoot any new scenes, so the effects team needed to repurpose as much previously shot footage as possible.

"Everybody at that point was wondering if this was going to come together," Chu recalled of those harried months. While Downey had a lot at stake personally with the movie, he recognized that Marvel had even more. "Kevin is the one who probably had to have an ice-bag on his stomach most nights," he said, "just hoping that his best-laid plans would all work out."

Feige responded, "Everybody deals with stress in different ways. If we talk about a metaphorical icepack—" He paused. "I don't think that works, putting ice on your stomach." He shrugged. "I'll try it now."

Iron Man premiered in May 2008 and was an immediate hit, with a $98.6 million domestic opening. It ultimately grossed over $585 million worldwide. Marvel had made one high-stakes gamble after another: mortgaging its characters to get the chance to make its own movies, hiring Downey, trusting Favreau to deliver a satisfying movie even when he seemed to be making everything up as he went along, and more. Those bets paid off so spectacularly that even Ike Perlmutter showed up for the Hollywood premiere. Perlmutter had to be dissuaded from slashing the budget for the catering at that event (he wanted to limit the menu to "only potato chips"). The press-averse Perlmutter had no interest in walking the red carpet or giving any interviews, and slipped into Grauman's Chinese Theatre in disguise, wearing glasses and a fake mustache.

Before its release, *Iron Man* had positive but modest buzz. After all, who would have anticipated a blockbuster from a new studio making a movie starring a second-string hero? So Marvel had the advantage of exceeding expectations: *Iron Man* was an entertaining movie with wit and heart, and it never condescended to its target audience. It wasn't the biggest superhero movie of the summer, a distinction that went to Christopher Nolan's second Batman movie, *The Dark Knight*. That movie was also concerned with 9/11 and its aftermath, although it explored those themes differently. Heath Ledger's Joker was a villain for the age of terrorism, with no motivation beyond spreading chaos and proving that even the best people in Gotham could be corrupted.

The filmmakers' intent with Tony Stark was to make him a sympathetic hero, despite his promiscuity, his self-indulgence, and his identity as America's leading weapons manufacturer. Along the way, the movie had some of its sharp corners smoothed down. Jon Favreau wanted to make sure that his flying superhero was plausible—but was forced by the demands of blockbuster film production (and the involvement of the Pentagon) to forgo commentary on the morality of a tech billionaire building a personalized weapons system to police the world.

The movie ends with Tony Stark declaring "I am Iron Man" in front of a room of reporters, shattering the assumption that a superhero's civilian identity must be kept secret at all costs. That was one sign that Marvel Studios was eager to question convention, even within the confines of mega-budget moviemaking. Other signs would soon appear.

CHAPTER SIX

Post-Credits Scene

I'm here to talk to you about
the Avengers Initiative.

Iron Man

KEVIN FEIGE HAD AN IDEA FOR ONE LAST SCENE IN *Iron Man*. He was inspired by an unexpected source: the 1986 John Hughes comedy *Ferris Bueller's Day Off*, starring Matthew Broderick. As an obsessive teenage film fan, Feige had always stayed until the very end of the credits, reading all the names of the people who had made the movie he had just seen. But at the end of *Ferris Bueller*, he got a surprise: Broderick came back to tell viewers that the movie was over and that they should go home. "It was the greatest thing in the world," Feige said. "I thought it was *hilarious*. It was like a little reward for me for sitting through the credits." (Movies with notable post-credits scenes before *Ferris Bueller's Day Off* include *Night of the Living Dead*, *The Muppet Movie*, *Meatballs*, and *Airplane!*)

Like cameos from Stan Lee, post-credits scenes became a trademark of the Marvel Cinematic Universe. They supplied moments of levity, stoked fan excitement about new characters, and provided connective tissue between films. "It always comes down to, what do we think would be a fun extra at the end of the movie?" Feige explained. "What do we think would be a fun thing *slightly* outside the narrative, but tied to the grander overall narrative, that would be the fun reward for people sitting through all our names?"

The very first MCU post-credits scene—featuring Samuel L. Jackson in an eyepatch as S.H.I.E.L.D. director Nick Fury, gruffly introducing himself to Tony Stark—was certainly a treat for fans. But it also had a larger purpose. Fury mentions "the Avengers Initiative," making explicit Feige's ambition for Marvel Studios to link all its disparate characters (the ones it still had the rights to, anyway) into one super-team.

In its previous two hours and five minutes, *Iron Man* had already introduced S.H.I.E.L.D. when Clark Gregg appeared as Agent Coulson and used the acronym in conversation with Pepper Potts. But in the post-credits scene, Marvel Studios essentially pitched its revolutionary interconnected future. The charismatic Jackson wasn't yet a well-paid spokesman for credit cards, but he drew on his talent for the hard sell and made the most of his thirty seconds on screen.

Throughout the *Iron Man* shoot, Jon Favreau had cooperated with the geek press—the network of movie-news websites that were becoming more influential around this moment—and tolerated the paparazzi, even when they were leaking pictures of the production. One night, when the crew was shooting reference footage for the final showdown with Ironmonger, a paparazzo even got a shot of an Iron Man suit. The flexible Favreau incorporated the photo into the movie (it's in the newspaper Tony Stark is reading in the final scene). On June 21, 2007, however, there was finally a leak that infuriated the director.

On the then-powerful movie rumors/reviews site *Ain't It Cool News*, writer Drew McWeeny, writing under the name "Moriarty," published a short item that concluded: "Today, though, [Robert Downey Jr. is] shooting scenes featuring an actor who is a set-up for a larger Marvel continuity, and it's exciting because I'm hoping this character can start showing up in other films, and we'll start seeing Marvel Studios creating a larger world, one that exists outside the frames of the individual movies. This is a major step towards making that AVENGERS movie we've been hearing about. So who's the actor? Who's the character? Sam Jackson. Nick Fury."

All the work that the *Iron Man* team had done to keep Jackson's presence secret had been for naught—and the movie wasn't going to be out for almost a year. Until then, everyone at Marvel Studios did what they could to keep quiet about the leak, to avoid bringing more attention to the story—everyone, that is, except for Avi Arad.

In June, when Favreau posted about the final day of shooting (at Caesars Palace) on his MySpace blog (it was 2007, after all), he ended his message with "I would also like to thank Caesars for their hospitality, and generosity, and Swank accommodations," capitalizing the *S* in *Swank*. It could have been a typo, or an inside joke about how one of the extras in the Vegas scenes, actress Stacy Stas, looks like the Oscar-winning actress Hilary Swank, but it sparked rumors of a secret *Iron Man* cameo by Swank. Arad, despite not being involved in the making of *Iron Man*, took the opportunity to spread some disinformation.

When the *MTV Movies Blog* asked Arad about whether Swank would appear in the movie—figuring that since he had a producer credit he would know—he snapped, "How do you know [about that]?" He then took a long beat and confided, "It's a cameo." Pressed on whether Jackson was also in the movie, Arad extemporized, saying, "I can't talk about that," before relenting: "The Sam thing was supposed to be the biggest secret of them all. It's amazing how it got out."

✳

SAMUEL L. JACKSON as Nick Fury had been a long time coming, for both the actor and the character. Fury had been considered as a possible subject for movie development ever since Stan Lee was in charge of Marvel's Hollywood office; the earliest mention of a possible Nick Fury movie was in a September 17, 1986, issue of *Variety* that claimed Paramount was trying to bring Fury to the big screen. Of the various properties that Marvel was touting for development,

Fury seemed the most accessible. In Marvel's lineup of superheroes with esoteric powers, he was a superefficient spy with an array of cool gadgets, basically a comic-book take on James Bond.

Nick Fury had been created by Stan Lee and Jack Kirby in 1963 as a World War II hero, the star of the war comic *Sgt. Fury and His Howling Commandos*. The character was popular enough that later that same year, Lee and Kirby introduced his postwar version: the top agent and leader of the spy agency S.H.I.E.L.D. Soon, in any given month, newsstands were selling the comic-book adventures of Fury in both the 1940s and the 1960s. A couple of years later, Marvel turned the title *Nick Fury, Agent of S.H.I.E.L.D.* over to the brilliant young writer/artist Jim Steranko, who gave the comic groundbreaking op-art visuals, epic battles against the evil organization HYDRA, and an undeniable 1960s cool.

Around 1995, David Goyer (who went on to write *Blade* for New Line) was commissioned to write a Nick Fury screenplay for 20th Century Fox. "I originally wrote a draft of *Nick Fury* as a feature film," Goyer said. "It was a fairly representative adaptation of the Steranko era, but updated with Baron von Strucker and the Satan Claw and all sorts of things like that." (Fury had collected a lot of supporting characters and fabulous inventions over the decades, not least the Infinity Formula that kept the World War II veteran youthful and spry.) "Nothing ever happened with it," said Goyer. "It went into development hell, and the studio that had it lost the rights. Years later, after *Blade* had been made, some people called me and said, 'Hey, we're gonna make a series of backdoor pilots for Fox, and good news, we've optioned the *Nick Fury* script that you wrote.'" The catch was that because they were making Goyer's script as a TV movie, the budget would be around $5 or 6 million, as opposed to the $20 million he thought would be the minimum necessary to realize the screenplay properly as a feature film. "I just said, 'Forget it, I don't want to be involved.' So they had someone else rewrite it, and I had absolutely zero involvement with the TV version."

The TV movie that came out in 1998, *Nick Fury: Agent of S.H.I.E.L.D.*, starred David Hasselhoff (of *Knight Rider* and *Bay-*

watch) in the title role. "At the time it did shoot, I was running my own short-lived series, *Sleepwalkers*," Goyer said. "I was also initially unenthused about Hasselhoff's involvement. I think the film was pretty mediocre, but Hasselhoff turned out to be the best thing in it. He got the joke. The script was meant to be very tongue in cheek, and Hasselhoff understood that."

Hasselhoff, hoping that he would get to play Nick Fury in the future, secured the informal blessings of Stan Lee and Avi Arad. "My Nick Fury was the organic Nick Fury that was written and discussed with Stan Lee before anyone got in there to change it," Hasselhoff said. "Nick Fury was written to be tongue-in-cheek, and he had a cigar in his mouth, he was a tough guy—he was cool. . . . Stan Lee said, 'You're the ultimate Nick Fury.' Avi Arad, when [Toy Biz took over Marvel], said, 'Don't worry, you're going to be Nick Fury forever,' and they lied." (As a consolation prize, Hasselhoff made a cameo appearance in *Guardians of the Galaxy Vol. 2* in 2017, credited as "The Form of David Hasselhoff.")

The TV movie got low ratings, and Fox canceled its plans to spin it off into a live-action S.H.I.E.L.D. series. About five years later, Arad asked Goyer to work on a new Nick Fury movie for Dream-Works. Goyer likely would have done it if Warner Bros hadn't already offered him the opportunity to write *Batman Begins* with Christopher Nolan. "I called Avi," Goyer remembered, "and I said, 'Listen, they've offered me Batman. Ever since I was a little kid, I told my mom that I want to go to Hollywood and make a Batman movie. I've got to do it.' And Avi said, 'No, you have to do it.'"

Arad and Marvel instead turned to Andrew W. Marlowe (later successful as the creator and showrunner of the TV series *Castle*) so they would have a Nick Fury script ready in case DreamWorks wanted to move forward. All parties involved were drawing heavily from the vintage Nick Fury comics, set around 1965. They didn't consider how the comic-book landscape—and Nick Fury himself—had changed in recent years.

After Perlmutter fired Marvel Enterprises CEO Eric Ellenbogen in July 1999, he replaced him with the more budget-minded Peter

Cuneo. He also named Bill Jemas the president of consumer products, publishing, and new media. Among his other responsibilities, Jemas had to take Marvel's printed comic books, which had been struggling ever since the boom years of collector speculation had ended, and make them profitable again.

Jemas, a graduate of Harvard Law School, brought up his degree as a cudgel in editorial meetings whenever he wanted to rail against overly complex comic-book continuity. "I went to Harvard Law," he would tell the Marvel editors. "If I can't understand it, it's not because of me." Jemas hated that after decades' worth of stories, characters like the X-Men and Spider-Man, who had started off as teenagers, were now full-grown adults, some of them with children of their own. As he saw it, this not only blunted their fundamental appeal, but put them out of sync with the movie versions. If a kid fell in love with the mutants or the webslinger in a movie, he reasoned, that kid should be able to pick up a comic book whose starring characters bore some resemblance to the big-screen versions.

Jemas contemplated blowing up the entire existing Marvel comics universe and starting from scratch. (DC Comics, which felt similarly encumbered by its own history, had done just that in 1985, on the company's fiftieth anniversary, with *Crisis on Infinite Earths*.) He was dissuaded and went with a less radical option: a separate "Ultimate" line of Marvel Comics that would take the characters back to basics, telling the tales of their earliest days—but updated for modern readers—and focusing on the most popular characters and storylines in Marvel history.

Aware that the X-Men movie was coming out in 2001 and the Spider-Man movie was slated for 2002, Jemas wanted the Ultimate comics to begin with those titles and assigned the project to editor-in-chief Joe Quesada. Marvel missed the window for an *Ultimate X-Men* tie-in, both because the initial comic-book script was rejected and because Fox unexpectedly moved the movie's release date up six months, to 2000. But Quesada recruited Brian Michael Bendis (a writer of independent crime comics who had also penned fill-in issues of *Daredevil* when its celebrity writer, director Kevin Smith, missed deadlines) to write *Ultimate Spider-Man* #1, with veteran Mark Bagley handling the art. The rebooted issue got a big push—Jemas made sure free copies were distributed to both comic-book shops and toy stores—and was an immediate success.

The Marvel publishing division still had plenty of troubles. Jemas complained about not being able to capitalize on the success of the X-Men movie: "The movie was for 20-year-olds and the toys were for 10-year-olds and the toys didn't sell. We had a TV show that was from hell [the animated *X-Men: Evolution*] that didn't tie into anything and we had merchandise that was from hell that didn't tie into anything, too. So, we had a movie success and a godawful financial failure and we were broke—like, can't-make-payroll broke."

Jemas and Quesada fired many of Marvel's longtime writers and editors, started up a new, edgier line of "MAX" comics in which characters like the Punisher could curse and blow heads off, and gave the green light to dozens of Ultimate versions of long-running Marvel characters, now published simultaneously with the traditional versions. They also brought in talent that was new to Marvel, including the team of English artist Bryan Hitch and Scottish writer Mark Millar. Hitch remembered the phone call he got from Quesada: "Look, the lunatics are running the asylum over here. Why don't you just come and have some fun?" Hitch laughed. "That was *literally* his pitch."

It worked: Millar and Hitch were given the task of reinventing the Avengers. They approached the job with gusto, going so far as to rename the team the Ultimates. Captain America was still a thawed Super Soldier from World War II, but Thor became an environmental activist who was mentally unbalanced enough to believe that he was the god of thunder, while the Hulk, for some reason, held a grudge against Freddie Prinze Jr. There were no MCU movies on the horizon when they launched the Ultimates in 2002, though the creators discussed how one might render the team in a modern movie as a way of coming at the property from a fresh angle, Hitch said: "Johnny Depp would have been Iron Man. Brad Pitt would have been Thor. And so on."

The 9/11 attacks altered the tenor of the entire Ultimate line, sending it in a darker direction. "It was 'super-terrorism,' not super-villainy," Hitch said. "And that changed the tone completely." It also made the figure of Nick Fury more important: he was the commander of S.H.I.E.L.D., Marvel's leading anti-terrorism agency.

In a different title, *Ultimate Fantastic Four*, Millar had established that the Ultimate Nick Fury was Black. He explained, "I wanted an African-American Nick Fury to be director of S.H.I.E.L.D. because the closest thing in the real world to this job title was held by Colin Powell at the time. I also thought Nick Fury sounded like one of those great 1970s blaxploitation names and so the whole thing coalesced for me into a very specific character, an update of the cool American superspy Jim Steranko had . . . based on the Rat Pack, which seemed very 1960s and due for some kind of upgrade."

The first time Hitch drew Fury 2.0, he rendered him as the spitting image of Samuel L. Jackson, "with the eyepatch and the Shaft beard." Hitch's style was ultrarealistic, drawing heavily from photo references, so it was obvious who had inspired him. Jemas and Quesada were worried—would this get them sued?—but decided the character looked cool enough to be worth the risk.

Jackson was a lifelong comics fan. Growing up in Chattanooga, Tennessee, in the 1950s, he was such a voracious reader of comics that his grandmother (who largely raised him) established a rule that for every five comic books he consumed, he had to read something more substantial. He had done some of his finest work in the 2000 movie *Unbreakable*, playing the owner of a comic-art gallery who becomes the supervillain Mr. Glass. And he regularly shopped at the Los Angeles comic-book store Golden Apple.

So it was no surprise that Jackson soon spotted his own face in the pages of *The Ultimates*. Flattered but confused, he called his agents: Had he given permission for this to happen? According to Hitch, "Sam's people got in touch with Marvel and said, 'Should we be suing you over this?'" Marvel avoided a lawsuit by saying that if Nick Fury was ever in a movie, Jackson could play the role. The actor accepted the offer. (Jackson's wife, LaTanya Richardson Jackson, even bought him an original page of Hitch's art as a birthday present.) From Marvel's point of view, it was a cost-effective solution. As Millar pointed out, "The idea that this might become a movie seemed preposterous, as Marvel was just climbing out of bankruptcy." But that deal is why, five years later, Marvel went with Jackson rather than honoring Arad's offhand promise to Hasselhoff. Of course, Jackson was also a bigger movie star and a better actor than Hasselhoff.

"We wanted Nick Fury to be the character to intertwine characters, but we didn't want to interrupt the movie," Feige said. "You know, if Sam Jackson in an eyepatch showed up in the middle, it might be jarring. I presumed the only people who would stay through the credits were people who would know who the guy in the eyepatch was."

As Favreau put it, "It was purely a love letter to the fans and something that would be a fun Easter egg for people who sat around until the movie was over."

The shoot, which took one day, happened on the still-standing Stark Mansion set a few days after the rest of the movie had wrapped. Brian Michael Bendis had scripted multiple versions of the same brief scene: Tony Stark returns home to find Nick Fury in his house, and Fury then tells him about the Avengers.

Some of the versions had extra dialogue from Stark, for example, "What are we avenging?" And one unused take even referenced two other successful franchises based on Marvel properties, plus the Hulk film that was about to start shooting. Jackson, as Fury, complained, "As if gamma accidents, radioactive bug bites, and assorted mutants weren't enough, I have to deal with a spoiled brat who doesn't play well with others and wants to keep all his toys to himself."

That line would have delighted fans but set an impossible standard for future Marvel movies. Feige didn't want to allude to characters he couldn't actually show on screen. "We don't have X-Men, we don't have Fantastic Four, we don't have Spider-Man, but we have everything else," he explained. "Even though everything else hadn't been turned into a big film before, or had the name recognition among non–comic book readers that other ones did, we had the opportunity to start putting certain heroes in other heroes' movies, which hadn't been done before."

Favreau acknowledged that Feige oversaw that final scene: "Kevin was definitely very involved with all of that, because exactly what Nick Fury said was going to have impact moving forward about the Avengers Initiative—it was a way to light that fuse. Kevin was laying out some larger plans."

*

WHEN MARVEL FINALLY SCREENED *Iron Man* for critics and preview audiences, the early prints didn't have the Fury scene at the end—one last attempt to preserve the surprise. Journalists who were expecting cameos by Hilary Swank and Samuel L. Jackson reported that they had spotted neither. The bonus scene was added when the movie opened for general audiences; word quickly spread not to leave the theater once the credits started rolling.

Feige reflected, "I thought it would just begin the potential conversation of hardcore fans going, 'Wait a minute. Could that mean . . . ' And instead, by that Monday, *Entertainment Weekly* was doing sidebars about Nick Fury and who he was and what that meant." He smiled and remembered his assessment of the public response: "That blew up much faster than I was anticipating."

CHAPTER SEVEN

Extraordinary Levels of Toxicity

You wouldn't like me
when I'm hungry.

The Incredible Hulk

THE HULK WAS THE STRONGEST ONE THERE WAS: MAR-vel's second-most-popular character after Spider-Man, who wasn't available to Marvel Studios. Created by Stan Lee and Jack Kirby in 1962 as a riff on Robert Louis Stevenson's *Strange Case of Dr. Jekyll and Mr. Hyde*, the Hulk was familiar to non–comics readers because of *The Incredible Hulk*, the TV show that ran on CBS from 1977 to 1982 (plus three TV movies in the late 1980s), starring Bill Bixby as the melancholy scientist Bruce Banner (renamed David on TV), who, when he became angry, transformed into the jade giant called the Hulk, played by Lou Ferrigno in green body paint.

Greg Pak, who wrote the comic-book character for many years, including the *Planet Hulk* issues adapted in *Thor: Ragnarok*, observed, "We all love the Hulk because he smashes—that's the visceral, vicarious thrill we get from seeing someone really cut loose in anger, the way we might fantasize about ourselves. But the stories resonate because there's always a price to be paid for lashing out in anger, no matter how justified it might be."

The character remained hugely popular, especially among young boys: Hulk toys were evergreen sellers. "Hulk was our second-biggest consumer product at the time," David Maisel said. The Marvel Studios leadership opted for a Hulk movie as one of its first releases without any dissension. "Hulk," Maisel concluded, "was a no-brainer."

Screenwriters call a dramatic choice "on the nose" if it's too predictable or obvious. The production of Marvel's Hulk movie played out like a real-life on-the-nose script, becoming a chaotic battle scene when its mild-mannered leading man transformed into an uncontrollable agent of chaos. A movie that seemed like a guaranteed smash almost fell apart, threatening not just the box office receipts of one summer movie, but the fate of a studio attempting to establish itself. *The Incredible Hulk*, starring Edward Norton and released in the summer of 2008, remains one of Marvel's least-loved projects. It's the movie that newcomers to the MCU are encouraged to skip. But it also taught Marvel Studios a valuable early lesson about the limits of collaboration. Put another way, Marvel learned that top-down authority and creativity are not necessarily in conflict with each other.

Marvel eventually boiled that moral down to its essence. "We have a no-asshole policy on our movies," one Marvel performer summarized.

Craig Kyle, who joined Marvel Studios as a producer back in the days of the kite factory, agreed: "It's a great policy."

*

THERE HAD BEEN another big-screen Hulk feature only a few years prior: *Hulk*, directed by Ang Lee and starring Australian actor Eric Bana, arrived in theaters in 2003. While some reviewers respected Lee's artistic ambition, the film was not well-loved by fans. Despite the mixed reactions, the movie was actually an asset when Marvel Studios selected the characters to use for its first four at-bats under Maisel's plan. "There'd already been a Hulk movie that had been made that had done a certain box office [$245 million worldwide]," Maisel explained. "When you make a sequel, you know it's going to do something in the range around the first film. It's very hard to dramatically increase it or dramatically decrease it. *Iron Man*, we were running for the fences. *Hulk* was something we knew."

The 2003 *Hulk* was produced and distributed by Universal Studios, after the head of Universal, Ronald Meyer (previously a cofounder of the Creative Artists Agency), had made a deal for the character with Avi Arad. One Saturday afternoon in 2005, Maisel called up Meyer, whom he knew well from their years together at CAA. They made some small talk about Universal and its parent company, General Electric, and then Maisel got to the point: "Are you guys going to ever make another Hulk movie?"

"Frankly," Meyer told him, "it's not in our plans."

Maisel suggested that Universal could distribute and market a Hulk movie that Marvel Studios produced (just as Paramount was doing with *Iron Man*). Marvel would spend around $100 million on the production budget; if the resulting movie did roughly as well as the 2003 motion picture, Universal would pocket between $20 and $30 million. What made the situation different from the Paramount deal was that Universal had renewed its option on the film rights to the Hulk after the 2003 movie. Marvel would have to use a character it didn't control—something that was anathema to the young studio. But Maisel had a strategy.

"I get the rights back for the character and tear up the old license agreement. We make a one-off Hulk distribution deal with you," he suggested. Meyer was intrigued, so they set up a meeting for the following week to discuss the details.

They agreed that Marvel would regain the film rights to the Hulk character, but Universal Studios would distribute any films in the Hulk franchise. That meant that the Hulk could make a cameo or participate in a team-up without the involvement of Universal, so long as the Hulk's name wasn't in the title of the movie. This turned out to be a crucial point of negotiation on Maisel's part: Universal had no idea of how much use Marvel could get out of the Hulk without the character headlining his own movies. The details of this contract would shape the MCU: this deal is the primary reason the Hulk has not starred in any further standalone movies, despite his prominence and popularity.

The arrangement was a boon for Marvel Studios and Marvel's other divisions, because now the company could control when new movies involving the Hulk would be released. The memory of Fox abruptly rescheduling the first X-Men movie, leading to dismal toy sales, still pained Ike Perlmutter.

Marvel Studios decided to film the Hulk movie right after the *Iron Man* shoot, with preproduction for both movies happening simultaneously throughout 2006. The Hulk property came with several scripts, all of which had been developed before Ang Lee worked with his longtime collaborator, writer/producer James Schamus. One of those screenplays was by Zak Penn, whom Kevin Feige knew from his work on *X2: X-Men United* and *X-Men: The Last Stand*. Marvel hired Penn to revise his old screenplay, while the studio's new squad of visual designers went to work on rendering the on-screen look of the green goliath.

Ang Lee's *Hulk* had been criticized for reasons ranging from the way the Hulk kept changing size, depending on his mood, to the director's efforts to mimic the look of a comic-book page with multiple on-screen "panels" at certain points in the film. But the overriding complaint of fans was that the movie didn't have enough action, so Marvel Studios turned to Louis Leterrier, a director better known for fight scenes than introspective drama, whose credits included *The Transporter* (codirected with Hong Kong action specialist Corey Yuen), *Unleashed* (starring Jet Li), and *The Transporter 2* (starring, as in the first installment, Jason Statham). His movies were heavy on practical effects, not CG creations, but he had shown himself to be a quick study, someone who could learn on the job.

Leterrier, a Paris-born protégé of French director Luc Besson, had first met with Arad and expressed his interest in directing *Iron Man*. When Feige informed him that the job was taken, Leterrier considered the Hulk. While the comic-book character had been reinvented many times over the decades, Leterrier found himself drawn to the visuals and emotions in the *Hulk: Grey* comics written by Jeph Loeb and drawn by Tim Sale. Leterrier signed on to direct *The Incredible Hulk*, but he wanted to start designing the main character as soon as possible, in the belief that no creative decision mattered as much as his look. Marvel Studios turned to Kurt Williams, a veteran visual-effects supervisor whose first superhero movie had been *Batman Forever* a decade earlier.

"My greatest memory," Williams said, "is walking into this war room for projects that they were going to be making in addition to *Hulk*. And I walked in there with Louis and with Kevin, and suddenly the future vision of Kevin burst out to me." Feige had the master plan; the detail-oriented Leterrier was already clipping favorite panels from Hulk comics to use for reference. Williams brought on concept artist and creature designer Aaron Sims (later famous for the faceless Demogorgon on *Stranger Things*).

The filmmakers knew they wanted to stay away from the look of the 2003 Hulk, who was oddly proportioned; Williams described him as a "big baby." Leterrier wanted a more muscular Hulk who was also capable of softer emotions, so they started by designing him not during a rampage, but at rest. "To have him calm through the design process at the beginning," Sims said, "that was probably the biggest challenge." Whenever Leterrier felt that he and Sims had nailed some aspect of the Hulk's look, he shared it with Williams and the Marvel producers. The meticulous process took almost a year, starting before there was a single actor cast, and not ending until postproduction was underway.

Williams also hired a visual-effects production company, Rhythm & Hues. Although it had worked on recent blockbusters such as *X-Men: The Last Stand* and *The Chronicles of Narnia: The Lion, the Witch and the Wardrobe*, it was the company's work on *Babe*, for which it had won an Oscar, that attracted Williams. On that film, Rhythm & Hues effects specialists had successfully mapped muscles onto CGI animals, making them appear as if they were actually speaking, and Marvel hoped they could do the same with the taciturn Hulk. (After all, the Hulk had a smaller vocabulary than Babe the sheep-herding pig.)

Although Eric Bana had done a credible job in the 2003 *Hulk*, Marvel Studios wanted to make it clear that this movie wasn't a sequel, so it needed a new Banner. Leterrier has claimed that when it came to casting his leading man, he wanted Mark Ruffalo, who had just finished filming David Fincher's *Zodiac* opposite Robert Downey Jr., who had been recently anointed as Iron Man. But Marvel believed it had a better option: Edward Norton.

The actor seemed like a natural for the role given the duality of his performances in *Fight Club* and *Primal Fear*. Norton, thirty-seven years old when *The Incredible Hulk* started filming, had already been nominated twice for an Oscar, once for *Primal Fear* and again for *American History X*.

If Marvel had followed what happened on *American History X* more closely, it would have seen a preview of how things would spiral out of control on the set of *The Incredible Hulk*. When Norton clashed with director Tony Kaye over the shape of their violent and disturbing film about the rise of neo-Nazi culture in America, New Line Cinema sided with its leading man. Norton was allowed to reedit the movie, adding about twenty minutes to what had once been a taut ninety-five-minute cut. Kaye complained that Norton had "generously given himself more screen time." Furious at having lost control of his film, Kaye tried to get his name removed from it and have it pulled from film festivals, efforts that didn't achieve much except for undermining his own directorial career. *American History X* was hailed as a triumph and Norton received that Oscar nomination for best actor.

Norton had experience as both a director and a playwright; he claimed that when his then-girlfriend Salma Hayek starred in *Frida* (2002), he had done an uncredited top-to-bottom rewrite of the screenplay. So before he agreed to star in *The Incredible Hulk*, he extracted a promise from Marvel that he would be able to revise Zak Penn's screenplay. Norton believed the Hulk could carry some serious dramatic weight and had ambitions for the character to be more than brand-name intellectual property in another popcorn movie. Marvel considered Norton's desire to get involved creatively to be a boon, not a burden, hoping his presence would give *The Incredible Hulk* the same sheen of prestige that Downey and Gwyneth Paltrow were providing on *Iron Man*.

Norton's other early concern was that the Hulk was a digital creature. He worried that he'd be handing over half his performance to another creative team he would have no control over. As Norton recalled telling Marvel, "If there's no way for me to play Hulk, then it's not really that interesting. Because as an actor, that's what sort of makes it complex." Williams assured Norton that they could use the latest advances in performance-capture technology, specifically a new system called MOVA, to allow Norton to play both Banner and the Hulk.

Norton signed on and started rewriting the screenplay, checking in periodically with the production while the rest of the cast was filled out. William Hurt, who was cast as General "Thunderbolt" Ross, proved to be a longtime fan of the Hulk. "He was always my favorite," Hurt said. "I keep asking my son why he's both of our favorites: I read the comic books, but he's a real fanatic." His son helped him prepare for the role by writing a report on Ross's comic-book biography and personality traits.

Liv Tyler was also drawn to the movie through family connections: as a young child, she had watched the TV show with her mother, Bebe Buell. In 2004, Tyler had given birth to her first son, Milo; now she was restarting her acting career. "My agent called me one night," Tyler recalled. "I had just put Milo to bed. It was like 9 o'clock at night, and I always get grumpy with them when they call me really late." Marvel Studios wanted her to fly out to LA the following day to discuss her taking the role of Betty Ross; she made the trip one day later, and after a meeting with Feige and Leterrier, signed on.

To play the movie's villain—soldier Emil Blonsky, who transforms into the CGI-powered Abomination in the final act—Leterrier wanted Tim Roth, best known for his work in Quentin

Tarantino movies. The director thought, as did Jon Favreau on *Iron Man*, that hiring character actors could prevent a comic-book movie from sliding into campy self-parody. Feige initially resisted casting Roth, wanting a bigger name, but Leterrier and Roth persuaded him. Feige's apprenticeship with Lauren Shuler Donner had taught him the importance of listening to other points of view, and according to Roth, he even thanked the actor for convincing him that he was the right man for the job. "I liken the Abomination thing to an independent movie," Roth said. "It was a very big-budget independent movie."

Discussing with Leterrier how he could embody the Abomination physically, Roth recommended movement coach Terry Notary, who had worked with him on *Planet of the Apes*, where Roth had played the vicious chimpanzee General Thade. Notary, Kurt Williams, and Rhythm & Hues launched into the pre-visualization process, doing rough drafts of whatever ideas Leterrier could come up with. When Leterrier suggested a sequence where the Hulk and the Abomination throw cars at each other, busting fire hydrants along the way, the visual artists quickly sketched out how that would look on screen. "Whatever you can come up with, we had a whole team of guys working for us right then and there," said an impressed Notary.

The pre-visualizations and the motion-capture data were passed on to Rhythm & Hues so the effects house could start work—and to the art department, where Aaron Sims was still refining the final look of the Hulk. The VFX artists tried to incorporate Norton's likeness into the CGI Hulk, Sims said, but "Edward Norton has very narrow features in his face, so if you elongate that or widen it in any way, it doesn't look like him. Then we started realizing it wasn't going to benefit us to force that. There could be some of him in the eyes a little bit, but that was basically it, because the rest of the structure—even the shape of his nose—the bone structure was so different that there's no way it's going to look like him."

As principal photography neared, Norton turned in his draft of the screenplay, which would serve as the shooting script. Leterrier agreed to let Norton have an unusual amount of control on set: he would be a combination of star, producer, and on-set writer. Leterrier was collaborative by nature, but he was also well aware that Norton had more clout than he did. Zak Penn, the original screenwriter, realized that he wouldn't be spending any time on location during the shoot. "It was kind of painful," he admitted. "All these people I was friends with were still working on it, and I understood. What could I do? What was I going to say? There's no point in the writer being there when the lead actor is the writer."

In July 2007, *The Incredible Hulk*'s production team decamped from Los Angeles to Toronto, where the movie would be shot. Two weeks later, the creative principals returned to California so they could participate in the Marvel Studios panel at the San Diego Comic-Con. The panel featured Feige, a very subdued Arad, Universal's Gale Anne Hurd, Norton, Tyler (who hadn't yet filmed any scenes), and limping onstage with his broken left foot in a cast, Leterrier. Catering to an audience of hardcore comics fans, everyone emphasized that the movie wouldn't be a continuation of Ang Lee's approach to the Hulk, with Feige referring to the current production as "part one." Hurd criticized the 2003 *Hulk*, even though she had produced it, promising that this time the Hulk wouldn't be "three different sizes."

When the conversation turned to Norton and the question of how the actor had ended up in a superhero project, he said, to audible surprise, "Well, I wrote the film."

From Penn's point of view, many of the changes Norton made to his script were cosmetic, possibly because much of the film had already been storyboarded and pre-visualized, possibly because Norton was trying to position himself for an eventual credit arbitration with the Writers Guild of America. "I had him walking east down the street wearing a blue hat and now he's walking west down the street wearing a red hat," Penn said. "And I had named his downstairs neighbor Lorina, and he changed it to Malina or something."

Penn conceded, "There was some stuff at the end that he really changed. I had a scene where, when Ross picked Banner up from the hospital earlier in the movie, he throws him out of the helicopter. It was a pretty shocking moment. They moved that to a moment when he chooses to jump into Harlem. So that's a big difference: I felt like [the original version] would have been a really cool scene, and I didn't totally understand why he would jump out into Harlem, given that he could theoretically kill a lot of people."

When the film's final credits were determined, there was, as expected, a WGA arbitration: the guild's ruling was that Penn would be the sole credited screenwriter, giving him both pride of public ownership and future residual checks. Regardless, Norton thought of the script as his own and believed he had imbued it with the mythic underpinnings of the Prometheus tale.

Before filming started, Leterrier said, "we did 'rehearsals' for three weeks." Among the other cast members, Norton particularly connected with Hurt, although the two actors had only two scenes together. And so, according to Leterrier, that "rehearsal" process was mostly "Tim, Liv, and I watching William and Edward talking."

While Favreau's *Iron Man* production was characterized by cocktail hours and the mantra of "plausibility," Leterrier's set was a cascade of manic activity, inspired by the approach of the Hong Kong filmmakers he had learned from. As Williams put it, "When you're working with Louis, his incredible energy tends to spread. And all you want to do is keep going." The shoot ran multiple units constantly: stunt teams, B-roll from helicopters, and even actors saying dialogue.

For the first month of the shoot, Leterrier had his foot in the cast, but that didn't seem to slow him down. With a cane in one hand and a red bullhorn in the other, he showed up wherever his attention was most crucial. When he needed to be elsewhere, he trusted his key actors to do their jobs, and so both Norton and Roth took control of significant scenes for their characters. "Louis can do action in his sleep," Williams said. "I think the more subtle scenes could have been a challenge for him. It seems easy to shoot, because the set's calm and you don't have two hundred people right there the whole time. But sometimes they can be delicate because of the dialogue."

Whenever Roth and Norton were free, they were summoned by

the visual-effects team for more reference footage. With the MOVA system, which was then cutting edge, they didn't have to perform green-screen scenes with dozens of dots on their faces. Instead, the actors were sprayed with iridescent dust. The reflected light, which resulted in thousands of accurate data points, was then captured to make a digital map of their performances. Williams explained the benefit: "The difference between a successful CG character and a not-successful CG character are the micro-movements in the eyes, the muscles in the facial expressions, the subtlety in fingers and those little muscles."

Although Norton had made his desire to play both Banner and the Hulk one of his key negotiating points before he signed on, when the digital team began to collect the data that would make the Hulk move, he wasn't actually interested in strapping on the bodysuit and wrestling with Terry Notary and his motion-capture buddies. Using MOVA on top of motion capture was a compromise intended to allow Norton to contribute to the Hulk's scenes, although Norton's MOVA facial data didn't translate well to a Hulk CGI model that didn't much resemble him. In any event, the workarounds were set aside when it became clear that Norton wasn't going to put in the hours necessary for a CGI performance.

All the Hulk's expressions were ultimately keyframe animated, meaning that they were rendered without any data captured from an actor. Keith Roberts, then animation director at Rhythm & Hues, said diplomatically, "Hulk doesn't have Edward Norton's expressions, but the two are eerily similar in facial timing."

Notary was blunter: "[Norton] wasn't really engaged, as far as the Hulk stuff goes, unless he was transforming from himself into the Hulk. He was not very present through the whole thing."

Roth, in contrast, relished working with Notary again, and periodically would get in the motion capture bodysuit himself. "Try this, mate!" he'd tell Notary, who described him as "one of those quintessential actors that likes to be involved, wants to make sure that he's going to look good and his character's going to look good."

Roth's MOVA data proved to be more useful to Rhythm & Hues,

Williams said, because "you could really see what he was trying to do with it."

While a huge amount of collective effort was focused on delivering a crowd-pleasing version of the Hulk, Roth and the production team had more of a free hand with the Abomination. "It was important to nail what everybody recognizes as the iconic Hulk," Sims said. "But the Abomination, even though he's an important character, we didn't have to be as true to the comic book with that design because he's not the star." They also didn't have to worry about making the Abomination resemble Roth, and according to Sims, "there was almost zero likeness" between the actor and his monstrous alter ego. Leterrier, however, noted a trace of Roth that delighted the actor: the Abomination had faint-but-visible versions of Roth's tattoos.

✶

PRODUCTION OFFICIALLY WRAPPED in November 2007, soon after filming Stan Lee's cameo as a hapless citizen who drinks some of Banner's blood out of a soda bottle. Leterrier began cutting the film with editor Vincent Tabaillon, with Norton working to shape the film alongside them. The visual-effects team raced to finish the movie by the summer of 2008. When the shoot started, they had planned on about 660 CGI shots, but now it looked like they would need closer to 750. Without intending to, Marvel Studios was establishing another tradition that it would become infamous for: the crushing demands it made of its CGI artists.

When Leterrier and Norton finished their cut of *The Incredible Hulk*, it was a ponderous 135 minutes. The major set pieces were all present, but the scenes of a morose Dr. Banner on the run overshadowed the action. To underscore that the movie was a fresh start for the character, Leterrier had shot footage of the Hulk's origins and scattered it through the first hour of the film in flashback sequences. Test audiences, confused, wondered if the scenes were from the 2003 *Hulk*—which was the opposite of the filmmakers' intentions. Marvel had wanted an exciting, crowd-pleasing Hulk movie, but it was getting something introspective and dour.

Marvel Studios wasn't yet two years old, but it already understood the importance of a climactic battle—on-screen and off. As they pushed for changes, studio executives faced a final confrontation with Edward Norton, the Hulk of their own making. Attempting to salvage the situation, Maisel, Feige, Leterrier, and Norton met. Norton was adamant that he had signed onto the movie because he was promised a large degree of control, and he was irate that Marvel was now trying to cut his emotional epic into a trivial summer blockbuster.

Norton frequently cited the Prometheus myth to explain his intentions with the Hulk. He thought of the movie as a portrait of a man out of control, establishing a complex character that could be developed further in the sequels that he said he wanted to make. Marvel Studios, for its part, felt that it had indulged Norton throughout development and production, often accepting his suggestions under its unofficial credo of "best idea wins." But now, Marvel believed, Norton had used his position in the editing room to push for an excessive amount of Banner footage; what he called character development, the Marvel executives considered to be self-indulgent chaff.

Although the visual effects were being tweaked until the last moment, there was no time to redo any of them from scratch: the movie's action beats were locked in. The argument concerned what would happen between them. Norton's edit of the movie, for example, began with Bruce Banner in the Arctic, attempting suicide—unsuccessfully, because he transforms into the Hulk before he can die. The Hulk then causes an earthquake that briefly reveals an Easter egg: a frozen Captain America underneath the tundra. Marvel believed the attempted suicide was far too bleak an opening for what was fundamentally an adventure movie. When several rounds of notes failed to solve the underlying problems, the studio wanted to reassert control. On *Iron Man*, giving the director and star free rein creatively had worked out brilliantly; *The Incredible Hulk* was demonstrating the risks of that approach.

Norton pointed out that he had been frank about his desire for an unusual amount of creative input and told the Marvel executives that they were breaking their promises. He got loud. Feige, unmoved, committed to a shorter, more commercial cut of the film, including Leterrier in the process but not Norton. (Three editors are credited on the movie: Tabaillon, Rick Shaine, and John Wright.) Although Leterrier's moviemaking instincts tended toward fast and frenetic, he learned from the mistakes of Tony Kaye and made strenuous efforts not to take the conflict personally, and to be diplomatic in public. "It's as much Marvel's fault as it is Edward's," the director said. "And my fault. It's everybody's fault! Or no one's fault, in a way. I regret that [Marvel and Norton] didn't come to an agreement where we could've all worked together." Norton cut back on his promotional appearances for the film to the contractually mandated minimum, likely to the benefit of all parties.

The Incredible Hulk, now 112 minutes long, was a modest success at the box office in 2008, boosted by *Iron Man*'s debut weeks earlier. Maisel was correct about sequels delivering in the neighborhood of original installments: after all the off-screen drama, *The Incredible Hulk* grossed $264 million worldwide, roughly the same as the $245 million for Ang Lee's *Hulk*. It was a result strong enough to validate the Merrill Lynch deal, even if it was dwarfed by the $585 million that *Iron Man* pulled in. (A final improvised scene featuring Downey as Tony Stark—to emphasize that the first two Marvel Studios movies took place in the same universe—was added to the film without Norton's involvement.)

Any plans to make further Hulk movies to be released by Universal were shelved, since neither Norton nor Marvel wanted to work together again. As the studio rolled out more movies and *The Avengers* started to look like an inevitability rather than a fever dream, fans assumed that Norton would be part of the team-up, playing the Hulk once more.

Feige, normally a staunch believer in keeping quiet about behind-the-scenes disagreements, did not extend that policy to Norton. In what stands as the frankest public statement he made during the first ten years of Marvel Studios, he issued a press release in 2010 that dismissed Norton from the role while name-checking most of the studio's other stars:

> We have made the decision to not bring Edward Norton back to portray the title role of Bruce Banner in the Avengers. Our decision is definitely not one based on monetary factors, but instead rooted in the need for an actor who embodies the creativity and collaborative spirit of our other talented cast members. The Avengers demands players who thrive working as part of an ensemble, as evidenced by Robert, Chris H, Chris E, Sam, Scarlett, and all of our talented casts. We are looking to announce a name actor who fulfills these requirements, and is passionate about the iconic role in the coming weeks.

"Yeah, which was cheap," Norton said. "It was brand defensiveness or something. Ultimately they weren't going for long, dark and serious. But it doesn't matter. We had positive discussions about going on with the films, and we looked at the amount of time that would've taken, and I wasn't going to do that. I honestly would've wanted more money than they'd have wanted to pay me. But that's not why I would've wanted to do another Hulk movie anyway. I went and did all the other things I wanted to do, and what Kevin Feige has done is probably one of the best executions of a business plan in the history of the entertainment industry. As a Disney shareholder, you should be on your feet for what they pulled off."

CHAPTER EIGHT

Some Assembly Required

What if I told you we were
putting a team together?

The Incredible Hulk

JON FAVREAU WASN'T JUST THE DIRECTOR OF MARVEL
Studios' first hit movie; he was also the new studio's de facto
human-resources manager. When he needed key personnel for
Iron Man, he brought on a slew of experienced hands from his previous movie, *Zathura: A Space Adventure*. Many of the people he hired
stayed with Marvel long after Favreau had moved on—and some of
them ended up running the studio.

Zathura was the largely unloved 2005 sequel to *Jumanji*. The
premise: some kids play a boardgame that sends their house into
outer space. It was a complicated shoot, full of practical effects (such
as sets that had to tilt 40 degrees when the house was caught in a
gravity field), but it had run smoothly, so one of Favreau's first calls
when he started working on *Iron Man* was to Louis D'Esposito, the
level-headed executive producer of *Zathura* who had also served as
the day-to-day unit production manager.

D'Esposito took a meeting in the spring of 2006 with Favreau,
Kevin Feige, Avi Arad, and Ari Arad. "Kevin, Avi, and Ari did not

say a word," he remembered, laughing. "It was just Jon and I talking. The next thing I know, they offered me the job."

D'Esposito, born in the Bronx in 1958, had spent decades in film production, working his way up from production assistant (on movies like *Endless Love* and the Rodney Dangerfield comedy *Easy Money*) to the second assistant director on big-budget flops like *A Chorus Line* and *Ishtar*. He became a first assistant director—the person who manages the set and the crew so the director can focus on making the movie—in 1987, on the gritty Abel Ferrera romance *China Girl*. He worked steadily as a first assistant director for the next fifteen years on more than twenty movies (ranging from *Major League* to *I Know What You Did Last Summer*). At that point, D'Esposito decided that he wasn't actually going to make the leap to director. He was, nevertheless, extremely gifted at solving problems on a movie set, so starting in 2003, he became a hands-on executive producer, working on the cop movie *S.W.A.T.* and the Will Smith drama *The Pursuit of Happyness*.

He established himself as the cool center of Marvel Studios production—literally, because D'Esposito liked to keep his office frigid, with his air-conditioning set 10 degrees below everyone else's. He was also an advocate of transcendental meditation, which has been practiced by creative types from the Beatles to David Lynch, and turned the other Marvel Studios executives on to its benefits. Practitioners say that it unlocks their creativity and helps them maintain a remarkable degree of focus. "You're given your mantra and you can't tell anyone, D'Esposito said. "Part of me thinks we all have the same mantra."

According to producer Craig Kyle, the two primary mantras shared by Marvel staffers were more worldly: "Pain is temporary, film is forever" and "If you're not going to bother to come in on Saturday, don't bother coming in on Sunday." Kyle noted, "These movies are really, really, really hard."

D'Esposito often showed up to sets wearing a T-shirt and jeans, and the more successful Marvel Studios became, the less likely he was to wear a tie to a movie premiere. He was comfortable operating in the background, making sure that productions ran efficiently and that Marvel cast the right actors. If you wanted to see your favorite character in a Marvel movie, you needed to talk to Feige; if you wanted to be in a Marvel movie yourself, you needed to talk to D'Esposito.

For *Iron Man*, D'Esposito hired some of his colleagues from *Zathura*, including production designer J. Michael Riva, set decorator Lauri Gaffin, and executive producer Peter Billingsley. (Billingsley, the former child actor famous for starring as Ralphie in *A Christmas Story*, also had a small role in *Iron Man* that he reprised in 2019's *Spider-Man: Far from Home*.) And D'Esposito knew a brash, unflappable visual-effects supervisor with superhero experience named Victoria Alonso.

Alonso was born in Buenos Aires in 1965. During her childhood, the Argentine government was run at various points by Juan Perón, his widow Isabel Perón, and a right-wing junta. "I'm a teenager of the military dictatorship," Alonso said. "I was very involved with the marches—I used to hold the banners in the front row." But at one protest march, because the banner was so heavy, she handed it off to someone else and stayed just slightly behind the vanguard of the march, which saved her life when soldiers opened fire on the demonstrators. "They shot at the first row and the second row," she said. "And by the time that the third row was about to be hit, we had a chance to run."

Alonso's father, a psychologist, died when she was six. "My mother never remarried," she said. "People were getting taken away and killed," but Alonso's mother was able to protect the family because of her position as a high-ranking official in the Ministry of Education. "She kept us safe; she kept us strong; she kept us open-minded."

When she was nineteen, Alonso came to the United States, enrolling as an undergraduate at the University of Washington, where she studied psychology—which made her feel closer to her absent father—and theater. She planned on being an actress, she said, "Because it was the only thing I knew I could be in the theater."

After graduation, Alonso spent six months auditioning for plays in Seattle without success. She then had two epiphanies: The first was that she loved the storytelling aspect of theater more than she loved acting. The second was that she would prefer to be a producer who made decisions, not a performer at the mercy of producers. She moved to Los Angeles and worked three jobs while she figured out how to break into producing: a morning shift at Alaska Airlines, an afternoon position as a page at Paramount Pictures, and a weekend gig as a waitress at the Black Angus Steakhouse. (She managed to barely get by, in part because she could eat the leftover first-class meals from Alaska Airlines.) She somehow found the free time to help produce a play about Frida Kahlo at the Bilingual Foundation of the Arts, which led to work as a film production assistant, and then to a steady job as a visual effects producer employed by the production house Digital Domain. For eight years, she traveled around the world, from one film production to another—everything from *Shrek* to *Big Fish*—until she wearied of the nomadic lifestyle.

Before *Iron Man*, D'Esposito and Alonso had been attached to the Will Smith superhero movie *Tonight He Comes* (later retitled *Hancock*), which went into turnaround for so long that both producers moved on to other projects. (*Turnaround* is when a production studio releases a project in preproduction to be developed and produced by a different studio than where it originated, keeping it alive but also delaying it.) When D'Esposito called Alonso up to offer her a job at his new gig, he mentioned that it was based in Los Angeles, and she accepted immediately, not even asking what the movie was.

Alonso was summoned to the Marvel Studios office above the Beverly Hills Mercedes dealership. While she waited for her formal interview to begin, she chatted with a curly-haired man who looked familiar, even if she couldn't quite place him. When D'Esposito entered the room, he said, "Oh, I see you met our director," and formally introduced her to Favreau.

Unfazed, she informed Favreau, "You're taller than I thought you would be."

"Yeah, I get that a lot."

Alonso asked, "What movie are we working on?"

"It's a superhero movie called *Iron Man*," Favreau said.

"Okay, let's do it. As long as it shoots in LA." (Favreau's insistence on keeping the *Iron Man* production based in LA led directly to Alonso, among others, working for Marvel.)

Short, outspoken, prone to talking with her hands, Alonso quickly became an indispensable liaison between digital effects houses, where hundreds of CGI craftsmen toiled at high-end workstations in unlit rooms, and the directors of Marvel's first two films, both of whom had little or no computer-graphics experience. It was Alonso who taught Jon Favreau how a director could guide the CGI process and get the most bang for the buck.

"She's a treasure," said Craig Kyle. "The secret of Marvel? It's that woman. She lives in darkness because her life is in post, but she is the most vibrant, irrepressible, and extraordinary woman I've ever met. She treats people like gold, and she makes the impossible possible."

Makeup artist Jamie Kelman remembered a moment when Alonso got flustered. Demonstrating the difference between flat and lustrous surfaces in computer graphics, Alonso brought out some small orbs for visual reference, with one side matte gray and the other side shiny chrome. But when everyone else called the reference objects "balls," she insisted that they were "spheres." Kelman said with a chuckle, "She didn't want to say 'balls.'"

By the time *Iron Man* hit the nation's cineplexes, Feige had learned how essential D'Esposito and Alonso were, and knew that Marvel Studios needed them to stick around. He offered D'Esposito the title "president of physical production." The producer accepted with some reluctance, having enjoyed the freedom that came with hopping from project to project, but later considered his "yes" to be the best decision of his professional life.

Alonso was similarly hesitant, telling Feige she was a producer, not a "studio girl." Feige told her she would still be making one movie after another, just with more responsibility and control. Alonso then countered with the proposal that she be put in charge of all postproduction, so that different departments wouldn't be working at cross-purposes. Feige agreed, and Alonso was made responsible not just for visual effects, but for each film's editing, sound mixing, score, and postproduction 3D conversion.

For the next sixteen years, Kevin Feige, Louis D'Esposito, and Victoria Alonso would be the ruling troika of Marvel Studios. In those early days, they were three driven personalities far more interested in launching a studio and getting movies made than in basking in the spotlight. While their responsibilities overlapped, they had their own spheres (definitely not balls) of influence. "There was some sort of kismet with these two men," Alonso said. "We recognized the knowledge that came from our different departments. If there was an issue in story, of course we were going to lean on Kevin. If there was an issue on production, we were going to lean on Lou."

Or as D'Esposito put it: "I'll be fielding more of the phone calls from agents concerning deals on actors, writers, directors, et cetera. Victoria will lean toward delivery and postproduction. Kevin is obviously everything creative."

★

X-MEN AND SPIDER-MAN had taught Feige the value of a producer who stayed with a project all the way from script development to postproduction, ensuring continuity of vision. Although Marvel Studios had access to plenty of specialists, he wanted to make sure that a creative producer was assigned to each movie. He didn't have to go far to look for eager young candidates.

Los Angeles native Stephen Broussard had started working at Marvel fresh out of Florida State University film school (where he had won a Student Academy Award for a short film called *The Plunge*); he was the assistant to both Feige and Ari Arad (Avi's son). Jeremy Latcham (David Maisel's assistant), who had hired Broussard, had told him that he shouldn't expect to be promoted out of the assistant position. A few months after Broussard started, however, Maisel finalized the Merrill Lynch financing deal. Latcham, previously pessimistic about his own job prospects, realized Marvel might now be a place where he could make movies, not just photocopies. When

Maisel told Feige about his assistant's aspirations, Feige agreed to hire Latcham as a junior producer.

Likewise, after a year of working as an assistant to Feige, Broussard was carrying a box out to his boss's car in the garage when he worked up the nerve to ask for a promotion: a moment that Marvel insiders call "the garage conversation." Feige was well aware of his assistant's ambition and ability; he promoted him.

"Suddenly, we were working on *Iron Man* and *The Incredible Hulk,*" Feige said. "So they both start doing notes and ideas for the scripts. At a certain point, I said, 'You can't work on both.'" Feige designated Latcham as the creative executive on *Iron Man* and assigned Broussard to *The Incredible Hulk*. Feige needed to look ahead to future Marvel Studios releases and couldn't spend as much time on the set of either movie as he would have liked, so he relied on each of the young producers to be his representative on set: the job he had once done for Lauren Shuler Donner.

On the last weekend of May 2008, between the blockbuster opening of *Iron Man* and the bullet-dodged release of *The Incredible Hulk*, Feige gathered the top creative producers at Marvel for a weekend retreat in Palm Springs, the desert resort town a couple of hours east of Los Angeles.

In the kite factory era, the bare-bones Marvel Studios staff had sometimes spent hours killing time while Avi Arad was out making deals. During those days of brainstorming and bullshitting, Feige had become friends with Craig Kyle. The chilled-out Kyle, who had worked on the cartoons *X-Men: Evolution* and *Spider-Man: The New Animated Series*, was in charge of Marvel's animated projects; he was a comics nerd down to his marrow.

Around the time Avi Arad left Marvel Studios, Feige and Kyle made a few visits to Palm Springs for weekend getaways with their wives. (Feige's wife, Caitlin, is a cardiothoracic nurse; they married in 2007.) Even then, Feige had been immersing himself in the fine points of Marvel mythology, turning himself into a comic-book expert. "He would bring stacks and stacks of hardcover trades and sit in the shade, because he hates sunlight, and he would just devour everything," Kyle remembered. Feige hadn't grown up obsessed with comic books the way Kyle had, but, Kyle said, "I got to see Kevin dive into such a deep, nearly boundless universe, and just consume it in such chunks until he became as knowledgeable as me and even exceeded me in some areas of the universe."

Now Feige was returning to Palm Springs with Kyle (who had recently moved from animation to live action), Broussard, and Latcham. With armfuls of their favorite DVDs and comic books, the four producers planned to lock themselves in a rental house and figure out what movies would come next. (Broussard was a little distracted: postproduction for *The Incredible Hulk* had been difficult, and two weeks before the movie's release date, the visual effects were still being finalized.) They went to see *Iron Man* at a local theater, the first time any of them had gotten to experience it with a crowd of civilians.

While they enjoyed themselves, they made sure to pay close attention to the audience's reactions. Back at the house, they discussed how *Iron Man* had a different tone from the superhero movies that had come before. Favreau, Robert Downey Jr., and editor Dan Lebental had found a way to balance the serious and the silly, landing big dramatic moments and then pivoting to a joke without diminishing the characters. To the producers, it felt like a template for future Marvel movies. (It was also a reminder of the alchemy and uncertainty of any movie production: even the people in charge of a movie couldn't control exactly how it would turn out.) They covered the walls with brown butcher paper and scribbled on them with multicolored magic markers while they brainstormed ideas for the future of Marvel Studios.

"The movie-specific conversation," Broussard said, "tended to be one part 'What do we want to see in a movie like this?' and one part 'What is really stupid in a movie like this?'" Feige was able to guide the studio toward movies that worked for newcomers and experts alike because, being relatively new to the world of comics himself, he approached the experiment with an outsider's perspective.

"Once Kevin took charge of the studio, he was truly able to say, 'Look, the costumes are in there, the sagas are in there, the character traits, the Easter eggs," Kyle said. "But he wasn't just catering to the fans; he was showing people how to stop being scared of what, maybe, they didn't grow up loving. I don't think Kevin's role could have been done by a comic-book geek, to be honest."

Soon the Palm Springs team had achieved consensus on the lineup for the next three Marvel movies—*Iron Man 2, Thor*, and *Captain America: The First Avenger*—and had a rough idea of what each could be. Feige assigned each creative executive a movie. As the *Iron Man* veteran, Latcham was the natural choice for *Iron Man 2*. Kyle, who had already produced animated Thor movies and was excited to make the character work for the multiplex, got *Thor*. That left Broussard with *Captain America: The First Avenger*; he was still finishing *The Incredible Hulk*, so he would get a short break before jumping into the man-out-of-time story.

Marvel wasn't using the "Phase One" terminology publicly yet: that language implied a "Phase Two," meaning that the Marvel saga would continue for many more years than fans could have possibly imagined. However, the Palm Springs producers knew they wanted to cap off the studio's first five movies with *The Avengers*, which would bring all of its Phase One heroes together—and privately, they were already planning on a Phase Two.

Thor seemed like the most difficult character to adapt, because the source material was steeped in a cosmic version of Norse mythology that would be hard to keep at a human scale on-screen. The best run of the comics, by writer/artist Walt Simonson between 1983 and 1987, had abandoned Thor's traditional human alter ego (Dr. Donald Blake) altogether. Marvel Studios had already commissioned a *Thor* screenplay, set among Vikings during the Middle Ages, but the producers wanted the thunder god to be able to team up with Iron Man, so they needed to find a way to make the character work in twenty-first-century Midgard (that is, Earth).

One early idea for *Iron Man 2* was a scene in which Iron Man would fly into Disneyland. That evolved into the "Stark Expo," set in

Queens on the site of the 1964 World's Fair (across the street from an apartment where Favreau had once lived). And it was imperative, the executives decided at the retreat, to roll out S.H.I.E.L.D. properly in the sequel. Somehow the espionage agency would need to be tied into whatever villain Tony Stark faced off against, who remained to be determined.

The producers discussed how best to handle Captain America, the Super Soldier whose origin story was inextricably tied to World War II. Their initial impulse was to split the movie in two, with the first half set in the 1940s and the second half set in the present day. The Marvel Entertainment executives in New York City had already made their view clear: they wanted as much of the movie set in the present day as possible and regarded a period movie as poison. But as the producers broke down the story, they found themselves being pulled to the past, when Captain America's identity was formed. They decided to push for *Captain America* to be entirely a period movie. Feige pointed out to the group that *Raiders of the Lost Ark* was a period movie, as was one of his favorite films from the 1990s, *The Rocketeer*.

Focusing on Steve Rogers' origin would give his debut more emotional weight, both for audiences and for the people working on the movie. "*Captain America* has a very dear place in my heart," Alonso said, "because of what it does for the younger kids in high school. The more different you are, the more you suffer from alienation or bullying."

✱

IN OCTOBER 2008, with development on all three films well underway, Marvel hired more personnel who would become key players at the studio. Feige's new assistant was Jonathan Schwartz, who had been working at the William Morris Agency, but had very little experience with actual moviemaking: he had never even seen a call sheet. And D'Esposito rehired Brad Winderbaum, who had been his assistant during the *Iron Man* shoot. His new job was to make an official timeline of the Marvel movies, reconciling the events of the two released movies and the rough drafts of *Iron Man 2* and *Thor*. Winderbaum realized that the movies inadvertently implied something he called "Fury's Big Week": the action of *The Incredible Hulk*, *Iron Man 2*, and *Thor* all overlapped during one frantic week for Nick Fury and S.H.I.E.L.D. Winderbaum also established the "zero point" for the Marvel timeline: Tony Stark's public declaration that he was Iron Man. Just as *Star Wars* fans and creators mark events as being before or after the Battle of Yavin (the climax of the first *Star Wars* movie, when Luke Skywalker blows up the Death Star), Marvel Studios kept its calendar by the time elapsed before or after Tony's admission.

There had been plenty of long-running movie series before. Recent examples included *Harry Potter*, *Star Trek*, and James Bond, although none of them had released as many installments as the now largely forgotten *Blondie* movies (based on the newspaper comic strip), of which there were twenty-eight between 1938 and 1950. Marvel Studios, however, was after something different than a conventional series. It had announced a slate of interconnected films, not traditional sequels. Making clear that the events in the movies were not identical to what happened in the comic books, and underlining that all of these movies were part of one larger story, Marvel Studios began to refer to its fictional world with a name that was a little grandiose but undeniably memorable, just like the movies themselves. The first public use of that term wouldn't come until 2010, when Feige let it slip while promoting *Iron Man 2*: The Marvel Cinematic Universe.

CHAPTER NINE

Demon in a Bottle

What's the point of owning a race car
if you can't drive it?

Iron Man 2

HE FELT HIS THROAT, MAKING SURE IT WAS STILL there. Then he looked around an empty rehearsal studio in Hollywood and ran his hands through his hair like he was looking for something he'd lost. *Iron Man 2* hadn't even begun filming yet, and Jon Favreau was already exhausted.

The weekend of *Iron Man*'s premiere, David Maisel and Kevin Feige took Favreau and Robert Downey Jr. out to Mr. Chow in Beverly Hills, an upscale Chinese restaurant decorated with art by Andy Warhol. To celebrate the movie's boffo box office, Maisel had something to offer his director and his star beyond the black pepper lobster: he had gotten permission from Ike Perlmutter to buy each of them their dream car. Even the obsessively frugal Perlmutter understood the importance of keeping Favreau and Downey happy.

Maisel had conspired with each of their wives to learn what car to buy: for Downey, it was a Bentley in a custom color, so it wouldn't arrive for a few weeks. But for Favreau, it was a top-of-the-line Mercedes, and it was waiting for him at the valet stand. "They both drove those cars for a long time," Maisel said.

The dinner was more than a celebration of a job well done. Marvel Studios wanted its third release to be *Iron Man 2*, and it wanted that movie pronto. After the success of *Iron Man* and *The Hulk*, Maisel saw that soon, Marvel Studios might no longer need its Merrill Lynch line of credit. Making a lucrative sequel seemed like the surest way to secure the studio's financial future. "Everyone in for *Iron Man 2* in two years?" Maisel asked at dinner. "If you are, I'll green-light it right now."

Favreau was uncertain. He was delighted that after all his hard work, *Iron Man* was a hit, but he had made popular movies in the past, so he knew not to get overexcited. "Fortunately, I'd had the experience of things connecting with audiences before, and I know how wonderful, but also disorienting, it is," he said. "Everything changes a bit. It's like the band that puts out a hit single: you go from playing in a garage to figuring out how you follow it up."

He also knew just how brutal a two-year timetable was, and how it wouldn't allow for the cocktail hours and bull sessions of the *Iron Man* production—not just exercises in camaraderie, but collaborative sessions where the creators had hashed out how to make the movie work. While he considered the offer, the studio announced that the sequel would arrive in theaters in April 2010. Marvel was so eager to turn a hit single into a franchise—and push toward an eventual Avengers movie—that it trumpeted the release date before it had official deals with Favreau and Downey.

Maisel dealt with the blowback: "I remember we got a lot of angry phone calls from the reps the next few days saying, 'Hey, you maybe should have kept us in the loop on this before you talked to our clients about committing to a movie in two years.'"

Favreau only grew more worried when he saw *The Incredible Hulk*, released a few weeks after *Iron Man*. The movie includes a post-credits scene where Tony Stark meets with General "Thunderbolt" Ross to tell him that they're putting a team together—to Favreau, it was a sharp reminder that he didn't have control over Stark's character. Feige mollified him, saying that they could work around the scene as necessary, and it didn't have to affect the story that Favreau told in *Iron Man 2*. That scene could have taken place anytime, Feige said, given that comic book narratives frequently jumped into the far future. (Ultimately, Marvel Studios decided that the post-credits scene happened in the same week as the action of *Iron Man 2*.)

It took two months to agree on terms, but in July 2008, Favreau agreed to direct the sequel. Downey also signed up after renegotiating his contract. He had played Tony Stark in the first movie at a discount rate for action-movie leading men, reportedly earning around $500,000, but he got a vastly improved payday on *Iron Man 2*, in the neighborhood of ten million dollars, and negotiated even more money for *Iron Man 3*. More significantly, he committed to an Avengers movie in exchange for another ten million dollars plus a healthy slice of the profits, which would turn out to be a brilliant move. Marvel Entertainment was willing to pay so much for Downey because *Iron Man 2* was a safer bet than *Thor* or *Captain America*, following Maisel's axiom that sequels to hit movies perform roughly as well as their predecessors.

★

ALTHOUGH FAVREAU and Downey didn't have the luxury of figuring out the story of the sequel in a leisurely fashion, at least they had already established an appealing tone—wry, nimble, jaded—in the first movie. As Downey put it, "There was a feeling in the first *Iron Man* of taking the subject matter seriously and not taking ourselves seriously."

To write the screenplay, Downey suggested Justin Theroux, then best known as an actor in David Lynch movies such as *Mulholland Dr.* He had met Theroux on the set of *Tropic Thunder*, an action comedy directed by Ben Stiller about the troubled production of a Vietnam War movie. Theroux was one of the writers; Downey played a method actor suffering from delusions that he was actually the Black character he was portraying.

Downey brought Theroux in for a meeting with Favreau and Feige. "It was super-organic. And it wasn't clearly well-orchestrated," Theroux said. "I explained what I loved about the first movie, ideas of where it could possibly go into, the themes that I thought were interesting." He got the job.

The brain trust's first impulse was to explore the excesses of Tony Stark's playboy lifestyle, adapting the famous 1979 *Demon in a Bottle* storyline from the *Iron Man* comic books that sees Tony succumb to alcoholism. Feige steered the filmmakers away from making Tony too dissolute; while Favreau and Downey didn't want to abandon the idea completely, they agreed to shift the plot's focus. In and out of his Iron Man armor, Tony would have to wrestle with his family's legacy and his own hubris.

Gwyneth Paltrow returned as the long-suffering love interest Pepper Potts. Terrence Howard, however, was no longer playing Colonel James "Rhodey" Rhodes, Tony's best pal and liaison at the US Air Force—and not by his choice. "There was no explanation," Howard complained. "Apparently the contracts that we write and sign aren't worth the paper that they're printed on sometimes. Promises aren't kept."

As the first actor to sign up for the original *Iron Man*, Howard had commanded a premium, with his prestige as a recent Oscar nominee establishing the movie as a credible project and earning him roughly $3.5 million for a supporting role (seven times Downey's reported salary). Now Marvel no longer needed his expensive veneer of respectability, but Howard blamed Downey's renegotiated deal: "The person that I helped become Iron Man," he said, "when it was time to re-up for the second one, [he] took the money that was supposed to go to me."

Howard had signed on as Rhodes partially because he expected the character would become a superhero, War Machine, in a high-tech suit of his own. In the first movie, that possibility was only hinted at, when Rhodes murmured "Next time" while looking at a silver suit of armor. But now that Marvel Entertainment could see the future of an extended MCU, it wanted War Machine to appear in multiple movies and didn't want to give the actor inside the suit steady raises from a base salary of $3.5 million.

A story leaked to *Entertainment Weekly*, suggesting that Favreau had been unhappy with Howard's acting in the first *Iron Man* movie and that he had reshot many of Howard's scenes because he couldn't put together an acceptable performance in the editing room. Although Howard has often been described as a difficult actor— talented but mercurial—Favreau was careful not to complain about him publicly. Friction on the set may have seemed, to Marvel, like a more palatable reason to let him go than financial concerns.

Don Cheadle, a standout in the ensembles of *Ocean's Eleven* and *Boogie Nights*, and recently Oscar-nominated himself for *Hotel Rwanda*, had been considered for the role of Rhodes two years earlier. With Howard out of the picture, Cheadle got the phone call offering him the part while he was at his daughter's birthday party. It was a six-movie deal, which he figured would take at least a decade of his life, encompassing projects that hadn't even been conceived yet, and he had one hour to decide. If he said no, the Marvel executive on the phone told him, they were going to the next name on their list.

"I'm at my kid's laser tag party right now," a slightly overwhelmed Cheadle said.

"Oh! Oh, take two hours," the Marvel executive said.

Cheadle discussed the pros and cons of joining the franchise with his wife as they played laser tag, dodging enemy fire. "You've never done anything like this before," she pointed out. "Big special effects, tentpole, four-quadrant movie. Do you *want* to do something like this?" While he pretended to be an action hero wielding a sci-fi blaster weapon, Cheadle decided that, yes, he wanted to play an action hero wielding a sci-fi blaster weapon—at a larger budget than a birthday party allowed. Cheadle was reportedly paid around $1 million for his work on *Iron Man 2*; Howard's deal would have netted him somewhere between $5 million and $8 million.

Ike Perlmutter's response to this recasting stands as one of the ugliest moments in Marvel's history. He reportedly told Andy Mooney, then the chairman of Disney consumer products, that nobody would notice because all Black people "look the same."

When faced with the overt racism of the Marvel CEO, most employees looked the other way, accepting it as the downside of a dream job, or even excused it. "Ike Perlmutter neither discriminates nor cares about diversity," said one person who worked with him. "He just cares about what he thinks will make money."

Another crucial piece of casting was Black Widow, the Russian superspy turned Western superhero, who seemed like a character with obvious crossover potential. The Black Widow, aka Natasha Romanoff, originally introduced as a villain in a 1964 *Iron Man* comic book, was conceived for the movie as a S.H.I.E.L.D. agent who could be one of the founding members of the Avengers.

Of the women that Marvel auditioned for the role, Favreau was most excited by the British actress Emily Blunt, who'd had a star-making turn in *The Devil Wears Prada* and had recently filmed the lead role of Queen Victoria in *The Young Victoria*. She was interested, but there was an obstacle: during the filming of *The Devil Wears Prada*, 20th Century Fox had signed Blunt to a multiple-picture deal, and now she was obligated to appear in a misbegotten comedic adaptation of *Gulliver's Travels*, starring Jack Black. It would begin shooting in the UK in March 2009, while *Iron Man 2* would start filming in Los Angeles the following month, and Fox wasn't inclined to change its production schedule to allow a Marvel movie to share Blunt's time.

"It's not that it's beneath me. It's not. I loved *Iron Man*, and I wanted to work with Robert Downey Jr.," Blunt said. "I was contracted to do *Gulliver's Travels*—I didn't want to do *Gulliver's Travels*. It was a bit of a heartbreaker for me because I take such pride in the decisions that I make."

Instead, Marvel signed up Scarlett Johansson. Twenty-four on the day filming began, she was a former child actress who had made the transition to nuanced adult work, largely in indie films, and was best known for her role opposite Bill Murray in *Lost in Translation*. For months, she threw herself into the physical training necessary to play

Black Widow, spending five or more hours a day working out, learning the techniques of on-screen combat, and practicing wirework stunts. Under the supervision of a nutritionist, she ate so much tuna sashimi that she joked she should sue Marvel for mercury poisoning.

"I was totally out of my element when it came to the physical part of this work," she said. She made up for her inexperience; Favreau praised her as the most dedicated member of his cast when it came to training for stunt work. Johansson wanted audiences to see her, rather than her stunt double, Heidi Moneymaker, risking her life as much as possible during fight scenes, and she savored the physical thrills of manhandling giant bodyguards. Johansson became so comfortable with her action scenes that she joked about the Black Widow's middle-of-combat hairflips, calling them her "Herbal Essences moments."

Johansson and Moneymaker both became expert at the Widow's trademark move of taking out an opponent by leaping up and scissoring her legs around his neck. On the set, they referred to the character tossing around larger adversaries as "Widow Throws." "I hadn't done the human jungle-gym stuff before," Moneymaker said. "It was fun for me—as a gymnast, you swing around the bars, but you never swing around people."

As Favreau hurtled toward the start of shooting, overseeing the work of hundreds of film technicians, he was well aware that Marvel had plans that extended beyond his movie and its very large budget. He knew that Kevin Feige was maneuvering everything into position to set up an Avengers movie. "Kevin was laying out some larger plans," he said. "There were also things in *Iron Man 2* that were included—when Tony Stark was looking into his father's history and opening up his locker—that was connected to things that were happening in *Captain America* that I wasn't aware of."

One of the simplest means of creating continuity from one movie to the next was to keep hiring Samuel L. Jackson to play Nick Fury. Jackson's representatives had some unexpected difficulty negotiating his deal—not so much because they felt Marvel's offer was insufficient financially, but more because Marvel wanted a nine-movie commitment from Jackson. Although Jackson was sixty years old when cameras rolled on *Iron Man 2*, he regularly made four or more movies a year, and he wanted to continue to take on as much work as he liked. "The average person goes to work every day except for maybe two weeks of vacation a year," he pointed out. "I do it and everybody says I'm a workaholic, but what's the difference?"

A scene originally conceived as Tony Stark getting summoned by Fury to a high-level meeting at a S.H.I.E.L.D. facility on the East Coast was reworked to be looser and funnier: instead, Fury sat down with Stark at a Los Angeles doughnut shop, barked "I am the realest person you're ever going to meet" at him, and revealed that Stark's new personal assistant was actually the Black Widow working as an undercover agent. At the end of the film, when Fury tells Stark he isn't Avengers material (leaving some room for the character to grow), video screens in the background play clips from Louis Leterrier's *The Incredible Hulk* as breaking news footage—establishing *Iron Man 2* as preceding that movie in the Marvel Cinematic Universe timeline, which was quickly becoming more complex than even Feige had expected.

Between *Iron Man* movies, Jon Favreau squeezed in a few hours in a recording studio, doing a vocal performance for *G-Force*, a 2009 animated movie about, yes, special-ops guinea pigs. Another rodent in the cast was Sam Rockwell, who had been considered as a possible Tony Stark before Downey's audition. During a *G-Force* recording session, Favreau asked Rockwell if he'd like to play Justin Hammer, Stark's sleazy counterpart: an arms manufacturer who is obsessed with replicating Stark's Iron Man technology.

Although Theroux was writing at a breakneck pace, Favreau didn't have a script to show Rockwell, because it kept changing. "I wasn't sure where the character was going," Rockwell said. But he respected Theroux—they knew each other from a theater festival in Williamstown, Massachusetts, many years earlier—and he signed on.

"I watched Gene Hackman as Lex Luthor, George C. Scott in *The Hustler*, I watched Bill Murray in *Kingpin*. I was trying to get a lot of different things to incorporate," Rockwell said of his villainous performance. One grace note that Rockwell added was Hammer's sweet tooth; in virtually every scene, he is consuming, without explanation, a sugary treat like a lollipop or a cake.

"Favreau just really wanted someone who could keep up with the verbal repartee that Downey has," Rockwell said. "I'm just barely able to do that. Downey is very quick. We went at it a little bit in the Senate room. [The scene where Tony Stark testifies before the United States Senate was full of back-and-forth ad-libbing.] It was like we were gunslingers," Rockwell said. "We were trying to see who's faster."

It was the very first scene shot for *Iron Man 2*, on April 6, 2009—almost exactly halfway through the movie's compressed production schedule. In attendance on the Senate chamber set were Downey, Rockwell, Paltrow, Cheadle, comedian Garry Shandling (playing a belligerent senator), dozens of extras, and blow-up dolls dressed in wigs and suits to fill out the crowd. (That was a budgetary move, albeit an unusual one: most movie productions are content to populate large crowds with cardboard cutouts.) Downey addressed the cast and crew, saying of Favreau, "You may see us occasionally acting like we're on the verge of performing sexual favors on each other and/or like we're not speaking. Do not be alarmed by either of these—it's just this symbiosis of working together." Favreau smiled wanly, already envisioning just how exhausted he was going to be at the end of that symbiosis.

For the movie's primary bad guy, the filmmakers needed somebody who would force Tony Stark to confront the disreputable aspects of his family history and, not incidentally, somebody who would blow things up. The result was Whiplash, aka Ivan Vanko, a former collaborator of Howard Stark (Tony's father) whom the elder Stark allowed to be written out of history. In a resonant bit of casting, Vanko was played by Mickey Rourke, a former golden boy who had spent years in exile from Hollywood.

Downey and Rourke were both nominated for Oscars in early 2009—for *Tropic Thunder* and *The Wrestler*, respectively—and at an awards-circuit banquet, Downey had convinced Rourke to join the

Iron Man 2 cast. Negotiations between Rourke and Marvel almost fell apart when the studio offered him just $250,000—despite the success of the first *Iron Man*, Marvel Entertainment was keeping a close eye on salaries. When Rourke nearly walked away, Marvel reluctantly increased the number.

If Rourke was going to play a comic-book supervillain wielding whips that crackled with destructive energy, he resolved to go all the way—and since he was filling out action beats as much as finished pages, the filmmakers largely indulged him. He wielded a thick Russian accent as if it were a serrated knife and played many of his scenes with a white cockatoo.

"The cockatoo that he has," Favreau said, "that wasn't in the original script." Favreau assented to Rourke's desire to have a pet on-screen, both to keep his star happy and because he liked how it made Vanko seem more like a pirate. Once the cockatoo was established, the movie supported its presence with new dialogue (for humans, not the bird). The filmmakers even shot a climactic scene where the bird shuffles off the mortal coil—Vanko snaps its neck—but decided it was too off-putting, especially for kids.

Rourke helped design Vanko's many tattoos, collected over his years in a Russian prison. This caused a minor kerfuffle after the movie was cut together and Feige noticed a tattoo on Vanko's neck that read "LOKI." Favreau explained it wasn't an allusion to the antagonist in the upcoming *Thor* movie, but a tribute to one of Rourke's dogs, which had died just before filming started. Feige insisted that the tattoo couldn't appear in the movie—it would be confusing to audiences—so the visual effects team had to erase the tattoo digitally in each of Vanko's scenes (although eagle-eyed fans nevertheless spotted it in a few flickering appearances).

Rourke also hired whip coaches, had his mouth fitted with gold teeth, and traveled the world to delve into Vanko's past. The week before he began filming with Rourke, Favreau said that he had met with the actor only once, but that Rourke had been phoning him and texting him from Russia. "He took it upon himself to fly to Russia and go to prison, which I thought showed some commitment.

He keeps faxing me lines that he wants to translate into Russian that he wants to say to his cockatoo, and I say, 'That's your prerogative.' "

The cast and crew of *Iron Man 2* stayed out of Rourke's way, with visitors to the set warned not to interrupt or approach the actor at any point. Rourke even insisted on not talking with Rockwell until after they had filmed the scene where their characters met. Rourke also did what he could to control how his performance would be edited; he made a habit of gesturing idiosyncratically or eating food in the middle of elaborate shots he knew would be expensive to retake.

"I wanted to bring some other layers and colors, not just make this Russian a complete murderous revenging bad guy," Rourke later said. Although he had been able to do this to his satisfaction on the set, he said that, despite his best efforts, most of the nuances of his performance had been clipped out of the movie. "Marvel just wanted a one-dimensional bad guy," he griped. "If you're working for the wrong studio or, let's say, a director that doesn't have any balls, then they're just gonna want it to be the evil bad guy."

Rourke wasn't the only movie star with unusual requests. In the first *Iron Man*, Downey had demanded that all the computers in the Stark laboratories have Classic Maya keyboards. Visual designer Ryan Meinerding was tasked with creating the props: "You could see the steam coming out of his ears," Marvel animatic editor Jim Rothwell said. "But it looked like a pro keyboard." Rothwell joked that if the ancient Mayan tongue ever became a living language again, Apple would just lift Meinerding's design.

Now Downey went even further. His personal philosophy was a mélange of beliefs that eluded even his own efforts at explanation. "I don't know where I fall," he said in 2004. "Spiritual Green Party? There were times when I was into the whole Hare Krishna thing, which is pretty far out. Now I would call myself a Jew-Bu, a Jewish-Buddhist. But there were many times when Catholicism saved my butt." When *Iron Man 2* filmed a sequence at the Monaco racetrack, at the actor's insistence his race car was painted with mystical symbols—an escalation from the first *Iron Man* film, where some crew members said they found crystals on the set that had been placed there by one of Downey's spiritual advisers.

✳

BECAUSE *IRON MAN 2* HAD started filming without a final script, and because Downey's spontaneous approach had paid off the first time, the actor now had even more freedom to ad-lib on the set. His quick-witted patter helped infuse Tony Stark with the intelligence and charm that audiences loved. The downside was that sometimes during the shooting day, the actors' improvisations would send the plot careening in new directions and then Theroux would have to spend the night revising the screenplay, trying to make sense of it all. The stress was so great that Theroux's back gave out and, for a time, he was confined to his bed.

The movie steadily moved away from its *Demon in a Bottle* inspiration. Early on, the production had filmed a scene with a bleary Stark vomiting into a toilet on an airplane, apparently feeling the effects of the night before, and Pepper telling him, "You look like you look every day. You look like you have a hangover." That scene was soon gone (although a brief excerpt, where Pepper throws the Iron Man helmet out of the airplane, forcing Stark to fly after it, made it into a trailer). Theroux said, "We didn't want to be the *Leaving Las Vegas* version of *Iron Man 2*."

Favreau, meanwhile, was busy with the movie's elaborate action sequences. For most of those scenes, the camera moves were locked in weeks in advance: in a small office at Marvel Studios, cinematographer Matthew Libatique had already used a digital rig to move a virtual camera through the world of motion-capture stunt footage. Favreau would supervise Libatique, giving aesthetic direction like, "There's too much convenience in the framing." Those sessions gave Victoria Alonso's visual effects team a much-needed head start on the special effects, both digital and practical.

The movie's final action scene, in a Japanese garden that had been digitally inserted into Flushing Meadows Park, was an elaborate battle that saw Iron Man and War Machine take on an army of Hammer Drones (prototypes of Justin Hammer's weapons hijacked by Ivan Vanko). To make sure the movie didn't become bogged down in a morass of CGI, Favreau approached a traditional animator, Genndy Tartakovsky, creator of the two-dimensional TV shows *Samurai Jack* and *Dexter's Laboratory* (not to mention a *Star Wars: Clone Wars* miniseries).

"Jon was a fan, and he liked the sensibility that I had on *Samurai*," Tartakovsky said. "I know what I would want from this situation, so I just tried to give it to him—and he could use all of it or none of it."

As on the original *Iron Man*, the climactic fight was one of the first action sequences to be conceived, and one of the last to be completed. This time, Favreau found the editing easier, because Tartakovsky had given him some distinct action beats that he could move around as modules. For example, Tartakovsky came up with a spinning Iron Man laser that cut multiple drones in half; Favreau moved that effect to the end of the fight (and added a tag where Cheadle said, "Next time, lead with that.")

Tartakovsky saw a rough cut that had substantially rejiggered his climactic fight. He thought that it basically worked but had become less surprising. "It became kind of normalized," he said. "And then the next time I saw it, it was put back together, more or less."

In January 2010, with the release date only months away, animation director Marc Chu had what he called the "come to Jesus" conversation with Favreau. What were they going to do to make that final sequence work? The answer was a reshoot that amped up Whiplash, putting him in a deluxe drone suit with extra-big whips. "That whole Japanese tea garden battle was one of those third-act reinventions in the final couple of months," Chu said.

By this point, Favreau was looking haggard and disheveled, sometimes wearing a half-buttoned plaid shirt draped over his frame. At Abbey Road Studios in London, where he was keeping an eye both on Dan Lebental editing the movie and John Debney recording the score, he groped for words: "A lot of things have to come together for this movie to work out," he said. "We're up against it, schedule-wise.

We've given ourself less time on this film than we did last time, and it's a much more ambitious project. This is part of the fear that I had when we started so late—less than two years to do this, to come up with this story. Set it up, prep it, film it, cut it, and do all the finishing touches. It's no excuse—we're going to have to do a great film—but it does put everybody under a tremendous amount of stress. It was ambitious to begin with, and now we have to knock it into overdrive. There's going to be a lot of people not sleeping. Hundreds of people not sleeping."

As planned, the movie premiered in April 2010. It was another hit, doing slightly better at the box office than the original *Iron Man*. (It cost around $200 million to make, about $60 million more than the original, and grossed $623 million worldwide.) The reviews were mixed, however, and audiences didn't love it to the same degree they had the original. While it had verve and some cool set pieces, the patched-together plot indicated how all the stress of the rushed production had shown up on the screen.

Favreau was done: he had no interest in figuring out how to make *The Avengers* work, no interest in fending off Marvel's increasingly frequent meddling, no interest in running himself into the ground any further than he already had for Ike Perlmutter's bottom line. He remained part of the Marvel ensemble as an actor, making half a dozen appearances as "Happy" Hogan, and even getting an on-screen romance with Marisa Tomei's Aunt May. And as a director, he took charge of other CGI extravaganzas, including *The Jungle Book* and *The Mandalorian*. But he never directed another MCU movie after *Iron Man 2*.

CHAPTER TEN

No Strings
on Me

The world has changed
and none of us can go back.

Captain America: The Winter Soldier

MARVEL STUDIOS VENTURED INTO THE WORLD OF theme parks in 2005, an effort that began with a proposal for a Spider-Man ride. Mohammed Khammas, the CEO of the Al Ahli Holding Group, was working on a massive real-estate development in Dubai. He had ambitious plans for residential properties and a huge indoor theme park, and he wanted one of the rides to feature the webslinger.

David Maisel said, "I went to Dubai, and I liked Mohammed so much that over the course of a week that evolved from a ride to a billion-dollar Marvel theme park." Khammas paid Marvel a large advance fee for the theme-park rights; Maisel and Kevin Feige eagerly began sketching out ideas for a Marvel park that might rival even Disneyland. "Kevin and I both love theme parks," Maisel said. "We had a blast for years designing rides for that park."

The park wouldn't have been legally possible in much of the United States, but in the United Arab Emirates, it was fair game. When Ron Perelman was running Marvel, striving for greater cashflow so he could keep acquiring other companies, he had signed a contract with Universal Studios that allowed for a Marvel-themed area in Universal's Orlando-based Islands of Adventure theme park. In unusually generous terms for Universal, the deal continued in perpetuity, so long as the Marvel characters were featured, and prohibited Marvel from featuring those characters in any competing theme-park attractions in North America east of the Mississippi River. (The Mississippi River was an arbitrary but effective way of dividing the United States in half: the two biggest theme-park territories are on opposite sides of the country, in Florida and California.) When Ike Perlmutter took over Marvel Entertainment, his team saw the deal as a huge liability, in large part because there was no legal trigger they could pull to get the rights back.

With the onset of the global recession in 2008, Khammas would have to cancel all his ambitious plans in Dubai. Maisel later described it as "a shame, but a real win for us, because we still got to keep the money." (Khammas would eventually revive the project when the economy improved, opening the Motiongate theme park in 2016, without any Marvel content.)

Also in 2005, Bob Iger became CEO of the Walt Disney Corporation, replacing Michael Eisner, and promptly turned his focus to the entertainment conglomerate's weak spots. His first priority was to resuscitate the Disney Animation brand. Disney's best-loved recent movies had come not from its own animation division, but from the films it distributed for Pixar Animation Studios. Iger wanted to buy Pixar outright, but its owner, Apple founder Steve Jobs, wasn't selling. The previous year, Disney and Pixar had been unable to come to terms even on a new distribution deal. When Iger broached the topic of an acquisition, Jobs invited him up to Cupertino, California, where he hosted a whiteboard session with the top minds at Pixar to discuss the pros and cons of a potential deal. The whiteboard soon filled up with the drawbacks of selling to the giant entertainment corporation, including "Disney's culture will destroy Pixar!" and "DISTRACTION WILL KILL PIXAR'S CREATIVITY."

Iger wasn't discouraged, because he was deeply impressed by his tour of Pixar, from the talent to the architecture. As he wrote in his autobiography, "What I saw that day left me breathless." Iger convinced Jobs that he didn't want to move Pixar's personnel 350 miles southeast to Los Angeles, and that he believed the studio should remain autonomous. Disney then bought Pixar for $7.4 billion of its own stock. The majority of that stock went to Jobs, making him Disney's largest single shareholder.

The deal, which closed in January 2006, worked as planned. Pixar's head of animation, John Lasseter, was named chief creative officer of both Pixar and Walt Disney Feature Animation, where he overhauled the Disney animation department. Although Lasseter was ousted in disgrace in 2018, Disney's two animation divisions would thrive for years in a friendly rivalry: Pixar hit new creative highs with *Up* and *Inside Out*, while Disney produced two of the highest-grossing animated films of all time with *Frozen* and *Frozen II*. With the Pixar deal in place, Iger soon started looking for other independent companies to expand the House of Mouse's portfolio of intellectual property.

In the fall of 2008, David Maisel requested a meeting with Iger; they knew each other from Maisel's brief tenure at Disney, after he had followed Michael Ovitz to the company. They had also spoken on the phone before the release of *Iron Man*, when Maisel warned Iger that he should move the release date of *The Chronicles of Narnia: Prince Caspian* so the two movies wouldn't conflict. According to Maisel, Iger's reply was "*Iron Man*? I'm not scared of *Iron Man*."

Hasbro had approached Marvel about a network it wanted to launch, called "The Hub," that might be an opportunity to push more Marvel toys. Maisel wanted to sit down with Iger to see if Disney could make a better offer for a TV partnership. If it couldn't, at least he'd know more about The Hub's main competitor. Neither party treated the meeting as high priority; Iger's office pushed back the appointment to February 2009.

"There didn't seem to be really any urgency for us to talk," Maisel remembered. The February meeting, when it happened, was a general conversation about TV strategy and how best to approach the impending death of the DVD market. "It was a relatively short meeting," Maisel said. "It was during the Academy Awards week and a lot of people were very busy." Pixar won best animated feature that year (for *WALL-E*), but none of Disney's live-action films were even nominated for best picture (although the Miramax division did pick up some acting nominations for *Doubt*). "They'd done very poorly in live-action movies at that time," Maisel said. "Obviously, strong in animation, but weak in live action."

Iger knew this all too well. Disney aimed to make entertainment for every age group: animation for young children, theme parks and Disney Channel sitcoms for tweens, ABC television and ESPN for teenagers and young adults—many of whom would start families of their own, starting the cycle of Disney tithing all over again. The weakest demographic for Disney was young men. Not enough of them, it seemed, were plugged into the ESPN ticker like it was an IV drip. With the animation division shored up by the Pixar acquisition, Iger was pondering how he could cater to young male movie fans—and his meeting with Maisel sparked his interest in the still-young Marvel Studios. (Marvel's fans weren't exclusively young men—its movies were and still are loved by many women and even some grandparents—but modern show-business economics has a tendency to consider entire artistic genres as delivery systems for specific demographics. This perspective, while effective in a brute-force way, often distorts both the art and the audience.)

Iger wasn't a comic-book fan himself, so he needed to educate himself on Marvel's roster of characters. He got the coffee-table book *The Marvel Encyclopedia* and began studying. He had another meeting with Maisel scheduled for May 2009, but in the intervening months, both men realized that the two companies could make an excellent match: Disney craved access to the young men devoted to Marvel, and Marvel needed Disney's marketing muscle. When Iger floated the idea of an alliance, an unsurprised Maisel asked the appropriate follow-up question. Did Disney, he asked, want to buy Marvel? Iger allowed that he was intrigued.

"Well, then, the next thing would be to talk with Ike," Maisel said. He told Iger that he hadn't yet broached the subject with Ike Perlmutter and "got Bob to agree that I would talk to Ike. If Ike was not interested, Bob would not pursue it."

It wasn't the first time Disney had contemplated buying Marvel. In 1995, when Ron Perelman owned Marvel (before it went bankrupt), Disney had kicked the tires on the Quinjet, but then-CEO Michael Eisner had turned down the opportunity. Disney's board of directors had worried that the Marvel characters were too mature and would tarnish Disney's family-friendly brand. Maisel remembered Eisner as having been angered by the very suggestion of acquiring Marvel, because he hated that the company had given up those crucial Orlando theme-park rights (which would have barred Disney from featuring Marvel characters at Walt Disney World). Iger, however, believed that Eisner was just intensely devoted to Disney's brand identity. "There was an assumption at the time," Iger said, "that Disney was a single, monolithic brand."

Iger had a more collaborative relationship with Disney's board, and a different perspective on how Marvel's identity might mesh with Disney's. "I had the opposite worry of those who were wary of acquiring a company that was decidedly edgier than Disney," Iger said. "Not what Marvel would do to Disney, but how loyal Marvel fans would react to their being associated with us. Would we possibly destroy some of their value by acquiring them?" Iger believed that he could convince the Disney board to buy Marvel, if Perlmutter could be persuaded to sell the first company he had ever wanted to hold onto.

After a briefing from Maisel, Perlmutter was curious enough to invite Iger to New York City for a meeting at the Marvel Entertainment office in midtown. Iger accepted, traveling by himself, rather than with a posse of Disney vice presidents. Iger described Perlmutter's office as "spartan"; the billionaire offered his guest a banana and a bottle of Kirkland-brand water from Costco, where Perlmutter and his wife still shopped on weekends to stock up on discount goods. Although both men knew the reason for Iger's visit, the Disney CEO approached the conversation gingerly, opening by telling Perlmutter about his own business background. When Perlmutter asked about the Pixar acquisition, Iger took the opportunity to explain how he made certain that Pixar had maintained its own culture after being acquired by Disney. Then he told Perlmutter that he was interested in doing something similar with Marvel.

Perlmutter didn't say yes, but he suggested they resume the conversation that evening at Post House, a steakhouse on East 63rd Street. Dinner went late, with Perlmutter sharing stories of how he had started by selling merchandise on the streets of Brooklyn. Iger outlined the possibilities of Disney-Marvel synergy, and what the sale could mean for both companies. "He stood to make a lot of money from a sale to Disney," Iger noted, "but he'd also taken control of Marvel when it was in trouble and turned it around. I think the notion that some other CEO would just come in and buy it up didn't sit easily with him, even though he knew he'd make a fortune off it."

The next day, Perlmutter told Iger that he was considering the matter, but he wasn't sure that a sale was a good idea. Iger realized this deal wasn't going to get hashed out on a whiteboard, so he invited Perlmutter and his wife, Laurie, back to the Post House a few days later to dine with him and his wife, Willow. They sat at the same table as before, but dinner was purely social, with no business talk. Perlmutter still didn't agree to the sale, but Iger could tell that he was warming to the notion. David Maisel started to discuss the details of a potential deal with Kevin A. Mayer (executive vice president at Disney) and Thomas O. Staggs (COO and CFO at Disney).

"Here's what Tom and Kevin are going to piss on," Maisel warned Iger before formal negotiations began. "We don't have the rights for Spider-Man. We don't have the rights for X-Men and Fantastic Four. We don't have theme parks east of the Mississippi, so you can't use the Marvel characters in your biggest theme park in Orlando. We have four movies left on our Paramount distribution deal, so you can't get your hands into those movies unless you buy them out."

Maisel was prepared to refute each objection. "Let me answer all those things for you. If we had the rights to Spider-Man, the price would be a billion dollars more. And it'd be higher if we had X-Men. And all the characters we have, we have a universe that doesn't require those. Theme parks east of the Mississippi, yeah, but you have them everywhere else." Maisel wanted to sell Marvel Entertainment for somewhere north of $50 a share, representing a 30 percent premium on the stock price at the time.

Perlmutter was still dithering, so Iger called Steve Jobs, "who claimed to have never read a comic book in his life," for help. By this point, Jobs trusted Iger implicitly, so he just asked, "Is this one important to you? Do you really want it? Is this another Pixar?" When Iger said that it was, Jobs made a personal call to Perlmutter, telling him how Disney had acquired Pixar without squelching the company's culture or creativity.

"He said you were true to your word," Perlmutter reported back to Iger. They had a deal. Disney agreed to a price that valued Marvel at about $50 a share, or $4 billion in total. Perlmutter's stake was valued at almost $1.5 billion. The offer, a mix of cash and shares, made Ike Perlmutter the second-largest individual shareholder in Disney—just behind Steve Jobs.

Before the official announcement, the companies were already busy behind the scenes preparing for the merger. Maisel, by his choice, would be leaving Marvel: he had executed his business plan, left his mark on the industry, and earned a small fortune from the sale. "I told Bob that in, I think, the first or second meeting," Maisel said. "I didn't want him to find that as a surprise. I told him I had confidence in Kevin running the studio."

When the deal was announced, some Marvel fans complained—as Iger had feared—about the prospect of their favorite superheroes turning into Disney characters. The comments section on Marvel's own website was flooded with concern, including one fan who fretted the brand would "become so watered-down and kiddie-fied that reading their adventures will become no more engaging than *See Spot Run*."

Feige met with Iger and pitched him the full scope of his plans for the Marvel Cinematic Universe: how the movies featuring Iron

Man, Hulk, Thor, and Captain America would set up *The Avengers*, and how that could lead to even more crossovers and sequels, with properties like Doctor Strange and Black Panther waiting in the wings.

Feige believed that crossovers weren't gratuitous fan service, but "completely inherent to the DNA of what Marvel is." As he pointed out, "Hardcore comics readers have had that experience for decades of Spider-Man swinging into the Fantastic Four headquarters, or new members of the Avengers joining, or Hulk suddenly rampaging through the pages of an Iron Man comic. There's something inherently great about that. We thought it would be fun for filmgoers to get that same rush, on a much bigger, more global canvas."

Iger's opinion of Feige's plans: "Seemed brilliant to me."

✳

IN THE SUMMER OF 2009, *Iron Man 2* had wrapped principal photography, *Thor* had signed up most of its principal cast, and *Captain America: The First Avenger* had director Joe Johnston (the man behind *The Rocketeer*, which Feige had cited as a favorite period film) ready to make a movie set in the 1940s. Marvel's creative producers were expecting to go on another weekend retreat in Palm Springs to plot out *The Avengers*, but instead Feige surprised them with an invitation to a Sunday-night dinner at a Scottish steakhouse in Los Angeles called Tam O'Shanter. There, he told them about the impending Disney acquisition and said that Iger had already been pitching him on what Disney's resources could mean for Marvel.

When the producers finally made it out to Palm Springs, after the deal was announced, they figured out how to thread "the Tesseract" (a magic item based on the Cosmic Cube in Marvel comic books) through their upcoming movies so that it would become a crucial element in *The Avengers*. They could establish its origin in *Captain America*: it would be hidden in a European village until the villainous Red Skull got his hands on it. Crucially, the Tesseract would make it easier to set the movie during World War II without having the battle sequences turn into bloodbaths, because instead of using guns, the soldiers of HYDRA would fight with energy weapons and flamethrowers. That pleased Marvel's New York office, since the resulting toys would be more interesting and—technically—not Nazi action figures.

Marvel Studios' first two movies had been made with a minimum of interference from New York. Jon Favreau got notes on the *Iron Man* script from the popular Marvel Comics writer Mark Millar, but the director also sought feedback from a wide range of people, including filmmakers not affiliated with Marvel, such as J. J. Abrams and Shane Black. After the success of *Iron Man* and *The Incredible Hulk*, however, New York wanted to exert more control over the moviemaking process. The stated reason was to ensure Marvel Studios wouldn't do anything that didn't synergize with the rest of Marvel Entertainment's efforts. But most people at Marvel Studios assumed that the underlying motivation was that the movies had suddenly become the most exciting and glamorous part of Marvel's business.

At Perlmutter's behest, Marvel Entertainment set up a group it called the Creative Committee. Its members were Dan Buckley, president of Marvel Entertainment; Joe Quesada, chief creative officer of Marvel Entertainment; Brian Michael Bendis, the star writer of Marvel Comics; Louis D'Esposito of Marvel Studios; Kevin Feige; and Alan Fine, newly promoted executive vice-president, office of the chief executive (generally understood to be Perlmutter's mouthpiece on the Committee). Perlmutter required Marvel Studios to obtain the Committee's approval on every major decision, starting with which movies the studio made and extending through casting and drafts of screenplays. Some of the Committee's notes were constructive, but in many instances, the Committee seemed to be impeding Marvel Studios. One early confrontation came over *Captain America: The First Avenger*. Fine believed that Marvel audiences wouldn't want to see a movie set largely in the 1940s. Feige and D'Esposito insisted that they needed to establish Captain America before making *The Avengers*: the movie had to show audiences that Steve Rogers was a man out of time, not just pay lip service to the notion. The meetings became "screaming matches," but Feige prevailed. That would not, however, be the end of his travails with the Committee. (Fine declined to answer questions about his tenure at Marvel for this book.)

According to Marvel producer Craig Kyle, Feige was looking for "what Pixar had. How do we develop a brain trust, where the most knowledgeable minds of the company can gather and offer insight to help us make the best choices at every stage, and then run cuts of the film by those same folks to get additional insights?" (At Pixar, the Brain Trust—the actual official name—included the studio's top directors and met every few months, producing unvarnished and incredibly helpful feedback among colleagues.) "The idea behind it was, let's just get our best together, speak frankly and productively, and make the best damn films we can," Kyle said. "The dream was a great one, because Pixar's model, most of the time, it's a beautiful and perfect one. Ours would not turn out to be that."

On August 31, 2009, Disney officially bought Marvel. After only two Marvel Studios movies, the whole notion of four at-bats from the Merrill Lynch deal had become moot now that Marvel had access to Disney's capital and financing. Marvel made enough cash from *Iron Man* and *The Incredible Hulk* that it easily paid back the money owed to Merrill Lynch, and the ten characters offered as collateral remained safely in Marvel's custody.

The distribution deal with Paramount, however, wasn't going to expire until after *The Avengers* and *Iron Man 3*. *The Avengers* was a crucial moment for Marvel—it would be proof of concept of the Marvel Cinematic Universe. With billions of dollars invested in Marvel, Disney was eager to handle the rollout itself, giving the movie the most powerful push possible and raking in the profits. For the biggest team-up movie in history, Disney wasn't interested in working with another distributor.

Paramount didn't want to let go of the Marvel properties. It had recently lost the rights to distribute DreamWorks SKG movies (when Viacom had purchased DreamWorks), and it was depending on the Marvel movies to buoy its bottom line. Working out a deal took a full year, but in October 2010, the studios agreed that for $115 million, Disney would buy out Paramount's distribution deal for *The Avengers* and *Iron Man 3*. If either movie overperformed expectations (as they both would), Paramount would receive bonuses (as much as 9 percent on *Iron Man 3*).

Marvel eventually found a way, too, to skirt the Universal Studios theme-park deal that featured Marvel's core heroes in the Islands of Adventure. Disney parks could feature Marvel content so long as they didn't include the specific heroes covered by that deal such as Hulk, Spider-Man, and the Fantastic Four, or use "Marvel" in the name of the attractions. The inclusion of Marvel in Disney parks started slowly, with a smattering of cast members in costume as Marvel heroes, but soon expanded, with Marvel-themed rides at Disney properties around the world. In Anaheim, the California Adventure Park featured the Guardians of the Galaxy in a rethemed version of the Tower of Terror ride, which eventually expanded into an Avengers Campus, with a Doctor Strange stage show and a restaurant called Pym's Test Kitchen.

Marvel wasn't the only Disney acquisition intended to help the company reach a male demographic. After Iger closed the Marvel deal, he moved on to Lucasfilm, home to the *Star Wars* and *Indiana Jones* franchises. In 2012, Disney laid out another $4 billion for Lucasfilm. Once more, Iger faced fan worries about the Disneyfication of those properties; again, he mostly left the profitable new subsidiary alone.

For his part, Feige was sanguine about Disney's acquisition of Marvel, and not just because he had fond memories of the childhood vacations his family took at Disney World every year. "I never had any experiences with somebody acquiring a company I was working for," he said, "but we just always trusted that they would be able to elevate what we were doing. We had fine studio partners before Disney, but we didn't have a family. As they have proved every year since then, Disney is the greatest marketing team in the business."

Our Brand Is Chrises

It's like his muscles are made
of Cotati metal fiber.

Avengers: Infinity War

THE *THOR* COMIC BOOKS DREW FROM VIKING MYTHOL-
ogy and the Norse Eddas, but they also regularly showcased
the thunder god facing off against modern supervillains like
the Absorbing Man. People liked to describe Thor's language in the
comic books as "Shakespearean," by which they meant that, verily,
Stan Lee hath sprinkleth Thor's dialogue with enough archaic flour-
ishes to make him feeleth like a man from another century.

The person hired to direct *Thor*, Kenneth Branagh, had directed
many plays by the actual William Shakespeare, on stage and on
screen, and saw connections that were deeper than Lee's faux-
Elizabethan language. "We're interested in what goes on in the
corridors of power, whether it's the White House or whether it's
Buckingham Palace," he said. "Shakespeare was interested in the
lives of the medieval royal families, but he also raided the Roman
myths and the Greek myths for the same purpose. I think Stan Lee
went to the myths that Shakespeare hadn't used."

Branagh recognized that although the stakes in a Thor story were cosmic, the actors were human: "If the actors take those stakes seriously it is passionate and very intense. That observation of ordinary human—although they're gods—frailties in people in positions of power is an obsession of great storytellers, including Shakespeare and including the Marvel universe."

Feige had a slightly more contemporary cultural touchstone in mind: *The Godfather*. "It's about fathers and sons, and it's about the actions that a father takes that his sons will have to answer for," he said.

Marvel Studios first approached not Branagh but Matthew Vaughn, who had debuted with the action movie *Layer Cake* and then directed an entertaining adaptation of Neil Gaiman's fantasy *Stardust*. And studio executives initially hired Mark Protosevich (*The Cell, I Am Legend*) to write a *Thor* script without giving him specifics about what they were looking for, because they weren't sure yet themselves. In the resulting screenplay, Odin banishes Thor to Earth in the Middle Ages, where he is enslaved by Norsemen until Lady Sif and the Warriors Three find him.

Marvel soon realized that it wanted *Thor* to be set in modern times, but with the 2007–2008 writers' strike in progress, the studio couldn't commission revisions on the Protosevich screenplay. By the time the strike was over, Marvel's option on Vaughn's services had expired; he left the project and made the ultraviolent vigilante-superhero movie *Kick-Ass*. Marvel commissioned a new outline from J. Michael Straczynski (creator of the TV show *Babylon 5*) and courted director Guillermo del Toro (*Pan's Labyrinth*, *Blade II*), but he opted to take on *The Hobbit* movies produced by Peter Jackson. (That was a bad decision: MGM Studios was in such financial distress, it couldn't actually move forward on *The Hobbit*. After waiting in New Zealand for two years, del Toro gave up and directed *Hellboy II*.) Marvel Studios had talks with thriller director D. J. Caruso before deciding that Branagh's experience directing a half-dozen Shakespeare adaptations on film (some including battle scenes) would serve him well on *Thor*. Branagh, the most famous and respected director of any Marvel film to that point, was almost fifty, but still had a reputation as a wunderkind: when he was in his twenties, his work on a movie version of *Henry V* had earned him Oscar nominations for both best actor and best director.

While Marvel Studios had been aiming for one movie a year, in early 2009 it pushed the release date of *Thor* back to 2011. Even on that timetable, production was rushed. Ashley Edward Miller and Zack Stentz, who had been a writing team on the sci-fi TV shows *Andromeda* and *Terminator: The Sarah Connor Chronicles*, got a call from their agent. As Miller told the story, "Marvel was looking for television writers because they were fast. Hopefully, they were a team because that was even faster. And hopefully, they knew science fiction and comic books, and hopefully hopefully hopefully, they knew Thor." Miller told Stentz, "I think we check off all the boxes."

Soon the writers were in a meeting at the Marvel Studios HQ, discussing their take on the thunder god in front of a full room, including one guy they didn't know, sporting a scraggly beard and wearing a T-shirt, jeans, and Chuck Taylor sneakers. But when he opened his mouth and spoke in a resonant, well-modulated British accent, the screenwriters realized it was Branagh. They got the job and started working with him, debating essential questions such as Thor's role in the modern world and the name of Thor's hammer. "One of my most vivid memories of those notes sessions," Stentz said, "was Branagh didn't like the name Mjölnir because it's difficult to pronounce. He turned to all of us and asked, 'Do we have to call the hammer 'Mjölnir'? I see that it's made out of some metal called 'Uru.' Could we call it Uru instead? Or would the fanboys string me up?' Kevin [Feige] just gave his little half-smile: 'Ken, the fanboys would string you up.' 'Alright. We won't be doing that, then.'"

While Miller and Stentz labored over the script, Branagh worked with Marvel casting director Sarah Halley Finn. Stentz recalled seeing pretty much every notable Hollywood actress between the ages of twenty-five and thirty as they came by the production office to read for the role of Jane Foster, earthbound scientist and Thor's love interest. He described Branagh's reaction immediately following a meeting with Natalie Portman. "He was very taken with her," Stentz said.

"Not in a romantic way, but with her intelligence. Jane is a physicist, and we needed someone who could convey that intelligence. That's what struck him about her: he said, forgive me, 'Because the last thing we need is nuclear physicist Denise Richards.'" (Richards had played the nuclear physicist Dr. Christmas Jones in the James Bond movie *The World Is Not Enough*, earning much mockery and a 1999 Razzie Award for "Worst Supporting Actress.")

Branagh was a draw for top-flight performers. Portman said she signed on because she figured that Branagh doing *Thor* was sure to be "super weird." Anthony Hopkins joined the cast, playing the All-Father Odin, because he was a fan of Branagh's theatrical work. But finding the right man for the title role proved more challenging. Finn said, "We were casting Cap and Thor in an overlapping period, and both of them seemed to be very risky."

✳

FINN HAD TRIED OUT for the job of casting director on *Iron Man*; once she got the position, she never left. Although the Hollywood studio system had once valued behind-the-scenes continuity—to name just one example, costume designer Edith Head worked at Paramount Pictures for forty-four years, from 1924 to 1967, winning eight Academy Awards along the way—that approach had largely been discarded in favor of letting producers assemble a new staff for each movie. But Marvel Studios, valuing consistency and reliability, preferred to hire talented professionals and keep them around. Finn, like Louis D'Esposito and Victoria Alonso, would be a critical pillar in the new Marvel studio system. The ambition to create a shared universe of movies required an emphasis on continuity that molded not just the final films but the organizational structure behind the scenes.

Along with Jon Favreau, Finn had been an early advocate for Robert Downey Jr. On *Iron Man 2*, she had been behind the decision to hire Scarlett Johansson for the role of Black Widow, even though the actress wasn't known for action movies or stunts. Finn said that Marvel had encouraged her to focus on the best actor for the character rather than securing the biggest name possible. Ironically, given her own status as a tenured employee of Marvel, she tended not to worry about the long-term trajectories for characters and encouraged the young actors she cast to do the same: "When you start to look at the comics, it can quickly get very confusing," she noted. "I learned to really key into the director's vision for the project and to try to understand their approach and the story they want to tell."

The casting of Downey set the terms for the Marvel audition process: in nearly all cases, the studio valued screen tests over reputation. When casting a role, Finn would typically bring in top choices for an audition with a small camera crew, the core Marvel Studios producers, and (ideally) the movie's director. The first round was the reading of a scene (known in industry parlance as "sides"), either in person or, if the actor wasn't in Los Angeles, on tape. Further testing could involve new sides to showcase different aspects of the character, another actor to test potential chemistry, and even costumes or sets to see how natural the performer looked in a world of superheroes.

In the name of continuity, Marvel Studios revived another practice from the old Hollywood system: signing actors to long-term contracts, typically for nine movies. While the immediate justification was that Marvel needed its superheroes on call for crossovers and team-ups, the underlying motivation was financial. After Downey used the success of *Iron Man* to negotiate gargantuan paydays, Marvel Studios wanted the cost certainty of young talent locked into affordable multiyear deals. (That was another reason Finn didn't focus on the biggest possible name for each role.)

Finn's challenge with Thor was finding "an actor who could play Asgardian, which we equated to Shakespearean, almost, and yet be completely earthbound and relatable." Back in 2004, when Avi Arad had almost set up a Thor movie at Sony, the leading contender for the role had been Daniel Craig. He still seemed like a strong candidate, but Craig quickly declined because he had committed to the James Bond franchise. Other actors Marvel seriously considered included Charlie Hunnam (*Sons of Anarchy*), Joel Kinnaman (a Swedish actor then largely unknown in the US), Tom Hiddleston (a British actor also little known in the US), Alexander Skarsgård (*True Blood*), and Liam Hemsworth (an Australian actor and another unknown). The guiding principle, according to Branagh: "Don't let it be like Fabio."

For any foreign actor trying to break into Hollywood, proper representation was key. Liam Hemsworth was handled by ROAR Management, whose cofounder William Ward had discovered him and his brother Chris when scouting for talent in Australia. Both Hemsworths were TV actors with greater aspirations. Ward had already flown Chris Hemsworth out to Hollywood and landed him an agent, Ilene Feldman, who had helped him get cast in the 2009 J. J. Abrams reboot of *Star Trek*. In a memorable opening sequence, Hemsworth played the brave but doomed father of Captain Kirk.

Chris Hemsworth had short brown hair, a clean-shaven face, and a Starfleet-slick American accent. Marvel Studios let him read for Thor but passed. Soon after, he went to Vancouver to shoot the horror movie *Cabin in the Woods*. Director Drew Goddard and producer Joss Whedon, who had encouraged him to pursue *Thor*, saw trade-magazine articles about the top contenders for the role and couldn't help but notice that Chris wasn't among them. "Why aren't you in the mix here?" they asked. "What happened?"

"I don't know," he told them. "I blew my audition, I guess."

Spurred on by Goddard and Whedon, and fueled by sibling rivalry—"frustration that my little brother had gotten further than me," he said—he agitated for a second chance. (Liam had gotten far enough into the audition process that he did one round of *Thor* tests in a borrowed Pepper Potts wig.) Chris shot a new set of sides in a Vancouver hotel room, with his mother reading Odin's lines, and many at Marvel suddenly saw the appeal. "When he came in for a screen test and told a story of Thor's exploits," Branagh said, "he did it with such relish, such fun, a sense of danger. He was able to occupy the character of Thor in a way that seemed just right to us."

Finn, Feige, and Branagh didn't want to lose Tom Hiddleston, who had originally gone on tape for Thor, but came back to audition for Loki, Thor's conniving brother. Branagh had previously worked with Hiddleston on the detective series *Wallander*, and Feige, having seen the actor in a production of Chekhov's *Ivanov* at Wyndham's Theatre in London, agreed with the director that Hiddleston had the range to play a role that Marvel had big plans for. Stentz said, "The singular mandate above all other mandates was that they wanted Loki to be the villain for *The Avengers*. They literally said, 'If you fail at everything else, please just give us a villain as good as Magneto in Loki.'"

Meeting at the Marvel Studios headquarters on a Saturday morning in May 2009, the *Thor* team made the final decision: Chris Hemsworth as Thor and Hiddleston as Loki. Feige anxiously paced around the conference table. "These will be the most important calls you make," he warned Branagh. The director was confident in his choices, although he had no way of knowing just how much chemistry the two actors would have.

Hiddleston played Loki, an abandoned frost giant boy raised to believe he is Thor's biological brother, with a quick wit and depth of feeling. *Thor* producer Craig Kyle recalled an early cast meal Branagh arranged where the director was quizzing the actors on their family dynamic. He turned to Rene Russo, who was playing Loki's and Thor's mother, Freya, and asked her if she would tell Loki the truth; she replied she wouldn't. "And we're all looking around the table saying, 'Of course not. It's Loki. He's evil,'" Kyle said. "She says, 'Because he's so sensitive.' She answered it as a mother of an emo kid. She's got this hot-shot, powerful husband and her quarterback son who was the spitting image of his father, and then you've got this kid who was standing in the shadow of two great men."

The shadow that Chris Hemsworth cast was about to get much bigger. "If you remember," Stenz said, "when they announced Hemsworth, it was like, 'Who? Captain Kirk's dad? This skinny Australian surfer?' The thing with Branagh is, he just has a freaking unparalleled eye for casting. He's so good at it. That's what we would tell people: 'If Ken says he's the guy, then he's the guy.' Indeed, he saw things in Hemsworth that I think not a lot of people had until that point. With these superhero movies, I think casting is seventy-five percent of it right there. You put the right actor in the role—as opposed to the almost-right actor—and it's magic."

Hemsworth immediately accepted the role, signing a multipicture deal. Whedon and Goddard had given him a collection of *The Ultimates* so he could get a handle on Thor. "I had read the comics," Hemsworth said, "and this guy's like 500 pounds."

Branagh advised him that he should get "as big as he can," so Hemsworth threw himself into a rigorous workout regimen to add lean body tissue. He already looked athletic, but the goal was to make him look godlike. Working with celebrity trainer Duffy Gaver, Hemsworth put on over twenty pounds of muscle in eight months. During that time, he also starred in the remake of *Red Dawn*, training with heavy weights several times a day when he wasn't on camera.

After that shoot, he returned for a final costume fitting as Thor: "Within a couple of minutes, my hands started going numb," Hemsworth said, "and everyone was like, 'Yeah, that's not cool.'" The measurements taken for his costumes only three weeks earlier were already so far off from his actual dimensions that the armor made to accentuate his muscles was instead cutting off his circulation. Branagh told the actor he was officially "big enough." Hemsworth shifted away from eating a lot of calories and training with high weight and embraced a kettlebell workout that maintained his muscle mass instead of building it.

Casting Thor was difficult because he was a god; casting Captain America was difficult because he had to embody old-fashioned American decency without being corny. "When I was casting Captain America," Finn said, "I did not understand where this was going to go—I really had no idea. When Kevin was first talking about *The Avengers*, that was mind-blowing to me."

With Thor and Loki, Marvel Studios had, through a mixture of skill and luck, gotten things exactly right with a pair of obscure actors. It was willing to look at some marginally better-known names to play Steve Rogers. "We knew the central core of qualities we were looking for," Finn said, "but the property was not well-known. People didn't get it, it seemed a bit 'B,' it seemed a bit dated." Ryan Philippe auditioned, as did Garrett Hedlund, Jensen Ackles, Chace Crawford, and (on a break from *The Office*) John Krasinski. Some of the finalists, including Krasinski, were brought in for screen tests that included dressing up in a Captain America costume on a period set. Krasinski, who would eventually appear in *Doctor Strange in the Multiverse of Madness* as the rubber-limbed superhero Reed Richards, later told the story of being half-dressed when a pumped-up Chris Hemsworth walked by in his full Thor costume. Krasinski regarded his own shirtless body and concluded that maybe he wasn't actually cut out for playing an Adonis.

Some of the other actors who auditioned for Captain America also ended up in the MCU with different roles. Wyatt Russell, son of Kurt Russell and Goldie Hawn, had his first-ever professional audition with Sarah Halley Finn. A decade later, he would finally get to carry Captain America's shield as John Walker (aka U.S. Agent) in the Disney Plus series *The Falcon and the Winter Soldier*.

Sebastian Stan also read for Steve Rogers. "But we saw something there that was a bit darker, a bit edgier," Finn said. "And as we continued to go through the process, it seemed like the best role might be Bucky." Captain America's sidekick Bucky Barnes had been one of the rare Marvel characters who died and stayed dead. In the comic books, he expired heroically at the end of World War II and remained deceased for five decades before writer Ed Brubaker came up with the plotline that revived him as the brainwashed Russian assassin called the Winter Soldier. It wasn't going to take Marvel Studios fifty years to turn Bucky into the Winter Soldier. Stan signed a nine-picture deal, which, for fans who kept up on Hollywood contract news, slightly undercut Bucky's apparent death in *Captain America: The First Avenger*.

Also reading sides for Captain America was *Parks and Recreation* cast member Chris Pratt. Finn was intrigued by the actor but decided "it wasn't quite a fit."

"Casting Captain America was super hard and it took a long time," Feige said. "I started to think, 'Are we not going to be able to find

Captain America, and if we can't get Captain America, what are we going to do with *Avengers*? Is the whole thing going to fall apart?'"

There was one performer the studio really wanted, but early on, he had declined even to audition. Chris Evans had already played a Marvel superhero, the cocky Johnny Storm, also known as the Human Torch, in the two Fantastic Four movies directed by Tim Story for Fox. Finn was very familiar with his work. "My oldest two boys and I had seen *Fantastic Four* maybe 50 or 60 times," she said. "We kind of went round and round and came back to Chris."

There were many reasons Evans seemed perfect for the role, Finn said. "He was American. We've cast a lot of Brits, but we wanted to cast an American. And a great actor and funny and charming and affable and all of that. But then beyond the obvious qualities, I think there were the other ones that were a little harder to discern: his humility, the sense that he had a moral compass, that he was very relatable. He has this vulnerability as well as strength, so we could take him from skinny Steve to Captain America."

Marvel Studios invited Evans to a meeting. "Bringing him in, showing him the artwork, showing him what was happening in this movie," Feige recalled. They offered him a nine-movie deal for Steve Rogers, no audition required. "He took a weekend to decide," Feige said. "That weekend was tough."

Evans made his decision and, once again, the answer was no. "Getting the offer felt, to me, like the epitome of temptation," the actor explained. "The ultimate job offer, on the biggest scale. I'm supposed to say no to this thing. It felt like the right thing to do. You see the pictures, and you see the costumes, and it's cool. But I'd now woken up the day after saying no and felt good—twice."

Evans added, "I like my privacy. The good thing about movies is there's a lot of freedom built in: you make a film and then you have time off. If one of those films hits and changes your life, you have the opportunity to . . . run away. If you want to. Take some time, reassess, and regroup." But if *Captain America: The First Avenger* was a hit, Evans knew he wouldn't have that opportunity, because he would be playing Steve Rogers again right away.

Robert Downey Jr. called Evans and encouraged him to take the role, telling him that the fame that came with it would expand his opportunities as an actor, not constrict them. To entice Evans, Marvel Studios rolled back his commitment to just six movies: a trilogy of Captain America movies and three Avengers films. Evans would still be locked into the role for roughly a decade, which scared him. But sometimes, he decided, "maybe the thing you're most scared of is actually the thing you should do." He took the part.

Marvel announced the casting decision in April 2010, but it took years for Evans to quell his worries. He later confessed to being roiled by fear and self-hatred while making his first Captain America movie. The mantra playing in his head: "This is it. I just signed my death warrant; my life's over. I can't believe I did this. This isn't the career I wanted." He relaxed once he realized that the Captain America movies were actually good. "The biggest thing I was worried about was making shitty fucking movies," he said. "I don't want to make shitty movies and be contractually obligated to make garbage."

Evans, too, embarked on an intensive effort to remake his body, one similar to Hemsworth's, centered on a couple of hours of daily high-weight training. For Evans the most challenging aspect of the program was the high caloric intake. "Just eating all the time," he complained. "You think it sounds nice, but it's not, like, cheeseburgers. You have to eat these bland, naked pieces of chicken and rice. You're just so full—it's a pretty uncomfortable feeling." Evans committed to the program, though, with impressive results.

Finn said she didn't have any profound insight into which actors would be able to make the accelerated physical transformations necessary to become superheroes. "Fortunately, that is not my job," she said. "My job is to find the embodiment of the character. Their [physical appearance is] somebody else's job. But I would say that informs the process, right? There has to be a willingness to submit to the kind of intense rigors that it requires of you."

She remembered her first meeting with Hayley Atwell to discuss the role of Peggy Carter, the superspy who would develop a relationship with Captain America, and the actress, "in her most perfect

British accent, saying she was tired of period pieces, and she really wanted to kick some ass. And then she worked very, very hard. So knowing they have that willingness is great, but it's never been a requirement. It's been about 'Let's find the person who makes this character come to life.'"

*

FINN IDENTIFIED the casting of another Chris as her proudest moment in her long career at Marvel: she realized that Chris Pratt could play Star-Lord in *Guardians of the Galaxy*, the 2014 movie directed by James Gunn about a gang of reluctantly heroic outerspace misfits. Pratt was famous as the dimwitted goofball Andy Dwyer on the NBC sitcom *Parks and Recreation*, but Finn remembered the spark he had shown in his audition for Captain America years earlier: "I was so excited, and I went to James [Gunn], and he said, 'Chris Pratt, no way, he's totally wrong.'"

Finn secretly kept Pratt on the short list for Star-Lord while casting the rest of the *Guardians* ensemble. She saw Chadwick Boseman for the role of Drax and Lupita Nyong'o for Gamora, and although both parts went to other people (Dave Bautista and Zoe Saldaña, respectively), each actor made enough of an impression to get a leading role in *Black Panther* years later. Another example of slow-burn casting was the Scottish actress Karen Gillan, who had auditioned for Sharon Carter (a secret agent and Peggy Carter's niece) in *Captain America: The Winter Soldier*. The role went to Emily VanCamp, but Finn realized the actress would be a perfect fit for Gamora's sister Nebula, because she had a cherubic look even when she was projecting menace.

Star-Lord remained uncast, so Finn prevailed on Gunn to at least let Pratt do a screen test for the role (remembering well how that had helped showcase Downey as a good fit for Tony Stark). Pratt was intrigued, if skeptical that he was actually the right man for the job. But his screen test was the type of moment casting directors dream of: "Chris walked in the room, and we have this audition, and it's really magical. Within ten seconds, James turned around and looked at me and said, 'He's the guy.'"

Pratt had further to go to achieve a superhero's body than the first two Chrises. He had intentionally gained weight to make his *Parks and Recreation* character appear more "schlubby." Marvel called Duffy Gaver, the trainer who had worked with Hemsworth. "I got a phone call and they wanted to see if I was available to train Chris Pratt. They said he'd just walked out of their office and found out he was the lead in their next franchise," Gaver remembered. He quickly Googled Pratt and agreed to do it. "I think Chris's body at the time was working for the type of actor he was, but it was time for a change."

Twenty minutes later, Gaver was on the phone with Pratt. They met for coffee the next day and began training the day after that. "Chris was very prepared to put the work in," Gaver said. Although Finn insisted that she didn't vet actors on the basis of how devoted they were to workout regimes, Gaver could only judge by the people who Marvel sent his way, and he could infer that at some point in the process, actors who didn't demonstrate the necessary level of commitment were getting screened out. "Marvel is hiring people for years and years, so they want people who are very dedicated and disciplined. The people I get called to train have already passed quite a litmus test to arrive where they are."

Gaver used Pratt as an example for his other clients, telling them how the whole gym would pay attention to him during his workout. "Not because he was a movie star, because at the time he wasn't," the trainer said. "He's dripping sweat, out of breath. He was just a guy who was killing himself in the gym."

Marvel also introduced Pratt to nutritionist Philip Goglia, who increased Pratt's caloric intake to 4,000 a day, plus one ounce of water for each pound the actor weighed. "I was peeing all day long, every day," Pratt said. "That part was a nightmare."

Within six months, Pratt had sculpted himself into a superhero. The writers of *Parks and Recreation* had written a scene for season seven where his character, Andy Dwyer, needed to take his shirt off. "We realized we couldn't do it," said showrunner Michael Schur. "Andy is not a guy who has a perfectly constructed human form with ripped abs and gigantic biceps."

On Instagram, Pratt posted a shirtless selfie of himself captioned "Six months, no beer." It was the first selfie of a Marvel star to go viral, as the world gaped at his physical transformation. Throughout its history, Hollywood has sold the female body to moviegoers, and young actresses have starved and surgically altered themselves to achieve impossible ideals. Marvel Studios didn't make the first movies that emphasized the male body, but in presenting one chiseled superhero after another in blockbuster after blockbuster, it created a world in which the male form is as malleable as the female form—and presented just as routinely as the object of fantasy. Like Dr. Abraham Erskine with his Super Soldier serum, Marvel Studios decided that it could make its own superior specimens of humanity and benefit from the results.

Superpowers, not being real, could work any way the creators of comic books and comic-book movies want: it's an extremely literal choice to say that with great power comes great muscularity. But Marvel leaned into that genre convention, so much so that the actors who didn't have rippling physiques felt the need to bulk up. Sebastian Stan admitted that when he arrived on the set of *Captain America: Civil War*, "I was so insecure being around these massive fucking guys so I started lifting really heavy and ate a lot. I remember I showed up, and I was a little bit bigger than I had been in *The Winter Soldier*. The [fake prosthetic] arm was a bit tight—I was losing circulation."

Although Robert Downey Jr.'s torso was typically concealed on-screen by a tailored suit or CGI armor, being in a superhero movie spurred him to remake his body too. He was already doing yoga and martial arts and weight training, but he started adding muscle: "I feel like I got a five-to-seven-year window and then if it goes past that, I'm sure all the optical stuff and CGI will have advanced to make you look better."

Chadwick Boseman, star of *Black Panther*, said that his Marvel workouts never stopped. "Even if you change the regimen—say, you have to get smaller for another role and you have to beef up again for this—there are certain things you have to keep doing."

Paul Rudd, like Pratt known as a comic actor, got in shape to play Ant-Man. "It's probably changed my life," Rudd said of his Marvel fitness regimen. "It's completely changed the way I eat food and work out. Fitness and diet have become something at the forefront of my life: that was never the case." Rudd planned to keep up the routine, to maintain both his viability as a movie star and his own well-being. "I feel way better," he admitted. "I owe the franchise maybe a few extra years of life."

Perhaps the most eye-popping Marvel transition of all belongs to comedian Kumail Nanjiani, who, after years of playing cuddly nerds, revealed his *Eternals*-ready muscles in 2019. "I will keep those opinions to myself," another comedian and Marvel actor said with a laugh when asked about Nanjiani's new physique. "He is very . . . ripped. He is extraordinarily ripped."

✳

SOME METHODS OF bulking up go beyond weight training and diet. Though forbidden by sports leagues, many steroid treatments are perfectly legal. Dr. Todd Schroeder, associate professor of clinical physical therapy and director of the University of Southern California Clinical Exercise Research Center at the USC Division of Biokinesiology and Physical Therapy, estimated that over half of Marvel's stars use some form of performance enhancing drug (PED) to get the physiques they want. "At least for the short term," he said. "I would say that fifty to seventy-five percent do." For an in-depth 2013 investigation into the industry's most popular performance-enhancing drug, human growth hormone (HGH), the *Hollywood Reporter* interviewed a number of talent agents and managers who considered PED use the "worst-kept" secret in Hollywood—just as commonplace, perhaps, as Botox and Restylane.

As Dr. Schroeder observed, "Nowadays, it's kind of expected

and, working under a doctor's care, it's really been accepted. A lot of actors won't talk about it openly, but they will work with a physician as well as a nutritionist and a trainer, and it's a team. It's not smart for an actor to do that alone. The big thing is, you can take steroids, testosterone, different androgens, growth hormone for a short period of time without any lasting effects on the body. It's not like you become addicted to it." Except, potentially, Dr. Schroeder noted, psychologically. If an actor loves the new shape of his body, and how people react to it, he might feel compelled to keep it.

A peak Marvel physique, however, isn't something that one can sustain indefinitely. "Especially as you get older," Dr. Schroeder said. "Like Robert Downey Jr., all the *Iron Man* [movies] he's done, and some of them he's gotten in really good shape for, but maintaining that is challenging. It's a tough, tough world out there. What people expect of you and how you need to look, and trying to maintain that. I feel for these actors, especially if you're in a Marvel role, where you're going to be in multiple films."

There's also the strain of trying to have a Marvel career while simultaneously looking less-than-super for other roles. Aaron Williamson, one of Hollywood's top trainers, has worked as a trainer and consultant for films like *The Fantastic Four*, *G.I. Joe Retaliation*, *Terminator Genisys*, and *Neighbors*. "Actors are trying to get on camera and blow everyone away," Williamson said. "Everyone's just maxed out, doing everything possible to look superhuman. . . . Someone might do a film where they have to look like a 'normal' person and then for their next project, they've got to look like this bulked-up, crazy-looking superhero guy. It's impossible to go from one extreme to the other overnight without some type of help."

"There's long-term health concerns, but short-term, there really isn't," Dr. Schroeder said. "So if you're preparing for a role, and you're going to get paid ten million dollars to look a certain way for a role? Then why wouldn't you do it under a doctor's care? Take some things that aren't natural but will change your body to look the way they want it to look, and gets you the recognition?"

Dr. Schroeder emphasized that he was speaking from his own

expertise and observation, not firsthand treatment of the Marvel stars. About Chris Hemsworth, he said: "He's always been in really good shape. His family, his genetics—they all, if they work out a little bit, they get in really good shape, and so he's taken it to the next level. A lot of people say, 'Oh, he does steroids, for sure.' And my opinion? I would say, 'No, he does not.'"

Marvel Studios didn't have to cast movie stars or even people in particularly good shape. Instead, like the toy company it still was, it simply made its own action heroes.

CHAPTER TWELVE

The Runaways

Anybody on our side hiding any shocking
and fantastic abilities they'd like to disclose?

Captain America: Civil War

THE JUNIOR SCREENWRITERS IN THE MARVEL WRIT-
ers Program had golden tickets to the best chocolate factory in Hollywood. When a Marvel movie was shooting,
they could visit the lot; when it wasn't, they might share an elevator
with Chris Evans or run into Paul Rudd in the hallway. On a daily
basis, they were eyewitnesses to the making of the Marvel Cinematic Universe—even if they had to figure out many of its mysteries
for themselves.

Writer Christopher Yost remembered one remarkable day of filming: "A few of the writers were on the lot, and a horse walked by in a
full mo-cap getup, with tracking dots all over it." He shook his head,
still flabbergasted. "We never found out what it was doing."

Much like that horse, the members of the Writers Program weren't
entirely sure how they had gotten there. The origins of the program
lay in the success of Marvel Studios' visual development (or "viz-
dev") workflow: as soon as one movie went into production, the
viz-dev team would reassign its staff to the next one, building up

libraries of images before a director had even signed on to the movie. That helped establish visual consistency across the MCU, whether movies were set in Malibu or Asgard, and it was one of the efficiencies that allowed the studio to release multiple movies in a year.

In 2009, producer Stephen Broussard was assigned a mission: build another assembly line, but with screenwriters. Many Hollywood studios and TV networks have fellowship programs for young writers; the studios benefit from a pipeline of promising new talent, while the writers spend six or twelve months on a studio lot, learning the industry. Soon, Broussard had a stack of sample scripts to read.

The chosen writers would each receive a year-long contract with Marvel Studios, during which time they would be on call to do emergency script polishes. More importantly, the studio wanted them to pitch movie ideas for unused superheroes from the Marvel comic books. To participate, writers had to sign a nonnegotiable 70-page contract that included a nondisclosure agreement and provisions stipulating that the studio owned all the work they did under the aegis of Marvel.

Edward Ricourt got a meeting on the strength of his spec screenplay *Year 12*, set on Earth twelve years after an alien invasion; it had made the prestigious Black List of promising but unproduced scripts. He met with Broussard and producer Jeremy Latcham, who put three comic books on the table in front of him and directed his attention to the one starring Luke Cage, aka Power Man, the blaxploitation-inspired superhero with unbreakable skin. As a Black man, Ricourt wondered if he was being sidelined on the project starring a Black hero. But "they said 'We really want to make this, we *really* want to make this.'" Ricourt conceded that he might have some ideas for it.

When Ricourt joined the Writers Program, he was assigned an office adjacent to Nicole Perlman. "They said how much they liked my scripts," Perlman remembered of her initial conversation with Marvel execs. They then told her, "But you probably never want to work on something popcorn like a superhero movie.'" Perlman, who is smart, sarcastic, and a little bohemian, assured them that although she hadn't read many Marvel comic books, she loved sci-fi and mass entertainment. That was good enough for Marvel, which signed her up. "We'd been told that we would have access to the slush pile—the less important properties—and we could choose one and just start working on it." Perlman said. "And as needed, they would pull us in to do rewrites on projects that were in production, or 'polishes.'"

Christopher Yost joined the Writers Program some months later, but he had history with Marvel stretching back a decade. In 2001, when he was a grad student in the USC film program, he cold-called the Marvel offices, looking for an internship. He joined Marvel during the Arad era, when Marvel was advising other studios on Marvel properties rather than making its own movies. Yost's job was to prepare dossiers on half-forgotten characters such as Werewolf by Night. After the internship, Yost finished his degree. As soon as he graduated, he got a call from producer Craig Kyle, who hired him for the animated *X-Men: Evolution* TV series. There, the two men created a new version of Wolverine: his young female clone, X-23, who proved to be so popular that she made the transition from the TV show to comic books (and eventually appeared in a major role in the 2017 movie *Logan*). By 2010, Kyle was working at Marvel Studios, and he invited Yost to apply for the Writers Program. For his interview, Yost had to pitch one of Kevin Feige's priority projects: a Black Panther movie. "It's important that we don't feel like a completely white, European cast," Feige said of the lineup of Marvel movie superheroes.

The Writers Program moved offices repeatedly. Whenever Marvel was filming a movie, it would rent space for production offices adjacent to the new soundstages and relocate the writers there, so they would be available for emergency rewrites. "The offices were always temporary," Yost said. "I didn't know that when I started: I decorated my office with images for inspiration and brought in stuff from my home office, and then got moved almost instantly. You always had the sense that you weren't the first person in this space, and you wouldn't be the last." In Yost's very first office, his desk phone still had labels on it for the staff of the TV show *Ally McBeal*, which had wrapped its last episode eight years earlier. "That should have been my first red flag," Yost admitted.

Wherever the writers were, they got used to being in the building—but also as far away from the action as was physically possible. Yost brought a scooter to work for the long trips to the other side of the office. "One time I found myself in an office where I was the only person on the floor," he said. "It was weird and creepy, and it had no snacks. But it was quiet and I got a lot of writing done."

Searching for an unloved property to work on, Perlman picked *Guardians of the Galaxy*. She had never heard of the comic, but it seemed like the title in the slush pile closest to pure science fiction. She asked Marvel's in-house librarian for every comic book the Guardians of the Galaxy had ever appeared in, expecting a handful of issues with guest appearances by this obscure interstellar team. Instead, the librarian showed up with a pushcart stacked high with *Guardians* comics dating back to 1969. "He brought out box after box after box," she said. She could pick any incarnation of the team she wanted—nobody else in the building cared about these characters—and she chose the lineup from the 2008 comic book by Dan Abnett and Andy Lanning, featuring the wisecracking Rocket Raccoon and Groot, the sentient tree.

While the first cohort of writers was expected to work regular hours, nine to five, their supervisor, Broussard, got pulled into production for *Captain America: The First Avenger*, and the studio's leaders—Feige, Louis D'Esposito, and Victoria Alonso—were too busy with movies in production to check in on the program. Left to their own devices, some days the writers would just sit around talking about movies and reading old comic books. They knew to keep an eye out for a good Doctor Strange story, since the character was one of Feige's favorites. Other days, they would go across the street to a Barnes and Noble bookstore and work there for a while, just for a change of scenery. This would be unthinkable a few years later, when Marvel would tighten up its security protocols to prevent secrets from leaking.

✶

MARVEL REALIZED it needed a producer who could keep an eye on the Writers Program and other projects that might take years to develop. Nate Moore, an executive producer on prestigious movies like *An Inconvenient Truth* and *The Kite Runner*, applied for the job. He had grown up in Southern California on a steady diet of blockbuster movies and now wanted to make some of his own. When he submitted his resume, it caught Kevin Feige's attention, because he realized they had actually met: Moore had been a production assistant on Sam Raimi's first Spider-Man movie. Instead of conducting a formal interview, Feige invited Moore out for coffee.

Jodi Hildebrand, a friend of Moore's who had been an executive at Sidney Kimmel Entertainment supervising indie films such as *Lars and the Real Girl*, applied for the same job. She and Moore didn't realize that they were competing against each other until after they had each had an encouraging meeting with Feige. When she came in for another round of interviews, Marvel informed her that they would be making offers to both of them.

Hildebrand took on the development of Edgar Wright's Ant-Man movie and a new project called *Runaways*, an adaptation of the Brian K. Vaughn and Adrian Alphona comic-book series about teenagers who discover that their parents are actually a cabal of supervillains. Moore was put in charge of the Writers Program. "I don't have the talent to write," Moore said. "I've tried writing screenplays and they're not good. I didn't really have the eye to direct. But I love being around storytellers and I love problem-solving. My brain loves puzzles. Doing a film is like putting together a really complicated puzzle."

Feige wanted to find screenwriters for *Black Panther*, *Iron Fist*, and *Doctor Strange*, but first Moore got the in-house writers brainstorming ideas for a reboot of *Blade* that would feel distinct from the three movies starring Wesley Snipes as the vampire hunter (not to mention the 2006 TV show on Spike starring Sticky Fingaz), hoping that it could be another opportunity for Marvel to diversify its lineup of heroes.

Perlman had been working on her *Guardians of the Galaxy* script, but without much feedback, since the top Marvel executives were usually out of the office, making movies. Once Moore was around to give her notes, she switched the protagonist of her script from the character Nova to Peter Quill, aka the Star-Lord. Perlman agreed with Moore that the lead character should be more of a rogue, like Han Solo; Nova had a distinct space-cop energy. Perlman gave Quill some prize possessions from the 1980s, the decade of her childhood: *Star Wars* toys, an Atari game, and crucially, a portable cassette player. After fourteen drafts of the *Guardians* screenplay, the studio told her that Marvel would be green-lighting the movie. It was a triumph for her, but also a validation of the Writers Program.

Joe Robert Cole got the attention of Marvel because of a hard-boiled police drama he had written, a script in the tradition of *Chinatown*. The studio invited him to pitch a movie for the War Machine character, and Feige pronounced himself impressed by Cole's take. But when Marvel devised other plans for the character, it tabled all work on a solo War Machine movie and offered Cole a position in the Writers Program instead. He immersed himself in a mountain of comics about the Inhumans, a superpowered race of humanoids who at various points in Marvel comics history have lived in a secluded mountain city and in an oxygen-rich pocket of the moon.

Hildebrand, meanwhile, was preparing a *Runaways* movie so that Marvel would have at least one non-Avengers project ready for production if *Guardians of the Galaxy* faltered. Feige and Hildebrand agreed that *Runaways* should feel like a John Hughes coming-of-age film, except that the parents would prove to be not just clueless but actual supervillains. By the end of the movie, the teens would discover their own powers, grow up faster than they had planned, and enter the larger Marvel Cinematic Universe. To direct, Hildebrand tapped Peter Sollett, who had made two indie films centered on characters in the same age range as the Runaways, *Raising Victor*

Vargas and *Nick and Nora's Infinite Playlist*; she was confident he was ready to make a blockbuster. For the movie's writer, they met with a variety of people, including Drew Pearce, who had created a British superhero comedy TV series called *No Heroics*.

When *No Heroics* was canceled after a single season, Pearce flew to Los Angeles, where he spent four weeks in 2009 developing a pilot for ABC. The pilot wasn't shot, so he returned home to London, where he married his wife, filmmaker Amy Barham, who was soon pregnant with their first child. Pearce visited LA again in April 2010 and took a general meeting at Marvel. He was amazed to find how in sync he was with the executives there.

"It reached a crescendo," Pearce said. "They asked, 'If there was one Marvel property you could do as a movie, what would it be?' I said, 'It wouldn't be a classic. It would be *Runaways*. It's just so cinematic.'" Surprised, the Marvel execs told him that they agreed, and that, in fact, they were already planning to make it as a movie. "My heart rose up. And then they said, 'But we've already got twenty writers coming in to pitch on it, so sorry.'"

Pearce didn't get hired at any of his other meetings while in LA, and his bad luck extended to his flight home to England, which was canceled when the Eyjafjallajökull volcano in Iceland erupted, belching a large cloud of ash into the northern Atlantic that made European air travel impossible. Pearce was grounded in Los Angeles for weeks.

Sleeping on a friend's couch, Pearce decided to turn his life around. "I sat there and wrote a *Jerry Maguire*–style document to all of my representatives: 'If I must be stuck here on a sofa in Los Angeles while my pregnant wife is at home, I really do need people to get the word out. I'm still in town for another two weeks: *Get me in rooms*.' And I heard nothing back." For twenty-four hours, Pearce queasily suspected he had pushed too hard. But then he got an email from Jodi Hildebrand at Marvel.

"Heard you were still in town," she wrote. "Just so you know, one of the writers that was going to pitch on *Runaways* has dropped out, so we have a slot."

Since his comic book collection was eight time zones away and under a cloud of volcanic ash, Pearce hustled over to Meltdown Comics on Sunset Boulevard and bought replacement copies of the first two volumes of *Runaways*. After spending the weekend reading them and dissecting the story, he pitched his version of a *Runaways* movie to Marvel. He made it through the winnowing process that reduced the field "from twenty to twelve, from twelve to five, from five to three, and then three to two," and started talking with director Peter Sollett.

Pearce got the job. "So I wrote my first paid screenplay for Marvel," he said. But although the work went well and the notes he received were encouraging, it became clear that Marvel's schedule was filling up with movies that would set up *The Avengers* and then other movies that would continue the stories of individual Avengers. In London, Pearce got a phone call and had to step outside to take it. Standing in the rain, just off Exmouth Market, he heard Hildebrand tell him, "It's not going forward." The Runaways movie was dead.

"*Runaways*' code name was *Small Faces*," Pearce revealed. (The alias was a reference to the influential rock band from the '60s.) Whenever he wanted to reminisce about the feature film that almost happened, he could look at a picture he took of the door to a Marvel office in Manhattan Beach, with his own reflection visible in the glass. "A production office with the Small Faces logo on it—done in the style of the Runaways logo," he said wistfully. "So yes, it was a real thing. I don't think people understand that, but it was going to be a 'go' movie, you know?"

When she wasn't working on *Runaways*, Hildebrand helped Moore and Feige recruit more candidates for the Marvel Writers Program. She nominated Eric Pearson, a friend of hers who had been bouncing around LA, working retail jobs while he tried to find writing gigs. For his interview, Pearson was asked to pitch a movie starring Cloak and Dagger, a pair of teenage runaways (yes, more runaways) who were fan favorites in the 1980s: Cloak (Black, male, stutterer) can teleport, while Dagger (white, female, rich) can throw energy daggers.

Pearson prepared a thorough pitch for Hildebrand, Moore, and Feige. It was *so* thorough that halfway through the third act, Feige interrupted him to ask exactly how long this proposed movie was going to be. But Feige admired Pearson's attention to detail and offered him a spot in the Writers Program the same day. Pearson was immediately given an assignment: polish a draft of a *Luke Cage* screenplay that Feige wanted to push into production as soon as possible.

Pearson quickly learned the mores of the Marvel offices: the vagabond life, the gray carpets, the spartan settings. When Shane Black, one of the highest-paid screenwriters in Hollywood history, famous for his work on action movies including *Lethal Weapon*, visited Marvel to discuss directing and writing a movie for them, he was taken aback by the lack of amenities. He made a point of mocking the budget-conscious culture that Ike Perlmutter insisted on. When Black took a bagel from the Marvel kitchen, Drew Pearce recalled, he left a note for top Marvel executive Louis D'Esposito and $1.25.

★

SOME OF THE IDEAS developed in the Writers Program went nowhere; many of them turned into something else along the way. Hulu commissioned *Runaways* as a TV series and ABC Family (operating as Freeform) launched a *Cloak & Dagger* show. The characters of Luke Cage and Iron Fist each got a TV series (on Netflix), as did the Inhumans (on ABC). The Writers Program eventually became a source of tension inside the company, with the Creative Committee trying to exert closer supervision over it. The company's Los Angeles executives shut it down in 2014. (It was revived in 2016.)

But even though it lasted for only two years in its original incarnation, the Marvel Writers Program didn't just let some talented young writers stow away on a spaceship, it gave them a chance to fly it. Some of the writers earned their wings and stuck around for years. Although his Inhumans movie didn't go into production, Joe Robert Cole cowrote the screenplay for *Black Panther* and its sequel, *Black Panther: Wakanda Forever*, movies on which Nate Moore served as executive producer. Eric Pearson became a steady contributor to the MCU, working on the screenplays for *Black Widow* and *Thor: Ragnarok*, not to mention a host of uncredited script polishes.

When Yost joined the Writers Program, he had his pick of the slush-pile characters to adapt. He was particularly interested in the Thunderbolts (a team of supervillains masquerading as superheroes), Power Pack (a family of superpowered preteens who, in an unexpected twist, are not runaways), and Captain Britain (Dr. Brian Braddock, a British man endowed with powers when Merlin gives him the Amulet of Right). But soon after Yost arrived, the entire Writers Program was pulled into production of the fourth MCU movie, *Thor*, doing rewrites.

"They'll throw some pages at me," Yost said, "and I'll turn them around and send them onstage with Kenneth Branagh and Chris Hemsworth, and they're shooting stuff that ends up in the movie. It was an amazing moment in time."

Perlman was even more excited, she said, "Because I had this massive crush on Kenneth Branagh. When I was in high school, I was actually in a Kenneth Branagh fan club. I had a T-shirt and everything." As often happens with women screenwriters, she was charged with enhancing the lead female character (in *Thor*, that was Jane Foster, played by Natalie Portman). "They gave me the whole script, and they said, 'We want you to do Jane's stuff. But if you have any other thoughts on scenes you want to alter, go ahead.' So I did a little bit of work on Odin and some work with Thor in the town."

Yost's favorite day on *Thor* was one of the last of the shoot: Jeremy Renner had been cast as Hawkeye, which meant the production could finally film his scene. Hawkeye was introduced as a government sniper—albeit one who uses a bow and arrow—who may need to stop Thor from reclaiming his hammer. "We were in a parking lot behind a Ralph's grocery store," Yost remembered. "We had set up a big crane and we were making it rain." Joss Whedon, who was already working on the screenplay for *The Avengers*, had written some dialogue for Renner, as had Yost, and the actor filmed his brief scene every way imaginable. Yost, who had his laptop out, was punching up dialogue on the spot. Feige sat next to Yost, watching the debut of the newest member of his Avengers ensemble.

"It was weird in the greatest way, just to see how it all comes together," Yost remembered. "It was the magic of Hollywood—in a parking lot behind a grocery store."

CHAPTER THIRTEEN

Earth's Mightiest Heroes

> What are we, a team? No, we're a chemical mixture
> that makes chaos. We're a time bomb.
>
> *The Avengers*

"**THE ESSENCE OF FILMMAKING IS KNOWING WHERE** you're going," Joss Whedon said. "The glory of filmmaking is never knowing how you're going to get there."

In the 1990s, Whedon was a successful screenwriter (earning an Oscar nomination for *Toy Story*) and highly paid script doctor (punching up *Speed*, *Waterworld*, and *Twister*). When the fledgling WB network launched a TV series based on his screenplay for the movie *Buffy the Vampire Slayer*, it offered him the chance to be showrunner, basically as a courtesy—but he surprised them by accepting. Whedon turned the show into something extraordinary: a genre series about a teenage girl staking vampires in a small California town, it used monsters from the Hellmouth each week as metaphors for the agonies of adolescence. The hero's journey of Buffy Summers across seven seasons (from 1997 to 2003) was witty, bawdy, and heartbreaking—often all at once.

Whedon wrote razor-sharp dialogue that was saturated with modern pop-culture references, but that crackled like old screwball comedies; he was formally inventive (one *Buffy* episode was a musical, while another was largely silent); he foregrounded the experiences of women. He was hailed as a feminist hero and a geek icon, and a popular T-shirt was emblazoned with the words (in the Star Wars typeface) "JOSS WHEDON IS MY MASTER NOW." (Decades later, when it emerged that Whedon had run his show cruelly and capriciously, and had taken advantage of his position to sleep with various young women, fans regarded it not just as a disappointment, but a betrayal. Whedon was far from the worst #MeToo offender in Hollywood, but he had always presented himself as someone better than the average sleazy TV producer.)

Shonda Rhimes, creator of *Grey's Anatomy* and *Scandal,* said she "rediscovered television" by watching *Buffy.* Russell T Davies, who rebooted *Doctor Who* for the BBC, said, "*Buffy The Vampire Slayer* shows the whole world, and an entire sprawling industry, that writing monsters and demons and end-of-the-world is not hack work, it can challenge the best. Joss Whedon raised the bar for every writer—not just genre/niche writers, but every single one of us."

Away from the adoring geek crowds, Whedon was more influential than successful. *Buffy* (and its spinoff *Angel*) never pulled in huge ratings, and subsequent series such as *Firefly* and *Dollhouse* were quickly canceled. By 2008, in the midst of the writers' strike, Whedon was selling a musical starring Neil Patrick Harris, *Dr. Horrible's Sing-Along Blog,* for download via the internet, and it looked as if he might spend the remainder of his career catering to his devoted niche following. That was when Kevin Feige decided that Joss Whedon was exactly the man Marvel needed.

★

WHEDON HAD GROWN UP in New York City a fan of comic books, especially *Uncanny X-Men* and the team's youngest member Kitty Pryde. "If there's a bigger influence on Buffy than Kitty, I don't know what it was," Whedon said. "She was an adolescent girl finding out she has great power and dealing with it." He not only wrote scripts for the *Astonishing X-Men* comic book between 2004 and 2008, but also polished the script of the 2000 *X-Men* film, contributing both the movie's best line (Wolverine proving his identity by telling Cyclops "You're a dick") and its worst (Storm declaiming "Do you know what happens to a toad when it's struck by lightning?"). Whedon said that the *X-Men* shoot was when he and Feige first discussed making a movie together. But for many years, Feige wasn't in control at Marvel Studios, and until *Serenity* (the 2005 movie that continued the *Firefly* story), Whedon hadn't directed a feature film.

In 2010, before *Thor* and *Captain America: The First Avenger* had even started shooting, Feige approached Whedon to ask if he would serve as a consultant on *The Avengers*. While Marvel had decided on some important moments in the movie—the studio knew, for example, that it would end with a huge battle against aliens in New York City, and had already started generating concept art for that sequence—it was unsure how to unite its disparate heroes as one team. Superteams were a Whedon specialty: when he had a solo lead of a TV show, he invariably surrounded that character with a group of powerful and colorful misfits. (In the case of *Buffy*, the sidekicks jokingly nicknamed themselves "the Scooby gang.")

"Everything I write," he said, "tends to turn into a superhero team, even if I didn't mean for it to. I always start off wanting to be solitary, because (a) it's simpler and (b) that isolation is something I relate to as a storyteller. And then no matter what, I always end up with a team."

"We pitched him sort of what we were doing in *Thor* and what we were doing in *Captain* and how we envisioned at least the bones on *Avengers*," Feige said. "He was into it." In the Marvel Studios offices, Feige showed off some of the art they had been generating for *Thor*, *Captain America: The First Avenger*, and *The Avengers*. The image that particularly grabbed Whedon's attention was that of a portal opening above Avengers Tower in Manhattan and Iron Man rushing up to meet it.

Feige hired Whedon to direct *The Avengers*—once again, he had zeroed in on a director who had the skills needed to solve the problems Marvel Studios was having with a movie, and he had found somebody who was accomplished but not at the apex of his career (and hence, affordable). Whedon insisted on writing the screenplay himself. "There was a script," Whedon conceded. "There just wasn't a script I was going to film a word of."

That initial *Avengers* screenplay was by Zak Penn, who was shunted aside again, just as he had been when Edward Norton signed on to *The Incredible Hulk*. "All the other directors we had been talking about, Joss wasn't on the list," Penn said. "I heard he was going to rewrite the script himself. He didn't even want to meet with me—which, by the way, I always call the writer I'm replacing. I feel like that's courtesy."

That snub was particularly painful because Penn had known Whedon for a long time; they were both Wesleyan graduates. Thinking that maybe the situation was uncomfortable for Whedon, too, Penn called him up. "He said to me, 'No, it's not awkward for me. I'm rewriting you,'" Penn recalled. "It became pretty apparent that he had less than zero interest in, in any way, having me involved with the movie."

Penn said that he balked when Whedon told him to take his name off the screenplay that he had spent years developing: "My kids have grown up while I've been working on it. They've all told their friends about it. What's going to happen when their friends are like, 'Your dad didn't work on *Avengers*'?" Whedon's response, according to Penn: "What's going to happen when my kids think that you wrote half the story?"

Penn didn't appreciate being booted off a Marvel movie yet again, although in this case, at least it was by an acclaimed writer, not the lead actor. "I think he's a dick. I think he's a bad person, and it was really surprising," Penn said of Whedon. "Remember, my bonus is based on my credit. So literally millions and millions of dollars, which is not the issue here, but that just came out of my pocket and went into Joss's pocket."

"I started on square one on the script," Whedon said, and indeed, the final movie very much reflects his voice and storytelling approach.

"I read [Penn's screenplay] one time, and I've never seen it since," he insisted. "I don't want to rag on it, but I fought that credit."

Unsurprisingly, there was another Writers Guild of America arbitration before the movie was released. Whedon got sole screenplay credit and shared the story credit with Penn, leaving neither of them happy.

Some of the big action beats had already been visualized by the art department. The Marvel Studios producers wanted Loki to wield the Cosmic Cube (the powerful comic-book artifact not yet renamed "the Tesseract"). They wanted S.H.I.E.L.D. to have a Helicarrier (a high-tech flying aircraft carrier). They wanted the Avengers to assemble in New York City for the final action sequence, looking up at the sky as an alien invasion descends upon them.

Whedon knitted these elements together. "We went through a lot of insane iterations," Whedon recalled. "I wrote entire drafts that had no bearing on what I would eventually film. There was a moment where we thought we weren't going to have Scarlett [Johansson], and so I wrote a huge bunch of pages starring the Wasp. That was not useful. I also worried that one British character actor [Tom Hiddleston] was not enough to take on Earth's mightiest heroes, and that we'd feel like we were rooting for the overdog. So I wrote a huge draft with Ezekiel Stane, Obadiah Stane's son, in it. Kevin looked at it and said, 'Yeah, no.' Louis D'Esposito actually at that point said, 'Yeah, Kevin, it's all wrong, but look how good it is. This is *really good wrong.*'"

Whedon wasn't reinventing the Avengers or giving them a postmodern spin. "I'm an old-fashioned storyteller to the point where I'm almost pedantic in my structure and moralism," he said. "I don't need to destroy the myth to build it up—that's been done. All I want to do is make people care about these characters."

In July 2010, Feige issued his bluntly worded press release formally announcing that Edward Norton would no longer be playing the Hulk. That put the studio under intense pressure: it had a big *Avengers* panel planned for the San Diego Comic-Con just two weeks later, and wanted to introduce the entire cast. Marvel offered the role of

Bruce Banner to Mark Ruffalo, who had been considered by Louis Leterrier for *The Incredible Hulk* years before. The actor's star had steadily risen since then, and he had just costarred in *The Kids Are All Right*, a performance that would earn him an Oscar nomination. Ruffalo was uncertain if he belonged in an action-movie spectacular, so Whedon, who was very much in favor of casting him, sneaked him some script pages, hoping to entice him. Ruffalo then called up Norton and got his blessing to take the part; the two joked that the Hulk was their generation's Hamlet, and eventually everyone would play the character.

Marvel Studios and Ruffalo's representatives negotiated the actor's contract until the last possible moment. The night before the Comic-Con panel, Ruffalo got a call from his agent: "Look out your window at five o'clock in the morning. If there is a car there, you got the part. If there's not, just go back to bed."

The next morning, a limousine was waiting. Ruffalo stumbled into it and went to the airport to catch a plane to San Diego. "I was happy," Ruffalo said. "And I was scared to death."

Like Norton, Ruffalo would use the MOVA technology to capture his facial expressions, but since the new Hulk design actually resembled Ruffalo, the data would be far more useful to the CGI team rendering the character. Ruffalo embraced the chance to play the giant green monster. "They made the radical decision to have the Hulk actually look like me," Ruffalo said, a choice that pleased him greatly. "It's always so dislocating to watch the Hulk turn into a totally different character."

Animation director Marc Chu remembered the first time he did motion capture with Ruffalo: "I have my animator dressed up in the mo-cap suit; Mark's in the mo-cap suit. One is Thor, and he's the Hulk, obviously. He just starts running and beating on my animator." Chu briefly wondered whether he needed to call Marvel's human resources department. What was the protocol for an actor and an animator attacking each other? "He wanted to tap into that animalistic Hulk, and he was just *going at it*," Chu said with amazement. (Ruffalo and the animator were both fine.)

Ike Perlmutter's main concern with *The Avengers* was that he wanted all the team's members to be men. While Disney now owned Marvel, Perlmutter had become one of Disney's largest individual stockholders; as Disney CEO Robert Iger had promised, Perlmutter was allowed to keep running Marvel as a personal fiefdom. Perlmutter knew his business—and even more than Marvel, his business was toys. He would brandish budget sheets with cherrypicked data to make his case that female action figures didn't sell, that female-led comic books underperformed compared to top-line male heroes, and that previous movies based on female superheroes had failed at the box office. Whedon, however, insisted that the Avengers had to include at least one woman, ideally Black Widow.

Feige supported Whedon. Ruffalo said that at one point, the studio head told him, "Listen, I might not be here tomorrow. Ike does not believe that anyone will go to a female-starring superhero movie. So if I am still here tomorrow, you will know that I won the battle." Feige stayed on the job; Black Widow stayed on the team.

Whedon announced publicly that he would be adding a second woman to the movie—when it came to gender in Hollywood, the benchmark for progress was set extremely low. That character was S.H.I.E.L.D. agent Maria Hill, played by Cobie Smulders. When Marvel rolled out the toys for *The Avengers*, there were multiple sizes and types of action figures for each member of the team, except for Black Widow, who had a single four-inch figure. Maria Hill did not get an action figure at all.

To keep his cast happy, Whedon contacted each of his stars early in the process, getting input on what they wanted and what was off-limits for them. Chris Evans trusted Whedon and told him to do whatever he needed to do. Scarlett Johansson said Whedon got "misty-eyed" when he related Black Widow's backstory and how young Natasha Romanoff had been forced into training against her will.

Robert Downey Jr., however, believed that Tony Stark should be the central focus of the movie. "I'm used to having people do everything I say, and so is he," Whedon said, laughing. Whedon eventually persuaded Downey that the movie would be stronger if it were an ensemble piece. On set, they found a comfortable working method. If Downey wasn't happy with some dialogue, Whedon could come up with three pages of alternate lines while the camera crew set up a new shot.

When Downey saw that Whedon was capable of short-order brilliance, he said, "Oh, that's easy. You do all the work, and I will pick from a menu."

As Whedon dryly observed, "I would give him stuff to say, and by and large, he would say it."

Whedon crafted sequences that would introduce each of his film's characters, bring them together, split them apart, and then unite them as the Avengers for the final battle. In a nod to the "Avengers Assemble" rallying call from the comic books, for a time Whedon even wanted to call the movie *Avengers: Some Assembly Required*. Perhaps his greatest creation was the incident that would force the team together: the murder of Agent Coulson (played by Clark Gregg), the S.H.I.E.L.D. agent who had appeared in *Iron Man*, *Iron Man 2*, and *Thor*, but who was revealed in *The Avengers*, before he died, as an unabashed fan of the newly unthawed Captain America.

Whedon preferred not to include too many other established Marvel properties in his movie, because they all came with long backstories and decades of associations. When it came time to pick which alien race would be invading New York City, for instance, he didn't want the blue-skinned Kree or the shape-shifting Skrulls, the two most famous alien races in the Marvel comic books. The studio was happy to save both of them for future projects. Whedon picked the Chitauri from the *Ultimate* line of comics, because they had very little history and so allowed him maximum creative freedom.

Marvel had considered using either Loki or the Hulk as the threat that brought the Avengers together. The studio had told Tom Hiddleston to make himself available during the shoot in case he was needed, but the actor didn't know until February 2011, when Whedon finished his screenplay, that he would be starring as the movie's antagonist.

In late April, the *Avengers* actors convened in Albuquerque, New

Mexico, the same state where *Thor* had been shot for tax reasons. Evans and Johansson had become friendly when they costarred in the 2004 movie *The Perfect Score* (a dud about high-school seniors stealing advance copies of the SATs), and on location they would play Game Boy together or sometimes find an evening to go out dancing. Evans became the off-camera leader of the team. When he summoned the actors to meet at a local bar, he sent group texts with the message "Avengers Assemble."

Ruffalo and Samuel L. Jackson both showed up in Albuquerque one day early. Jackson wanted to file a complaint. When Whedon had consulted with Jackson before writing the screenplay, the then-sixty-two-year-old actor had made only one request about Nick Fury: he didn't want to run. But now he pulled out his script and pointed to a stage direction where Fury ran onto the deck of the Helicarrier with a rocket launcher. "What's this say here? It says I run!"

"Just that once," Whedon assured him. "You only run once."

Jackson called Whedon a "motherfucker," which felt like an official benediction from the actor who used that four-syllable word better than anyone else on the planet.

✳

THE LATEST TREND for summer blockbusters was the simultaneous release of a 3D version that could command an increased ticket price. *Thor* and *Captain America: The First Avenger* had both gotten 3D releases, and Marvel wanted *The Avengers* to have one too. Whedon had never directed in 3D before, so as a test run, he used a 3D camera rig to shoot a post-credits scene for *Thor* featuring Tom Hiddleston and Stellan Skarsgård. When it took several hours to get the camera working correctly, Whedon decided that the *Avengers* shoot couldn't afford to work at that slow pace. The movie would have to be converted to 3D in postproduction.

To facilitate the 3D conversion, Whedon shot his non-action scenes in a straightforward fashion, favoring depth over camera movement. That left the producers on *The Avengers*—Feige, D'Esposito, Victoria Alonso, and Jeremy Latcham—concerned that the film wouldn't provide the visual spectacle of previous Marvel movies. Marvel sent a steady stream of producers to the New Mexico set to monitor Whedon's work, which irked him. He felt that the constant oversight reflected a lack of confidence, and he was correct. While the executives trusted Whedon's storytelling sense and gift for dialogue, they were much less confident in his visual acumen, and after years of making TV shows with limited budgets, the director quietly shared some of their doubts. But the director and the studio achieved a détente by agreeing to plan the shots for action sequences as meticulously as possible.

Whenever Whedon and his director of photography, Seamus McGarvey, weren't working from detailed animatics (basically, animated storyboards), the producers applied an extra level of scrutiny. Almost every shot that made it into the film was carefully choreographed—and that level of preparation became essential once the action featured the digital Chitauri.

Production was its toughest when filming the Battle of New York, shot in New Mexico, where vast indoor sets stood in for midtown Manhattan. Every action sequence required Whedon to conduct multiple departments in perfect harmony for hours, given that even simple scenes were rendered complex by the demands of 3D conversion and the multitude of CGI special effects.

"It happened to be the worst time of filming," Whedon recalled. "The most problematic, when the producers really had the least confidence in what I was doing. For the most part that was not a problem, but it became a bit of a thing during that particular time. There was some worry that my work was not kinetic enough. It was in the middle of the shoot, we were all at ebb, and I would come to work and everything would be flames and sulfur. And I was like, *Could hell not be so literal?*"

All of the actors, including those in gray motion-capture suits standing in for the CGI Chitauri, endured multiple takes, often getting pummeled by dust and debris from explosions. The Avengers' costumes ended up with realistic battle wear, and the performers found themselves exhausted and a bit shellshocked.

Whedon had an idea for the movie's post-credits scene, one that stemmed from his deep knowledge of Marvel comics. In a vignette, he revealed that Loki's Chitauri army was on loan from Thanos, one of the most terrifying villains in the Marvel cosmos, a large purple alien with a corrugated chin and a serious infatuation with death. Whedon wasn't trying to set up Thanos as the Avengers' next foe. Rather, he just wanted to provide an explanation for where Loki's army came from, seasoned with a bit of fan service. For its part, Marvel Studios was so focused on making sure that everything came together for *The Avengers* that it approved the inclusion of Thanos without much thought about what that might mean for the movies to come.

Photography wrapped on time, and Whedon went into the editing bay with Lisa Lassek (who had edited *Serenity* and *Cabin in the Woods*) and Marvel's regular editor, Jeffrey Ford. Whedon's dialogue-heavy scenes played as smoothly as he had hoped, but the Battle of New York came together slowly and painfully. One particular shot of all the Avengers using their powers simultaneously was particularly difficult to get right; late in postproduction, Whedon wanted to abandon it. Marvel's leadership had to remind him that comic-book movies were fundamentally a visual medium and that it was essential in a superhero team-up movie that the superheroes actually team up.

The Battle of New York "is why we all showed up. It's why the audience showed up, it's why I showed up," Whedon agreed. But he took the most pleasure in the scenes when the Avengers found personal moments of connection and disconnection: "The intimate stuff is the most fun to sort, and certainly the most fun to film, because filming this was . . . the opposite of fun."

All that pain paid off. When *The Avengers* debuted in May 2012, it was an immediate smash, shattering various box office records on its way to becoming Marvel Studios' first billion-dollar movie. It grossed a billion dollars faster, in fact, than any motion picture ever, and with total global box office of $1.5 billion, it ranked then as the third-highest grossing motion picture of all time.

For Ike Perlmutter, *The Avengers* vindicated every single bet he had made on Marvel in the previous two decades. For Disney and Bob

Iger, *The Avengers* was a live-action film that reached their weakest demographic, almost singlehandedly validating the Marvel acquisition. For Robert Downey Jr., *The Avengers* was a huge windfall; the profit-sharing deal he had negotiated yielded him approximately $50 million. For Kevin Feige and the rest of Marvel Studios' leadership, the movie represented the brilliant and immensely profitable execution of a long-term plan. It meant that for the foreseeable future, every Marvel movie would play like a sequel with a built-in audience, with the hype building from one film to the next.

The rest of Hollywood watched Marvel's success closely. There had been cinematic crossovers before, ranging from *Alien vs. Predator* to *Abbott and Costello Meet Frankenstein*, but none had succeeded financially like the Marvel Cinematic Universe. Other studios began chasing the potential of "shared universe" films, although they would discover that it wasn't as easy as Marvel had made it look.

Sony struggled for years to do a series of films featuring Spider-Man villains who would join forces as the Sinister Six; the studio periodically canceled and revived the project. Universal tried to launch a "Dark Universe" featuring its horror characters, but shelved it after only one movie and one awkward photoshoot. Warner Bros. labored mightily to have the DC heroes come together as the Justice League, an effort that lost it a lot of money three times (once with director George Miller's aborted attempt to launch the superhero team-up in 2007, once when the studio hired Whedon to salvage director Zack Snyder's unfinished *Justice League* movie in 2016, and then again when it paid Snyder to put together an extended director's cut in 2021). After the industry-shaking release of *The Avengers*, Disney started working on a live-action film franchise called *Descendents*, which brought together the children of various villains from its animated movies, eventually consigning it to the Disney Channel, where it was a modest success. One of the rare shared universes that worked was one that many people did not even compare to Marvel: Legendary Entertainment's Monsterverse, which launched with money-making Godzilla and King Kong movies (starring MCU actors Elizabeth Olsen, Aaron Taylor-Johnson, Tom Hiddleston,

Samuel L. Jackson, and Brie Larson) ahead of the kaiju monsters facing off in 2021 with *Godzilla vs. Kong*.

Surveying the failures of his competitors, Feige offered some wisdom: "Don't worry about the universe. Worry about the movie," he said. "Everyone within Marvel Studios knows the individual movie trumps the overall picture. If we're going to plant a seed in this movie that was going to be awesome and pay off three movies later, but that seed is not working and that seed is screwing up the movie, goodbye. We'll do something else later. Make the movie work."

As for Joss Whedon, *The Avengers* was remarkable proof of his vision and ability as a filmmaker, and he didn't want to walk away from Marvel after its release. Other Marvel directors, including Jon Favreau, Kenneth Branagh, and Joe Johnston, had all quickly burnt out on the Marvel enterprise, but Whedon was willing to jump right back in, not only to prepare an *Avengers* sequel but to help shape the entire Marvel Cinematic Universe. Marvel Studios was eager to continue with him, too. The studio hired Whedon to do a pass on all the screenplays leading up to his next Avengers movie, making him, effectively, the central creative figure for Phase Two of the MCU. Whedon had always believed that he wasn't a niche artist but an entertainer who could deliver hugely successful movies that had both flash and substance. Now he had the box-office receipts to prove it.

"It's my favorite thing, the popcorn movie that you take home with you. Not 'I went on the ride and now I feel dirty,'" he said. "I want the movie to give you enough so that you know it was about *something*." Sometimes that message could be "Dear God, please see my movie," Whedon joked. "But I try to make that just the subtext."

PHASE TWO

✦

CHAPTER FOURTEEN

House of M

This is monsters and magic
and nothing we ever trained for.

The Avengers

WHEN PETER JACKSON SHOT ALL THREE *LORD OF the Rings* films simultaneously in 1999 and 2000, principal photography lasted fourteen months, with units working on soundstages and in locations scattered all over New Zealand. Some days, Jackson would supervise multiple sets remotely from the movie's Wellington headquarters, performing the jobs of filmmaker, wizard, and air-traffic controller all at once. Thousands of people labored to make the trilogy possible, but no group was more important than the design team at Weta (Jackson's production company). The artisans at Weta ensured that the production's disparate efforts could eventually be cut together seamlessly, and that all three films would look like they were taking place in the same version of Middle-earth.

It was a feat unparalleled in filmmaking history—and then Marvel not only matched it, but surpassed it. Marvel's visual development department hasn't just brought a comic-book world to life across dozens of movies and television episodes. It has given the

Marvel Cinematic Universe strong visual continuity, even though that universe ranges from a gladiator arena on a distant planet to a self-storage unit in San Francisco, and countless settings in between.

Like so many aspects of Marvel Studios, the viz-dev department had its roots in ad hoc decisions made during the production of the first *Iron Man* movie. By the time Jon Favreau agreed to direct the film, Marvel already had a roomful of artists churning out cinematic images of both Iron Man and the Hulk, all variations on how the characters had appeared in the comics. When Favreau took charge of an *Iron Man* concept-art team, he made sure that it included two men who had worked with him on his ill-fated attempt in 2005 to make a *Princess of Mars* movie: Phil Saunders and Ryan Meinerding.

Both were excited to work on a big superhero movie, particularly a Marvel one: When Meinerding was a kid, his mom had bought one Spider-Man beach towel, which he and his brother would always fight over. (Meindering still has the towel today.) They moved into Marvel's crowded Beverly Hills offices. Not only did they have direct access to Favreau there, but they could show off their work to whatever producers and movie stars dropped in for a visit. "If you were lucky, you could say, 'Yeah, I loved you in *Hustle & Flow*,'" artist Jim Rothwell remembered of the time he met Terrence Howard. At first, Saunders focused on the Mark III armor that would become Iron Man's trademark look. He was building on the work of Adi Granov, who had come up with an especially sleek version of the Iron Man suit for the *Extremis* storyline in the comic books; Marvel Studios had also hired Granov.

"I wanted to do a believable and three-dimensional suit of armor where it looked like a live human being could be inside," Granov said. For comic books, he had needed to simplify his designs so they would be practical to draw page after page, but "in designing for the film," he said, "I was able to do all those things that I wished I could have done in the comics."

Meinerding worked on the Mark I armor, the clunky first suit that Tony Stark builds out of spare parts. Saunders took the lead on the silver Mark II armor, drawing inspiration from Howard Hughes's shiny aluminum-plated airplanes. The industrialist used to insist on shaving down all the external rivets on his aircraft, both for aerodynamic purposes and for visual appeal.

When it came time for Stan Winston Studios (since renamed Legacy Effects) to make physical suits of Iron Man armor, the craftsmen wanted the input of the designers who had been laboring over so many versions of those suits. "The fabrication of the first suit was where we got a sense of how a real suit worn by an actor would move," Saunders said.

Once again, Marvel Studios emphasized the value of continuity. At many studios, concept artists would be engaged for an initial pitch, or for some weeks of preproduction, and let go once cameras started rolling. Marvel, however, kept its designers on staff when their work on *Iron Man* was done, in large part because they needed them to start as soon as possible on the next slate of movies (*Iron Man 2*, *Thor*, and *Captain America: The First Avenger*). Because of that, the artists were also available for postproduction on the first *Iron Man*, meaning that when Marvel built digital models of the armor so that CGI could bolster the practical effects, Meinerding and Saunders were on hand. They knew every bulge and crevice of each suit so well that they could help correct (or cheat) the virtual proportions.

Susan Wexler, a visual artist who worked at the desk next to Meinerding's, said, "There aren't enough words in the English language to describe how brilliant Ryan is."

Joss Whedon raved, "He has a way of taking comic books and really bringing them to life, even beyond Alex Ross, in a way that I've never seen."

With three more movies on the way, Marvel Studios finally moved out of its Beverly Hills office above the Mercedes-Benz dealership into a larger space at Raleigh's Manhattan Beach Studios, in part because Louis D'Esposito advocated for the value of having preproduction, production, and postproduction all under the same roof.

Meinerding knew that Marvel needed more artists if the studio wanted to develop three movies simultaneously. (He hoped to reduce his crushing workload, but his gambit failed: During *Iron Man 2*,

Favreau was so reliant on Meinerding that the artist ended up with a dozen different viz-dev assignments. For a while, he stopped going home at night and instead napped under his desk.) Meinerding went to Kevin Feige and Craig Kyle and recommended a designer he knew from his time working in videogames: Charlie Wen. Feige promptly brought Wen in for an interview.

"I was sold when [Feige] spoke to me about the long lead time, where I could be developing super-early work on *The Avengers*, years before development or writing would actually start," Wen said. "But when I came on board, the first agenda was to design the world of *Thor*."

Wen's first job on *Thor* was to design Mjölnir, Thor's hammer. Ordinarily, a viz-dev artist would begin with the lead characters, but Marvel considered the hammer to be the most iconic aspect of Thor's look. Wen drew dozens of versions of Mjölnir. Some were simple rectangular blocks clearly derived from the comic-book designs, but others had more elaborate shapes, resembling blunted axes or orbs with flattened sides. Wen wanted to give the filmmakers as many choices as possible, but he privately worried that if they selected one of the more ornate options, the whole look of the movie would become rococo, because all the other design decisions for the movie would stem from the look of Mjölnir. Wen said, "I was fortunate that Kevin Feige and Kenneth Branagh responded to something that wasn't too outlandish and preferred the simpler version of the hammer."

Meanwhile, Wen and concept artist E. J. Krisor designed a suit of medieval armor, ten feet high. It was called "The Destroyer" and would fight Thor in the movie's final act. The Destroyer was going to appear onscreen as a digital effect, but Legacy Effects sculpted and fabricated a full-size version of it, both to gather lighting reference for the CGI team and to give the actors a notion of what they were up against.

When Meinerding began work on *Captain America: The First Avenger*, his first sketches were black-and-white portraits of Cap in World War II that saw the artist searching for a middle ground between the comic-book version of his costume and an outfit that wouldn't look ridiculous in a realistic 1940s setting. He took inspiration from *The Adventures of Captain America*, a four-issue series from 1991 that retold the early adventures of the superhero before he spent decades in hibernation. Meinerding loved how artist Kevin Maguire had rendered one particular version of Steve Rogers, already the recipient of the Super Soldier formula but still in civilian clothes. "The first pass," Meinerding said, "was based on that concept . . . Cap in a black leather jacket, and a helmet."

Joe Johnston, the director of *Captain America: The First Avenger*, was at home with the Marvel viz-dev department. He had broken into Hollywood working on the *Star Wars* movies as a concept artist and effects specialist (he designed the look of Boba Fett, for example). Production designer Rick Heinrichs said, "Joe seemed happiest and most comfortable when he was in the art department and getting away from the budget concerns and all the difficult decision-making that had to happen."

At Johnston's request, the *Captain America* production team built him a secret room, hidden behind a group of set designers. Andy Nicholson, the movie's supervising art director, said, "When Joe wanted to hide from everybody else and just draw, he could go in there for a day and no one would find him. The producers would come walking through and go 'Where's Joe?' And we're all trained to say, 'Well, I haven't seen him.' He'd be sitting in an office drawing, because that's how he liked to operate, and he'd come out with twenty pages of beautiful hand-drawn art."

✷

IN LATE 2010, Marvel Studios officially put Charlie Wen and Ryan Meinerding in charge of the new visual development department, which also included Andy Park, Rodney Fuentebella, and Jackson Sze. The studio would still hire freelancers as necessary, but the designs of the core heroes were now in the hands of artists with Marvel experience. Marvel Studios leaders trusted its artists so completely that it started building movies around the splash-page images they created, an extraordinary inversion of the usual Hollywood approach where visual artists are hired to render images after a screenplay is written.

"We formed the visual development department, which is a made-up thing that doesn't really exist in Hollywood," Park said. "We're a full-time team of artists, typically it's been six or seven of us, and we get to design the characters and the costumes. A lot of times it's costumes, because they're real actors, but it's also CGI characters like Thanos and the Hulk. We claim this pool of characters from the comic world, and translate that into the real world. Of course, eventually they do hire a costume designer, and we have to collaborate with them."

Alexandra Byrne, the costume designer on *Thor*, had been nominated for an Oscar four times, winning in 2007 for her work on *Elizabeth: The Golden Age*. But at Marvel, her job was to bring the visual development team's imagery to life, from the hero's winged helmet to his cape: the first cape for any MCU character. Inspired by the flowing mantle in the viz-dev renderings, she experimented with various crimson wall-covering fabrics. (Which meant that Iron Man's gibe in *The Avengers*—"Doth mother know you weareth her drapes?"—was pretty much on target.) Byrne constructed the garment with supports that would allow it to arch up dramatically over Chris Hemsworth's shoulders, and she sewed weights into the bottom to make sure it could sway and move but still keep its shape. She was working off viz-dev sketches, but creating a physical version was more complicated than anyone had guessed. The process involved so much trial and error that Byrne referred to the rejects as the "cape graveyard."

"We're designing, essentially, the look and feel of the film," Park said. As he saw it, the culture of Marvel Studios felt more like a tech start-up than a traditional studio: "They don't necessarily adhere to the norms of Hollywood." When he was hired, Park promptly went to work on *The Avengers*. Because there was no more office space, he was stationed in a dressing room designed for an actor, complete with well-lit mirrors, a private bathroom, and a star on the door. "They just threw a table in there," Park said, chuckling.

Weekly viz-dev meetings for each movie evolved into weekly meetings for the entire visual development department, where Wen and Meinerding would present the work of the team to all of Marvel's creative producers (plus directors and production and costume teams, for films that were actively in preproduction). Each meeting centered on a slide show, showing off renderings of heroes, villains, weapons, and environments. Designs that got no response were quietly dropped.

An important step for the viz-dev department once it had locked in some design decisions was a "keyframe" for each important sequence in a movie, intended to showcase a particular look or mood. (Keyframes were Meinerding's favorite part of his job.) For *The Avengers*, Avi Granov was asked to oversee a crucial test: Given their wildly different backgrounds and conceptions, could the heroes even stand next to each other realistically? Granov's image of Captain America, Thor, Iron Man, Hawkeye, Black Widow, and the Hulk, all shoulder-to-shoulder in a circle, convinced the studio that the movie was going to work. When that tableau, generated by the art department, came to life in a camera shot that dramatically circled around the heroes, it became one of the iconic moments of Joss Whedon's movie.

Rodney Fuentebella began his career at Marvel Studios with keyframe work for *Captain America: The First Avenger* and *The Avengers*, illustrating Cap leaping into his battle with his shield and Tony Stark falling from Stark Tower and suiting up as Iron Man in midair. Whenever Whedon would invent a new action scenario in a draft of his screenplay—say, the Hulk leaping through a smashed Helicarrier window toward a Quinjet—Fuentebella would be charged with visualizing it.

"When working on the keyframe illustration of Loki meeting Captain America, with this sea of people bowing to Loki," Fuentebella said, "I took a lot of reference pictures of my wife and I bowing from all different angles. I had a great time changing how we looked to create a diverse scene with all types of people. [With] the pose for Captain America, I had to imagine how I would look as a superhero." He confessed, "I did not have a very 'superheroic' physique, so looking at reference pictures of myself and imagining those poses I shot as Cap made me laugh a little."

When Fuentebella was posing as Captain America, Meinerding was standing in for Loki, and the rest of the viz-dev team helped out by playing the crowd of terrified onlookers kneeling before the Norse god. They went outside to get the shots; Meinerding carried out a standing lamp from the office to use in place of Loki's staff. In the middle of the photo shoot, Kevin Feige and Louis D'Esposito walked by and saw most of the Marvel visual-development team kneeling before Meinerding. Unsurprisingly, the studio heads wanted to know what they were doing.

"Reinforcing corporate culture," Meinerding told them.

★

WHILE MARVEL'S COMIC BOOKS encompassed an almost impossibly wide range of artistic styles, the visual development department at Marvel Studios was founded on photorealism. The viz-dev artists would look through decades' worth of different versions of a superhero costume, but always with an eye to how it might work onscreen. Specifics of a costume's construction—fabrics, meshes, pieces of armor—needed to be decided long before they were fabricated for on-screen use or added digitally in postproduction. Preparing for *The Avengers*, each artist spent a full week polishing a visual pitch for one of the core Avengers, with Meinerding, Wen, and Park supervising the process. The final results were determined by the notes generated during the weekly meetings.

As the relevant technology advanced, so did Marvel's processes. By the time of *Avengers: Infinity War* (2018) and *Avengers: Endgame* (2019), the viz-dev team could do full 3D renders on computers. Department heads viewed the characters from all angles, and when a look was approved, the visual development department could pass the computer model directly to the relevant production departments.

Marvel's visual workflow also changed when the studio started relying more on preproduction processes such as storyboards and animatics. Many moviemakers of all genres employ storyboards and have done so since Walt Disney pioneered the process in 1933. Pixar, for example, will do an entire movie in storyboards, and redo it as necessary, before it spends any money to make its characters move. Animatics are crude animations of those storyboards, or as Marvel animatics editor James Rothwell put it, "We start by making a Saturday-morning-cartoon version of the feature film." Animatics give directors a sense of how scenes actually play, and, Rothwell said, "it's a tool to help the director get what he wants from the producer at an earlier moment." Some shots can have hundreds of different VFX elements in them, raising the question of whether a live-action Marvel film is secretly an animated movie.

Animatics evolved into the pre-visualization process of rendering a movie's action in 3D (and then overlaying virtual camera movements). At first, Marvel employed pre-viz only for occasional tests of difficult shots, but 2014 was, quietly, a watershed year for Marvel Studios. On *Captain America: The Winter Soldier*, the studio used the technique to provide a blueprint for the movie's biggest action sequences, including Steve Rogers's battle with a Quinjet, Nick Fury's epic car chase, and the climactic crash of the S.H.I.E.L.D. Helicarrier. Almost two-thirds of the movie existed in pre-viz before it was shot, taking the guesswork—and the spontaneity—out of the production process. The cinematography and pacing were largely determined beforehand. Marvel never went back to its old methods.

All of Marvel's movies since *Winter Soldier* have received a first draft created in collaboration with the Third Floor, a 3D pre-viz company founded in 2004 by a group of visual effects artists who had worked together on *Star Wars: Revenge of the Sith*. Pre-viz became a tool to weed out ideas that don't work. For example, in an early version of Fury's car chase in *Winter Soldier*, Fury's car was going to fly. As Rothwell recalled: "It was going to take off in the air, and it was going to become an airborne chase. Then Kevin said, 'There are no flying cars in the Marvel Universe,' and that was the end of that."

Marvel's increasing use of pre-viz made for more elaborate action sequences and helped streamline the moviemaking process. But it also led to criticism that the studio had squashed the improvisational magic that can happen on a movie set and that it was running an assembly line. Favreau, Whedon, and Branagh had all made some personal, idiosyncratic choices in their films; now, some critics argued, it no longer seemed to matter that much who was directing the movie.

"I've seen movies where you can see they just shot the pre-viz," Whedon said. "And the movie either gets radically better, or worse, depending on the talent surrounding the pre-viz."

When Lucrecia Martel met with Marvel Studios to discuss her directing *Black Widow* (a job that would ultimately go to Cate Shortland), Marvel told her that it was looking for a female director because it wanted somebody who would be focused on Scarlett Johansson's character. As she recalled, "They also told me, 'Don't worry about the action scenes, we will take care of that.' I was thinking, 'Well, I would love to meet Scarlett Johansson, but also I would love to make the action sequences.'"

The Marvel pre-viz approach prompted some MCU directors to take pains to emphasize their own contributions—effectively telling the world that they had actually directed the biggest sequences in their own movies. Chloe Zhao, who directed *Eternals*, declared, "My God, for a year and a half, three times a week for a couple hours a day, I was sitting in front of a big screen making decisions for every detail of how visual effects could look in the real world."

James Gunn, who directed *Guardians of the Galaxy* and *Guardians of the Galaxy Vol. 2,* insisted that "although some Marvel directors use pre-viz to design the action sequences, others use it as a tool in designing their own. On both *Guardians* films, the pre-viz was fully built off of my personal storyboards."

"Our creative process really hasn't changed—it has solidified," Victoria Alonso insisted. She believed that Marvel's culture and workflow were strong, but her challenge was to make sure that all the outside VFX vendors—Marvel hired more such companies as the MCU expanded—were working in concert. "Before, we were finding our groove," she said. "[Now] you bring nine to thirteen companies to come and help you—so you've got to find your groove with each and every guest that comes to the table."

The artists and executives who ran outside effects houses, many of whom logged countless hours on conference calls with Alonso over the years, often cited her as their staunchest advocate in the face of indecisive or inexperienced directors. However, contractors further down the chain of command, executing the last-minute notes and requests for VFX miracles that Marvel had relied on ever since it overhauled the *Iron Man* ending, learned to think of Alonso's name as synonymous with an unbearable workload.

Inside the Marvel Studios offices, the viz-dev team felt like part of the family. Meinerding had gone from sleeping under his desk to becoming one of the most influential creative minds at Marvel Studios. "We're very lucky to have someone at the highest levels of the company like Kevin Feige, who really respects and appreciates the artwork developed for a film," he said. "Anywhere else in Hollywood, people like us are down the food chain."

CHAPTER FIFTEEN

The Forbidden City

You're in a relationship with me.
Nothing will ever be okay.

Iron Man 3

I
N 2007, THE TOTAL BOX-OFFICE TAKE AT MOVIE THE-
aters in the People's Republic of China was $255 million; by
2013, it had grown by an order of magnitude, to over $3.6 bil-
lion. That wasn't just a measure of the country's booming economy.
China had embarked upon a major program to build movie theaters
and had started playing "enhanced" movies in lucrative formats,
such as IMAX and 3D. Those efforts made people in China the
second-largest moviegoing audience in the world—and the country
was obviously on its way to number one. American studios desperately wanted to reach China's hundreds of millions of movie lov-
ers, but it was no simple matter to get a film into Chinese theaters.
The government exercised strict oversight on content—a movie that
displeased Chinese censors would be blocked, which is why a Chinese villain is hardly ever seen in a twenty-first-century Hollywood
movie—and did everything it could to protect and favor its bur-
geoning domestic movie industry.

American movies often faced a blackout period after their initial release dates, ranging from weeks to months, before playing in China (giving bootleggers ample time to sell black-market DVDs), and foreign companies were limited in what percentage of the Chinese box office they could collect after the theaters took their cut: only 15 percent, as opposed to 45 percent for Chinese companies distributing non-Chinese films. The MCU was gradually becoming more popular in China; while *Iron Man* had grossed only $15.2 million there, *The Avengers* sold $86.3 million in tickets. Marvel's 15 percent slice of that *Avengers* figure, however, was just $12.9 million.

For years before it acquired Marvel, Disney had been slowly and delicately expanding its presence in the Chinese market. It had opened Hong Kong Disneyland in 2005, in the semiautonomous city that was formerly a British colony. But Disney wanted a larger presence on the mainland, one that would be regarded more favorably by the Chinese government than its Hong Kong venture. Disney was denied permission to construct a theme park on Chinese soil, however, until it partnered with a Chinese firm, the newly created Shanghai Shendi Group, to run Shanghai Disneyland. Once a Chinese company owned the majority stake in the $3.75-billion park, Shanghai Disneyland was approved; construction began in 2011.

With so much money at stake in the Chinese movie market, fixers sprang up, eager to help studios navigate a foreign bureaucracy and to explain China to Hollywood. (The familiar truths of American movie theaters aren't universal: buttered popcorn isn't popular in Chinese movie theaters, while dried plums and sunflower seeds are.) One of those middlemen was DMG Entertainment, founded by American producer Dan Mintz with his Chinese partners Bing Wu and Peter Xiao. DMG started by making Chinese TV commercials for American brands and then moved on to distributing movies such as *Twilight* (the company was sufficiently Chinese to qualify for the 45 percent cut of box-office receipts).

The production company Endgame Entertainment had been working with director Rian Johnson on his sci-fi time-travel movie *Looper*; in 2011, Endgame brought on DMG as its partner. The movie had been slated to shoot most of its scenes in Louisiana, with a couple of weeks in Paris for idyllic flashbacks featuring the main character, Joe (actor Joseph Gordon-Levitt), and his wife. Now the Paris sequence was relocated to Shanghai and the Chinese actress Summer Qing was cast as Joe's wife.

For a movie to be considered an official Chinese coproduction, one-third of the movie's cast had to be Chinese or one-third of its running time had to take place in China. Audaciously, the *Looper* producers applied for that status anyway. The government didn't grant it, but it did call *Looper* an "assisted production"—which was almost as good. It meant the movie had no blackout period and the producers were allowed to keep 100 percent of the box-office receipts. *Looper* was a hit, earning $176.5 million worldwide, albeit not on the scale of *The Avengers*, which came out the same year and earned $1.5 billion worldwide. In China, however, the favored status of the production meant that *Looper* yielded $20.2 million to *The Avengers'* $12.9 million.

DMG pitched its *Looper* success to Marvel; Mintz promised, "We will build your brand, and we'll position it as one that is global." Ike Perlmutter liked the idea, but the Marvel Studios executives in California felt that the studio's next movie already had enough problems without worrying about the Chinese market.

✳

DIRECTOR JON FAVREAU didn't want to make *Iron Man 3*. After filming *Iron Man* and *Iron Man 2* essentially back-to-back, he was spent—and not thrilled with Marvel's emphasis on crossovers and team-ups. "In theory, *Iron Man 3* is going to be a sequel or continuation of *Thor*, *Hulk*, *Captain America*, and *Avengers*," Favreau said in 2010. The notion of the Marvel Cinematic Universe held no allure for him: "I have no idea what it is. I don't think they do either."

When Favreau bowed out, Robert Downey Jr. nominated Shane Black, who had directed him in *Kiss Kiss Bang Bang*, the 2005 mystery/comedy costarring Val Kilmer that had launched Downey's comeback. Before becoming a director, Black had made his name with the script for *Lethal Weapon*, which made him one of the highest-paid screenwriters in Hollywood.

Black had a good relationship with Downey, which was important. As Downey put it: "As far as I'm concerned, I have everything approval." And after Joss Whedon's success with *The Avengers*, the Marvel brass liked the idea of hiring another writer/director: if a single person took care of story and character and performance, the studio's visual virtuosos could handle the rest. Black arrived at Marvel's Manhattan Beach offices to discuss *Iron Man 3* with Kevin Feige and Stephen Broussard.

"Marvel was very gracious," Black said. "They didn't know who the villain was. They had kind of expressed a desire that it be the Mandarin at some point, but they were willing to let it not be the Mandarin. They wanted it to be about, sort of, the destruction of Tony Stark, and the one scene I remember being given on day one was his entire house and his entire laboratory are sort of decimated and taken out from under him."

Writer Drew Pearce had also been working on ideas for the next Iron Man movie. After Marvel abruptly canceled *Runaways* in 2010, his first child, Noah, was born and he stayed home in London, living off the money he had been paid for his drafts of the screenplay. Pearce regularly woke up to do Noah's 3:30 a.m. feeding—and over the course of six weeks, he used that time to brainstorm ideas for the *Iron Man* franchise, holding his newborn son with one hand and typing with the other. "I don't know if it was because of the extraordinary lack of sleep or the hormones of having a new kid and desperately wanting to provide and tell stories, but I wrote this story for *Iron Man 3*," he remembered.

Pearce called up the Marvel producer Jodi Hildebrand, who confirmed his suspicions that it was bizarre for a professional screenwriter to work, unpaid, on a character that belonged to somebody else. "She quite rightly said, 'That's fucking bananas. I legally probably can't even accept it.'" (Hollywood studios make sure not to see unsolicited treatments of the IP they control, in case they independently come up with a similar idea later and get sued.) Undeterred, Pearce sent her his Iron Man treatise, telling himself that since she hadn't asked him for it, everyone was in the clear.

Although Pearce's reasoning wasn't, in fact, legally sound, his tactics worked. In January 2011, he got a call from Marvel telling him that Feige was in London (checking on the recording sessions for the *Thor* score at Abbey Road). Did Pearce have time to meet with the studio president? He did. The last time Pearce had spoken with Feige, before *Runaways* was canceled, they had discussed the possibilities for Marvel One-Shots, smaller stories that would take place between Marvel's tentpole movies, and so the writer assumed that was what Feige wanted to discuss.

At a Starbucks near Abbey Road, Pearce quickly spotted Feige in his baseball cap, but when he greeted the studio president, he discovered that the document Feige had loaded onto his iPad was Pearce's Iron Man manifesto. "And my first instinct is to panic," Pearce said, "because I suddenly realized that I don't remember a single word of it because I wrote it in total sleep deprivation, at a point of absolute madness."

Feige began the conversation by letting Pearce down: "Well, obviously I'm not going to do this story." But they discussed the character for two hours, and a few weeks later, Pearce officially had the job to write *Iron Man 3*. Two days after that, however, he got the news that the studio had also hired Black as the director. Pearce assumed he would be fired, but Broussard insisted that Marvel wanted them to work together. Pearce remained skeptical: "I'm a scrub and he is an incredibly famous screenwriter. Are you sure this is going to work?"

Feige and Broussard invited Black and Pearce to Simi Valley, where director Joe Johnston was doing some reshoots for *Captain America: The First Avenger*. The production had found a patch of forest that matched scenes from principal photography and was filming sequences in which the Captain threw his shield, taking out HYDRA agents. The meeting started just as Pearce had feared. "I didn't know Drew was on the project when I took this thing, so I rebelled," said Black. "I said, 'Excuse me, there's a British guy with a beard in this room, what's he doing here?' And they said, 'Well, he'll be writing the draft with you,' and I said, 'Well, that's good, but no he won't.'"

Black had a writing partner of his own he wanted to bring onto the project, but Marvel convinced Black to try working with Pearce for a week before making a final decision. During that week, Pearce showed up at Black's home every morning with a 7-Eleven coffee and a cookie. "The cookie was for his dog and the coffee was for him," Pearce said. "I was shameless." They discovered that they had similar senses of humor and bonded over their mutual love for *The Seven-Ups*, the 1973 action movie starring Roy Scheider as a dirty cop.

One week later, Black and Pearce went into the Marvel offices to brief Feige and Broussard. The Marvel execs seemed happy with their progress—but as the meeting ended, Pearce realized how tenuous his situation was, both because Black had much more clout than he did, and because Pearce had already had one Marvel project killed. Although Pearce was terrified, he knew that he needed to stand up for himself in that moment. "It was a very big-boy-pants moment," he said.

Pearce literally stood up. He told everyone in the room, "Guys, this has been a really brilliant and productive week with Shane, and I would love and feel honored if I could write *Iron Man 3* with him. But it has to be me and him and it has to be a partnership. I will give him the best version of the movie that he wants to make, but it has to be the two of us."

There was silence. "Direct confrontation is not necessarily a tenet of the Marvel production process," Pearce noted. Which isn't unusual in Hollywood: the industry has long operated on smiling expressions of enthusiasm face-to-face, and rejections delivered by intermediaries.

According to Pearce, "Shane stood up himself and said, 'I've been working with him all week. I've found him to be both a gentleman and a man of honor, and I would be happy to write *Iron Man 3* with him.' And then what's crazy is, between then and two and a half years later, when the movie came out, no one else touched a keyboard on *Iron Man 3* other than Shane or I." It was one Marvel movie that didn't end up with a WGA arbitration.

That level of control over the script was unusual at Marvel, but the studio was happy with the story the pair came up with: Tony Stark, shellshocked after the events of *The Avengers*, lets the world believe he is dead while he hides out in Tennessee. He takes on an unlikely sidekick (a local boy named Harley Keener) while he investigates the powerful but dangerous technology called Extremis and reconsiders the value of his own life after almost dying in the defense of Earth in *The Avengers*. There were the necessary action moments, too, including Iron Man's daring midair rescue when the bad guys blow up *Air Force One* in flight, a set piece the writers called the "barrel of monkeys sequence."

Black had confided in Pearce that he didn't particularly like people, but he loved dogs. So when the writers worked on the barrel of monkeys, Pearce said that Black "imagined that scene as twenty dogs being blown out the back of a jumbo jet rather than twenty people. And that is what made him believe in the stakes."

The Creative Committee at Marvel Entertainment's New York offices was less enthusiastic about the screenplay. "Not to throw anyone under the bus, but the notes we got from the Creative Committee were more extensively brutal. From what felt like Ike-access, if you know what I mean," said Pearce, referring to Ike Perlmutter. "There was definitely a giant pushback that we were just making, I think they called it, 'an eighties buddy-cop movie.' And I was like, 'Cool. Let's make an eighties buddy-cop movie.'"

The biggest question was the villain. Marvel fans expected it to be the Mandarin, whom Jon Favreau had mistakenly touted as the antagonist in the first *Iron Man*. Before Favreau decided not to return to the franchise as a director, he told the press that he expected *Iron Man 3* to feature the Mandarin, who had long been the biggest bad guy in the *Iron Man* comic books. "You've got to do the Mandarin," Favreau said. "The problem with the Mandarin is that the way it's depicted in the comic books, you don't want to see that. He has ten magical rings—that just doesn't feel right."

And as Black pointed out, the Mandarin, a scheming Chinese warlord, was based on racist Asian stereotypes. He was a thinly rewritten version of Fu Manchu, a pulp-novel character that debuted in 1912 and had become one of the most notorious, and pernicious, of those caricatures. Chris Fenton of DMG Entertainment, trying to ease Marvel's entry into the Chinese market, warned Marvel executive Tim Connors, "The Mandarin scares the shit out of us." He explained: "The Mandarin looks and acts like the stereotypically derogatory Chinese man. Not only does he have a long spiny beard that he's constantly straightening with his fingers, he regularly speaks in uber-'Chinglish,' constantly saying Chinese-cliché types of proverbs."

Black and Pearce tried to minimize the issues with the Mandarin without writing him out of the movie altogether. In one early draft, Iron Man would have fought five different supervillains, reducing the impact of any individual bad guy. Pearce was using the bathroom at Black's house when the solution came to him. "I pitched the twist with Shane to Kevin two days later," he said. "Kevin loved it from the beginning and backed it right the way through." The film version of the Mandarin would have nothing in common with the comic-book version beyond his name; he would be a terrorist of vague ethnicity. Halfway through the movie, Stark would discover that the Mandarin was a paid British actor, sponsored by an evil think tank to help it cover up the dangerous Extremis experiments. The true villain would be the mastermind of that think tank.

Black and Pearce wanted that villain to be female. Black hoped to cast Jessica Chastain in the role of Maya Hansen; when she declined, he signed up the British actress Rebecca Hall. "We had a female character who was the villain," Black said. "We had finished the script and we were given a no-holds-barred memo saying 'That cannot stand and we've changed our minds because after consulting, we've decided that the toy won't sell as well if it's a female.'" He exhaled with frustration. "So we had to change the entire script because of toymaking. Now, that's not Feige. That's Marvel corporate."

Caught in the middle of this conflict was Hall, who saw her character steadily diminished as the production went forward. "She wasn't entirely the villain—there have been several phases of this—but I signed on to do something very different to what I ended up doing," the actress said. Halfway through the film's shoot, she was asked what she would think if her character were abruptly killed, instead of lasting to the end of the movie as originally planned. "I grappled with them for a while and then I said, 'Well, you have to give me a decent death scene and you have to give me one more scene with Iron Man,' which Robert Downey Jr. supported me on."

With Maya Hansen killed off and the Mandarin, played by Sir Ben Kingsley, revealed as a fake, the role of principal villain fell to Guy Pearce as genius scientist Aldrich Killian: the last big name standing in the supporting cast.

*

BEFORE FILMING BEGAN, Fenton and Mintz of DMG Entertainment kept pitching Marvel Studios on how they could tailor *Iron Man 3* for the Chinese market and take advantage of coproduction rules. But in a meeting with Feige and Louis D'Esposito, they got shot down. Perlmutter had reluctantly withdrawn his support for the Chinese initiative because Disney didn't want Marvel to do anything that might interfere with its huge Shanghai Disneyland project.

Fenton and Mintz persisted, touting the value, culturally and economically, of building a bridge between the world's two biggest superpowers. What if Harley Keener, the kid whom Tony Stark befriends in Tennessee, was actually a Chinese exchange student? Chinese leader Xi Jinping had basically been an exchange student in the United States himself, living with an Iowa family back in 1985.

According to Fenton, D'Esposito told him, "Your Chinese-kid idea is not happening. Because we're not interested in having the sidekick from *Indiana Jones* [*and the Temple of Doom*] in *Iron Man 3*."

Feige's alternate suggestion: A Chinese doctor, who could be the one to remove the shrapnel from Tony Stark's chest that endangered his life. "And his name will be Doctor Wu." When asked if that was a Marvel reference, Feige said, no, it was just a "great song by Steely Dan."

Running the risk of angering Disney, Marvel took on DMG as a coproducer, but did as little as possible to target the Chinese audience, publicly minimizing the amount of Chinese content in the movie. At the 2012 San Diego Comic-Con, Black even told a room full of fans, "We're setting aspects of the film in China, but the first unit won't be filming there. But don't tell anybody."

According to Fenton, Feige assured DMG that they would make Dr. Wu a "crucial character" in the movie, standing right next to Tony Stark at the end of the movie when Stark hurls his now-unnecessary arc reactor into the sea. That didn't happen, but Feige nevertheless promised, "We'll figure out how to get you something in China. Let me work on it."

Most of *Iron Man 3* was filmed in Wilmington, North Carolina. The character of Harley Keener was played by Ty Simpkins, who was eleven years old when the shoot began. He played almost all his scenes opposite Downey, who took the young actor under his wing when he arrived on location.

"Robert reached out," Simpkins remembered. "He was like, 'Hey man, let's hang out for a day so we can get to know each other more. And we can go over some of the stuff that we're going to be working on. Do you like pizza?'"

Simpkins allowed that he did. When he got to Downey's rental beachfront house, he discovered that it was fully equipped with pool floats and Super Soaker water guns. And Downey had laid out an array of fifty mini-pizzas. Downey explained the excessive spread: "I didn't know what kind you like."

Unfortunately, halfway through the *Iron Man 3* shoot, Downey broke his ankle filming the final action sequence, set on an oil rig. Guy Pearce recalled, "He had to do a stunt where he jumped from one platform down to another platform and be on a cable. They wanted to rehearse it, and he said, 'I don't need to rehearse it.'" Downey jumped before the crew member holding the cable was ready, landed hard, and the shoot shut down for five or six weeks.

When filming resumed, Downey was still limping, so Black shot him from the waist up (and when necessary, used CGI to paste his face digitally onto a stand-in). The injury removed any possibility of Downey filming a scene in Shanghai. Instead, Marvel Studios shoehorned in extra footage filmed in China with the Chinese actors Wang Xueqi (Dr. Wu) and Fan Bingbing (his unnamed assistant). In the American cut of the movie, Dr. Wu performs the operation and is never seen again, but the Chinese cut extended the sequence, added a scene where Dr. Wu drinks milk and calls J.A.R.V.I.S. (Stark's AI) on the phone to pledge his support against the Mandarin, and included a commercial for the milk drink Gu Li Duo at the beginning of the movie. (The Chinese milk market was in turmoil at the time; a major dairy company had just recalled some of its baby formula because of mercury contamination, and so the industry needed to convince citizens to trust milk again.)

The new footage, seen nowhere but in China, added four minutes to the running time of *Iron Man 3*. Many Chinese fans deemed it a cynical move on Marvel's part. Young Chinese film fan Liu Kunpeng complained, "The Chinese version treated Chinese audiences like idiots. I want to see the same version that the rest of the world sees."

Nevertheless, the additional footage made the difference. Marvel was allowed to release *Iron Man 3* in China without a blackout period and to keep a full cut of the Chinese box office. The movie did better in China than any MCU movie that had come before, grossing $121 million after it was released in May 2013. (It was a hit in the rest of the world, too, pulling in $1.215 billion total.) Marvel wouldn't partner with DMG or other Chinese companies after that, but its movies would continue to do big business in China.

Marvel benefited from perfect timing, with the studio hitting its stride at the exact moment when the Chinese market exploded, and it released a steady stream of movies that were exotic but understandable to Chinese audiences. "People love Marvel precisely because it's so different from local content," said Sky Shi, a Chinese movie producer. Older franchises, such as *Star Wars*, weren't as successful in China because the foundational movies were decades in the past and so the series never had a chance to build up an audience.

Over the next seven years, Marvel's box office numbers kept

climbing in the People's Republic, culminating with a $629.1 million Chinese gross in 2019 for *Avengers: Endgame*. Soon after that triumph, however, one Marvel movie after another found itself unable to get past the Great Wall of China. In most cases, the studio never received an official explanation for the blackout from the China Film Administration (which is part of the publicity arm of the Chinese Communist Party), but it could guess what had happened.

Shang Chi and the Legend of the Ten Rings (2021) had long sequences set in China and was full of Chinese mythology, but its star Simu Liu had called China a "third world" country in 2017. The film was blocked. Similarly, Chloé Zhao, the Chinese-born director of *Eternals* (2021), had called China "a place where there are lies everywhere" in a 2013 interview. Her movie also never made it into Chinese theaters. (Her fleeting inclusion of a gay couple may not have helped.)

By that point, the Chinese Film Administration seemed to be making a point: even if the MCU was massively popular, China didn't need it. *Doctor Strange in the Multiverse of Madness* (2022) was also banned—maybe because of the brief glimpse on a New York City street of a yellow newspaper box holding copies of *The Epoch Times*, published by the Falun Gong movement, which opposes the Chinese Communist Party. *Thor: Love and Thunder* (2022) didn't make it either, possibly because of passing references to the supporting characters Valkyrie and Korg not being heterosexual. (Neither of them is actually human, but that doesn't seem to have mattered.)

Marvel Studios had steadily grown through its short history, whether one measured by cultural impact, by box office, or by the number of releases. Now it faced a retrenchment, and not one of its choosing. Almost four years passed without any Marvel Studios movies in China; the ban was lifted in early 2023 for *Black Panther: Wakanda Forever* (a couple of months after it debuted in the rest of the world) and *Ant-Man and the Wasp: Quantumania*.

When it hit a rough patch, Marvel Studios was willing to do whatever it took to shore up its global box office receipts. To placate China and other conservative countries, Marvel had removed the fleeting references to homosexuality in its movies. That meant cutting a blink-and-you'll-miss it relationship in *Wakanda Forever* and excising the queer-friendly signs and flags in the background of the San Francisco scenes of *Quantumania*.

The latter decision required some digital tweaks by the VFX department, but it frustrated Victoria Alonso, a queer woman, so much that she refused to make the edits. So did everyone on her team. D'Esposito then went around her and outsourced the job to a VFX contractor. This was a crack in the unified front of Marvel's leadership team, one of many that would lead to a messy and public fracture.

But Marvel was back in China. While the Chinese government didn't issue an explanation for the return of the MCU, observers noted that in 2022, the Chinese box office had dropped 36 percent from the prior year, falling behind the North American market. China had succeeded in making some homegrown franchises of its own, such as the war movie *The Battle at Lake Changjin* and the sci-fi blockbuster *The Wandering Earth* (and their sequels), but Chinese theaters still wanted Hollywood releases to keep their seats filled.

China needed Marvel and Marvel needed China and almost everyone on both sides was willing to bend their principles to make that work.

CHAPTER SIXTEEN

Remote Control

Challenge incites conflict and
conflict breeds catastrophe.

Captain America: Civil War

I N APRIL 2013, AROUND THE TIME *IRON MAN 3* WAS
opening around the world, Marvel Studios relocated its offices
yet again, this time to Walt Disney's Burbank headquarters,
which is famous for its carved stone statues of the seven dwarfs from
Snow White. The new office space wasn't as grotty as the studio's
previous locations, although the furniture was still mismatched and
threadbare. Also housed at the Burbank location was Marvel Television. Tellingly, Marvel Studios was at one end of the campus, while
Marvel Television was at the other. Although they allegedly shared a
common purpose, the two corporate divisions were stationed as far
away from each other as physically possible.

Marvel Entertainment created Marvel Television in 2010, the
same year that *Iron Man 2* arrived in theaters. Ike Perlmutter and his
right-hand man Alan Fine promoted publisher Dan Buckley, giving
him a new title (president of print, animation, and digital) and the
critical assignment of launching a new television division. The New
York executives conceived it not as a subsidiary of Marvel Studios,

but as a separate division that would take orders from them, via the Creative Committee. After the surprisingly lucrative *Iron Man* movies, Marvel Entertainment saw an opportunity to make money on the small screen and wanted to stay in control of that enterprise.

Buckley hired Joseph "Jeph" Loeb III to be Marvel TV's executive vice president and head of television. Loeb, who had been making movies when Kevin Feige was still in junior high school, had credibility as both a filmmaker and a comics nerd. Loeb grew up in the suburbs of New York and Boston and got a master's degree in film from Columbia University in 1979. After graduation, Loeb and his writing partner, Matthew Weissman, moved to Los Angeles. They had no contacts, so to pay the rent while they wrote scripts, Weisman worked at a videogame arcade and Loeb bartended at a T.G.I. Friday's. But they sold their first screenplay—*Commando*, which became a hit for Arnold Schwarzenegger in 1985—and followed it up with *Teen Wolf*, an even bigger hit for Michael J. Fox, the same year. (The "van surfing" scene in *Teen Wolf* was based on Loeb's drunken antics as a Columbia student.)

In 1991, Loeb pitched Warner Bros. an idea for a movie starring the Flash. Although the film never happened, that pitch led to him writing comic books through the 1990s, for both DC and Marvel, on high-profile characters including Batman, Superman, and the Hulk. In 2002, he returned to Hollywood work with the young-Superman show *Smallville*, ultimately writing and producing for *Lost* and *Heroes*. Loeb's work sometimes verged on goofy—he was a fan of "dad jokes"—but it acquired a sorrowful tinge after Loeb's teenage son Sam died of bone cancer in 2005.

After it was bought by Disney, Marvel had access to a broadcast TV network, ABC—if it could come up with shows. Director Guillermo del Toro expressed interest in making a Hulk series, but opted to spend his time on the movie *Pacific Rim* instead. Writer Melissa Rosenberg developed a series centered on Jessica Jones, the super-powered private detective created by writer Brian Michael Bendis and artist Michael Gaydos, but the deal fell apart when ABC wanted to retool the show to focus on Jessica Jones's pal Carol Danvers (the future Captain Marvel).

Loeb and Marvel Television then created two series for the ABC Family cable network, *Cloak & Dagger* and *Mockingbird,* but both shows languished in development. (In 2018, seven years after work on *Cloak & Dagger* began, the series premiered on the Freeform network, where it lasted for two seasons.) They worked up a *Punisher* series for Fox, which passed. The only programs Marvel Television could get on the air were animated series such as *The Super Hero Squad Show.* But *The Avengers* changed everything.

While the billion-dollar movie was still in theaters, ABC and Marvel Television discussed how best to bring the Marvel Cinematic Universe to TV. The conversation happened without Marvel Studios, which wanted its movies to feel like events: one blockbuster after another, not just episodes of TV shows on a larger screen. The Marvel Studios leaders regarded a TV spinoff as forced synergy.

Nevertheless, Marvel Television pitched a series to Joss Whedon: *Agents of S.H.I.E.L.D.,* about the adventures of secret agents in the organization run by Nick Fury. The show could capitalize on the MCU's buzz, but on a TV budget (i.e., without too many elaborate special effects). Whedon was already negotiating a three-year deal to return as writer-director of an *Avengers* sequel and to be an advisor on the other Phase Two movies leading up to it. In August 2012, he signed a huge contract for those projects, plus *Agents of S.H.I.E.L.D.,* reported to be in the neighborhood of $100 million. (He contested that number—"Jeepers, I'm not getting $100 mil on *Avengers 2,*" he wrote on a fan website—sidestepping the question of whether he might be making that much overall in a multiyear deal.)

Marvel Studios planned to reveal that S.H.I.E.L.D. was riddled with traitors a few movies down the line, and it wasn't going to alter those plans to make life easier for Marvel Television. "They had said early on, 'Hey, we're thinking about doing this show about the agents of S.H.I.E.L.D.,'" Kevin Feige recalled. "And Joss said, 'I think I might do this.' I said, 'That's cool. God bless you. But you should know that we're destroying S.H.I.E.L.D. in *Winter Soldier*. You guys do whatever you want. But know that's what we're going to do."

Whedon moved ahead anyway, writing the series pilot with his brother Jed Whedon and Jed's wife Maurissa Tancharoen. They centered the show on Agent Coulson (Clark Gregg), who had been stabbed through the heart by Loki in *The Avengers*. He was dead in the movies, but mysteriously alive on television. Joss Whedon directed the pilot, and in May 2013, ABC ordered it to series. "[Marvel Studios] didn't actually want me to make [the show]," Whedon admitted later. "It's like, 'Uh, Joss, we really wanted you to do *Avengers 2*. Instead you created a TV show, you moron.' 'I thought you wanted me to!' 'No, we just wanted you to make a movie.' 'Oh. My bad.'"

To make the series feel more essential, the Creative Committee pushed for *Agents of S.H.I.E.L.D.* to react to developments from the MCU movies. The show's first cross-promotional test was the November 2013 sequel *Thor: The Dark World*. Marvel Television wanted a story involving Asgardians, but although Marvel Studios granted access to some of its sets and props, the movie division was unwilling to loan out any of the MCU characters. Instead, the show set an episode in London in the aftermath of the movie's final battle: the S.H.I.E.L.D. team is helping clean up when they encounter an unrelated Asgardian artifact and an "Asgardian Berserker" (guest star Peter MacNicol).

The next movie crossover, in April 2014, was a far greater challenge. In *Captain America: The Winter Soldier*, all of S.H.I.E.L.D. comes crashing down when Steve Rogers discovers the organization has been infiltrated by the evil quasi-Nazis of HYDRA. Most of the cast of *Agents of S.H.I.E.L.D.* learned about the essential plot twist only when they saw an early screening of the movie. (Underscoring Marvel Studios' lack of regard for Marvel Television: a movie centered on S.H.I.E.L.D. didn't mention, even in passing, that Agent Coulson, who hadn't appeared in the MCU since *The Avengers*, was actually alive.) In the final episode of its first season, the series had to reinvent its premise. Marvel Studios reluctantly approved a cameo by

Samuel L. Jackson as Nick Fury, who named Coulson the new director of S.H.I.E.L.D. and told him that he had to rebuild the agency "from the ground up."

Joss Whedon had become the creative face of the MCU, more prominent than even Feige. He was developing the *Avengers* sequel, doing script polishes for Marvel's Phase Two movies, and managing the Creative Committee's desire to see *Agents of S.H.I.E.L.D.* link up to the MCU. "There was a period where it got . . . complicated," Whedon said. "A lot of people who aren't connected with the show were like, 'Oh, yeah, you have to have this guest star, and you have to work around this.' Sometimes it makes your head spin. I mean, it's hard enough when they're like, 'And by the way, in *Iron Man 4*, he's going to be played by Linda Hunt as a human spider. And you're like, 'Oh, OK! I guess I'll have to work that in.'" After the first season of *Agents of S.H.I.E.L.D.*, Whedon stepped away from the show-running responsibilities he had been sharing with his brother and his sister-in-law, leaving the show in their hands. The show quietly continued for seven seasons, lasting until 2020, but after the first year, barring a few guest appearances, Marvel Television mostly gave up on integrating its action with the MCU movies.

*

THE CREATION OF Marvel Television didn't stop Marvel Studios from commissioning shorter programs of its own. Studio copresident Louis D'Esposito, indulging his one-time dream of becoming a director, went behind the camera to shoot some short films as part of the Marvel One-Shot series. Usually included on DVDs and Blu-rays as bonus programming, the One-Shots explored moments or characters that the full-length movies didn't have time for. *Agent Carter*, included on *Iron Man 3* discs, starred Hayley Atwell reprising her role from *Captain America: The First Avenger* as a 1940s secret agent. Based on the positive reaction to that fifteen-minute short, ABC commissioned a full *Agent Carter* series, created by *Captain America* screenwriters Christopher Markus and Stephen McFeely.

The *Agent Carter* production team had less friction with Marvel

Studios than *Agents of S.H.I.E.L.D.* had, maybe because the show had been sparked by D'Esposito, maybe because it was set seventy years before the main action of the MCU. Atwell then returned for a cameo in *Captain America: The Winter Soldier*, playing an aged version of Peggy Carter. The actress spoke enthusiastically about how her show could follow the life of Peggy through the years, maybe advancing one decade in each new season. But after two critically acclaimed seasons, the show was cancelled due to low ratings.

In 2012 and 2013, some of the licensing deals Avi Arad had made during his tenure at Marvel finally concluded, years after his departure, and a clutch of superheroes returned home. When New Line declined to make any more *Blade* sequels, Marvel regained the rights to the vampire hunter. Similarly, Fox let its rights to Daredevil and Elektra lapse a decade after the much-maligned movies starring those characters, and Sony let its option expire on the character of Luke Cage without ever making a movie about the Black superhero with unbreakable skin. Nicolas Cage had starred as one of Arad's favorites, the demonic motorcycle stunt rider Johnny Blaze, in *Ghost Rider* (2007) and *Ghost Rider: Spirit of Vengeance* (2011); although the first movie was a surprise hit, the widely panned sequel made $100 million worldwide, half the box-office take of the original. In 2013, when Cage announced he was done playing the character, the rights quickly reverted to Marvel.

Kevin Feige had dossiers on all these characters in the filing cabinets of Marvel Studios, as well as ideas on how he might integrate them into the Marvel Cinematic Universe. The Creative Committee, however, decided that Feige was busy with the Avengers characters, not to mention the upcoming *Guardians of the Galaxy* movie, and, ignoring the protests of Marvel Studios, it assigned all the wayward characters to Marvel Television. A new version of Ghost Rider (not Johnny Blaze, not Nicolas Cage) soon made a guest appearance on *Agents of S.H.I.E.L.D.*, but Loeb had a bigger plan for the other characters.

Marvel Television and Marvel Entertainment aimed to create the TV equivalent of *The Avengers*: four different television series whose characters would come together on one all-star team. The *Agents of S.H.I.E.L.D.* ratings were good enough that Marvel could ask a streaming platform for a long-term commitment; after secretly shopping the ambitious proposal around, Marvel announced a deal with Netflix in November 2013.

Netflix was a logical home for the shows. The streaming service had just begun a serious effort to expand its original content, having debuted its first prestige show, *House of Cards* (starring Kevin Spacey and Robin Wright) in February of that year. And the year before, Disney and Netflix had signed a deal making the streamer the first stop after theatrical releases for Disney movies, including Marvel movies. "Marvel is a known and loved brand," said Netflix chief content officer Ted Sarandos. And so, Netflix committed to an astonishing sixty episodes of television: full seasons of *Daredevil, Jessica Jones, Luke Cage*, and *Iron Fist*, leading to a team-up called *The Defenders*. The shows would not only be set in New York City, they would film there, since the city gave Marvel Television a great deal on production costs.

Loeb saw the value in "street-level" Marvel heroes who could star in small-screen stories that didn't require flashy superpowers—or, put another way, expensive special-effects shots. Marvel Television would make shows about heroes who punched their way out of problems.

Joss Whedon, immersed in the *Avengers* sequel, wasn't available for further TV work, so to reboot the character of Daredevil, Marvel Television hired Whedon's frequent collaborator Drew Goddard (director of *Cabin in the Woods* and writer of *Cloverfield*) instead. Goddard argued that Netflix was a better venue for Daredevil than the movie screen, not only because the smaller budget fit the scope of the character, but because a TV series could explore the character of Matt Murdock in greater depth and venture into R-rated territory.

"The thing about Matt Murdock is, he's not saving the world. He's just keeping his corner clean," Goddard said. "So it would feel wrong to have spaceships crashing in the middle of the city. But because of that, Marvel on the movie side is not in the business of making $25 million movies. They're going big, as they should. [We] have more freedom to make it on the small screen and make it more adult."

Goddard, announced as the *Daredevil* showrunner in December 2013, wrote the first two episodes of the series but quit just four months later. He had also been working with Amy Pascal, cochairperson of Sony Pictures Entertainment, on a Sinister Six movie, implementing the studio's plan to expand the *Spider-Man* franchise into its own universe. Goddard wrote a screenplay that would feature Spider-Man (then played by Andrew Garfield) as a side character in a movie featuring a smorgasbord of Spider-Man villains. The studio hoped it could come out in 2016, on the heels of *The Amazing Spider-Man 2*, and offered Goddard the job of directing it. Goddard eagerly accepted what promised to be his highest-profile job ever. He believed he had discharged his obligations to *Daredevil* with his two scripts; Marvel had already lined up a new showrunner, Steven S. DeKnight (yet another Whedon associate).

Nevertheless, when he decamped for Sony, Marvel reacted with rancor. "Been in meetings with Marvel all day," Goddard emailed Pascal in March 2013. "They're slowly working through the seven stages of grief." Over the next couple of months, Goddard and Marvel negotiated the terms of his departure. The haggling over Goddard's payment and title was mundane. What was unusual was that it involved not only Jeph Loeb at Marvel Television but Alan Fine at Marvel Entertainment and even Marvel CEO Ike Perlmutter.

"I tried to help," Pascal wrote in an email to president of Columbia Pictures Doug Belgrad, during Goddard's negotiations. "Didn't volunteer but Ike kept calling me. . . . I think Ike is trying to scare everyone and they don't really have a leg to stand on."

DeKnight took over as showrunner of *Daredevil*, and the resulting series—visceral, existential noir with a side of Catholic guilt—was a hit. While the Marvel Cinematic Universe routinely had bloodless brawls, in *Daredevil* the violence was intense and had consequences, given that characters used bullets, not repulsor beams. Charlie Cox, who played Matt Murdock and his alter ego Daredevil, often appeared on-screen with bruises and stitches. Vincent D'Onofrio, who gave the series' standout performance as crime lord Wilson Fisk (aka the Kingpin), crushed a lackey's head by repeatedly slamming it in a car door.

Netflix promptly commissioned a second season of *Daredevil*. When the Sinister Six movie was delayed indefinitely, Goddard even returned to the show as a consultant. Meanwhile, Marvel Television revived *Jessica Jones* (aka *A.K.A. Jessica Jones*), the series that Melissa Rosenberg had developed for ABC a couple of years earlier. Krysten Ritter starred as Jessica Jones, the superpowered private investigator with a drinking problem. In a harrowing but thoughtful plotline, the show explored themes of sexual assault and rape.

The Marvel Television shows made winking references to their existence in the same universe as the Avengers. Characters referred, for instance, to Thor as "the man with the hammer" and the Hulk as "the big green guy." Marvel Studios, however, obdurately refused to loan the shows its characters or actors. (And the Marvel movies continued the tradition of ignoring all developments in TV shows. The Defenders weren't invited to the party in 2019, when every other superhero on Earth showed up to defeat Thanos in *Avengers: End-game*.) The heads of the two rival divisions were careful not to say anything publicly that would draw attention to the rift. "We don't want to ever do something in our show which contradicts what's happening in the movies," Loeb stated. "The movies are the lead dog. They're setting the timeline for the MCU and what's going on. Our job is to navigate within that world."

"The future's a long time," Feige said, truthfully but vaguely. "There are a lot of TV shows being made, and hopefully we'll continue to make a lot of movies. At some point, there's going to be a crossover. Crossover, repetition, or something."

While the lack of cooperation was a significant drawback for Marvel Television, the TV shows had advantages that came with smaller-scale projects. Because Netflix didn't release viewership data, a Marvel show was considered a success if people believed that it was doing roughly as well as *House of Cards* or *Orange Is the New Black*, or at least creating a similar amount of buzz. The shows weren't expected to move toys: when *Jessica Jones* was released in 2015, it became the first Marvel project centered on a woman (unless one counted Fox's ill-fated *Elektra* movie), and the following year, *Luke Cage*, with Mike Colter in the title role, was the first Marvel project centered on a Black character. Feige had fought for years to make movies starring women and nonwhite characters, and had been constantly stymied by Perlmutter and the Creative Committee; now Loeb's TV shows made it on the air with no resistance from Marvel's New York offices.

Of all the comic-book heroes to flourish in the Black Lives Matter era, perhaps none was better suited to the moment than Luke Cage, a man who got his powers after being falsely imprisoned and subjected to horrible experiments. Luke Cage made his Marvel Comics debut in 1972; in the twenty-first century, after police officers had killed Eric Garner, Michael Brown, Tamir Rice, and many other Black people, the notion of an invulnerable Black man resonated widely. As *Luke Cage* showrunner Cheo Hodari Coker put it to riotous applause at the 2016 San Diego Comic-Con, "The world is ready for a bulletproof Black man."

"I could not have predicted that," Coker said of how his comment became widely distributed via GIFs and memes. "As people are talking about the relevance of the show compared to Black Lives Matter, my feeling is that all Black art that is consciously Black is ultimately about humanizing the Black experience and saying that our lives matter. It goes beyond a hashtag."

Edward Ricourt's version of Luke Cage never made it out of the Writers Program. The writer was, however, brought on to *Jessica Jones*, the series that introduced Cage, to advise on the character while the Coker series was being developed. The first seasons of both *Jones* and *Cage* were well-liked by audiences and critics alike.

The Defenders Initiative crashed, however, when it introduced its fourth hero, the immortal Iron Fist, a white man swaddled in old-fashioned Asian mysticism (the hero Danny Rand got his kung fu powers from the magical city of K'un-Lun). "It seemed like these were not, like, the greatest superpowers," conceded showrunner Scott Buck. "All he can do is punch really hard."

Although some fans hoped the series would reinvent the protagonist by making him Asian, Marvel Television cast the white English actor Finn Jones (*Game of Thrones*), along with Jessica Henwick, an English actress of Chinese Singaporean descent (also best known for *Game of Thrones*). Jones said that before the show started filming, he went through three weeks of intense weight training and martial arts instruction, but that once shooting started, he wasn't given enough time to prepare for action sequences properly. "I was learning the fight scenes fifteen minutes before we actually shot them because the schedule was so tight," Jones said. "The stunt director would talk me through the choreography and I'd just jump straight into it."

In a 2021 interview that stunt coordinator, Brett Chan (*Warrior, Marco Polo*), recoiled when the subject of *Iron Fist* was raised. He said, "You know, [we] spent twenty-one- to twenty-two-hour days trying to make it work and having directors say, 'Ah, no,' or having Marvel say, 'Ah, no. Everyone is fighting and the actor doesn't want to train.' That's probably why the best sequences were with Jessica Henwick, because she trained four hours a day—and she had zero martial arts experience."

Iron Fist was not well-received, with its action seen as mediocre and its racial optics woefully behind the times. "One of the most troubling things about *Iron Fist* is that Danny Rand is the classic white savior," NPR culture critic Eric Deggans observed. "These are white characters, usually male, often misfits who find their true calling by coming to an environment filled with people of color and leading them. In *Iron Fist*, Rand trained in a hidden city with Buddhist monks and becomes their greatest warrior. While he saves the day with fighting styles birthed in Asian culture, Asian actors play as mentors, a love interest, sidekicks and villains."

Loeb didn't help matters by beginning a 2018 Comic-Con presentation dressed in a karate robe and headband, saying that he had been taught the secrets of the Iron Fist from Mr. Miyagi (the mentor character in *The Karate Kid*). The bit was clearly an attempt at a joke, with actress Jessica Henwick playing along, but went over like a lead balloon. (Loeb declined to answer questions about his tenure at Marvel Television for this book.)

The Defenders, filmed immediately after *Iron Fist*, brought all the Netflix Marvel characters together to fight for the fate of the Manhattan neighborhood of Hell's Kitchen. In an unexpected coup, Marvel Television convinced Sigourney Weaver to play the villain Alexandra. Marco Ramirez, who shared showrunning duties with Douglas Petrie, said, "It was crazy to talk about a character for four months as 'She's a Sigourney Weaver type' and then have Jeph Loeb of Marvel TV be like, 'Oh, she's on the phone.'"

Jessica Jones, *Luke Cage*, and *Iron Fist* all made it to second seasons, while *Daredevil* got a third. Even the Punisher, the vigilante introduced as a supporting character in *Daredevil*, was made into a two-season Netflix series. But after *The Defenders* didn't perform well, the Netflix experiment was effectively over. Streaming services like Netflix run on hype, always searching for shows that would entice new subscribers. With *The Defenders*, however, the buzz was terrible.

✱

NOT EVERY wayward character had returned to Marvel. Fox had green-lit Josh Trank's *Fantastic Four* movie, but then took the troubled project away from the director, shooting new sequences and reediting the film, resulting in an utter mess. (The patchwork movie was released in 2015, around the same time Marvel started airing its Netflix shows.) The studio did better with the *X-Men* franchise, however, rolling out spinoffs and prequels and crossovers, including hits such as *X-Men: Days of Future Past* and *Deadpool*.

Marvel Entertainment (meaning Perlmutter and Fine) deeply resented that Fox retained the rights to those properties. *Fantastic Four*, the book that launched Marvel Comics, had been the company's flagship title since 1962—but in 2014, it ceased publication rather than give free publicity to a Fox movie. Similarly, although *X-Men* comics had long been among Marvel's most popular books, the company suddenly did everything it could to deemphasize its mutant characters and de facto replace them with the similarly enhanced Inhumans. That royal family of a superpowered race living outside of human society had been supporting characters in Marvel comics since 1965, but a 2013 plotline increased their prominence by turning unsuspecting human beings into Inhumans (with the "Terrigen Mists").

"That has everything to do with the fact that the film rights are controlled by a rival corporation," longtime *X-Men* writer Chris Claremont said at New York Comic Con in 2016. "The corporate publishing attitude is 'Why would we go out of our way to promote a title that will benefit a rival corporation's films when we could take that same energy and enthusiasm and focus and do it for our own properties?' Hence the rise of the Inhumans as the new equivalent of the mutants. I could wish for something else, but it ain't my five billion dollars."

Marvel Studios had been developing an Inhumans movie for years, but Feige was never satisfied with the script and wasn't eager to do battle with Fox on Perlmutter's behalf. (One proxy fight, against Marvel Television as the cat's-paw of the Creative Committee, was enough for him.) As soon as Feige pulled the Inhumans movie from the release schedule (in April 2016), Marvel Entertainment ordered Loeb to fast-track Inhumans content on TV. Just two months later, the Inhumans appeared on *Agents of S.H.I.E.L.D.*

Marvel Television immediately began work on an Inhumans television series, and by November 2016, ABC had committed to airing an eight-episode season with IMAX as a production partner. That meant that the first two episodes of *Inhumans* were filmed in the IMAX format and aired on IMAX screens in September 2017. The embarrassing reviews were matched by the dismal box office, and theater owners pulled the *Inhumans* episodes in favor of the IMAX version of *It* as quickly as possible.

The show didn't do any better on the small screen. Because of budgetary constraints, many of the Inhumans were swiftly depowered. Medusa, the Inhuman queen, had her prehensile red hair—

expensive to render in CGI—shaved off her head. The teleporting dog Lockjaw had to be grievously wounded so most of the action could stay in a single location (the show filmed on the Hawaiian island of Oahu). The series was quickly cancelled. One of the stars quipped, "At least I got a trip to Hawaii out of it."

How determined was Marvel Studios to minimize any connection with Marvel Television? When it developed a movie starring another obscure superteam, the Eternals, the creators were instructed that none of it could take place in Hawaii. The studio didn't want any risk that audiences might be reminded of the Inhumans.

In 2017, Anthony Mackie, who played the Falcon in Marvel movies and would, four years later, go on to star in one of Marvel Studios' first TV shows, was asked about the possibility of greater integration between the movie and TV divisions of Marvel. After all, seven years after the creation of Marvel Television, there hadn't been much in the way of visible corporate synergy beyond a couple of Samuel L. Jackson cameos on *Agents of S.H.I.E.L.D.* Mackie said bluntly that fans shouldn't expect those crossovers anytime soon. "Different universes, different worlds, different companies, different designs. Kevin Feige is very specific about how he wants the Marvel Universe to be seen in the film world. It wouldn't work. It wouldn't work at all."

CHAPTER SEVENTEEN

On Your Left

★

Air conditioning is
fully operational.

Captain America: The Winter Soldier

"**W**E TRY TO BE HONEST IN EACH SITUATION," SAID screenwriter Stephen McFeely, speaking of himself and his writing partner Christopher Markus. He meant that they strived to mix light with dark, in their work and in their lives. "Even if I'm at my grandfather's bedside and he's dying of cancer, I will make a joke in the hallway," he said. "That's the only way I'm going to get to the vending machine."

That approach served them well on the *Captain America* franchise, where heroism always had an undercurrent of tragedy: Steve Rogers could save the world again and again, but almost everyone he knew and loved had died many years before. After McFeely and Markus wrote the screenplay for the 2011 movie *Captain America: The First Avenger*, Marvel Studios hired the partners for the sequel, even before the release of the first movie.

The sequel didn't have to directly follow the events of *The Avengers*, which was in production as they went to work, but it needed to be set in the twenty-first century, not the 1940s. (Joss Whedon's

Avengers screenplay had some good comedic beats playing off Cap's unfamiliarity with the modern world, as when the unfrozen man proudly notes, "I understood that reference.") And the studio wanted to bring back Sebastian Stan as Bucky Barnes. More precisely, it wanted Bucky's villainous incarnation as the Winter Soldier, the brainwashed assassin kept in deep freeze by the Soviets for decades.

Markus and McFeely reread the comic books by writer Ed Brubaker and artist Steve Epting that launched the Winter Soldier, and then pitched multiple ideas to Kevin Feige. He told them to focus on their idea for a movie in the mode of a political thriller, saturated with conspiracy and corruption. In some ways, the MCU had forged its own genre: modern superhero stories that took the characters seriously but had a light touch, letting audiences revel both in heroism and absurdity. But the MCU had a voracious appetite: it swallowed other genres whole. *Thor* had veered toward Shakespearean summer stock, while *Iron Man 3* borrowed the tropes of buddy-cop movies. Feige, wanting to upend the audience's expectations, now planned to go further.

Jon Favreau compared the superhero movie's market dominance to Westerns in the mid-twentieth century: "There's a certain comfort level in very challenging times for theatrical distribution, [knowing] that people will show up for a good superhero film." That gave directors the potential to stretch the boundaries of the genre, he said: "What John Ford was doing with Westerns shifted dramatically from the early days, through *Stagecoach*, through *The Searchers* and *Cheyenne Autumn*."

For the eighth MCU movie, Markus and McFeely would draw on classics of paranoia, including *The Parallax View*, *Marathon Man*, and *Three Days of the Condor*. They nicknamed their script "*Three Days of Captain America*."

The writers thought Captain America should spend the movie on the run, being chased by mysterious forces until he learned that the world wasn't what he believed it to be. An actual 1970s thriller would have ended on an ambiguous note, suggesting that the world was irredeemably corrupt and that the protagonist's greater knowledge of it didn't change anything. In the MCU, Captain America needed to take the fight to the grand conspiracy and win. McFeely and Markus spent most of the spring and summer of 2011 struggling with how to achieve that, until they had a crucial meeting with Feige, who told them, "I think we're ready to take down S.H.I.E.L.D."

That unlocked the entire movie, McFeely said, "because, honestly, at that point we were struggling to figure out what the big third act was."

They were given a free hand to include any Marvel characters who weren't going to star in their own Phase Two movies after *The Avengers*, and once they were certain their story was about S.H.I.E.L.D. being riddled with traitors, they drafted Nick Fury, Black Widow, and Hawkeye, the three biggest names with S.H.I.E.L.D. affiliations. Along the way, Hawkeye's scenes were reassigned to Black Widow, because Jeremy Renner was filming *American Hustle* and *Kill the Messenger*, making it complicated to schedule the actor. Dropping Hawkeye came with the advantage of sharpening the contrast between Captain America and Black Widow, pitting his old-fashioned ethics against her more nebulous, more modern morality.

After running the Marvel Writers Program, Nate Moore had risen through the ranks of Marvel's producers, and attended the 2012 creative retreat after the release of *The Avengers* alongside Feige, Louis D'Esposito, Jeremy Latcham, Stephen Broussard, and Craig Kyle. There, he advocated for the Guardians of the Galaxy space opera that Nicole Perlman had been developing, but lost out on producing it to Latcham, who had seniority. Instead, Moore was assigned to the next Captain America movie. When he discussed the movie's lineup of characters with Markus and McFeely, he advocated for the man who had been one of his favorite Black superheroes growing up, a long-term partner to Captain America in the comic books: the Falcon.

"We have to introduce the Falcon, because as a kid, that was a character I remember loving," he told them.

They were skeptical, believing that the winged character looked ridiculous. "The guy with the wings?" they asked Moore. "Do people like the Falcon?"

He replied emphatically: "*People love the Falcon.*"

Director Ryan Coogler, who would work closely with Moore on both *Black Panther* and its sequel, said, "He's a comic book fan. He's also a Black man, and I think he felt a responsibility once he got to Marvel to shepherd these specific characters—Falcon and Panther—into the MCU."

Moore prevailed. Sam Wilson (also known as the Falcon), introduced in 1969, was Marvel Comics' first African American superhero—T'Challa, the Black Panther, is not American—and one of only a handful of early Black comic-book heroes to not have "Black" in his superhero name. Sam Wilson shared top billing with Steve Rogers between 1971 and 1978, a period when, for eighty-eight issues, the comic was called *Captain America and the Falcon.*

Marvel pursued Anthony Mackie (*Half Nelson, The Hurt Locker*) for the role; Mackie was eager, having become an actor because he wanted to be both a cowboy and a superhero. He knew just how much cultural weight came with the character. "When I heard I got the role I broke down in tears," he said. "I realized two years from that date, some little brown boy was going to be at my door in a Falcon costume on Halloween. When I was a kid, I didn't have that."

Although Feige was pleased with how *Captain America: The First Avenger* had turned out, he wanted a director for the sequel who would be more available to Marvel Studios producers than Joe "Secret Room" Johnston had been. And for Phase Two of the MCU, he was searching for directors who were comfortable with the emergent Marvel method, which entailed close collaboration with Marvel's in-house visual departments. Feige, described as a "vibe guy," liked to have open-ended meetings with directors to feel them out before discussing any particular project. He narrowed his list down to three candidates for the Captain America sequel: George Nolfi, the writer-director of *The Adjustment Bureau*; F. Gary Gray, a music-video director who had made the transition to features such as *Fri-*

day, *The Negotiator* and *The Italian Job*; and the brothers Joe and Anthony Russo.

✳

"**WE GREW UP IN** a big Italian family," Anthony Russo said. "We like the notion of community, sitting around a campfire and telling a story." They grew up in Cleveland, Ohio; Anthony was born in 1970, Joe in 1971. From an early age, they loved movies (everything from the Bowery Boys to François Truffaut) and dreamed of making their own; as they got older they discovered that working together brought that impossible task within their reach. While they were graduate students at Case Western Reserve University, the Russos made an independent comedy, *Pieces*, that was accepted in the 1997 Slamdance Festival.

Though never released, *Pieces* won the attention of director Steven Soderbergh, who produced (with actor George Clooney) their next movie, the 2002 heist film *Welcome to Collinwood*. "We were really up-our-own-ass artistic filmmakers when we got into the business," Anthony Russo said with a laugh. "Only Steven Soderbergh would have responded to our first film—thank God he did. Frankly, he taught us how to make commercial movies."

First, however, they made sitcoms. They won an Emmy for directing the 2003 pilot of *Arrested Development*, the groundbreaking single-camera sitcom about the self-centered Bluth family, and then served as the show's executive producers while directing thirteen more episodes of the series. They also directed the 2009 pilot of *Community*, the genre-hopping single-camera sitcom about a study group at a community college, and again served as executive producers while directing thirty-four more episodes of the series. (The Directors Guild of America requires a special waiver for two people to be listed as the director of a TV episode; although the Russos worked in close collaboration, all the episodes of these shows they directed, except for the pilots, were credited to one brother or the other.) Both programs had unusually large casts, and the brothers demonstrated a skill for making sure none of the actors were neglected.

Anthony Russo laid out the brothers' shared aesthetic: "We understand ensemble storytelling, we understand multiple brands, we're ambitious, we like the cutting edge, we're also—this is a dirty term, so I don't use it anymore—populists." Anthony was more inclined to speak off the cuff, while Joe was somewhat more measured, but when they worked together on a set, they achieved a total mindmeld. It didn't matter which of them gave instructions to the cast or crew because, without speaking with each other, they already agreed on what was needed.

The Russos encouraged Dan Harmon, the creator of *Community*, to use his sitcom as a vehicle for parodies of other film and TV genres, and some of the show's finest episodes were pitch-perfect takes on historic documentaries and claymation holiday specials. The first splashy one: a 2010 action-movie parody called "Modern Warfare," set during a college paintball competition. That episode was directed by Justin Lin (already well-known for his work on the *Fast and the Furious* franchise), but the Russos directed two follow-up episodes the following year: the Western spoof "A Fistful of Paintballs" and the action-franchise pastiche "For a Few Paintballs More." Those episodes were funny, but also demonstrated a deep understanding of the films they were satirizing. Kevin Feige, an avid watcher of comedy TV, loved the paintball episodes and set up a meeting with the Russos. ("Kevin is a big comedy lover—he likes a lot of really interesting comedy and alternative comedy," said Paul Rudd, who was impressed by Feige's familiarity with the niche Neil Hamburger character created by comic Gregg Turkington.)

Feige and the brothers got along immediately, sharing an obsessive nature that was notable even in the movie business, which attracts more than its fair share of intense personalities. After the paintball episodes, the brothers wanted to make an actual action movie. Another studio head might have scoffed, but Feige agreed that they were ready. F. Gary Gray made Feige's decision easy by committing to another project (the N.W.A biopic *Straight Outta Compton*), and in June 2012, Marvel announced that the Russo brothers would be the directors of *Captain America: The Winter Soldier*. Feige told a crowd at the San Diego Comic-Con that if they didn't know them already, they would very soon.

During his time as showrunner of *Community*, Harmon was embroiled in constant conflict with NBC, and the network fired him from his own show for a season before fans and cast members demanded his return. (After *Community*, he went on to create the animated show *Rick and Morty* for Adult Swim.) He recognized that the Russos had the diplomatic acumen he lacked, letting them fit in at the highly collaborative Marvel Studios. "You've got to be a bit of a politician as well as a creative in order to navigate these waters. Or a healthy way of looking at it is you have to not be a megalomaniac," Harmon said. "Orson Welles is not going to work well at Marvel," he observed. But the Russo brothers? "They were collaborators always, first and foremost."

The open secret of Marvel Studios was that Kevin Feige was a shadow director for all its movies. His hands-on approach to shaping and refining every installment of the MCU extended well beyond that of a typical studio executive—and even exceeded the creative involvement of most producers. The system worked well enough as long as the directors he hired played along and there weren't too many projects demanding his attention.

As soon as they took the job, the Russos met with Ed Brubaker to discuss the secrets of the Winter Soldier. Joe Russo said that when he read comics as a kid, he had always found Captain America to be too much of a Boy Scout and had imagined the actor Steve McQueen as the character, because that gave him more of an edge. "But what Brubaker did was so brilliant," he raved. "He completely deconstructed the mythology, and made him very relevant. And putting it in an espionage genre, he married it to a genre that could support the character and make the character more interesting. We were very fortunate to have that source material."

The brothers then jumped into the development process, which was already in progress with Markus and McFeely, Marvel's top creative producers (Feige, D'Esposito, Moore, and Victoria Alonso), and Marvel's visual artists. Early drafts of the screenplay opened with a World War II flashback, but that was soon jettisoned in favor of a modern assault on a hijacked military boat: Captain America would jump out of a plane without a parachute and fight a villain known in the comic books as Batroc the Leaper. Batroc had long been an absurd French blowhard, but here he was remade from a Gallic punching bag into a credible threat.

For every action sequence, the brothers brought in a portfolio of visual references for their collaborators to study. For the boat sequence, the Russos collected the most frenetic action clips they could find, from Jason Bourne fight scenes to MMA bouts. Anthony Russo was fascinated by how fast MMA fighters punched, and while watching MMA fights, the Russos spotted Georges St-Pierre, a Quebecois UFC champion, and cast him as Batroc.

It had long been a truism in the Marvel Comics office that every new writer wanted to script an issue in which a S.H.I.E.L.D. Helicarrier crashed. There was something irresistible about giant weapons of war plummeting out of the sky. Now the Russos would make that happen on screen. The Helicarriers would be new vessels, designed by Tony Stark, manufactured by S.H.I.E.L.D., and hijacked by the quasi-Nazis of HYDRA, capable of making a targeted lethal strike anywhere on the planet.

The inspiration for those Helicarriers came during a visit to the *Sea Launch Commander*, a ship docked in Long Beach, California, which the Russos scouted as a location for the opening Batroc sequence. When they learned that the ship was so large because it was a launching pad for sending satellites into space, the brothers decided to make government surveillance and drone strikes central to the movie's plot. Those concerns would become front-page news in 2013, later in the movie's production, when the whistleblower Edward Snowden leaked thousands of classified documents about National Security Administration (NSA) surveillance programs and reality caught up with a movie already in progress.

"It's hard to make a political film that's not topical," Anthony Russo said. "That's what makes a political thriller different from just a thriller. And that's what adds to the characters' paranoia and the audience's experience of that paranoia. But we're also very pop-culture-obsessed and we love topicality, so we kept pushing to [have] scenes that, fortunately or unfortunately, played out when Snowden outed the NSA. That stuff was already in the zeitgeist. We were all reading the articles that were coming out questioning drone strikes, pre-emptive strikes, civil liberties—Obama talking about who they would kill. . . . We wanted to put all of that into the film because it would be a contrast to [Captain America]'s greatest-generation [way of thinking]."

Although the Russos worked closely with the Marvel production machine, in some respects they were at odds with the usual methods of the studio. For example, the brothers insisted on as many phys-ical settings and practical effects as possible, even if scenes would ultimately be augmented digitally. Anthony Mackie praised their approach: "The Russos, what they did that was so great was they wanted to stay with live action, which is a dying art form. If they can build it, they built it. If we could do it, they did it. They wanted to do as little CGI as possible. That's why the movie looks so great." Ironically, the Falcon was the character in the movie whose perfor-mance ended up being the most dependent on CGI, according to Industrial Light and Magic. Whenever the Falcon unfurls his wings in *The Winter Soldier*, the character is actually a digitally rendered double of Mackie.

When *Iron Man 2* was released, Samuel L. Jackson said, "We still haven't moved Nick Fury into the badass zone. He's still just kind of a talker." In *The Winter Soldier*, there was finally good reason to give Fury an action sequence, because the movie was about the battle for the future of S.H.I.E.L.D., and the stakes rise dramatically when S.H.I.E.L.D.'s leader gets physically involved. The movie's creators were operating under the same limitations as Whedon on *The Aveng-ers*, in that Jackson, sixty-five years old on the first day of principal photography, still didn't want to run. In *The Winter Soldier*, at least, he wouldn't have to: he stayed behind the wheel of a high-tech car as assassins pursued him through the streets of Washington, DC.

Markus and McFeely included a car chase in their early scripts, but when the Russos came on board, they greatly expanded it. Their visual portfolio for the epic sequence included classic cinema car chases (*The French Connection*), modern entries (the Jason Bourne series again), and real-life car chases. The Russos told Marvel's concept artists and animatic editors to build out the sequence as a "moment of tension," where the audience would see Nick Fury stuck in an escalating situation for longer than expected.

The other "moment of tension" in the Markus-McFeely script that the Russos wanted to emphasize was the elevator fight when Steve Rogers, escaping S.H.I.E.L.D. headquarters after learning the organization has been corrupted, takes out an entire squad of HYDRA loyalists. For the movie's hand-to-hand combat sequences, the Russos and the Marvel visual staff developed an extensive collection of storyboards and montages, dictating the overall look and key shots, but the actual fight choreography was handled by James Young (also the stunt double for Sebastian Stan).

After studying the Russos' portfolio for each fight, Young choreographed it with his team of stuntmen, shooting the action with a consumer-grade camera or a cellphone. The Russos watched his videos and pointed out attacks they particularly liked or shots they wanted him to modify in the next pass. Eventually, the Russos would approve the choreography; Young and his team would then teach the fight to the actors. In the case of the elevator fight, Evans had to do most of the action himself: given the confined quarters, it was difficult to swap in a stunt double without being obvious about it.

Anthony Russo said that he and his brother loved action set pieces that emphasized the character of Captain America, a human being in a world of superhumans, empowered by morals as much as muscles. "Essentially, he's a man, only more so," he said. "It's not flying across the sky, or transforming into something else. So we sort of came up with an approach of a hard-hitting, hardcore-realism version of what a superhero movie can be on an action level."

As creative assets like storyboards, concept art, and costume design rolled in, the Russos picked their favorite elements and incorporated them into their animatics; then they could see what worked and what didn't, and retool as necessary. Monty Granito, the pre-viz supervisor on *The Winter Soldier*, said the Russos repeatedly asked him to rebuild the animatics for the movie's final action sequence, where Steve Rogers has his final showdown with Bucky Barnes while the Falcon brings down multiple Helicarriers over Washington, DC: "They would take one or two shots, and they would say, 'Great, these are good, [these] one or two shots. Rebuild the entire sequence around these one or two shots.' And then I would build the whole sequence again, and they would say, 'Great, these are great, [these] four shots. Rebuild the entire sequence around these four shots.'" That pre-viz work could save a lot of effort in postproduction—if not for the way Marvel Studios kept revising movies until the last possible moment.

The Russos' experience as executive producers was as crucial as their experience as directors, given that the Marvel method of filmmaking favored strong managers, not auteurs. The brothers followed the advice that Steven Spielberg gave to young directors who approached him for counsel before making a movie. "He'd say, 'Get a personal trainer and get in shape,'" Anthony Russo recalled. "Because it's an endurance test." They kept exercise equipment in the production offices; on the set, they consumed bright-green health drinks.

"Joe and Anthony had the stamina and the demeanor to bob and weave," said Feige.

Principal photography on *Captain America: The Winter Soldier*—given the code name *Freezer Burn* during the shoot—lasted three months in the spring of 2013, with filming in DC, LA, and the Russos' hometown of Cleveland. The cast included Robert Redford as Alexander Pierce, a treacherous senior official at S.H.I.E.L.D. Redford was chosen not only because he was a movie icon but because he was a living link to the political thrillers of the 1970s, having starred in *Three Days of the Condor* and *All the President's Men*.

Samuel L. Jackson had never acted with Redford before, but their characters were supposed to be longtime friends and colleagues. On the morning of their first scene, Jackson sought out the older actor: "We talked about golf. We talked about life. We talked about movies. So by the time we got on set, it did look like we spent some time together, or had some past."

The shoot went smoothly, confirming Feige's belief that the Russos had been ready to trade in paintballs for live ammunition. He remembered, "Joe and Anthony, they were very clear and had very lofty ambitions, saying things like 'We want to do the best car chase in any Marvel movie, and maybe the best car chase of all time.' I said, 'Well, that sounds good. Let's try that.'" Feige smiled. "Damned if they didn't pull it off."

Feige was also pleased by the brothers' eagerness to include connections to the greater Marvel Cinematic Universe, the type of request that had always rankled Jon Favreau. *The Winter Soldier*, for instance, has a mid-movie infodump that would be revisited in a later Russos-directed movie, *Captain America: Civil War*, where it is revealed that Bucky Barnes killed Tony Stark's father. "If you are a comic book geek like me, you get off on that stuff," Joe Russo said. "It's a weird sort of, I don't know, tapestry of writers and directors working together to create this universe."

Captain America: The Winter Soldier was one of the very best MCU movies, a taut action thriller where a man dressed in red, white, and blue has to confront a world colored in shades of gray. The movie grossed $714 million worldwide, almost exactly doubling the box office of *Captain America: The First Avenger*; by this point, Marvel Studios had released so many sequels that exceeded projections, it had rewritten the Hollywood rules of how long-running franchises might be expected to perform. As soon as they finished their work on *The Winter Soldier*, Feige signed up the Russos to direct the third Captain America movie and hired Markus and McFeely to write a script that would conclude the trilogy, wrapping up the story of Steve Rogers and Bucky Barnes.

That was the plan, anyway—until the day when Feige stopped by the office at Marvel Studios shared by Markus and McFeely to say two crucial words: "Civil War."

CHAPTER EIGHTEEN

We Are Groot

We're all standing up now.
Bunch of jackasses, standing in a circle.

Guardians of the Galaxy

YEARS LATER, THE STARS OF THE AVENGERS MOVIES were asked to identify the turning point in the history of Marvel Studios, the moment when the enterprise transformed from Kevin Feige's lucky start-up experiment into an entertainment behemoth that seemed too big to fail. None of them named their own movies, even the ones that broke box-office records. Rather, they pointed to a swashbuckling adventure starring a genetically altered raccoon and a talking tree.

"*Guardians of the Galaxy* opened up another door in the Marvel Universe," Mark Ruffalo said. "It could go into space, it could be funny, it could be colorful, it has a style that's totally disconnected from the rest of the Marvel Universe."

"*Galaxy* in some ways is the best Marvel movie ever," Robert Downey Jr. conceded. "And it's odd for someone with—on occasion—an ego the size of mine to actually say that."

Feige called the movie "the best example of the audience validating even our most esoteric instincts . . . of how far they are willing to go with us. Just the ridiculous pairing of a tree and a raccoon and a guy that doesn't understand metaphors. We just loved the idea of doing that."

"It seems so simple now," said an insider who worked at Marvel during the development and release of *Guardians*. "But don't forget that selling a talking tree and a raccoon was the dumbest thing you'd ever heard. We were terrified. One of the phrases we always used was 'We're terrified we're drinking the Kool-Aid that nobody else is.' We were like, 'This is so good, but are people going to agree with us?'"

Screenwriter Nicole Perlman, who had left the Marvel Writers Program in 2011 after completing her two-year stint, was hired again almost immediately to do some revisions on her *Guardians of the Galaxy* script. She couldn't believe that Marvel was really going to make her bonkers sci-fi movie. In fact, although the studio was enthusiastic about it, Marvel's New York office was much more skeptical, and worried that it starred a group of characters with close to zero name recognition. The viz-dev staffers in Los Angeles, however, were busily creating digital renderings of her team—the puckish protagonist Peter Quill, aka the Star-Lord, the irascible Rocket Raccoon, Gamora the green-skinned assassin, the literal-minded Drax the Destroyer, and the sentient tree called Groot—so she conceded that the studio appeared to be serious.

"For years, I told my parents, 'I'm working on a movie about a raccoon—well, not about a raccoon, but it has a raccoon and a talking tree.' And they were like, 'Oh, you poor thing. We're going to be so supportive when you have your first major flop.'" But when one Marvel executive suggested that Rocket Raccoon could end up as a debacle along the lines of Jar Jar Binks, Feige supported Perlman, insisting, "No, no. Got to keep Rocket in there."

For an early sequence where Quill steals a precious Orb, Feige asked Perlman to invent an alien planet, later called Morag, that hadn't been seen in movies before. She reached back to her childhood, remembering a visit to Disneyland when she couldn't go on the *20,000 Leagues Under the Sea* submarine ride because it had been closed for cleaning. "They had these plywood boards up so that you wouldn't look at it," she said, "but they had a little hole in the plywood, and I put my eye up to it. I saw this land with shipwrecks, but completely devoid of water. It always stuck with me. So when Kevin asked for a science-fiction planet, I was like, 'What about a world that had all of the oceans removed? Maybe it lost its moon and that pulled all the tides away.'"

Perlman assumed she wouldn't be the last writer on the screenplay. "I always knew they were going to bring in a writer-director," she said. "That was always sort of the plan. I'm not primarily a comedy writer, but it needed to be a comedic project. Like, this is a project that has always been irreverent; it's always been tongue-in-cheek."

During Feige's good-vibes speed-dating tour with the membership list of the Directors Guild of America, he had been looking out for people who might have the talent and off-kilter humor to handle a group of outer-space misfits. His short list included Peyton Reed (*Bring It On*), the team of Anna Boden and Ryan Fleck (*Half Nelson*), and James Gunn.

Gunn grew up in and around St. Louis, Missouri, obsessed with low-budget horror movies like *Night of the Living Dead* and *Friday the 13th*, and by the age of twelve, he was making 8-mm movies that featured his four brothers getting devoured by zombies. (Those brothers all ended up in show business; one of them, Sean Gunn, had a recurring role on *Gilmore Girls*.) "We would use tissue paper and Karo syrup and red food-coloring dye—that's how you made gore," Gunn said.

Over the years, he was lead singer for a punk-rock band, a hospital orderly, and a published novelist (*The Toy Collector*). He got an MFA in fiction from Columbia University, but said that he learned more about storytelling by moving to Hollywood in 1998 to work for the low-budget horror studio Troma Entertainment (*The Toxic Avenger*) for $400 a week.

At Troma, Gunn enthusiastically threw himself into every aspect of the business, from scouting locations to designing poster art. He wrote the Shakespearean black comedy *Tromeo and Juliet* and the superhero satire *The Specials* before booking his first two major-studio jobs: the screenplays for the 2002 live-action *Scooby-Doo* and the 2004 reboot of *Dawn of the Dead*. He also costarred in the 2004 mockumentary *Lollilove* with his then-wife Jenna Fischer (not yet famous as Pam on *The Office*); the couple divorced in 2008 but remained friendly. "We weren't the best at being married, but we're the very best at being divorced," Gunn said.

Gunn directed his own screenplays for *Slither* (2006) and *Super* (2010). The first was a horror movie about alien parasites, while the second was about a short-order cook who becomes a vigilante, but both were full of blood and black comedy. Gunn had a punk-rock splatter-horror attitude: he knew how to entertain you, but took just as much pleasure in grossing you out.

None of this would seem to make Gunn a natural match for the Marvel Cinematic Universe, but he nevertheless met with Feige soon after the release of *Iron Man*. "I knew he liked what I had done, and he knew I was a Marvel fan," Gunn remembered. "I loved loved loved *Iron Man*. I think it changed the genre. But I didn't have any idea it would grow into what it became."

In 2011, Feige called in Gunn for another meeting and showed him concept art for *Guardians of the Galaxy*, including a shot of Rocket Raccoon, a three-foot-tall raccoon in a jumpsuit. Gunn wasn't interested at first, but after the meeting was over, he kept thinking about the project and realized that it would allow him a great deal of freedom. The history of Marvel comics offered an analogy. Gunn remembered that when he was a kid, "there were the basic Marvel comic books that were more generic and worked in the everyday way. And then every once in a while, someone like Frank Miller would come around—who started drawing *Daredevil*—and it was very visionary and very much its own thing. And yes, it was connected to the Marvel Universe, but it was also a work of art unto itself. Some of the movies are a bit more basic and some of them, they want to take a bigger risk with. I wanted to make it both a Marvel movie and a James Gunn film. And I didn't want to make it less than 100 percent either of those things."

Now that he wanted the job, Gunn wasn't sure how to get it.

But he had Joss Whedon's email address. (They knew each other socially; Whedon had cast Sean Gunn in an episode of his TV series *Angel* and even named one of the principal characters on that show, Charles Gunn, after the Gunn brothers.) "I wrote him an email and said, 'Hey, I'm trying to get this job. Can you help me?'"

Whedon emailed back: "You're fucking late. I already talked to all of those guys about you."

*

WITH SOME HELP from Whedon, who touted *The Specials* as one of the best superhero movies ever made, Gunn got the *Guardians* job in September 2012. He was paired with producer Jeremy Latcham and given the latest version of the script. As Perlman had expected, she wasn't the last writer on the movie; over the summer, Chris McCoy had punched up her draft. Then the director immediately started rewriting it to reflect his own sensibility. "I don't think there's a huge difference between writing and directing a film—not for me," he said. "When you're directing, it's just putting the visual aspect to it." He allowed that Perlman "definitely got the ball rolling," but didn't give her much credit beyond that. "The original concept was there, that was sort of like what's in the movie, and then there's the story and the characters—those were pretty much recreated by me."

Once again, a Marvel movie ended up in a WGA arbitration. The official ruling was that both Gunn and Perlman had contributed significantly and that they would share the screenplay credit equally. Gunn wasn't pleased: "In Nicole's script everything is pretty different . . . the story is different . . . the character arcs are different. It's not about the same stuff. But that's how the WGA works. They like first writers an awful lot."

Perlman declined to challenge Gunn publicly, saying, "I credit everybody on that movie, including James, for making it so beautiful." However, her friend Zack Stentz (cowriter of the *Thor* screenplay) objected on her behalf: "Nicole had to knife-fight for her credit on *Guardians of the Galaxy*. But she is probably the preeminent female action tentpole writer now because she was the first woman to have her name on not just a Marvel movie, but on a Marvel movie that people really love. She threw a party when the movie came out literally called the 'Fuck James Gunn' party because she had won that very bruising credit arbitration. The thing that I'm still angry about, and I say this as a fan of James Gunn as a director, was that he very clearly was selectively leaking stuff to his friends and the fanboy media circles to undermine her credit. When Matthew Vaughn decided to have a temper tantrum over the fact that we got screen credit [on *X-Men: First Class*], at least he did it under his own name."

One thing everyone agreed on was that while Perlman had originated the story device of Peter Quill's Walkman, James Gunn placed it in the center of the movie: a physical symbol of the character's connection to his dead mother, which crucially also served as the delivery system for a soundtrack of 1970s pop and rock music, including decades-old hits such as 10cc's "I'm Not in Love" and Blue Swede's "Hooked on a Feeling."

"I started the process by reading the *Billboard* charts for all of the top hits of the '70s," Gunn explained. "I downloaded a few hundred songs, and from that made an iTunes playlist of about 120 songs which fit the movie tonally. I would listen to the playlist on my speakers around the house—sometimes I would be inspired to create a scene around a song, and other times I had a scene that needed music and I would listen through the playlist, visualizing various songs." Gunn filled his version of the screenplay with very specific needle drops.

Marvel Studios loved the movie's mix tape, but the Creative Committee did not, and gave notes demanding the music's removal. Feige and Latcham had to run interference, insisting that the music was part of the charm of Gunn's vision. Whedon also gave the filmmakers feedback, which they paid more attention to. The early drafts of the screenplay followed the established mythology of Peter Quill in the comics: his father was revealed to be J'Son, emperor of the planet Spartax, making Quill intergalactic royalty. Whedon strongly objected, insisting that for audiences to care about him, Peter Quill needed to be an average person, not a space prince. "Joss sent me a memo in all caps, 'IN NO UNCERTAIN TERMS: YOU DO NOT HAVE A MOVIE,'" Latcham said.

Whedon also felt that the script's dialogue had a rhythm and humor too similar to other MCU projects. "Joss was happy, but he wasn't as happy as everybody else," Gunn recalled. "I was like, 'Whoa, man!' And he's like, 'Well, I really loved this and this is great, and the story's been cracked. But I just really want there to be more James Gunn in the script. There are things that are too conventional, and I want more James Gunn in it.' And I was like, 'Alright, your funeral.'" The jokes became edgier, pushing the boundaries of what one might expect from a Marvel movie in the Disney era.

Gunn had vague ideas of which performers he wanted for the movie, but casting director Sarah Halley Finn provided him with candidates whom he might not have considered, including Chris Pratt for Star-Lord. The role of Drax required a physically imposing actor, such as Jason Momoa (later Aquaman, then best known as Khal Drogo on *Game of Thrones*). But when Momoa passed on the movie, feeling that he had played versions of the character before, Finn turned to the former wrestling star Dave Bautista, who was trying to break into acting.

Bautista read some sample scenes but was utterly bewildered by the metaphor-impervious character. "I didn't get Drax at all," he said. So Bautista called his acting coach, who luckily was a huge comic-book fan and helped him find the dry humor of the character. Bautista had to fly to London to audition for Gunn—preproduction had already started there—but got the role. (*Guardians of the Galaxy* was based in London because *Thor: The Dark World* had filmed there; when the *Thor* shoot was over, Marvel Studios rolled many of the crew members directly onto the next film on its production calendar.)

Gunn had decided that Rocket Raccoon and Groot would be CGI characters, performed on set by stand-ins. Of the five core Guardians, that left only Gamora to cast. Marvel offered the role to Amanda Seyfried (*Mamma Mia!*), who passed: "I didn't want to be part of the first Marvel movie that bombed. I said, 'Who wants to see a movie about a talking tree and a raccoon?'" She added, "The script was great. It was all based in not wanting to be 'that guy.' . . . Because if you are the star of a giant movie like that, and it bombs, Hollywood does not forgive you. I've seen that happen to people and it was a giant, giant fear and I thought, is it worth it?"

Zoe Saldaña also declined the role; having starred in the 2009 *Star Trek* movie and James Cameron's *Avatar*, she didn't want to get pigeonholed as a sci-fi heroine. Gunn, however, prevailed on her to read the script. "I was not that excited about the script from Gamora's standpoint," Saldaña said. "You want me in every scene, but I don't speak in any of them. So I'm just going to go there for six months, go through five hours of make up every day, six days a week, to just be like a fly on the wall in every scene?" When Gunn promised that he would expand the role, she joined the cast.

Karen Gillan, known to *Doctor Who* fans as the companion Amy Pond, was cast as Gamora's sister Nebula, both of them adopted by the supervillain Thanos. Before being offered the role, Gillan had to agree to shave her head. But she didn't throw away her long red hair; rather, it was made into a wig by "the people who are making the monsters for *Star Wars*," Gillan said. Using it, she was able to wear her own hair while filming her short-lived ABC sitcom *Selfie*.

Although Gunn insisted on practical sets whenever possible, the *Guardians* shoot had a lot of blanks that would later be filled in with CGI. "It's a complete kind of act of imagination," said Lee Pace, who played the principal villain, Ronan the Accuser. "But in the hands of James Gunn, so it's very much a creation of his and I found myself being, like, 'Alright, let's do it. You tell me what you're into here.'"

Somehow, on a multimillion-dollar production rife with green-screen technology, Gunn managed to recreate the freewheeling vibe of his low-tech adolescent zombie movies. He hired his own brother, Sean, to stand in for Rocket Raccoon. The actor donned a motion-capture suit and spent much of the shoot crawling around on his knees so that other actors could have a good eyeline. (Sean got to stand up, however, in the supporting role of the querulous space pirate Kraglin Obfonteri, one of the Ravagers.) Groot was played by the London-based Polish actor Krystian Godlewski, who wore a blue motion-capture suit with a bust of the character's head on top of his own skull. Chris Pratt, who had worked on the improvisation-friendly set of *Parks and Recreation*, was initially concerned about ad-libbing on *Guardians*, knowing just how expensive every minute of production time was on a major motion picture, but he soon found that his director wanted the actors to be as playful and collaborative as possible.

James Gunn established an unusual reward system for people working on the film: "I would keep a pile of little Play-Doh containers on set and if someone did an especially amazing job that day—whether it was an actor, a grip, a stunt man, or a PA [production assistant]—they'd get a canister of Play-Doh. I probably only gave about 40 containers out over the entire shoot—on an 85-day schedule with a crew of a couple hundred, that isn't much." Each one of Gunn's gifts evoked the spirit of play he was trying to foster. "Opening a new container and smelling it puts me in a creative, child-like place," the director said. "And who doesn't love playing with Play-Doh?"

Despite her conflict with Gunn, Nicole Perlman visited the London sets and had the surreal experience of stepping into real-life versions of her dreams. She said, "There were so many things that just were so much more beautiful than I had even pictured when I wrote them."

For one of the final shots of *Guardians of the Galaxy*, featuring Baby Groot dancing in a flowerpot, Gunn cast himself. "Baby Groot dancing is 100 percent me," he admitted. "I was too embarrassed for anyone to be there, so I made everyone leave the room and I set up a camera and I videotaped myself dancing. Then I sent the video to the animators and had them animate over that. I begged them not to leak the video!" Gunn thought that he had rendered himself unidentifiable, but when his friends saw the finished movie, they recognized his dance moves.

After principal photography, Gunn cast Bradley Cooper (recently Oscar-nominated for *The Silver Linings Playbook*) to perform Rocket's voice. The animators drew on three different sources for Rocket's movements: Sean Gunn on the set; Cooper, filmed while he recorded his voice sessions; and an actual raccoon named Oreo.

For the voice of Groot, Marvel approached Vin Diesel of *The Fast and the Furious* franchise, since both Gunn and Feige were fans of his basso profundo work as the title character in the animated film *The Iron Giant*. Diesel was hesitant about playing a character whose dialogue largely consisted of three words (*I, am,* and *Groot*), but when he showed his children a picture of the Guardians of the Galaxy and asked them which part they thought Marvel wanted him to play, they pointed at Groot. Diesel signed up to voice the tree.

When Marvel showed a rough cut of *Guardians* to preview audiences, it didn't test well, in part because the CGI for Rocket and Groot wasn't finished. But early audiences enjoyed two essential elements—the soundtrack and Chris Pratt's performance—so Marvel didn't feel the movie needed major surgery. The biggest change during additional photography was the decision to have Thanos appear. He had previously been lurking in the narrative shadows, with Ronan seeking one of the Infinity Stones on his behalf, which made Ronan come off as the middle manager for a holy war.

Whedon had been working to establish Thanos as the ultimate threat for the Avengers; with his approval, the Mad Titan would finally get some real screen time. "We wanted to focus on the creation of the Guardians team itself," Feige said, "so we didn't want to spend too much time with Thanos, but [we] wanted to showcase that there's a guy behind the guy behind the guy." One priority for the studio head: getting "one of my favorite shots in the whole movie, him leaning back on his throne and smirking, which he does on every cover of every Thanos comic book, which is cool."

Looking for an actor with enough gravitas to play the MCU's arch-villain, Finn reached out to Josh Brolin, who had recently been nominated for a Best Supporting Actor Oscar for his work in *Milk*. Brolin had never performed a motion-capture character, so he turned to his friend Mark Ruffalo for advice, asking "What do you think, man? Is this cool? Is this fun?"

Ruffalo told him, "Look, you're gonna feel more ridiculous than you've ever felt. You have a onesie on, you have dots on your face, you have a helmet with a headcam, it's hard not to cross your eyes when you're acting." The actor's bottom line, however: "When you see it eventually, your mind will be blown."

Brolin signed up. He filmed his scenes, his face shining with a veneer of iridescent paint, surrounded by an array of cameras. Brolin couldn't even see Gunn giving him direction; the actor found the process so distracting and confounding, he worried he would forget his lines and so kept his script between his knees while he was seated.

In July 2014, Brolin was announced as Thanos at San Diego Comic-Con, and strolled onstage wielding a foam Infinity Gauntlet. Just one week later, *Guardians of the Galaxy* was released. It was the tenth MCU movie. "I will never forget it," said Louis D'Esposito. "I had friends tell me, 'Lou, if this film isn't a success, you've had a great run.' No one thought *Guardians* would work. So when it did, it felt even more successful."

It starred characters unfamiliar even to most Marvel comic-book fans, but *Guardians* had an opening weekend of $94 million, ending up with $773.3 million in worldwide box office. Despite the skepticism of the Creative Committee about Gunn's music choices, the soundtrack—*Guardians of the Galaxy: Awesome Mix Vol. 1*—went platinum, selling 1.75 million copies (the second-best-selling movie soundtrack of 2014, behind only *Frozen*).

As Robert Downey Jr. observed, "The *Iron Man*s and the *Thor*s and the *Captain America*s and the *Avengers* movies have afforded Marvel the opportunity to essentially take what was a third-tier, minor, kind of upstart bit of potential from one of their comic-book series and say: 'Look!'" Downey was amazed by the improbability of it all: "It's like you have a great quarterback, and his brother plays for another team, and then you say: 'Look, this is their second cousin and we think he has a great arm and he should start.' And then he goes and wins the Super Bowl."

The second-cousin quarterback in this analogy was the Guardians team, but Gunn was just as unlikely an underdog. Somehow he had found the way to give Marvel exactly what it needed while doing exactly what he wanted. "We have a really great relationship where they let me go and do my thing," Gunn said of Marvel, "and I truly listen to their notes and ideas. I've never been told to put in any character or plot element at all. I can't tell you the amount of times I've read stuff on the Internet from people who think they understand how Marvel works, when they don't at all. When they trust you—and I think I've earned their trust over the past few years— they give you a wide berth. I truly love them and love working with them. Like a good marriage, we just fit." He spoke like a man who expected, from that day forward, for better or for worse, to be partners with Marvel.

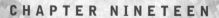

CHAPTER NINETEEN

Where's Natasha?

The truth rarely makes sense
when you omit key details.

Black Widow

MARVEL STUDIOS KEPT MOST OF ITS INTERNAL battles—the turf war with Marvel Television, the grinding long-term conflict with the Creative Committee—as secret as the Sanctum Sanctorum. One exception was an ongoing confrontation over the MCU's treatment of its female characters. For years, every powerful female character in the MCU provoked the same tired argument within the offices of Marvel Entertainment: *Was it really necessary to have female superheroes?*

Fans didn't need to read insider blogs or gossip websites to realize that Marvel wasn't making a big push for female superheroes: they could see that for themselves in the nation's multiplexes and toy aisles. But the character who made that conflict unavoidable for Marvel was Natasha Romanoff, aka the Black Widow.

Scarlett Johansson made her red-wigged MCU debut as Natasha in *Iron Man 2*. That version of Agent Romanoff, in full honeypot mode, with voluminous curls and a skin-tight catsuit showing off her cleavage, was still formidable—she could dispatch a dozen security guards in a hallway at Hammer Industries without breaking a sweat—but nothing like the fan favorite she would become.

"I didn't feel like I owned that suit until the first *Avengers*," Johansson said. "I didn't know how people would react to me in that role, if they would accept me as the character." The Black Widow's look got upgraded for *The Avengers*, becoming more practical—an action-ready haircut, more weapons, tactical padding, and a higher collar—but more importantly, actual thought was given to her character. "Joss Whedon and I talked about her past," Johansson said. "Who is she? How does she get to be a mercenary? What path do you follow in order to get to that place? We both wanted to see the darker side of her—why did she have to learn those skills?"

Whedon supplied Natasha with a backstory, a meaningful friendship with her fellow S.H.I.E.L.D. agent Hawkeye, and the motivation to remove "red" from her moral ledger. Although she had no superpowers, when she stood next to Thor, Captain America, and the Hulk, she looked like she belonged. Which raised an obvious question: If those characters were starring in solo movies, why wasn't she?

"There's no definitive plans," Kevin Feige said in 2011 when asked about a Black Widow movie. "But we have started talking, and talking with Scarlett, about what a Widow movie could be."

For her part, Johansson saw the possibilities of an MCU spy thriller. "I personally think there's an awesome [potential] Black Widow movie," she said. "A *Bourne* [*Identity*] type of film that would take the comic-book genre in a completely different direction."

The Black Widow's greatest obstacle wasn't HYDRA but the Creative Committee of Marvel Entertainment, which clung to the belief that female superheroes wouldn't move merchandise. "Toymakers will tell you they won't sell enough," Whedon said in 2013. "And movie people will point to the two terrible superheroine movies that were made and say 'You see? It can't be done.' It's stupid."

It wasn't the first time a Black Widow project had to answer for the failure of other people's movies. Back in 2004, the Black Widow had been seen as one of the *easiest* Marvel characters to adapt for film, because she fell squarely in the familiar action-espionage genre.

The Lionsgate studio optioned the rights to the character and hired *X-Men* screenwriter David Hayter to write and direct the movie. "Unfortunately, as I was coming up on the final draft, a number of female vigilante movies came out," Hayter remembered with a wince. "We had *Tomb Raider* and *Kill Bill*, which were the ones that worked, but then we had *BloodRayne* and *Ultraviolet* and *Aeon Flux*. *Aeon Flux* didn't open well, and three days after it opened the studio said, 'We don't think it's time to do this movie.' I accepted their logic in terms of the saturation of the marketplace, but it was pretty painful. I had not only invested a lot of time in that movie, but I had also named my daughter, who was born in that time period, Natasha."

A decade later, in 2014, *Captain America: The Winter Soldier* featured the Black Widow as the second lead. By that point, Johansson felt emboldened enough to demand script changes to protect her character so that she would do more than fulfill the audience's sexual fantasies. "When we were doing *Captain America: The Winter Soldier . . .* she first drives up in this beautiful car and picks up Cap, and initially in the script, it was like, she arrives in her tennis whites with a blonde wig. It was very quickly killed," Johansson said. "You work with a lot of male writers. Things were shifting—you have to be part of the change."

The Creative Committee had no interest in becoming part of the change. Ike Perlmutter believed that toys of female superheroes didn't sell, and so, tautologically, he proved it by not making them available for sale. This had been Perlmutter's philosophy since the early 1990s, when he was running Toy Biz; the popular 1991 line of X-Men action figures designed by Avi Arad had included only one woman, "Power Glow Storm," which was manufactured in lower quantities than any of the others.

Alan Fine, Perlmutter's deputy in New York, had correctly assessed Disney's priorities: Disney acquired Marvel (and later, Lucasfilm) because it wanted to sell to boys and men. Disney already had a dominant share of the market for licensed products aimed at young girls. It didn't need Marvel to reach girls and women, and it certainly wasn't going to push its subsidiary—which it had promised to leave alone—on that point.

On August 8, 2014, Ike Perlmutter sent an email to Sony executive Michael Lynton, continuing a conversation about female-led superhero movies. Arguing that they were bad investments, Perlmutter cited three in particular, even providing links to their grosses on boxofficemojo.com: *Elektra* ("Very bad idea and the end result was very, very bad"), *Catwoman* ("a disaster"), and *Supergirl* ("another disaster").

Seven days before Perlmutter sent that email, Feige was asked—yet again—when Marvel was going to make a movie with a female lead. Echoing Whedon's complaints from the year before, he said, "I very much believe in doing it. I very much believe that it's unfair to say, 'People don't want to see movies with female heroes,' then list five movies that weren't very good—therefore, people didn't go to the movies because they weren't good movies, versus [because] they were female leads. And they don't mention *Hunger Games*, *Frozen*, *Divergent*. You can go back to *Kill Bill* or *Aliens*. These are all female-led movies." Although Feige didn't mention the Creative Committee or Perlmutter by name, this counted, for him, as unusually blunt criticism of them.

✳

IN THAT SAME MOMENT, *Guardians of the Galaxy* was the number-one movie in the country. Fans who loved it enough to head to a toy store and pick up a pack of Guardians action figures soon noticed that nothing had changed with Marvel toys. The Guardians four-pack was missing a key character: the green-skinned Gamora. Her absence from the comic-book merchandise was all the more noticeable given that Zoe Saldaña's performance, in what was arguably the movie's second lead, had been wildly popular.

On the feminist website *Jezebel*, one woman wrote about how her young daughter loved *Guardians of the Galaxy*, so together they visited a chain store, the Children's Place, and tried to buy a T-shirt that featured Saldaña's character. When the mother discovered that

Gamora shirts didn't exist, she sent a complaint to the store and received this response: "We rely on advice from our licensors on our licensed tees. The *Guardians of the Galaxy* shirt in particular is a boy's shirt, which is why it does not include the female character Gamora. We try to have a diverse assortment but unfortunately cannot represent each movie and character." When reported, the blandly corporate message sparked widespread outrage.

"Remember when *The Avengers* came out two years ago, and Black Widow was missing from merchandise and toys?" writer Amy Ratcliffe blogged. "It sadly looks like Marvel and Disney licensees didn't learn from their mistakes because there's a sad lack of Gamora in the *Guardians of the Galaxy* product on the market. New hashtag: #wheresgamora." The hashtag went viral. Ratcliffe's post examined numerous cases of *Guardians* merchandise that excluded the movie's female lead.

After the howling absence of Gamora in *Guardians* products, fans were ready to scrutinize Black Widow merchandise when *Avengers: Age of Ultron* was released in May 2015. If Marvel Entertainment had wanted to respond to the Gamora protests by increasing Black Widow's presence among the *Age of Ultron* toys, it likely wouldn't have had enough time, because toy design, manufacturing, and distribution usually takes much longer than nine months. There's no evidence, however, that Marvel Entertainment had any interest in addressing those issues.

When Marvel saturated the planet with *Age of Ultron* merchandise, the only Black Widow action figure on sale was part of a large Lego set. The only clothing item the Widow appeared on was a men's T-shirt. She was, however, featured on a tote bag. Soon #WheresNatasha started trending on social media, often accompanied by photos of toy aisles filled with merchandise from Marvel's billion-dollar *Avengers* franchise, always lacking the Black Widow. Four days before the release of *Age of Ultron*, Mark Ruffalo joined the cause, tweeting, "@Marvel we need more #BlackWidow merchandise for my daughters and nieces. Pretty please."

It was a very modern protest campaign: It played out largely on social media and it centered on people who were trying to give their money to a corporation worth more than $150 billion. Also: It spotlighted questions of identity and it strived to force old men to let go of some of their prejudices. Author and activist Patricia V. Davis started an online petition to add Black Widow to the Avengers action figure pack, writing, "Little girls need better messages from toy companies than that women's contributions don't count or that a female is less of a superhero. Currently, females make up 46% of the viewing audience for superhero movies like *The Avengers*." If her numbers were basically correct—and they were—then Marvel was snubbing almost half its audience.

Once people saw *Avengers: Age of Ultron*, the lack of Black Widow toys seemed even more egregious. The movie features a sequence in which Black Widow drops out of an Avengers Quinjet on a motorcycle and chases after Ultron (a murderous artificial intelligence in a vibranium body). Whedon shot the stunt practically, although Johansson wasn't able to participate because she was pregnant. Her stunt doubles had to wear rubber Scarlett masks that would be replaced digitally. "It looked exactly like her face, and it even had the whites of her eyes," said Johansson's longtime stunt double, Heidi Moneymaker. "It's very creepy to look at somebody wearing that, because they have no facial expression at all, but then you just see this little piece of eye moving behind this thing." The motorcycle drop, the centerpiece of the *Age of Ultron* trailers, inspired two different toy sets. Incredibly, one replaced the Widow with Captain America, while the other featured a motorcycle ridden by Iron Man—a character who can fly.

The image of the Avengers as a boys' club was reinforced by answers actors Jeremy Renner and Chris Evans gave to a question during the *Ultron* press junket about Natasha's affection for their characters, Hawkeye and Captain America. "She's a slut," Renner said. "She's a whore," Evans agreed. After the moment went viral, Evans quickly apologized, saying he had spoken "in a very juvenile and offensive way that rightfully angered some fans." Renner, notably less contrite, told Conan O'Brien that he had no regrets about making the joke.

In *Age of Ultron*, Natasha's romantic partner was neither Clint Barton nor Steve Rogers but Bruce Banner. Whedon created a connection between the spy and the scientist, each of them soaking in regret. Whedon fought to include a scene where Natasha Romanoff tells Bruce Banner about her traumatic "graduation ceremony" from the Red Room, the Soviet program that trained her: a forced sterilization. The monologue ends with her asking if he still thinks that he's "the only monster on the team." The implication—that women who can't have children are in some way aberrant, if not terrifying—didn't sit well with some viewers. Whedon helped turn Black Widow into a more formidable character, but he had limitations of his own.

"*Age of Ultron* sees Black Widow yet again employing her feminine charms to help advance a fellow male teammate's personal growth," wrote Jen Yamato for the *Daily Beast*. "The Hulk can now finally control his rage-outs, but her soothing female touch and cooing ministrations are literally the only things that can calm him. In exchange, the nerdly Bruce Banner ignites Romanoff's long-suppressed lady feels, or something—Whedon gives his favorite character the kind of female troubles only a man can write. The result is an overdue character exploration for Black Widow that still manages to reduce the baddest bitch in the MCU to a shell of a superheroine who's sad she can never be a complete woman."

Johansson eventually responded to the controversy: "You know, I'm happy that people scrutinize the Widow's storylines and care about it and are invested. I'd much rather it be like that than have a kind of 'meh' reaction. . . . Everything that I've done with the Widow, to me, makes sense."

✳

THE IRONY OF Marvel Entertainment's toy-focused approach to making movies was that although Perlmutter's Toy Biz had swallowed up Marvel, the company hadn't been exposed to the boom-

and-bust cycles of the toy business for many years. "The board put a lot of pressure on Perlmutter to get out of the toy business," recalled Marvel lawyer John Turitzen. "They're essentially Christmas products, and you make your investment and your decisions in February or March, and you hope that you sell them at the end of the year."

Back in 2006, soon after David Maisel made the financing deal with Merrill Lynch that launched the Marvel Cinematic Universe, Marvel granted a broad license for toys and merchandise to Hasbro and sold the name "Toy Biz" to a Chinese company. So long as there was a steady flow of new movies featuring Marvel characters, Marvel Entertainment was guaranteed substantial royalty payments from Hasbro.

Once Hasbro controlled the Marvel toy line, it created a special team dedicated to making superhero action figures. The Marvel Entertainment offices coordinated the toy team's efforts with film production, not only keeping Hasbro apprised of film schedules, but giving the action-figure designers access to the files from Marvel Studios' viz-dev department, including costume designs and scans of actors. Hasbro sometimes pitched toy concepts to Marvel, although David Maisel said it never dictated what appeared in the product line, let alone the movies. "I remember some conversations with Hasbro about what their dream would be," he said, "if there's things that they thought could be toyetic. But always just taken as fun." If a toy line earned more than the benchmarks of the minimum royalty payments, Marvel collected a percentage of profits; if a toy line flopped, Hasbro shouldered the loss.

The deal was worth it for Hasbro because Marvel merchandise sold in vast quantities. In fact, Hasbro's toys typically grossed over $800 million in a calendar quarter when Marvel had a movie out, a significant spike from its usual quarterly figure of around $700 million. Even though it had outsourced production, Marvel Entertainment remained focused on the money from toy sales and maintained a licensing staff. Ultimately Marvel Entertainment decided which characters became action figures and which ones appeared on other merchandise (like T-shirts), while its licensees shouldered production costs. And even as movie revenue outpaced toy royalties, Perlmutter maintained a blinkered focus on the merchandise because it had, for so long, paid the bills.

These priorities didn't really make sense, but Marvel Entertainment had created a structure that made it almost impossible for Marvel Studios to disprove the entrenched belief that female characters wouldn't sell in plastic figurine form (and hence shouldn't be the stars of movies). Perlmutter wasn't going to start making toys of female characters because he suddenly became enlightened about the ethics of gender representation—the best way to convince him to change strategies was to show him that by ignoring the huge market of girls, he was leaving money on the table. But apparently that was a proposition he wasn't even willing to test.

CHAPTER TWENTY

Marvel Studios vs. the Committee

> I recognize that the Council has made a decision,
> but given that it's a stupid-ass decision,
> I've elected to ignore it.
>
> *The Avengers*

MARVEL STUDIOS WAS THREE THOUSAND MILES AWAY from Marvel Entertainment's headquarters in New York City, but its executives couldn't escape Ike Perlmutter. When Disney acquired Marvel in 2009, Perlmutter received assurances from Disney CEO Bob Iger that the corporation wouldn't interfere with Marvel's culture. In practice, that culture consisted of two main elements, neither of which was intended to foster creativity. The first was coordination among the various divisions to ensure the largest toy sales; Perlmutter's vehicle for that effort was the Creative Committee. The second element was extreme frugality.

"They were cheap. They were *very* cheap," James Gunn remembered. When he first went to the Marvel Studios offices for a meeting about *Guardians of the Galaxy*, he couldn't believe that he was in the headquarters of a studio making billion-dollar movies. "I was sitting in an office that seemed to be constructed of cardboard and scotch tape."

Marvel Entertainment pored over the bills from Marvel Studios' office spaces, from the kite factory to the Beverly Hills Mercedes-Benz lot to Manhattan Beach, leading to cost-saving measures that left the working environment, as one Marvel screenwriter called it, "shithole-adjacent."

When distributor Chris Fenton visited the office, he described it, more tactfully, as "unassuming and a bit disheveled." The reception area had no seats, so Fenton was told to wait in a conference room furnished with a large table and a dozen chairs. "None of them matched," he observed. Fenton sat down in one chair, which collapsed underneath him. "Shit," the receptionist said, "I forgot to warn you about the chairs."

When Marvel's films went into preproduction on studio lots, staffers would smuggle in drinks and snacks from the offices of other productions on the same lot, because the cupboards at Marvel were always bare. Office managers weren't allowed to order boxes of Kleenex; employees were expected to use their napkins from lunch if they needed to blow their noses.

When producer Jodi Hildebrand started working in the Marvel Studios office, she noticed that many notes and interoffice memos were written in violet ink. "You like our purple pens?" Kevin Feige asked her. The first time Hildebrand opened the office's supply closet, she understood: there was a vast stockpile of purple pens because the Marvel staffers had used all the black and blue pens in the multi-packs, and the office wasn't allowed to order more until all the purple ink had been used up.

One top Marvel executive remembered being berated by Perlmutter over his writing implement: "Why do you need a new pencil?" the CEO demanded. "There's two inches left on that one!"

Perlmutter, at least, held himself to the same standards. "He used to do this thing in our office that people would laugh at," Avi Arad said. "If there was some used paper or a memo lying around, he would rip it into eight pieces and he would have a new memo pad."

For press junkets, Perlmutter would routinely slash budgets, even if they were already spartan. Once, for example, he complained that journalists had been allotted two sodas each instead of one. A press event for *The Avengers* revealed the Marvel culture of thrift: hungry reporters liberated food from a nearby suite, where Universal was hosting a junket for *The Five-Year Engagement*. Unsurprisingly, the reporters tweeted about it.

✳

PERLMUTTER AND his lieutenants could tabulate the dollars and cents spent by Marvel's various divisions with ease. Controlling the work of fractious creative personalities was more complicated, but that didn't stop Marvel Entertainment from trying.

Perlmutter allowed *Iron Man* and *The Incredible Hulk* to be made with very little supervision. After all, Marvel Studios was spending Merrill Lynch's money. After those movies, however, he established the Creative Committee to exert control over the studio.

According to a Marvel Studios insider, "The first two films we made were the best as far as the relationship with New York goes, because New York had no idea what we were doing. So they just sat back and watched. Sadly, after the second film came out, after *Hulk*, they had Hollywood all figured out. They had it all dialed in, and they knew how to do it better. And then with every success, *Oh my God, oh my, it's so easy. So, so easy. We just take the action figure rules, apply to Hollywood, take as much money as you can from everyone. It's easy.* And now with every future success came more oppressive notes and oversight."

Marvel Studios at least avoided one of Perlmutter's more noxious forms of supervision: the surveillance cameras, at least twenty in number, he installed throughout the New York offices of Marvel Entertainment.

The stated purpose of the Creative Committee was to make sure that the various divisions of Marvel weren't working at cross-purposes, and especially to coordinate schedules so that toy manufacturing, which had a long lead time, was aware of the movies in development. In practice, the Creative Committee started micromanaging the operations of Marvel Studios, demanding changes on scripts, edits, and any other creative decisions made on the West Coast.

The problem only grew after Marvel Studios established *The Avengers* as a billion-dollar property. The more money Marvel Studios made, the more the Creative Committee wanted to control it.

As Marvel Studios entered Phase Two, the Creative Committee became a production chokepoint, insisting on reading all scripts but taking longer than ever to respond to them. The notes coming out of New York coalesced around a single idea: the Marvel Cinematic Universe should exist to sell merchandise. Marvel insiders familiar with the Committee's inner workings lay the blame at the feet of one man, former Toy Biz executive Alan Fine, who was now executive vice president and chief marketing officer of Marvel Characters, Inc., and who was understood by the other members of the committee to be a proxy for Perlmutter.

"That wasn't the whole Creative Committee," one insider insisted. "That was Alan Fine who comes from toys." Many genre stories over the years have been driven by toyetic opportunity. The comics and cartoon character He-Man, invented by the toy company Mattel, rides an oversized tiger called Battle Cat only because Mattel had a surplus of unsold giant tiger toys that could be packaged and sold with the muscle-bound warrior. While the powers that be at Marvel Studios considered themselves storytellers first and foremost, this insider said, "Alan Fine's whole thing was that, whether it's comic books or movies, these are all loss leaders for the merch, which is where the real money is."

Marvel often manifested its hidebound attitudes about gender and race through the Creative Committee, via Fine in particular. The lack of Black Widow merchandise was just the most prominent example of that dynamic. "Where he comes from, boys will not buy girls' dolls, period," the Marvel insider continued. "*Elektra* tanked and *Catwoman* tanked, ergo, it can't happen. That is not the Creative Committee. That's Alan fucking Fine. I guarantee you, that is not the position of either Joe Quesada or Brian Michael Bendis" (both of whom were also on the Committee).

When *Runaways* was canceled, screenwriter Drew Pearce figured the decision had been made because *The Avengers* had taken the slot for a team in the MCU, but producer Craig Kyle said it was actually toy-based. "We were doing heroes that were white and in their mid-twenties to mid-thirties—that was the sweet spot. That's what moved plastic. And that's what our stories had to be. *Runaways* got thrown to the side because they're not in their twenties and there are some girls and minorities in that group. So that's out.'"

Also stricken from the lineup at the behest of the New York office: a Power Pack movie (the Power siblings were too young) and the intended villain of the 2013 *Thor* sequel, *Thor: The Dark World*, Hela, the Norse goddess of death. Kyle, who produced *The Dark World*, said, "In our original film, yes, it was a Hela story, and she was our big bad. But at that point in the process, so many of our decisions were being driven by the New York office. They forbid us from going that direction. And the short version was, 'Boys don't buy female action figures.' That is truly the reason why that version of the film was not allowed to be developed. I was also told that people don't buy Black action figures."

Thor star Natalie Portman, reluctant to play Jane Foster again in the sequel, urged Marvel Studios to hire Patty Jenkins (the director of *Monster*), who was interested in making a superhero movie. "Word got out that I wanted to do a superhero film, and to Marvel's credit—on a movie that didn't require a woman at all—they hired me," Jenkins said.

Jenkins wanted *The Dark World* to focus on the star-crossed romance between Jane Foster on Earth and Thor in Asgard. The Creative Committee, however, didn't think that a superhero romance would drive toy sales. When Jenkins received a revised draft written by Christopher Yost that deemphasized her planned love story in favor of an action-figure-ready villain, Malekith the Dark Elf, and a cosmic MacGuffin called "the Aether," she quit. "I did not believe I could make a good movie out of the script that they were planning on doing," Jenkins said. "It would have looked like it was my fault. It would've looked like 'Oh my God, this woman directed it and she missed all these things.'" Jenkins would become the first woman to direct a superhero movie for a major studio—four years later, with Warner Bros., where she helmed the hit *Wonder Woman*.

Portman had signed on to the *Thor* sequel specifically because of Jenkins's involvement; she took pride in helping to expand the opportunities in Hollywood for women. When Jenkins left the movie, Portman was contractually obligated to continue, but she declared herself done with the franchise, not even making time for reshoots. When the movie needed to shoot a climactic kiss, the production conscripted Chris Hemsworth's real-life wife Elsa Pataky (who wore a long brunette wig for the scene).

To take over the troubled project, Marvel Studios hired director Alan Taylor, best known for his work on TV programs such as *The Sopranos* and *Game of Thrones*. According to Taylor, the Marvel executives mostly left him alone during the shoot, but that changed during postproduction. The Creative Committee was convinced that Loki didn't get enough screen time and that his scenes weren't much fun. The solution was to airlift Joss Whedon from the *Avengers* editing room to the *Dark World* studios in London so he could rewrite all the Loki scenes for reshoots. The opening scene of Loki in chains was part of those reshoots—otherwise the popular character wouldn't have appeared until nearly an hour into the film. The mid-credits scene, shot by James Gunn, introduced Benicio del Toro as the Collector in a tease for Gunn's *Guardians of the Galaxy*. In a flimsy TV tie-in, the post-credits scene involved a frost monster from another realm, left behind on Earth so that *Agents of S.H.I.E.L.D.* could deal with it. The resulting film felt like it was serving the needs of other Marvel projects more than its own viewers.

Taylor made no friends at Marvel Studios during his time there. "Kevin is an all-powerful force, but films at the end of the day live and die by the director," said Kyle. "Sometimes it works out great, sometimes it doesn't, and *The Dark World* speaks very much to the unfortunate side of the wrong person for the wrong franchise."

Guardians of the Galaxy was so far outside the main action of the MCU, with only Thanos and an Infinity Stone to connect it with the larger continuity, and so plain weird, that the Creative Committee mostly left it alone, other than trying to remove the 1970s soundtrack. It issued a round of notes on Gunn's version of the screenplay, but when Feige and D'Esposito pushed back on those notes, it didn't fight the producers, believing that the inevitable failure of this strange movie would allow the New York office to rein Feige in. (At moments like this, the Committee's opinions weren't necessarily monolithic, but among all its members, Alan Fine's voice was the loudest.)

"Every problem I had on the first movie was because of this weird entity that would stop the conversation between director and producer," Gunn said. "I'm really grateful to have Kevin be the guy. At the heart of it, Kevin loves movies. And that's all we're trying to do: make great pop cinema."

As for his opinion of the Creative Committee: "They were a group of comic-book writers and toy people. Kevin and I were brain surgeons performing surgery, and we were surrounded by a group of podiatrists."

✲

THE MARVEL STUDIOS brain trust saw the Creative Committee as an impediment to making good movies. When they gathered around a speakerphone in the Los Angeles offices, studio executives would literally roll their eyes at the latest dumb suggestion from New York. But while the Creative Committee was a hassle, it mostly just slowed down Marvel Studios. The studio's producers regarded fending off the Committee as an unpleasant part of the process that ultimately let them make most of the movies they wanted to make.

After *Guardians* wrapped, however, the Creative Committee made clear that its notes needed to be acted on, not hand-waved away. Joss Whedon entered production for *Avengers: Age of Ultron*, and although that sequel was virtually guaranteed to be lucrative, the increased budget (the cast, all of them stars now, had gotten significant pay bumps), meant that New York expected the sequel to substantially exceed the billion-dollar grosses of the original so that its profit margin wouldn't diminish. While Whedon filmed *Age of Ultron*—in locations including South Korea, England, and Italy—

the leaders of Marvel Studios were busily planning for the Phase Three movies that would follow it.

Robert Downey Jr. was essential and expensive: he had earned $50 million for his work in *The Avengers* and $70 million for *Iron Man 3*. At those prices, Marvel didn't want to make a fourth *Iron Man* movie, but Downey was willing to accept somewhat less for supporting roles in other MCU films. Feige wanted Downey to appear in the third *Captain America* movie, which would be called *Captain America: Civil War*. In Marvel's *Civil War* comic books, the Marvel superheroes had divided into two factions, led by Captain America and Iron Man, riven by the question of whether they would comply with the Superhuman Registration Act. *Captain America* screenwriters Christopher Markus and Stephen McFeely, working again with the directors Joe and Anthony Russo, were given the job of figuring out which heroes might band together with Captain America and which would follow Iron Man—and who they could bring into the movie without getting bogged down in a litany of origin stories. The two strongest Avengers, Thor and Hulk, didn't seem to fit into this intramural battle, so Joss Whedon made sure they wouldn't even be on Earth when *Age of Ultron* ended.

Once the Russo brothers assured Downey that Iron Man wouldn't be the movie's bad guy, the actor liked the idea of *Civil War*, not least because he would effectively be the costar of a Captain America movie. The Creative Committee was less pleased, worried that the movie's budget would swell to *Avengers* proportions. It demanded a lower-budget draft of the movie—specifically, one that achieved cost savings by not including Iron Man. Markus and McFeely, however, had built their script around the idea that Bucky had killed Tony Stark's parents, driving the split between Iron Man and Captain America. Removing Tony from the movie would mean starting from nothing, and they strenuously resisted.

"Kevin always had to pick his battles because we were fighting on all fronts, we were fighting to develop the films to come," Craig Kyle said. "We were fighting on the films we were making. And the Creative Committee had become such a septic place. It went from,

'Hey, here are some things to think about that could improve the story' to, 'No, no, no, no.' They wanted notes on their notes and then they wanted proof that they went in. And when I say 'they,' I really am just talking about one guy and then a few of the people that were just in the room with him. So it became unbearable. We all had to swallow it. We put up with it for too many years."

Kevin Feige could stand his ground, but he nevertheless reported to a group that was loyal to Ike Perlmutter. And nobody had more authority within Marvel than Perlmutter—except for Disney CEO Bob Iger. So, in a meeting with Iger and Alan Horn, the chairman of Walt Disney Studios, Feige brought up the challenges he was facing, namely that various projects were stalled and Marvel "culture" was stymieing Marvel Studios' efforts to make movies. Soon after, Iger made a brief but emphatic phone call. "I called Ike and told him to tell his team to stop putting up roadblocks," he wrote in his memoir *Ride of a Lifetime*. "I've been in the business long enough to have heard every old argument in the book, and I've learned that old arguments are just that: old, and out of step with where the world is and where it should be."

Iger not only instructed Perlmutter to let *Captain America: Civil War* proceed with a prominent role for Robert Downey Jr., but told him that it was time to move forward with *Black Panther* (starring a Black hero) and *Captain Marvel* (starring a woman). Although Iger had promised not to interfere in Marvel when Disney purchased it, he saw the risks of doing nothing. Feige had established himself as a reliable moneymaker at the highest echelons of Hollywood, and so his clout had grown dramatically in just a few years. To Perlmutter's surprise, Feige's power within the company had eclipsed his own.

★

IN AUGUST 2014, the successful release of *Guardians of the Galaxy* vitiated the criticism from the Creative Committee. One Marvel insider remembered the response at the Marvel Studio offices: "We were flying high, but it was also a sigh of relief. *It actually worked—we were right.*"

Armed with the *Guardians* box-office bonanza and operating under the protective aegis of Iger, Feige asked Disney's PR team to put together a presentation that would usher in not just Phase Three of the MCU, but a new age for Marvel. It would be something halfway between a press conference and a fan event. Internally, it became known as "Kevin-Con."

Back in 2006, Feige had made his first presentation at the San Diego Comic-Con to a half-empty room. "Absolutely nobody cared," one fan recalled. "Everybody was trying to get into the *Spider-Man 3* panel instead. They had an *Iron Man* teaser poster signing with Jon Favreau and they practically couldn't give them away." Onstage, Feige wore an oversized button-down shirt that made him look like a kid dressing up as a studio president.

Eight years later, Feige had figured out his day-to-day uniform, and rarely appeared in public dressed any other way. "He'll still have his baseball cap and his sneakers on and a sports jacket thrown over a Marvel or Disney T-shirt," Chris Hemsworth said affectionately of Feige. "He's like a fanboy with such an open honesty and warmth to him that you don't usually find with people who are as successful and established as he is."

On a Tuesday morning in October 2014, Feige took the stage of the intimate El Capitan Theatre, on Hollywood Boulevard in Los Angeles, an ornate movie house owned by Disney. He had largely avoided publicity, but the newly empowered Feige understood that if he was to be the captain of the MCU, he needed to be more of a public figure. "He gets why it's important," a Disney insider said, "if it makes sense to tell a story."

The theater was filled with fans, a handful of journalists, and some of Marvel's directors, such as Joss Whedon and the Russo brothers. (Whedon might have been the czar of Phase Two, but notably, at this event about the future of the MCU, he wasn't onstage.) Feige touted the success of *Guardians*—the number one movie of the year worldwide—as well as Marvel's overall box-office record. "Ten films, over seven billion dollars," he bragged.

Then he laid out the Marvel Studios plan—*his* plan—for the

next five years, announcing no fewer than eight different movies, including *Doctor Strange* and *Captain Marvel*. "We have planted a lot of flags," Feige said. But with the exception of one film—*The Inhumans*—all those projects would happen as scheduled.

Feige announced the two-part conclusion of the epic Infinity Stones saga, which would require a pair of *Avengers* movies, prompting gasps and applause, but that wasn't the climax of his presentation. He brought Robert Downey Jr. and Chris Evans onstage to introduce the actor he saw as the future of the MCU. "Black Panther himself," Downey drawled, "ladies and gentlemen, Mr. Chadwick Boseman." As Boseman strolled onstage, the crowd erupted, and Downey pumped his fist.

Ten years earlier, Black Panther had been one of the ten characters put up as collateral to secure a line of credit from Merrill Lynch; now, Feige was finally able to announce a *Black Panther* feature film, the Black-led superhero movie that he had long fought for. On the way out of the El Capitan, everyone attending Kevin-Con was given a Black Panther poster.

✳

FEIGE'S CLASHES WITH the Creative Committee did not mean that he was unconditionally supportive of Marvel's filmmakers. Joss Whedon had added a slew of heroes to *Avengers: Age of Ultron*, swelling the cast with Pietro and Wanda Maximoff (known in the comics as Quicksilver and the Scarlet Witch), not to mention the artificial intelligence J.A.R.V.I.S., which became corporeal in the form of the Vision. Wanda fit into a familiar Whedon archetype: a high-powered, emotionally traumatized teen in a short skirt and thigh-high stockings. While Whedon's work didn't suffer from the traditional Madonna/whore dichotomy, he did sometimes lean on a killing machine/sexual fantasy dichotomy.

Whedon wanted to include even more characters; he had heard about *Captain Marvel* well before the Kevin-Con announcement, and he knew that Sony chair Amy Pascal, after a number of disappointing *Spider-Man* movies, had been talking with Feige about bringing the character to the MCU. So Whedon proposed that those two characters, Captain Marvel and Spider-Man, appear in the final scene of *Age of Ultron*, to provide an even greater thrill for comics geeks than the appearance of Thanos at the end of *The Avengers*. Feige told Whedon that Spider-Man was absolutely not going to make his MCU debut with a cameo at the end of an Avengers movie, but he did let Whedon shoot some Captain Marvel footage.

The film's closing sequence took place at the Avengers headquarters in Upstate New York, with Captain America reviewing his new recruits, including the Vision, the Falcon, and War Machine. Whedon shot footage with an uncredited extra taking the place of Carol Danvers, so that when Marvel cast an actress in the role, she could be edited into the film and onto the new Avengers team. "The way we reveal Scarlet Witch [in costume] at the end of the movie?" Feige later recalled. "Those were Captain Marvel plate shots. Joss said, 'We'll cast her later!' And I said, 'Yeah Joss, we'll cast her later.' [*Whispers to an invisible associate who isn't Whedon*] 'We're not putting her in there.'"

After the movie wrapped principal photography, Feige asked the director if he'd be interested in taking on the next two *Avengers* movies. Whedon declined. "What I said was 'I'm tapped out,'" he remembered. "I think they knew that even if I could give them something, it wasn't going to be anytime soon." An exhausted Whedon could barely see his way to the end of his current Marvel movie, let alone two more.

Whedon moved into a rented home in Burbank near the facility where *Age of Ultron* was being edited. The rough cut achieved the rare feat of uniting the East Coast and West Coast Marvel executives: They all agreed that the movie was a ponderous mess. The middle act, as Whedon conceived it, features Thor and Dr. Erik Selvig (Stellan Skarsgård) searching for more information about the Infinity Stones, while the rest of the Avengers recuperate at Hawkeye's farmhouse but are subjected to individual nightmares, courtesy of Wanda. "The dreams were not an executive favorite," Whedon said. "The dreams, the farmhouse—these were things I fought to keep."

The studio had instructed Whedon to include a sequence with Thor in a cave, designed to set up the thunder god's future adventures in *Thor: Ragnarok*. Whedon hated the cave sequence, but Marvel Studios was insistent. "They pointed a gun at the farm's head and said 'Give us the cave, or we'll take out the farm,'" Whedon said. "I respect these guys, they're artists, but that's when it got really, really unpleasant."

In Hollywood, significant reshoots are often a symptom of a troubled production, but at this point in the Marvel filmmaking process, weeks of reshoots were routinely built into the production schedule. They gave Feige a way to guarantee that individual MCU installments would fold easily into the larger saga. "Kevin says, 'We are writing this film until they rip it out of our hands,'" reported Craig Kyle. "He is not kidding. Doesn't matter how many drafts we have of that script—while we're shooting, our job is to continually go back to those old drafts and say, 'Is there a line? Is there a moment that we missed?' Once it's all shot, then the pieces come home."

By "home," Kyle was referring to Marvel HQ in Los Angeles, where Feige would pore over footage and rough cuts to poke and prod and find the missing magic that made a Marvel movie sing. "When shooting, you rarely see Kev," Kyle said. "If he visits the set, he's a lovely presence, but he spends very little time there. He's usually just catching up on emails, preferably in another country so he can do it while people are sleeping, then he goes home. He says, 'Look, just bring it all back and then we're going to make a movie. Just give me all the pieces, I'll make the puzzle.'"

Shooting additional footage didn't solve Whedon's problems with the *Ultron* cave sequence; eventually it was shortened and turned into a CGI-heavy Thor vision. After truncating as many of the farmhouse side stories as it could, Marvel finally decided that the sequence was short enough not to derail the movie.

By the time *Age of Ultron* was finished, Whedon was something of a broken man. He had already told Feige of his intentions to move on from the MCU, but he emerged from the editing room hoarse and hollow-eyed; his bottom lip was split and scabby. "I have been to the other side of the mountain," Whedon said. "I gotta say, it's been dark. It's been weird. It's been *horrible*. About a month and a half ago, I said goodbye to my kids, and I've been living in Burbank next to the studio. I feel every day like *I didn't do enough, I didn't do enough, I didn't do enough. I wasn't ready. Here's failure. Here's failure. Here's compromise. Here's compromise.*"

The more a wrung-out Whedon talked with the press, the clearer it became that he had grown frustrated with Marvel Studios. "With so much at stake, there's gonna be friction," he said. "It's the Marvel way to question everything. Sometimes that's amazing. And sometimes"—Whedon growled through gritted teeth, his hostility clear—"that's *amazing*."

Unwittingly, Whedon was aiding the arguments of the Creative Committee, which was convinced that any problems with *Age of Ultron* stemmed from Feige refusing to bring the director to heel, or to demand that Whedon implement the Committee's notes. Whedon would not be the czar for Phase Three of the MCU; he would not direct any more movies for Marvel. One of Feige's cardinal rules for Marvel Studios was *Don't air your problems publicly.* And Whedon broke it.

Simultaneously, *Captain America: Civil War* was running up against obstacles created by the Creative Committee, even after Iger's phone call to Perlmutter. The movie's centerpiece was a battle royale between Team Iron Man and Team Cap at a German airport, but the Committee proposed a different version in which the heroes team up to fight a bunch of unfrozen Super Soldiers. As Kyle remembered it, "We were discussing *Civil War* and the question posed to us is, 'Who wants to watch a movie with heroes fighting heroes?' Everybody. *Everyone.* So that encapsulates what we were facing for years."

The Russo brothers delivered an ultimatum: they would make the version of *Civil War* they had been planning, with Captain America pitted against Iron Man, or they would walk off the movie, even though it was well into preproduction. With Feige and Perlmutter facing off and the future of Marvel Studios on the brink, Disney's CEO stepped in. "Kevin is one of the most talented film executives in the business," Iger wrote in 2019, "but my sense was that the strained relationship with New York was threatening his continued success. I knew I had to intervene, and so in May 2015, I made the decision to split Marvel's movie-making unit off from the rest of Marvel and bring it under Alan Horn and the Walt Disney Studios. Kevin would now report directly to Alan, and would benefit from his experience, and the tensions that had built up between him and the New York office would be alleviated.'" Iger later said that while he had told Perlmutter that he could continue to run Marvel after Disney bought it, he didn't promise that he would get to do so forever.

Iger waited until 2023, when he and Perlmutter were battling over the composition of the Disney board of directors, to tell the unvarnished story: To assert his control over Marvel Studios, Perlmutter had tried to fire Feige. "I thought that was a mistake and stepped in to prevent that from happening," Iger said. "He was not happy about it."

★

THE MOOD AT Marvel Studios, once the staff learned of the regime change, was jubilant. "It was such a long time coming," Kyle said of that day. "I wasn't sure it was ever going to come."

"The minute the Creative Committee was gone, there was a sense of freedom," one Marvel insider recalled. "Almost a gleeful 'I'm free, I'm free, Dobby is free' kind of feeling."

Kyle said he sent out emails to Marvel staffers with the message, "Holy hell, ding dong, the witch is dead."

After Disney's official announcement, Feige immediately promoted Victoria Alonso to executive vice president of physical production, an endorsement as her role of one of the three essential executives at Marvel Studios, and a move that had been blocked by the Creative Committee.

Even after Iger's restructuring, Marvel's New York executives continued to grouse that their approach would lead to higher profits. *Avengers: Age of Ultron* was the fourth-most popular movie in the world in 2015, grossing $1.4 billion, but Alan Fine insisted that it would have done even better if he had been in charge. Kyle remembered the carping from the East Coast: "[Kevin's] a rock when it comes to that stuff. But he got to the breaking point, I believe it was *Avengers 2* that really set him off. It was a big success financially, but according to what I've heard, Ike was told that the movie would have made another half a billion dollars had they listened to Alan [Fine]." Kyle shook his head, impressed by the patience of his friend and colleague. "Kevin can take on so much. The amount of BS he will stomach for the greater good is crazy."

Avengers: Age of Ultron was released worldwide in May. By the end of the summer, the Creative Committee had disbanded. Feige had won, and a new era at Marvel Studios had begun—not exactly how he had planned, but in a way that he could only have hoped for. And finally, Marvel Studios could buy new pens.

CHAPTER TWENTY-ONE

Wright Man, Wrong Time

Baskin-Robbins always finds out.

Ant-Man

EDGAR WRIGHT STARTED WORKING ON MARVEL MOVIES around the same time as Kevin Feige, but to less effect. In the year 2000, Avi Arad convinced Artisan Entertainment, the mini-major studio that had a colossal hit in 1999 with *The Blair Witch Project*, to partner with Marvel. The two companies created a joint subsidiary and endowed it with the screen rights for a host of Marvel's characters, many of them lesser-known: Captain America, Thor (earmarked as a TV show), the Punisher, Black Panther (Wesley Snipes was already attached to produce and star), Deadpool (the irreverent mercenary), Man-Thing (a shambling swamp monster), Luke Cage, Iron Fist, Morbius (the vampiric Spider-Man villain), Power Pack, Longshot (a genetically engineered marksman from another dimension), Mort the Dead Teenager (a comedic character who had appeared in just four issues of Marvel comics), and Ant-Man (a superhero who can shrink to the size of an insect). On a visit to Los Angeles, Wright—then a young British TV director hoping to break into the big time—took a meeting with Artisan. When the

278

studio asked if he was a fan of Marvel Comics, he admitted that he was.

"I said that I always was a Marvel Comics kid," he remembered. "And they said, 'Are you interested in any of these titles?' The one that jumped out was Ant-Man, because I had the John Byrne *Marvel Premiere* #47 from 1979 that David Michelinie had done with Scott Lang that was kind of an origin story. I always loved the artwork, so when I saw that, it just immediately set bells going off." Wright and his friend Joe Cornish wrote a treatment for a heist movie starring Ant-Man, which Artisan promptly rejected. It had been hoping for family-friendly entertainment more along the lines of *Honey, I Shrunk the Kids*.

In 2003, Lionsgate Entertainment bought Artisan for $160 million, which scuttled the Marvel/Artisan partnership. Artisan had hired writers for some of the Marvel properties but had gotten only one film (*The Punisher*) into production. In the interim, Fox's *X-Men* movies had demonstrated that there was a healthy appetite for Marvel superheroes, but Lionsgate wasn't interested in what it regarded as Marvel's dregs. Lionsgate let all the Marvel characters (including Ant-Man) revert to the publisher, except for the Punisher; the studio released the Artisan-produced *The Punisher* in 2004 and then rebooted the franchise a few years later in 2008's *Punisher: War Zone*.

Wright was too busy to lament the Ant-Man movie that didn't happen. The British sitcom he was directing, *Spaced*, was a hit, and he was writing a screenplay with its male lead, Simon Pegg. That script became the movie *Shaun of the Dead*, an instant-classic zombie comedy, directed by Wright and starring Pegg and another *Spaced* alum, Nick Frost.

Wright brought *Shaun of the Dead* to the 2004 San Diego Comic-Con for an advance screening. During the convention, he also took a meeting with the two men who were running Marvel Studios at the time, Avi Arad and Kevin Feige. "Weirdly enough, I did something for you," Wright told them. "Do you want to read the thing that we did three years ago?" Neither Arad nor Feige knew about the pitch, so Wright gave them a copy. They were impressed: Wright and Cornish had taken two different Marvel characters who used the name Ant-Man and elegantly merged them in a single film. His proposed movie started with a flashback to the original Ant-Man, Hank Pym (in the comics, a genius scientist and founding Avenger who debuted in 1962). Then the movie jumped into the present day, when a younger thief, Scott Lang, steals the Ant-Man suit from Pym. It was a loose adaptation of Wright's favorite story from *Marvel Premiere* #47, "To Steal an Ant-Man!"

Feige and Arad weren't yet in a position to green-light the Wright version of *Ant-Man*. Over the next couple of years, Marvel Studios transformed itself under David Maisel's leadership, becoming more than a production company that licensed out intellectual property. Feige held onto the Wright/Cornish treatment, and when Marvel Studios had the money to make its own feature films, Ant-Man was on the short list of characters it considered for its "four at-bats" with Merrill Lynch's money.

It didn't hurt that Wright's career had thrived in the interim. *Shaun of the Dead* had been a hit, critically and commercially. He was already prepping his follow-up, *Hot Fuzz*, a spoof that transplanted the clichés of buddy-cop action movies to small-town England. The characters of Pym and Lang weren't as well-known as the Hulk—but before the *Iron Man* movie, neither was Tony Stark. Why not give Wright a shot at making *Ant-Man*?

Wright was all for it: "It's not like a secret power. There's no supernatural element, there's no gamma rays. It's just, like, the suit and the gas," he said of the Ant-Man character. "We could do something high-concept, really visual, cross-genre, sort of an action and special-effects bonanza, but funny as well." The director, who had grown more comfortable with action sequences during the *Hot Fuzz* shoot, saw the potential in fight scenes in which the hero could spontaneously change sizes. Wright and Cornish agreed to turn their treatment into a screenplay for Marvel as soon as Wright was finished with *Hot Fuzz*.

In 2006, Wright and Feige both returned to San Diego for

Comic-Con. Wright did a panel on *Hot Fuzz* (where he showed off advance footage to an excited crowd), while Feige appeared onstage in his first Marvel Studios panel, trying to drum up excitement for *Iron Man* and *The Incredible Hulk*. Marvel convinced Wright to join Feige onstage so they could announce *Ant-Man*, which let Feige hint at the not-yet-named Marvel Cinematic Universe: "If you listen to all the characters that I name that we are working on currently and you put them all together, there's no coincidence that they may someday equal the Avengers."

Wright and Cornish delivered their completed *Ant-Man* script to Marvel in 2008. But in the intervening two years, a lot had changed at Marvel Studios. Arad was gone; Feige was head of production. More importantly, the massive success of *Iron Man* had altered the studio's strategy. Instead of experimenting with a range of characters and seeing what worked best, it was filming an *Iron Man* sequel and working toward an Avengers movie by establishing the identities of Captain America, S.H.I.E.L.D., and Thor. Marvel Studios still wanted to make *Ant-Man* with Edgar Wright, and commissioned another draft of the screenplay, but both parties had other priorities: *The Avengers* (without Ant-Man) for Marvel, and a film adaptation of a different comic book (*Scott Pilgrim vs. the World*) for Wright.

The next revision of the screenplay wasn't finished until 2011, because Wright had been working on *Scott Pilgrim*, while Cornish had made his directorial debut with *Attack the Block*. It had now been more than a decade since Wright wrote his initial *Ant-Man* treatment; in that time, he had made three feature films of increasing ambition and visual complexity. On *Scott Pilgrim*, he created a distinct look by eschewing the usual wide-angle "coverage" for each scene, instead framing individual shots like comic-book panels. Wright had established himself as an ambitious young auteur who controlled every frame of his films.

Marvel Studios had also established itself as a studio that demanded control. Admittedly, it had given free rein to Jon Favreau and Edward Norton in its early days (at least for a time), but Feige, Louis D'Esposito, and Victoria Alonso had since built up a Marvel house style: a visual grammar and a workflow that facilitated the relentless extension of a multi-movie superhero saga. Marvel Studios was ambitious in the scope of its storytelling, even if some of the visuals and story beats had become homogenized, even interchangeable between one movie and another. (Gwyneth Paltrow famously lost track of which of her scenes happened in which movies, forgetting that she appeared in *Spider-Man: Homecoming*.)

Marvel Studios liked the latest screenplay by Wright and Cornish, which was a sleeker version of the same story, a heist movie that featured both Pym and Lang trying to keep the Ant-Man suit away from a villain who wants to use the technology for nefarious purposes. Marvel knew that Wright was also developing *The World's End*, the third film in his "Cornetto trilogy" (three comedies starring Pegg and Frost, so named because each includes a passing appearance by a British brand of ice cream novelties), but the studio was hoping to include *Ant-Man* in Phase Two of the MCU as one of the movies leading up to *Avengers: Age of Ultron*. To that end, Marvel paid for Wright to film a day of test footage in June 2012. He shot a scene where Ant-Man (played by a stuntman) takes on two men in a hallway, shrinking and growing as he fights—showing off the Ant-Man suit created by the Marvel visual-development team. Seeing an obvious promotional opportunity, Feige planned to bring the footage, complete with CGI, to the San Diego Comic-Con in July.

Before Comic-Con, however, Eric Fellner was diagnosed with cancer. Fellner was the cofounder and cochair of Working Title, the production company that partnered with Wright on his Cornetto films. He told Wright about his illness when the director handed in the screenplay for the third movie in the trilogy, *The World's End*. "That changed everything: Eric was our knight in shining armor on *Shaun of the Dead*," Wright said. (When the movie's original production company went out of business, Fellner stepped up to rescue the project.) "I felt [that] if we didn't make this film and something terrible happened, I would never forgive myself."

Wright told Marvel executives that he still wanted to make *Ant-Man*, but out of loyalty to Fellner, he needed to make *The World's*

End next. "To Marvel's credit," he recalled, "Kevin Feige and Louis D'Esposito said they understood. 'We'll see you in a couple of years,' they said." (Fortunately, Eric Fellner not only got to see *The World's End*—he beat cancer during the production of the movie.)

Wright showed up at the 2012 Comic-Con anyway, walking onstage during Marvel's presentation, brandishing an issue of *Marvel Premiere* #47. Wright joked with the crowd that he was taking "the Terrence Malick approach to superhero films"—the revered director had a twenty-year gap in his filmography between *Days of Heaven* and *The Thin Red Line*—and showed off the minute of *Ant-Man* footage he had shot two weeks earlier. "I shot a little test, because when I say 'little test' it was genuinely to test what it looks like when he's little," Wright explained. That was the only footage Wright would ever shoot for *Ant-Man*. When he completed *The World's End* and returned to his diminutive hero in 2013, nine years after he first met with Feige, he discovered that—once again—much had changed at Marvel Studios.

The problem wasn't how the MCU timeline had advanced in the past decade. "It is pretty standalone in the way we're linking it to the others," Wright said of his movie. "I want to put the crazy premise of it into a real world, which is why I think *Iron Man* really works." Marvel Studios, however, was no longer fueled by improvisation and guesswork: it had settled into a road-tested system for making movies. If Marvel Studios didn't have a formula, then it at least had a recipe. And it certainly had a process—one that involved lots of oversight and feedback and discussion. Wright soon discovered that he would be getting notes not only from Feige, but from Joss Whedon and from the Creative Committee in New York.

In October 2013, Marvel set a July 2015 release date for *Ant-Man*, saying that the movie would kick off Phase Three of the MCU, and began casting. Simon Pegg, Wright's frequent collaborator, was rumored to be up for the lead, as was Armie Hammer (*The Social Network*). The final decision, however, came down to Paul Rudd and Joseph Gordon-Levitt (*Inception*). Although the latter denied he was on the shortlist, Marvel was pushing for him to play Scott Lang because the studio wanted to add some younger blood to its future Avengers. Rudd, whose prolific film career had begun in 1995 with *Clueless*, was twelve years older than Gordon-Levitt, but Wright wanted Rudd, seeing in him the same mixture of charm, vulnerability, and comedic timing that characterized the director's prior protagonists. The December announcement of Rudd's casting was soon followed by Michael Douglas (in the role of Hank Pym), then Evangeline Lilly, Michael Peña, and Patrick Wilson.

Wright prepared for principal photography, scheduled to start in May 2014, assembling a trusted coterie of department heads who had collaborated with him on his other films (including cinematographer Bill Pope and production designer Marcus Rowland). There was some friction between Wright's chosen personnel and the in-house Marvel staffers—each crew had its own working methods—but nothing insurmountable.

Wright and Cornish were already addressing what seemed like an endless stream of new notes from the Creative Committee. Before Wright went into preproduction, the message from New York was that they loved the director's take on Ant-Man and his script was in excellent shape. Once the movie had an actual release date, the Committee wanted to find ways to connect Ant-Man with the rest of the Marvel Cinematic Universe. It peppered the writers with questions: If Hank Pym had been active in the past, wouldn't S.H.I.E.L.D. have contacted him? Shouldn't Pym have interacted with Howard Stark, Tony's father?

Feige accepted these questions as not only a necessary evil created by Marvel's corporate structure but part of the architecture of the Marvel Cinematic Universe. As he observed, "Filmmakers we've worked with before, or new filmmakers coming in, inherently understand the notion of the shared sandbox more than the initial filmmakers did, because the sandbox didn't exist." Wright had come up with his story before the sandbox existed, but now he found himself up to his neck in sand.

Wright and Cornish were happy to make revisions that would inch their story closer to what Marvel wanted, but they were adamant that they needed to maintain the tone of the movie they had written. Every time they thought that they had addressed the final notes from Marvel, they would receive more. In March, Wright and the Creative Committee agreed to postpone the beginning of production to July so the script issues could get sorted out. Marvel Studios handed off the script to an in-house writer who did a pass that addressed all of the Creative Committee's notes. In mid-May, around the time that filming was originally supposed to start, Marvel showed that revised draft to Wright—and he was horrified.

The story hadn't changed significantly, but swaths of dialogue had been altered, and references to the wider MCU had been shoehorned in. Wright hated the new script and felt betrayed by its very existence: he and Cornish believed that they had been working in good faith to address Marvel's notes and find a middle ground.

The efforts of Marvel Studios to push the process forward so Wright could start shooting the movie had backfired spectacularly. On May 23rd, the studio and the director announced they had parted ways "due to differences in their visions of the film." Most of Wright's department heads decamped at the same time, both out of loyalty and out of recognition that the movie was not going to start shooting in July. The production also lost Patrick Wilson, who had other commitments in the fall.

"I wish it wasn't as late in the day as it was," Feige said, "but it just had become clear that there was an impasse that we had never reached before. We've worked with lots of unbelievably talented filmmakers like Edgar before, and of course there are disagreements along the way. We had always found a way around it, a way to battle through it and emerge on the other side with a better product. It just became clear that both of us was [*sic*] just being too polite over the past eight years, I guess! Then it was clear that, 'Oh you're really not gonna stop talking about that note?' 'Oh, you're really not gonna do that note?' Alright, this isn't working."

Whedon, then still one of the central figures of the MCU, seemed as confused by what had happened as anyone else. "I thought the script was not only the best script that Marvel had ever had, but the most Marvel script I'd read. I had no interest in Ant-Man," he said. "I read the script, and was like, 'Of course! This is so good!'"

Wright tweeted, and then deleted, a Photoshopped image of Buster Keaton, looking sad and holding a Cornetto ice cream—Keaton had been notoriously regretful about working with big film studios and the compromises to his artistic vision that he had made as a result. A few years later, Wright tried to give a polite overview of where things had gone wrong. "I wanted to make a Marvel movie but I don't think they really wanted to make an Edgar Wright movie," he said. "Having written all my other movies, that's a tough thing to move forward. Suddenly becoming a director for hire on it, you're sort of less emotionally invested and you start to wonder why you're there, really."

*

FEIGE TOOK STOCK. Although losing Wright was a high-profile embarrassment, he still had a project that he regarded as very close to ready, and Marvel Studios still had Rudd and Douglas under contract. The studio didn't move the release date after Wright quit, insisting that *Ant-Man* would still come out in July 2015; it just needed a new director, one willing to board a moving train and follow the Marvel method. Rudd suggested Adam McKay, who had directed him in *Anchorman*.

"[Rudd] called me when Edgar Wright stepped away from the project and told me what was going on," McKay said. "I was a little dubious just because I'm friends with Edgar and I didn't know what the story was, and then when I kind of heard what happened, that Edgar had parted ways, and then I saw their materials. I was like, 'God, this is pretty cool.' Ultimately I didn't want to jump in as a director—I had too many other projects going and it was too tight—but I thought, 'You know what, I can rewrite this, and I can do a lot of good by rewriting it.'" Rudd and McKay agreed to revise the screenplay together, as quickly as possible, while Marvel searched for a new director. For the first time since Edward Norton on *The*

Incredible Hulk, Marvel Studios was paying a movie star to rewrite the film he would be headlining.

McKay and Rudd sequestered themselves in a series of hotel rooms, periodically getting a change of scenery by flying to a new city. According to McKay, "It was like six to eight weeks: we just ground it out and did a giant rewrite of the script. I was really proud of what we did. I really thought we put some amazing stuff in there and built on an already strong script from Edgar Wright."

One thing they added was more substance for Evangeline Lilly's character, Hope Van Dyne. Lilly (one of the stars of *Lost*) had an unusually strong bargaining position—because her contract was still being finalized when Wright left, she hadn't signed it yet. "I think everyone was a little uncomfortable because we all loved Edgar and were very passionate to work with him," she said. She almost quit the movie, but Rudd and McKay made Hope an expert in hand-to-hand combat and established a more complicated daughter-father relationship with Hank Pym. After Lilly read the revised pages, she signed her deal. "In a film of this size, I don't think you necessarily expect your voice to be heard, especially if you're not one of the superstars in the franchise," she said. "I was honored that my opinions were seriously considered."

"The idea, the trajectory, the goal, and the blueprint of it all, is really Edgar and Joe," Rudd maintained. "It's their story. We changed some scenes, we added new sequences, we changed some characters, we added new characters. If you took the two scripts and held them up together they'd be very different—but the idea is all theirs." Wright and Cornish received final screenplay credit alongside McKay and Rudd. To slake the Creative Committee's thirst for greater integration with the MCU, Rudd and McKay inserted a flashback appearance for Peggy Carter of S.H.I.E.L.D. and created a scene in which Ant-Man would face off with the Falcon (Anthony Mackie) on the new Avengers Compound, a location established at the end of *Age of Ultron*.

Rudd took a break from his rewriting duties to attend the 2013

Comic-Con, doing a panel with the established stars of the MCU, an experience he compared to "going to a music convention with the Beatles." He had played an extended guest role in the final seasons of *Friends*, in episodes airing from 2002 to 2004, and this new experience felt similar to him, even if Marvel was hoping he could be a crucial part of its next generation. "I'm just on the periphery of a beloved group of people," he said. "I'm enjoying this surreal and fun experience, but I feel like Cousin Oliver to the rest of the Brady Bunch."

Feige still had to find a comedy director who could handle a large production that was already well underway. The studio vetted Rawson Marshall Thurber (*We're the Millers*), Ruben Fleischer (*Zombieland*), and David Wain (*Wet Hot American Summer*) before landing on Peyton Reed (*Bring It On*), who had also been on the shortlist for *Guardians of the Galaxy*. Reed was willing to helm the project if Marvel would push back production one month to give him just enough time to get oriented and to replace the department heads who had left en masse with Wright to work on his next movie, *Baby Driver*.

Film journalist Eric Vespe wrote on the *Ain't It Cool News* website that while he would always mourn the Edgar Wright movie that didn't happen, he was excited to see what Peyton Reed would do with the project. After he published that comment, he said, "I got a salty DM from Edgar going, 'Yeah, well, let's see if they let Peyton bring any personality or character to this movie.'"

In the short period before the cameras rolled, Reed made some significant contributions. Working with Rudd and McKay, he came up with the climactic sequence where Ant-Man enters the Quantum Realm. He also decided to employ microphotography, which has shallow depths of field, for some sequences, helping establish Ant-Man's wee stature in a real-world setting. Working with Sarah Halley Finn, he filled out the cast: Corey Stoll (*House of Cards*) replaced Patrick Wilson in the villainous role of Darren Cross, aka Yellowjacket.

Principal photography finally began in August. To quell the bad buzz after Wright's departure, Marvel Studios invited press to the set. Between takes, Reed, Rudd, and Feige emphasized Marvel's talking points: the movie was on track and wasn't an afterthought to the studio. Feige went so far as to explain that *Ant-Man* was no longer the first movie in Phase Three of the MCU; it was now the last movie of Phase Two. "The truth is, the phases mean a lot to me," Feige said. "*Civil War* is the start of Phase Three. It just is."

On its completion, *Ant-Man* was a likeable movie with one genius sequence, a Wright/Cornish invention, in which a miniaturized Ant-Man and Yellowjacket battle on a child's train table, threatened by the toy Thomas the Tank Engine barreling toward them. It was a respectable hit, earning $180.2 million in North America and $519 million worldwide. That wasn't close to *Avengers* money, but it was good enough to merit a sequel and to establish Ant-Man so he could appear in *Civil War*.

∗

EDGAR WRIGHT HAD dreamed of making a movie starring a Marvel character, but he didn't want to make a Marvel Cinematic Universe movie. As the MCU entered Phase Three, the Wright incident left Marvel Studios with a reputation that it was unfriendly to directors who wanted to leave a personal imprint on their movies. "There seemed to be a period," Vespe said, "when Marvel was bringing in all these journeymen directors who would do what the studio wanted, or these people who they could, frankly, bully."

The truth was somewhat more nuanced. Marvel Studios was in the business of producing a steady supply of broadly appealing superhero movies that had narrative and visual continuity with its other block-busters. Directors who were willing to cede a measure of control in those areas were granted a relatively free hand with other aspects of their movies, so long as they could make the results entertaining.

James Gunn had the good fortune of working on an offbeat project so many parsecs away from the mainstream of the MCU that he didn't need to worry much about integrating his story into it. Joe and Anthony Russo were enthusiastic company men with the talent to execute a Marvel movie at the highest level. They would make as thrilling a film as possible within the parameters set by the studio, and they had no particular ambitions to go beyond those boundaries.

Joss Whedon was, at heart, a comics-continuity nerd who loved elaborate crossovers and callbacks; he made TV shows full of them. He sometimes complained about the MCU's shifting storylines, but Marvel trusted him enough to make him the hall monitor of its own continuity. And since Whedon lacked the visual acumen of some other big-name directors, he ceded the spectacle and action beats to Marvel's craftsmen. When he tried to get artier than one might expect in a summer popcorn movie, however—the farmhouse sequence in *Age of Ultron*, for example—his relationship with Marvel Studios foundered.

Edgar Wright wanted to make an Ant-Man movie, but he wanted it to reflect his vision, not the larger needs of the MCU—so much so, he walked away from his own film. It marks a significant "*What If . . . ?*" moment in the history of Marvel Studios: If Wright had filmed his Ant-Man script in the early years of Marvel, he likely would have been able to make it his way, and he might have even shifted the trajectory of the Marvel Cinematic Universe, infusing it with his own sensibility and humor. He just waited too long.

PHASE THREE

★

Tangled Web

✴

Anyone can wear the mask.

Spider-Man: Into the Spider-Verse

CAPTAIN AMERICA: CIVIL WAR WAS SCHEDULED TO begin filming in May 2015, but in March, screenwriters Christopher Markus and Stephen McFeely still weren't sure which Marvel heroes would be facing off against each other. They knew that Robert Downey Jr. would reprise his role as Tony Stark, in a deal that would ultimately earn him $64 million in salary and profit-sharing, and that Chadwick Boseman would be making his debut as Black Panther. The writers had opted to include Paul Rudd as Ant-Man (and to debut his Giant-Man powers), but not Evangeline Lilly as the Wasp, since her character would get her in-costume debut in the planned *Ant-Man* sequel. As the MCU entered its third phase, the complexity of its story onscreen was mirrored by the complexity of behind-the-scenes negotiations, especially when it came to Marvel Comics' most famous character.

There was a gap in Tony Stark's team of heroes that the writers hoped to fill with Spider-Man, who had long been unavailable to the MCU. Kevin Feige had told them not to be optimistic. He had been discussing a Spider-Man deal with Sony, but he wasn't sure whether it would come together. Markus and McFeely had written drafts of the screenplay both with and without Peter Parker, making Spider-Man a bonus, not an integral part of the main plot. Then Feige appeared in the doorway of the writers' office. He didn't say anything, but he held both his hands up with his fingers splayed out, except for the ring and middle fingers curling back on his palm, the internationally recognized hand gesture for shooting web fluid. Markus and McFeely understood they finally had a workable draft of the movie—the Spider-Man draft.

Thirty-one years after Marvel had licensed the Spider-Man film rights to Menahem Golan, twenty-six years after James Cameron became interested in the webslinger, and eighteen years after Sony consolidated its claim on those movie rights in a $10 million deal, Spider-Man would be making his debut in the Marvel Cinematic Universe. Every strand in the process was tangled and sticky, of course.

In 2007, Sony had released *Spider-Man 3*, with a lineup of villains that included Sandman (Thomas Hayden Church), Venom (Topher Grace), and a new version of the Green Goblin played by franchise star James Franco. It was critically lambasted but grossed $894 million worldwide, the most of any *Spider-Man* movie to that point. The steadily increasing box office for the character kept pace with the growing cost of production: retaining director Sam Raimi and the stars Tobey Maguire and Kirsten Dunst was becoming more expensive with every sequel.

Nevertheless, Sony Pictures and Avi Arad (who had left Marvel Studios in 2006 but retained his position as producer on the Spider-Man movies) put together a package for *Spider-Man 4*. Anne Hathaway would play Felicia Hardy, who would become the antihero Black Cat from the comics; John Malkovich would join the franchise as the Vulture; and Angelina Jolie was briefly attached to the film playing the Vulture's daughter, who would don the wings as the Vulturess after a fight with Spider-Man kicked Vulture out of the movie (by literally kicking him off a building).

Raimi, however, was overwhelmed by the pressures on him. He

not only would have to outdo himself yet again but faced the daunting task of delivering profits on a movie that might cost close to $400 million. In January 2010, on a late-night phone call to Amy Pascal, the head of the Sony Pictures film division, a stressed-out Raimi quit the movie. In a 2013 interview, Raimi recalled telling her: "I don't want to make a movie that is less than great, so I think we shouldn't make this picture. Go ahead with your reboot, which you've been planning anyway."

Raimi could stop making Spider-Man movies, but Sony couldn't—the franchise was too popular for Sony to wrap it up. Ideally, Pascal might have waited some years before making another installment, to avoid oversaturation, but that wasn't possible. Sony's contract with Marvel specified that after the release of a Spider-Man movie, the studio had to start production of the next one within three years and nine months, and get it into theaters within five years and nine months. Otherwise, the hugely valuable Spider-Man movie rights would revert to Marvel.

Ike Perlmutter had long been irritated that Sony had paid just $10 million for the American film rights to Spider-Man in 1998, when Marvel was at its most vulnerable. He routinely called high-ranking Sony Pictures executives, including Pascal and CEO Michael Lynton, to hector them about a minor point or a perceived slight. After the first *Spider-Man* movie was a hit in 2002, Marvel sued Sony over the merchandising deal. (Sony countersued.) The 1998 deal had mandated that Marvel would get a lump payment for any Spider-Man film plus just 5 percent of the profits. Sony had the rights to sell toys based on the movie, while Marvel retained the rights to "classic" Spider-Man product (there was also some profit-sharing in both directions). The 2002 suit was eventually settled. Sony gave up some of its merchandising rights, and the distinction between "film" and "classic" toys was eliminated; Marvel would control all Spider-Man merchandise from that point forward. In the immediate aftermath of any Spider-Man movie, Sony would get 25 percent of Marvel's profit from that merchandise.

Within days of Raimi's late-night call, Sony announced that while the director was leaving the *Spider-Man* franchise, it planned to reboot the series with a new director and actor. That enraged Perlmutter, who had hoped Sony would let the character return to Marvel. To assuage him, Sony amended the Spider-Man deal once again in 2011: for $175 million, Marvel bought out Sony's 25 percent share of the merchandise profits. In addition, each time Sony made a Spider-Man feature film, Marvel would pay Sony $35 million. The movies sold so much merchandise, Marvel was willing to help finance them.

To relaunch Spider-Man, Pascal turned to the aptly named Marc Webb, who had directed just one feature film, the inventive indie romance *500 Days of Summer*, starring Joseph Gordon-Levitt and Zooey Deschanel. His new leads were the lanky, up-and-coming Brit Andrew Garfield (*The Social Network*) as Peter Parker—whose casting was announced abruptly at an impromptu press conference in Cancun, Mexico—and the rising American star Emma Stone (*Easy A*) as Gwen Stacy. (In the comic books, Gwen Stacy was Peter Parker's most serious love interest before Mary Jane Watson.) Sony retained the production staff that had been hired for *Spider-Man 4*, reassigning them to a movie now called *The Amazing Spider-Man*.

The movie retold the origin of Spider-Man and then pitted him against the Lizard, a large reptilian monster played in its human form by Rhys Ifans. Webb and screenwriter James Vanderbilt originally included a subplot about how Peter Parker's deceased parents had arranged for him to have "special" blood, meaning that any other teenager who got bitten by a radioactive spider wouldn't have developed his remarkable powers. Teaser posters for the movie promised an "Untold Origin" that wasn't in the final movie; producers Avi Arad and Matt Tolmach, another former Sony executive who, like Pascal, had stepped into the world of producing, ultimately decided that the film needed to hew closer to Spider-Man canon.

The Amazing Spider-Man, which appeared in theaters in July 2012, made $758 million worldwide: a lot of money, but also the least of any Spider-Man movie that Sony had produced. Pascal was trying to develop a library of tentpole releases based on brand-name intellectual property rather than A-list movie stars, but her strategy wasn't yielding as much money as she hoped for. That same year, the studio's *Men in Black 3* grossed $624 million worldwide, but contractually, $90 million of that money had to be redistributed to star Will Smith and producer Steven Spielberg. Sony also released the James Bond movie *Skyfall*, which grossed $1.1 billion worldwide, but the studio earned just $57 million from the release. (MGM still owned the Bond franchise, but when MGM came out of bankruptcy in 2010, Sony had cut a deal in which the larger studio would shoulder 50 percent of the production costs of Bond movies and get 25 percent of the profit back.) "Even though we were #1 at the box office," Pascal wrote about 2012, "it was a shitty year."

Pascal cast around for a plan better than "make another Spider-Man movie every two years with diminishing returns." Marvel Studios' massive success with *The Avengers* in 2012 suggested a new strategy, albeit one that had become popular all over Hollywood: Sony could launch spinoffs of secondary Spider-Man characters like Venom and Kraven the Hunter, ultimately bringing them together for the supervillain team the Sinister Six. Pascal also considered an all-star team of female supporting characters, such as Black Cat, Silver Sable, and Silk—or maybe a movie about the adventures of Aunt May and Uncle Ben before Peter Parker was born. Sony publicly characterized Spider-Man IP as a "rich universe"—the contract with Marvel detailing which comic-book characters Sony could use in its movies listed 856 in total, from A'Sai to Mickey Zimmer—even as privately Pascal complained, "I have only the Spider universe, not the Marvel universe, and in it are only his villain and relatives and girlfriend. No superhero team-up here." A lack of access to top-tier characters hadn't stopped Marvel Studios' rapid expansion when it launched Phase One, but Sony was stymied.

The Amazing Spider-Man 2, released in 2014, brought back Garfield and Stone, while Webb executed the mandate from Sony to include as many supervillains as possible: Electro (Jamie Foxx), Harry Osborn aka the Green Goblin (Dane DeHaan), the Rhino (Paul Giamatti). As if the movie didn't have enough going on, it ended with tragedy: as in the comics, Gwen Stacy died in a fall and

Spider-Man was unable to save her. That bummer ending destroyed the best thing about the *Amazing* franchise, the onscreen chemistry between the real-life couple Andrew Garfield and Emma Stone.

Although Kevin Feige was not involved in the development of the film, it was nominally a Marvel Studios coproduction, and so Pascal periodically reached out to get his feedback. Feige sent notes laying out his concerns with the movie, including his worries that Andrew Garfield's performance was scattershot and emotionally inconsistent. He particularly criticized the "special blood" plotline, which had been revived:

> We're distracted by the idea that Peter became Spider-Man b/c of his father's blood—all this special back story with his super-scientist dad fights with the idea that Peter is normal kid from Queens who becomes the greatest super-hero in the world . . .

Pascal could see for herself that the movie was overstuffed and disconnected. In an email to Doug Belgrad, president of Sony Pictures, two months before its release, she enumerated the problems: "Uneven, schizo tone . . . weird, disjointed, no one single great set piece because action is just big and not storytelling, not funny . . . if I'm really honest, wrong director and wrong casting." She concluded, "We will almost get away with it and we can never go back."

"Almost get away with it" was an accurate prediction. Although the movie was projected to make $865 million and Sony hoped that it would join the "billion dollar club" of top-earning superhero films like *The Avengers* and *Iron Man 3*, the worldwide gross was just $709 million. The franchise's numbers were steadily shrinking.

Marvel was disappointed and confused by how the Sony studio and producers Avi Arad and Matt Tolmach were stewarding the Spider-Man character. Alan Fine of Marvel Entertainment (and the still-active Creative Committee) emailed his thoughts to Feige after reading a screenplay for *The Amazing Spider-Man 2*: "This story is way too dark, way too depressing. I wanted to burn the draft after I read it."

For his part, Feige told Fine, he was dismayed by the lack of continuity between the Raimi films and the Webb films: "I saw the spider bite in Sam Raimi's movie and it was totally different than the Spider bite in ASM. They have rebooted," Feige wrote. "In a million years I would not advocate rebooting the Iron Man MCU. To me it's James Bond and we can keep telling new stories for decades even with different actors."

Fine agreed that it was a dicey maneuver with a film franchise: "Okay for comic books but I wouldn't even do it with cartoon animation. Had I known, I would never have approved that strategy. Avi is totally nuts. More confirmation to me that he never knew what he was doing."

✷

WHEN *THE AMAZING SPIDER-MAN 2* underperformed, Marvel saw an opportunity: Sony wasn't going to abandon its claim to Spider-Man, but maybe there was a way that the two studios could work together, to the benefit of both. To broach the idea of collaborating, Marvel decided, Perlmutter would court his counterpart, Lynton, while Feige would approach his, Pascal.

Feige convened a top-secret summit of Marvel's creative producers at a hotel in Santa Monica. The brainstorming session was built around two questions. First, if a deal with Sony to share Spider-Man was possible, what could that deal look like? Second, if Marvel Studios finally had control of its long-off-limits flagship character, what stories would it want to tell?

Soon after the summit, Feige visited Pascal on the Sony lot. The two executives had lunch—gourmet sandwiches—on the porch connected to her office. Pascal thought they were meeting so that Feige could give notes on Sony's plans for *The Amazing Spider-Man 3*. Feige had a different agenda. As he remembered it, she said, "I really want you to help on this next movie. We have these great ideas for the next one. It's amazing stuff."

Feige replied, "I'm not good at that—giving advice and leaving." He made his pitch: he knew that Pascal and Sony were struggling with how to go forward with Spider-Man but believed that Marvel Studios knew how to handle the character. Feige told her, "The only way I know how to do anything is to just do it entirely. So why don't you let us do it. Don't think of it as two studios. And don't think of it as giving another studio back the rights. No change of hands of rights. No change of hands of money. Just engage us to produce it. Just pretend it's like what DC did with Christopher Nolan. I'm not saying we're Nolan, but I am saying there is a production company that is doing this pretty well. Just engage the services of that production company to make the movie."

Pascal did not respond well to Feige's proposal. More specifically, she threw her sandwich at him and said, "Get the fuck out of here."

Michael Lynton was more receptive to Perlmutter's overtures, especially after Bob Iger went over Lynton's head and mentioned a possible Spider-Man deal to Kaz Hirai, chairman of the Sony corporation (who was surprised to learn of *The Amazing Spider-Man 2*'s problems). "Michael [Lynton] had no ego about who creatively oversees Spider-Man," said Michael De Luca, then a Sony executive. "He felt this is a giant asset for the studio, so let's get the best movie made. I think Amy felt personally guilty the fans didn't love the last Andrew Garfield movie and felt she owed Peter Parker a better outing. She wanted to deliver that outing."

Sandwich-hurling aside, Sony's leadership was open to a deal, but Perlmutter squeezed too tightly. He insisted that if Marvel produced the next Spider-Man movie, it should have a 50 percent share of the profits, but he was willing to offer only a 5 percent share of any MCU movie where the character made a guest appearance. Sony rejected the offer out of hand. As far as Sony could tell, those numbers were an expression of Perlmutter's lingering bitterness over the 1998 deal in which Marvel got only 5 percent of any Spider-Man movie profits.

In November 2014, hackers released a vast trove of internal Sony Pictures documents, including over 200,000 email messages. (The US government concluded that the culprits were sponsored by the North Korean government, in an act of retribution for Sony releasing *The Interview*, a Seth Rogen comedy about a journalist who gets recruited by the CIA to kill the North Korean Supreme Leader, Kim Jong-un.) Among the countless problems that resulted from Sony emails ending up on WikiLeaks was that movie fans now knew that Marvel had proposed to integrate Spider-Man into the MCU but Sony had turned the studio down.

By the time the emails were released, negotiations between Marvel and Sony had ended. Pascal shuffled Sony's release schedule, switching the announced 2016 date for *The Amazing Spider-Man 3* and the 2018 date for *The Sinister Six*, hoping to build some buzz around the franchise with a successful spinoff. When she hired writer/director Drew Goddard away from the showrunner job at *Daredevil*, Ike Perlmutter made Goddard's departure as difficult as possible—not just because he wanted Marvel Television to succeed, but apparently because he was still salty that Sony hadn't accepted his Spider-Man proposal. Goddard got to work on a *Sinister Six* script; by the end of 2014, he had a draft that took Spider-Man and his villains to the Savage Land (in the Marvel comic books, a prehistoric pocket of jungle life hidden in Antarctica), where Spider-Man would ride a T-rex.

Although Pascal hadn't reacted well to Feige's proposal that she subcontract Spider-Man back to Marvel, the more she thought about the plan, and the more online clamoring she saw for it after the Sony leaks, the more sense it made to her: if Spider-Man appeared in a popular movie, that would lead filmgoers to his next solo film. For years, Marvel had been proving this maneuver worked—and an MCU movie seemed like a safer bet than *The Sinister Six*. It helped that Pascal genuinely respected Feige. She remembered well how in the Sam Raimi era of Spider-Man movies, he showed up at all the meetings, got everyone coffee, and remained silent. "Which makes you love somebody," she said, because "when they do open their mouth, you realize that they've been thinking all these big thoughts and are really smart, but never had to hear themselves talk."

Pascal invited Feige over to her house for dinner, and this time she refrained from throwing food. The two executives discussed what a new Spider-Man franchise could be if they rebooted the character together. If Peter Parker was a teenager again, they agreed, they should emphasize the inherent drama of that age, making something like a John Hughes high school movie set in the MCU. Feige suggested that if the new Spider-Man debuted in *Captain America: Civil War*, his suit could be made by Tony Stark.

In January 2015, Perlmutter, Feige, Lynton, and Pascal had lunch at Perlmutter's condo in Palm Beach, Florida. Since Perlmutter had backed off on his demand that Marvel receive half the profits from any Spider-Man movie, a deal came together quickly. The current actors would be replaced and a new Spider-Man (cast by Marvel) would debut in Marvel Studios' *Captain America: Civil War* in 2016 before starring in his own movie in 2017, the first of at least two movies to be produced by Marvel Studios but paid for and released by Sony Pictures. The question of how to split profits was sidestepped entirely: each studio would finance its own movies and keep all the profits. (Marvel would still owe Sony $35 million for each Spider-Man movie in consideration of the toy rights, but if any of those movies grossed over $750 million, Marvel would receive a bonus that would defray that $35 million payment.) *Civil War* was all Marvel's, and the solo Spider-Man movie was all Sony's; the benefits of integrating Spider-Man into the MCU were significant enough that Marvel was willing to produce Sony's movies to make it happen.

The current Spider-Man producers, notably Avi Arad, wouldn't be involved with the new shared incarnation of Spider-Man, but they would continue to develop properties for Sony based on Spider-Man's friends and foes. Pascal knew that she would struggle to hold onto her job as studio head: the email hack had been too embarrassing for Sony and had released too many of her frank personal messages. As an exit strategy, she arranged to coproduce the new Spider-Man movies with Feige, meaning she would be an active on-set presence. In a sign of Feige's respect for Pascal's talents, he shared the title of lead producer with her—the first time he had shared that credit in nine years, since the first *Iron Man* and *The Incredible Hulk*. Less than a week after the Palm Beach meeting, Pascal was fired from Sony Pictures. She formed her own production company, Pascal Pictures, to produce franchise movies featuring the likes of Spider-Man and Ghostbusters for Sony without being the head of the studio.

Sony held a summit of its own in January 2015 with producers Avi Arad and Matt Tolmach to determine its post-Pascal plans for Spider-Man. *Sinister Six* was set aside indefinitely, but the studio proceeded with two other feature films. The first was a solo *Venom* movie; it had been intended to tie into *The Amazing Spider-Man* franchise, but now it would feature the anti-hero without a cross-over. The other movie was wall-to-wall crossovers: an animated picture called *Spider-Man: Into the Spider-Verse*, produced by Phil Lord and Christopher Miller (*Cloudy with a Chance of Meatballs*, *The Lego Movie*). Their story was inspired by the "Spider-Verse" run of *Spider-Man* comics where, beginning in 2014, writer Dan Slott had brought together just about every Spider-being from every possible medium, including even Peter Porker, the Spectacular Spider-Ham (a comedy character from the 1980s: Peter Porker was a spider who was bitten by a radioactive pig).

Feige, Pascal, and casting director Sarah Halley Finn began looking for candidates to play the new Peter Parker and quickly settled on a favorite: British actor Tom Holland, who had only a handful of film credits (including 2013's *The Impossible*), but who had played the title role in the musical *Billy Elliott* in a production in London's West End. Finn noted the teenager's work ethic. "I knew that he had been dancing eight hours a day since he was nine years old. He had already shown that he was a professional and could go on a set and show up for work every day."

Marvel brought its two top contenders, Holland and Asa Butterfield (*Ender's Game*), to Atlanta, where *Civil War* was already filming, for a screen test with Robert Downey Jr. Since Pascal and Feige were planning to show a close relationship between Tony Stark and Peter Parker, a chemistry test seemed vital. Pascal said that it was usually hard to watch people screen-test with Downey, since the actor had a natural penchant for stealing scenes, but Holland more than held his own. After his test, Downey walked over to the monitor where Feige and Pascal were watching and gave them an enthusiastic thumbs-up. Holland was in.

The *Civil War* scene introducing Peter Parker was slimmed down during production rewrites, but Downey successfully advocated for restoring its original length (a suggestion he couched as being to the benefit of Holland and the Spider-Man character but that incidentally increased Downey's own screen time). While *Civil War* filmed, Marvel Studios gave the Spider-Man solo movie a slot on its Phase Three release schedule—July 2017, pushing back *Thor: Ragnarok* and displacing the Inhumans movie entirely—and then rushed to make that date. The movie was soon titled *Spider-Man: Homecoming*, a sly nod to the character returning to Marvel. To direct it, the studio hired Jon Watts, who had proved he could work with young actors in his sophomore film *Cop Car*, a thriller where two young boys steal a police vehicle. Watt's marching orders: to the greatest extent possible, make *Homecoming* feel like a John Hughes movie. Once again, the MCU proved that it was capable of swallowing other genres whole.

Marvel had considered the team of John Francis Daley (the *Freaks and Geeks* actor) and Jonathan Goldstein to serve as writers/directors of the movie—they had made *Vacation*, the 2015 installment of the *National Lampoon's Vacation* series—but after picking Watts, hired them to write a draft of the screenplay. "We wanted to depart from some of what was in the comic books," said Goldstein, "We definitely didn't want to rehash the death of Uncle Ben. We felt like the origin story had been told so many times that either you knew it or you didn't, and if you didn't, you figure it out pretty quickly. When you start your movie with a death in the family, then you spend a lot of the movie sort of dealing with that emotionally and recovering from it, and it's just not a ton of fun, obviously." That attitude permeated the production: Marvel needed to deliver a version of Spider-Man that was different from what audiences had seen before. (But not *too* different: Sony and Marvel had a seventy-one-page license agreement detailing which aspects of Spider-Man comics Sony could use and listing Spider-Man's powers from "Super-Human Jumping Ability" to "Super-Human Adherence." According to the license agreement, Spider-Man could not torture, smoke tobacco, or have sex before the age of sixteen; Peter Parker had to be heterosexual, Caucasian, and raised in Queens.)

The Marvel Studios plan for Peter Parker: place him in the middle of the Marvel Cinematic Universe. While the Sony incarnations of Spider-Man had typically battled evil scientists with ties to the Osborn or Parker families, the MCU Spider-Man would face off against villains who had a grudge against Tony Stark, pulling Peter Parker away from high school and into the orbit of the Avengers. In *Homecoming*, Michael Keaton played Adrian Toomes, who becomes the villainous thief called the Vulture after Stark puts Toomes's clean-up crew out of business following the Battle of New York (the climax of *The Avengers*).

Ryan Meinerding of the Marvel visual-development team had the idea of turning the eyes of Spider-Man's costume into working lenses rather than fixed apertures, letting the character emote better while in costume. "In the past, designers were hesitant to embrace having the eyes surrounded by the thick border. Once you add a calligraphy to the eyes there's an impression of a masquerade mask—which, understandably, is a direction not many costume designers would want to explore," Meinerding said. But when they decided that the Stark technology in Spider-Man's suit would dynamically change how the eyes worked, that gave the filmmakers more control and freedom of expression: "He could squint and struggle to see, and that black line would get a lot thicker. His eyes didn't have to be constant and static objects."

The studio strived to avoid scenes of Spider-Man cutting through the Manhattan skyline, swinging from one construction crane to the next, since that had been done extensively in past movies. The *Homecoming* set pieces would take place in the suburbs, on the Washington Monument, on the Staten Island ferry, and on top of a large cargo plane.

The movie debuted in July 2017 and grossed $880 million worldwide, a significant increase over the declining numbers of *The Amazing Spider-Man* version of the franchise. Sony was delighted that

Spider-Man's box-office trajectory was headed upward again, while Marvel was thrilled to have Spider-Man in the MCU ensemble. Spider-Man returned in *Avengers: Infinity War* (released the following year), and although he was a supporting character in a cast of dozens, the studio made sure he had plenty of on-brand moments: Peter Parker ditches a high school field trip to stow away on a spaceship; he is moved more than he wants to admit when Tony Stark officially makes him an Avenger by off-handedly knighting him during a dangerous trip halfway across the galaxy; he trades pop-culture wisecracks with Star-Lord; he gets in a fight with somebody vastly more powerful than him but holds his own; and he delivers one of the movie's most poignant lines ("Please, sir, I don't want to go"—dialogue improvised by Holland) before he dematerializes in Stark's arms.

✳

MARVEL STUDIOS, at a new pinnacle of cultural power, could not only push Avi Arad aside—for the second time—it could bend another studio to its will, at least for a while. In 2019, Tom Holland appeared as Spider-Man in two billion-dollar movies: one for Marvel, one for Sony. First he rematerialized for a brief appearance in *Avengers: Endgame*, then he starred in *Spider-Man: Far from Home*. The second solo Spider-Man movie Marvel Studios produced for Sony was also the final movie in Phase Three of the MCU. Jake Gyllenhaal played Mysterio, another disgruntled ex-employee of Tony Stark, while Samuel L. Jackson showed up as Nick Fury so he could growl at Peter Parker and tie the action more firmly to the MCU. The plot involved a school vacation to Europe, in part because relocating to another continent ensured the movie would avoid repeating the look of any previous Spider-Man adventures. The movie made $1.132 billion globally, busting into the billion-dollar club and validating Avi Arad's long-ago estimate of the character's inherent value. Marvel Studios had made Sony's highest-grossing film ever.

The MCU version of Spider-Man was working exactly as Feige

and Pascal had hoped—but the Spider-team at Sony, led by Arad and Tolmach, was also doing better than ever. In 2018, the studio finally produced a Spider-Man villain spinoff: *Venom*. Reimagining the parasitic alien black goo as the star of a buddy comedy, featuring two wildly divergent performances by Tom Hardy, *Venom* was a hit, grossing $856 million worldwide—and with a mid-credits scene featuring Woody Harrelson, set up a sequel featuring the symbiote called Carnage. "Sony did a fantastic job with *Venom*," Pascal conceded. "Everything is about characters. If you have a great character, you can make a great movie."

Later that year came *Into the Spider-Verse*, featuring a bevy of alternate Spider-heroes, including a film noir version from a 1930s universe (voiced by Nicolas Cage) and a young Japanese girl with a spider-like robot from an anime universe. The central Spider-Man was Miles Morales, a Black Latino character created by Brian Michael Bendis and Sara Pichelli to replace Peter Parker after he died in the *Ultimate Spider-Man* comic books. "Many kids of color, when they were playing superheroes with their friends, their friends wouldn't let them be Batman or Superman because they don't look like those heroes but they could be Spider-Man because anyone could be under that mask," Bendis said when the print character debuted. "But now it's true. It's meant a great deal to a great many people." *Into the Spider-Verse* was a moderate hit ($375 million worldwide) but got rave reviews for its humor and its inventive, layered visuals, winning the Academy Award for Best Animated Picture (the first non-Disney movie in seven years to take that trophy, much to Disney's dismay). Its success put the lie to Pascal's complaint that there wasn't enough material in the Spider-Verse to merit a superhero team-up.

Feige and Pascal expected that the Sony/Marvel Spider-Man deal would cover a trilogy of films, although only two were contractually mandated. But after the success of *Venom* and *Into the Spider-Verse*, Sony felt confident about its own Spider-Sense. (Or its "Peter Tingle.") Midway through the *Far from Home* shoot, Sony told Marvel that it would be reclaiming the Spider-Man solo franchise, reasoning that it didn't need Kevin Feige as producer to make a hit *Spider-Man* movie starring Tom Holland. Marvel kept that bombshell secret from the cast and crew, but after the (insanely profitable) release of *Spider-Man: Far from Home*, the news leaked. Sony would not be renewing the Marvel deal.

CHAPTER TWENTY-THREE

Long Live
the King

Wakanda will no longer watch
from the shadows.

Black Panther

LONG BEFORE CHADWICK BOSEMAN PLAYED A KING, HE
carried himself like one. When Boseman was an undergraduate at Howard University, he studied to be a director and
a playwright, but he shifted his focus to acting with the encouragement of Phylicia Rashad (then a visiting teacher) and the financial support of Denzel Washington (who later jokingly asked for his
money back). One of his earliest professional gigs was a role on a
soap opera, but Boseman became concerned that his part might be a
crude racial stereotype, so he asked the producers to detail his character's family history. He was informed that the character's mother
was a heroin addict and that his father abandoned the family long
ago—and then Boseman was fired for being "difficult." That experience clarified his sense of purpose: if he was going to act, he would
do so on his own terms and would not take roles that played into
pernicious assumptions.

In *42*, Boseman portrayed Jackie Robinson, who broke baseball's
color line. In *Get on Up*, he embodied James Brown, one of the great-

est musical geniuses of the twentieth century. He had a completely different physical presence in each role, but he didn't do a cheap impersonation in either case; both performances were riveting. With his body and his word, Boseman insisted on each man's dignity and importance and humanity. And he brought that same approach to the fictional character T'Challa, the Black Panther.

When Marvel asked Boseman to do the role with an American or British accent, he refused, because he believed that if he did, every line he uttered would imply that Wakanda, the utopian African nation where T'Challa is ruler, had been colonized at some point. "It felt to me like a deal-breaker," he said. "I was like, 'No, this is such an important factor that if we lose this right now, what else are we gonna throw away for the sake of making people feel comfortable?'"

Instead, Boseman employed an accent colored by Xhosa, one of the native tongues of South Africa. "I found a dialect coach from Paytel, South Africa," Boseman said. "We developed a relationship and continued to explore what T'Challa would be. I also worked with Sarah Shepherd, the dialect coach within Marvel, so I'd find something that people would feel is authentic and real, and that hopefully most people will understand. That was the main thing."

Sebastian Stan faced off against Boseman in *Captain America: Civil War*—his character, the brainwashed Winter Soldier, was framed for the assassination of T'Chaka, T'Challa's father—and was immediately impressed. "I was like, 'Oh my God, this guy's going to blow everyone away,'" Stan remembered. "There was such commitment and dedication to everything he was doing. We had a lot of these fight sequences, and we really went for it. I was like, 'He's really showing up. I got to stand tall, too.'"

Boseman played a character who was driven by both vengeance and compassion, and made that contradiction feel true when he confronted the film's villain, Baron Zemo, played by Daniel Bruhl, in the movie's climax. "The turn in the scene towards the end of the movie when I decide not to kill Zemo," said Boseman, "that's the most difficult transition."

The Marvel Studios leadership could see that Boseman had the charisma and the ability to be the standout performer in a new generation of MCU heroes that included Ant-Man, Doctor Strange, and Captain Marvel—he just needed a movie that matched his talent. As soon as *Civil War* wrapped filming, producer Nate Moore worked to make a solo Black Panther movie happen. Moore had long been an advocate for Black characters in the MCU, from the Falcon to Luke Cage, and so he was the natural choice to be the creative producer developing *Black Panther*. Instead of putting out a general call for screenwriters, Moore reached out to a select handful, ultimately hiring Joe Robert Cole, a graduate of the by-then-defunct Marvel Writers Program.

Cole regarded the assignment as more than his next paying gig. "As a kid I played a lot of make-believe and I would change every hero to black," he said. "Instead of James Bond I was James Black; instead of Batman, Blackman. Little brown kids, including my own, don't have to do that. That's amazing to me. This is the movie I wish I'd had to look up to."

By May 2015, the *Black Panther* script was in good enough shape that Moore and Feige went looking for a director. They publicly courted their first choice, Ava DuVernay, a former film publicist who had risen quickly to A-list status after *Selma*, her 2014 feature about the civil rights movement. "I really have a thing about Black people thinking on screen—I think it's important," she said. "Films affect the way we see ourselves as Black people and the way that we are seen by other people." Marvel Studios offered her the choice of two projects that they hoped would break new ground in representation: *Black Panther* and *Captain Marvel*.

DuVernay gravitated toward *Black Panther*, recognizing its potential importance in popular culture, but ultimately declined the job. "I'll just say we had different ideas about what the story would be. Marvel has a certain way of doing things and I think they're fantastic and a lot of people love what they do. I loved that they reached out to me. I loved meeting Chadwick and writers and all the Marvel execs," said DuVernay. "In the end, it comes down to story and perspective. And we just didn't see eye to eye. Better for me to realize that now than cite creative differences later."

Marvel also had discussions with F. Gary Gray (the studio had previously considered him for *The Winter Soldier*) and Ryan Coogler (*Fruitvale Station*), who made the shortlist after the November 2015 release of *Creed*. That movie, a *Rocky* spinoff, demonstrated that Coogler could deliver a hit movie based on preexisting IP. When Gray decided to direct *The Fate of the Furious* (the eighth film in the *Furious* franchise), Coogler quickly became Marvel's top choice.

Moore remembered Coogler's crucial meeting with Feige: "One of his questions to Kevin was, 'You realize that this movie is going to be predominantly a Black cast?'"

Feige's matter-of-fact response: "Yeah, obviously. That's why we're doing it."

To get the job, Coogler also needed to pass muster with Boseman. "The way he works, I feel like he's very methodical," Boseman said about Coogler, "He's cerebral, and there's almost an intuition that he has in terms of working with all the different departments. I think he brings the independent filmmaker to a big budget movie, and that brings a certain amount of grit and reality to something that is fantasy."

Coogler, officially hired in January 2016, wanted the hidden nation of Wakanda to feel both plausible and Afrofuturist. He convinced Marvel Studios that to get that balance right, he needed to bypass the studio's in-house artists in favor of his own crew of department heads, notably cinematographer Rachel Morrison (the first female director of photography on a Marvel Studios movie); production designer Hannah Beachler, who had worked on *Moonlight* and on Beyoncé's "visual album" for *Lemonade*; and the revered costume designer Ruth E. Carter, who had made a dozen movies with Spike Lee, dating back to 1988's *School Daze*, and who had received Oscar nominations for her work on Lee's *Malcolm X* and Steven Spielberg's *Amistad*.

During preproduction, the *Black Panther* team made multiple trips to Africa. Carter spent time in Central Africa, while the movie's composer, Ludwig Göransson, went on tour with the Senegalese musician Baaba Maal. Coogler and many of his department heads made a pilgrimage up the continent's east coast, starting in the South African province of KwaZulu-Natal. Along the way, they visited with scientists to discuss the concussive and sonic properties of the fictional metal of vibranium (the extremely valuable ore found only in Wakanda; Captain America's shield is made from vibranium), scouted for locations, and gathered visual references. "When I came back we reworked everything," Beachler said. "There was a lot achieved because of my experience of being able to touch and feel and be there and see."

The most radical aspect of Wakanda, as established in the comic books, wasn't the vibranium: it was that the nation had remained untouched by rapacious colonial powers. "It was such a challenge because knowing that this is a nation that had never been colonized and never experienced slavery—there's not a lot of representation for that anywhere in the world," Beachler said. Wakanda was a technological utopia, and therefore a pointed critique of Western European empires: to imagine the country is to ask what Black people could have achieved in Africa if they hadn't been removed from the continent in chains.

"You might say that this African nation is fantasy," Boseman said. "But to have the opportunity to pull from real ideas, real places and real African concepts, and put it inside of this idea of Wakanda— that's a great opportunity to develop a sense of what that identity is, especially when you're disconnected from it."

Working with Coogler, Beachler mixed traditional design from sub-Saharan African nations (such as Nigeria, Kenya, and Burundi) with speculative technology; she put mag-lev hovercrafts, which she guessed were still twenty-five years away in the real world, next to "thatched roofing on skyscrapers." She generated a 515-page "Wakandan Bible" that outlined not only design influences but also the different cultures of Wakanda and how they interacted visually. Colors carried thematic weight—purple was royalty and wisdom, blue was colonization, green was connection to the Earth. When Carter designed the clothes of Wakanda, she further developed these visual motifs. "I would say the Afrofuturistic model is the one characteristic that goes throughout the Wakandan community," Carter said.

Boseman's performance as T'Challa enriched the portrayal of Wakanda—and that relationship went both ways. "I think the thing that distinguishes him is the fact that he's the ruler of a nation," said Boseman, "and his interest is primarily for whatever is good for that nation, whatever is going to be positive for that nation."

With the Creative Committee no longer interfering, Marvel Studios gave Coogler a relatively free hand to make the movie he wanted. It didn't even pressure him to incorporate other MCU characters. (He ultimately included Sebastian Stan as the Winter Soldier in a post-credits scene.) Coogler cast his frequent collaborator Michael B. Jordan as the morally complex antagonist Erik Killmonger, comparing the Boseman-Jordan dynamic to Denzel Washington facing off against Wesley Snipes. He filled out the cast with Lupita Nyong'o, Angela Bassett, Forest Whitaker, Daniel Kaluuya, and Letitia Wright. Danai Gurira joined as Okoye, leader of the Dora Milaje, the all-female security force—color-coded in deep red. Boseman's choice of a Xhosa accent in *Civil War* became the vocal template for the actors playing other Wakandans.

At some point in 2016, Boseman was diagnosed with stage three colon cancer; he kept his condition secret. Only a few of his closest associates knew, including his producing partner Logan Coles, his longtime agent Michael Greene, and his personal trainer Addison Henderson. During the production of *Black Panther*, Coogler was not aware of his leading man's serious health condition. Boseman's brother Derrick said that Boseman didn't want people to worry about him; the actor also appears to have been confident that he was going to beat cancer and didn't want the diagnosis to stop his work or even slow it down. That wasn't the vanity of a man looking for more time in the spotlight, but the intensity of an artist who believed in the importance of the role he was playing.

Spike Lee, who directed Boseman in the Vietnam drama *Da 5*

Bloods, filmed three years after the cancer diagnosis, said that the actor never complained about a grueling shoot in the jungle. "He did not look well, but my mind never took that he had cancer," Lee said. "I understand why Chadwick didn't tell me, because he didn't want me to take it easy. If I had known, I wouldn't have made him do the stuff. And I respect him for that."

✳

BLACK PANTHER PRODUCTION began in January 2016 at Pinewood Atlanta Studios (later renamed Trilith Studios) in Georgia, which had recently become a primary hub of Marvel filming. Beachler built large sets, including a majestic waterfall fighting arena dubbed "Warrior Falls": 120 feet wide and 40 feet tall, it had over 125,000 gallons of water cycling through it. The production filmed at the outdoor Warrior Falls set for two full weeks; it was the setting for two of the film's major showdowns, fight scenes that would occur in six inches of standing water.

Angela Bassett recalled long, hot days at Warrior Falls. "We did ten-hour days, which they call 'French hours,' which really means, 'Get your lunch when you can,' " she said. By the second day, many cast members were blinking more than usual and wondering if there was too much chlorine in the water. "And the third day, I'm looking at Daniel and Lupita, and their eyes are getting really, really red—they were bloodshot red." The day after that, the actors had trouble opening their eyes. The producers had the water tested for pH balance and pathogens, but everything seemed to be clean. They finally figured out the culprit: the high-intensity light reflecting off the water. "Our eyes got sunburned!" Bassett said. All the actors made a habit of donning sunglasses between takes.

Also shooting in Atlanta at the same time was *Avengers: Infinity War*, directed by the Russo brothers, which had a major third-act battle set in Wakanda. That meant that the *Infinity War* crew could draw on the expertise of their *Black Panther* counterparts to get the look of Wakanda right, and that the actors who were cast in both films could do double duty. Letitia Wright, Danai Gurira, Winston

Duke, and Boseman were the Wakandan ambassadors on the *Infinity War* set.

"I remember Chadwick taking Anth and I aside and explaining to us the mythology they'd been developing," Joe Russo said.

"He would go off and work with some of the other actors on the sort of Wakandan formation," Anthony Russo said.

"He would take them through the chants, the pronunciation, the diction, the form that they would take, how they would hold their body in attack stance," Joe added.

Anthony summed it up: "He was the leader of Wakanda."

Coogler wanted to open and close the story of *Black Panther* in Oakland, California, his hometown. With some digital tweaks to the background architecture, an Atlanta apartment complex stood in for Oakland. Across the street was the King Center, the foundation also known as the Center for Nonviolent Social Change that continued the work of Martin Luther King, Jr. Bernice King, his daughter, visited the set, reminding the cast and crew of how much impact their collective effort could have. "[She] shook everybody's hand and blessed the project," Coogler recalled. "It was pretty intense."

Filming finished in South Korea—a car chase through the streets of Busan—and in Africa, where the second unit gathered location footage in Uganda, Zambia, and South Africa. In April 2017, Coogler went into the editing room with Michael Shawver (his collaborator on *Fruitvale Station* and *Creed*) and Marvel veteran Debbie Berman (*Spider-Man: Homecoming*). "We worked on separate sections," said Berman. "On such an effects-heavy film it can be useful to have ownership of a section. But we always collaborated and commented on each other's scenes." The movie had numerous important female characters, and Berman said she was protective of them: "I cared a lot about the women in the film. They were my ladies and I had their backs."

When Berman visited the set during some routine reshoots, the diversity of *Black Panther* hit her full on. "When I was on the set for additional photography, I suddenly had this flash," said Berman, "Ryan and Rachel [Morrison, the director of photography] and I were standing together discussing a shot, and I suddenly saw there was an African American director, a female DP, a female editor, and we were making a $200 million film together."

The representation of women in the movie was profoundly important to many of the people working on it. Letitia Wright, who played Shuri, T'Challa's tech-genius sister, said, "Thumbs up to Ryan [Coogler] and Joe [Robert Cole] and the folks at Marvel for not making the men the ones who are always saving the day. Women doing amazing things on screen—I didn't see a lot of that when I was growing up."

Given Marvel's history with female and non-white characters, the pressure to deliver with *Black Panther* was enormous, Boseman said. "Because it's the first of its kind, this movie, that you want to make sure you do well. There's a fear that if it doesn't do well, it'll be a long time before it happens again. So it's not even just for you, it's for other artists that will come after you."

Every day, the Marvel Studios staff in Burbank watched the dailies uploaded by Coogler and his team, and soon realized they had a hit on their hands. In June 2017, the studio debuted the *Black Panther* teaser trailer during game four of the NBA finals; online, it was streamed eighty-nine million times in twenty-four hours, the most views for any trailer ever, other than the one for *Star Wars: The Last Jedi*. A month later, at San Diego Comic-Con, Coogler debuted a sizzle reel, showing off the casino fight that led into the Busan car chase. Boseman and the other cast members, sitting on the stage in Hall H, craned their necks to watch the footage behind them; it was the first time any of the actors had seen a completed scene. At the end of the clip, the crowd gave them a standing ovation. "I saw Chad crying," said actor Daniel Kaluuya, who spontaneously started hugging the rest of the cast. "To be a part of something like this, I feel so blessed, man. I feel mad privileged."

Responding to the early enthusiasm, Marvel Studios ramped up its advertising for the film, ultimately spending around $150 million on promotion, an amount it usually reserved for *Avengers* movies. *Black Panther* opened on February 16, 2018, in the middle of

Black History Month, and got the best reviews the studio had ever received, with Coogler's Afrofuturist vision hailed as authentic Black pop art. The movie became the first film since James Cameron's *Avatar* to hold the number one spot at the American box office for five weeks in a row. It ended up grossing $1.347 billion dollars worldwide, defying the expectation that February was a time for unsuccessful genre movies, and more importantly, disproving the belief in Hollywood that movies with Black leads couldn't do huge business internationally. *Black Panther* was the highest-grossing film by a Black director, the highest-grossing solo superhero film, and the ninth-highest-grossing movie of all time.

Though Coogler had brought in the composer Göransson, who had collaborated with him on *Fruitvale Station* and *Creed*, to score *Black Panther*, the director also wanted to work with rapper Kendrick Lamar. "I've been a massive Kendrick fan since I first heard him, since his mixtapes," Coogler said. After he showed an early cut of *Black Panther* to Lamar, the rapper responded by contributing three songs to the soundtrack and curating an entire album inspired by the movie. "Corrupted man's heart with a gift / That's how you find out who you dealin' with," Lamar rapped on "All the Stars," his collaboration with the singer SZA, which led off the album.

Marvel and hip-hop had a long history, but the dialogue had previously been one-way: artists drew inspiration from the comics but received little acknowledgment in return. Rappers such as MF Doom and Eminem made Marvel references, but the most prominent MC who was a Marvel fan was probably Dennis Coles, who performed in the Wu-Tang Clan as Ghostface Killah. On his debut solo album, *Ironman*, he drew heavily from the comics character's mythology, even renaming himself "Tony Starks." Ghostface, who also sometimes calls himself "the kid," filmed a cameo in the first *Iron Man* movie eleven years later. "It was a good look for the kid because Robert Downey Jr. recognized me as soon as I seen him," said Ghostface, "He was like, 'Yo, Tony!' "

Ghostface's cameo was cut, however, and although Marvel Comics put out a few alternate covers inspired by graffiti and hip-hop culture between 2015 and 2017, it seemed reluctant to explore the bond between the rap community and its Black heroes. Lamar's big-budget mixtape, *Black Panther: The Album*, changed that: it topped the American album charts and made Lamar an official voice of Wakanda, further cementing the movie's place in Black culture.

★

AVA DUVERNAY didn't direct *Black Panther*, but she didn't stop thinking about the movie and why it so moved audiences, especially Black people. "Wakanda itself is a dream state," she said, "a place that's been in the hearts and minds and spirits of Black people since we were brought here in chains."

Although the movie had opened thirteen months before the March 2019 Academy Awards ceremony and was also not the typical prestige fare that the Oscars favored, it seemed like a viable candidate for award recognition. It was high-quality cinema, it was hugely popular, and it was an antidote to the Oscars' long-running issues with race (as captured by activist April Reign's popular hashtag #OscarsSoWhite). "Do I think it merits a best picture nomination? That's not for me to say," commented Michael B. Jordan. "But I'm okay listening to other people say it."

Disney, unfettered from New York's cost-conscious ways, spent the money for a serious *Black Panther* Oscars campaign, an expense that Ike Perlmutter had always avoided with Marvel's other movies. *Black Panther* ended up with seven nominations, including Best Picture (the first superhero movie nominated for that award) and Best Original Song, for "All the Stars." The movie would ultimately win three Oscars: Ludwig Göransson for Best Original Score, Ruth E. Carter for Best Costume Design, and Hannah Beachler for Best Production Design (the first time a Black person had even been nominated in that category).

Marvel Studios had sought out directors who could take the studio's orders, or at least cede control when it came to crossovers and complex action scenes. Marvel's methods resulted in consistency and reliability, but also gave the studio a reputation as heavy-handed and unfriendly to auteurs. As a consequence, gifted directors such as DuVernay avoided the studio. In Phase Three, however, chastened by its public rupture with Edgar Wright or emboldened by no longer needing to answer to the Creative Committee, the studio hired more directors out of the independent-movie world and empowered some of them. Taika Waititi would go on to rejuvenate the *Thor* franchise when he refashioned the third installment, *Thor: Ragnarok*, as a quirky comedy in the vein of his vampire movie *What We Do in the Shadows* (it helped that he was happy to turn the action sequences over to Marvel's visual department). To ensure that his movie was immersed in the visual traditions of Africa, not Burbank, Ryan Coogler had insisted on hiring Black artists and designers—and demonstrated how Marvel Studios could benefit when it hired the right person and got out of the way. *Black Panther* not only made over a billion dollars at the box office; it raised the stature of the entire superhero genre, insisting that a movie about a costumed hero could be a legitimate cultural event, not just a trashy distraction.

Even without a Best Picture statue, *Black Panther* changed the trajectory of the MCU. With Robert Downey Jr. and Chris Evans nearing the end of their multi-movie runs, Marvel Studios believed that it could count on the radiant Chadwick Boseman as T'Challa, king of Wakanda. Coogler was quickly hired to direct a *Black Panther* sequel and to develop a Wakanda-based television series. The coronavirus pandemic temporarily shut down film production, but the sequel was scheduled to start shooting in March 2021. And then, on August 28, 2020, Boseman died of complications from his colon cancer. Up until a week before his death, he was convinced that he would defeat the disease.

In an official statement, Coogler said, "I spent the last year preparing, imagining and writing words for him to say, that we weren't destined to see. It leaves me broken knowing that I won't be able to watch another close-up of him in the monitor again or walk up to him and ask for another take." The director and the studio decided that they wouldn't recast the character of T'Challa, because asking another actor to replace Boseman seemed like a hopeless task for all involved. Instead, they retooled the movie. It would depict Wakanda coping with the offscreen loss of its protector and king, reflecting the real-life sorrow of the movie's cast and crew.

Marvel would release the sequel, titled *Black Panther: Wakanda Forever*, in November 2022; it would be the final movie in Phase Four of the MCU. Centered on the female leaders of Wakanda, especially Letitia Wright's Shuri, it also introduced two major new MCU characters: Mexican actor Tenoch Huerta Mejia played the imperious underwater monarch Namor (aka the Sub-Mariner) and the American Black actress Dominique Thorne as Riri Williams, a young MIT student inspired to build her own Tony Stark–style armor and call herself Ironheart. Namor was king of a lost city that had once been ravaged by colonialism, while Riri was a budding genius, the technological heir to Iron Man.

Riri, Namor, and Shuri were all part of a newly vibrant Marvel Cinematic Universe that Boseman had every reason to believe he'd be at the center of. On the set of *Endgame*, he appreciated that Robert Downey Jr. took the time to say, as Boseman put it, "Hey, you're here. Here's what I can bestow upon you or impart to you." But Boseman particularly valued spending time with other members of the new class, like Tom Holland and *Captain Marvel* star Brie Larson; they all expected that the success of *Black Panther* was a harbinger for their future. "Brie and Tom Holland and I were talking about it a few hours ago," he said in 2017. "Just that it's special. That it's exciting."

Logan Coles, Boseman's producing partner, said that in one of their last conversations, the actor urged him to keep talking about their accomplishments. Boseman instructed him, "Tell 'em what we did. Tell them all the work that was done and what I had to go through to tell those stories."

CHAPTER TWENTY-FOUR

Higher, Further, Faster

What happens when
I'm finally set free?

Captain Marvel

LOOKING BACK AT HER OWN CAREER, VICTORIA ALONSO
marked *Captain Marvel* as a crucial moment. She had over-
seen Marvel Studios' postproduction apparatus since the earliest days of the studio, but *Captain Marvel* was the movie where she
pivoted from proving herself to embracing her own legacy. "I always
say that both *Black Panther* and *Captain Marvel* were the two columns that have held my house—my house of filmmaking," she said.
"They are the columns of the legacy that I could potentially leave my
daughter. . . . They have said that it is absolutely OK to be different
and still have the power, which is what I think is what *Black Panther* did—inspired others to live that noble life. And to have *Captain
Marvel* come along and actually [help you] find your voice. When
people tell you that 'you feel too much' or 'you have too many emotions,' or 'you don't know what you want because you don't know
how you feel' . . . you realize that you do know. And what you want
is not what the other person wants."

Actress Brie Larson had spent many years filling her inner self with the inventions of other people, playing one fictional woman after another. "My identity was tangled up in the parts that I had played since I was a child," said Larson. "I would go through my closet and only see audition clothes: Brie looking older, Brie looking '60s, Brie looking '40s, Brie looking younger in the future. I realized that if you've been acting since you were 7, there are a lot of stories inside you that are not actually yours. It's a blessing to play all these different characters, but it's also confusing. And overwhelming."

So when she considered the role of Carol Danvers, aka Captain Marvel, in 2016, right after winning an Oscar for her performance as an abducted woman in *Room*, Larson was initially reluctant. She ultimately decided that the perfect way to take advantage of the blurry boundaries between her art and her identity was to play a hero.

Kevin Feige had announced a Captain Marvel movie at Kevin-Con in October 2014, when he revealed the Phase Three schedule at the El Capitan Theater. But the studio didn't settle on writers for the project until April 2015, when it partnered Meg LeFauve (one of the writers on Pixar's *Inside Out*) with Nicole Perlman (the Marvel Writers Program graduate who wrote fourteen drafts of the screenplay for *Guardians of the Galaxy*). "They brought me back in and we started talking about it," Perlman recalled. "And Meg and I have a really good relationship. I hold her in such high regard. And she and I just really hit it off when it came to writing. We had a lot of great discussions about character and about how important it would be for us that it wasn't a story about a woman finding her power—it's a story about a woman understanding that strength comes from emotion and humanity."

LeFauve and Perlman had plenty of time to contemplate their screenplay's themes, because as Marvel Studios hurtled toward *Avengers: Infinity War* and *Avengers: Endgame*, it kept tinkering with its plans for how Phase Three would work, and how Captain Marvel would fit in. "That process went on for well over a year and a half. They would talk about it whenever they had time between shooting everything else," Perlman said. "And every time we talked about it, something different had changed with what they were going to do with the Avengers. So it wasn't a straightforward 'Just come up with a great story.' It was, 'Come up with five different versions of what this could look like.' And 'Here are five and then we'll talk about what's working from each of them and then we'll do it again.' It was iterative."

Carol Danvers had debuted in Marvel Comics in 1968 as a minor supporting character, an officer in the United States Air Force. In 1977, she acquired superpowers and became the miniskirted Ms. Marvel, whose civilian job was editor-in-chief of *Woman* magazine. The character represented Marvel's efforts to respond to the "women's liberation" movement—"This Female Fights Back!" promised the cover of her first issue—but Carol was mostly written by men, some of whom seemed baffled by feminism, or simply hostile to it. (In one storyline, when Ms. Marvel was an Avenger, she was impregnated and abducted by an alien while the rest of the team stood passively by.) At various points, Carol lost her memories and her powers, and even abandoned the Ms. Marvel name for years, going by Binary and Warbird.

In 2012, however, Marvel Comics rebooted the character and renamed her Captain Marvel, a title with a resonant but complicated publication history. The flagship hero of Fawcett Comics in the 1940s was a superpowered man-child called Captain Marvel, but DC sued the publisher, saying the character was too similar to Superman. After a protracted lawsuit, in 1953 Fawcett agreed to stop publishing the character; in 1967, Marvel realized that the rights to the name had lapsed and successfully trademarked its own Captain Marvel, a male warrior of the alien Kree race named Mar-Vell. (In 1972, DC acquired Fawcett's intellectual property and integrated Captain Marvel into its own comics, usually under the name Shazam.) Mar-Vell had various cosmic adventures, sometimes swapping realities with his human sidekick, Rick Jones, before dying of cancer in a 1982 graphic novel. After that, a variety of other characters, including Monica Rambeau, were known as Captain Marvel for brief periods of time, mostly because Marvel wanted to maintain an active character with that name so it wouldn't lose control of the trademark.

Making Carol Danvers the new Captain Marvel gave Marvel a chance to reconsider her character—and her appearance. "If you look at the comics, the further you go back, the less clothes Carol Danvers seems to be wearing," Feige observed. "Oftentimes it's a one-piece bathing suit, basically." Writer Kelly Sue DeConnick commissioned artist Jamie McKelvie to redesign Danvers's look, resulting in a superheroic take on a flight suit. Marvel didn't authorize McKelvie's work, but DeConnick promised McKelvie that she'd pay him herself if Marvel didn't. Ultimately, the publisher came around.

DeConnick's run on the *Captain Marvel* title succeeded beyond its sales: by treating Carol Danvers as one of the top-flight heroes of Marvel, she inspired a legion of fans who called themselves the Carol Corps. When she heard that Marvel Studios would be making a movie based on her iteration of the character—Carol Danvers as Captain Marvel—she decided that was a good time to leave the book. "I quit about a week after the film was announced," she explained. "I'm a slow writer, so I was having trouble with deadlines to begin with. If I was going to take something off my plate, that was the book I didn't own. There was a bit of a Machiavellian sense to it: I either have to dig in and stay on this book for three years and the quality cannot drop, or I leave right now and get the credit for making the movie happen and walk away at the high point." She soon discovered that while she might be done with Captain Marvel, Captain Marvel wasn't done with her.

Marvel Studios contacted DeConnick at her home in Portland, Oregon, and flew her down to LA for a meeting with Feige, Jonathan Schwartz (Feige's former assistant and the movie's creative producer), and Mary Livanos (a fast-rising development executive). They met for a couple of hours, discussing all things Carol. The meeting went well, but on DeConnick's flight home, she kept thinking about something that she felt she hadn't adequately explained. "I said, 'The thing about Carol is she always gets back up.' Kevin was like, 'No, that's Cap.' He even says that: "I could do this all day," right?' I was like, 'Yeah, but it's Carol,' but I didn't articulate the difference very well, which bothered me."

Then DeConnick realized she knew how to explain it. "The difference is, Steve gets back up because it's the right thing to do. Carol gets back up—well, the thing I say has a curse word in it, which Disney loves—but Carol gets back up because *fuck you*. Carol gets up not because it's righteous or just, but because she's full of piss and vinegar."

At home, DeConnick composed a long email, based on her theory of how classic cinematic triangles worked. "Kirk is Spock plus McCoy. Harry is Ron plus Hermione. Luke is Han plus Leia. That's the formula. And Carol is Steve plus Tony. She's got Tony's spunk and swagger and she knows how to flip a wrench, but she's also a soldier like Steve is and she has that sense of duty." She sent Marvel the email, which resulted in Marvel keeping her on retainer while they made the movie, so the studio could contact her whenever they needed her to talk about the character.

The studio was having trouble hiring a director, because it was hard to attract talent to a movie whose concept was still inchoate and clearly secondary to the two upcoming Avengers movies. "We're trying to get a little more of the story set before we bring a filmmaker on," Feige said in October 2016. Asked if *Captain Marvel* needed to have a female director, Feige filibustered. "The issue is," he said, "we need to find the best director for any given movie. And that's really where we always start. If diversity is part of that, it's great. It's important. You will start to see things across the industry as a whole change as more filmmakers come up through the ranks and become part of making movies like this . . . you look back sometimes, and it's just the nature of this industry, or the nature of the culture. But there's a big shift happening. What's exciting about Marvel, go back and look at the source material: It's been diverse in a cutting-edge way going back to the '60s, and I think we've represented that effortlessly and accurately in the movies we've made up to this point, but certainly with *Black Panther* and *Captain Marvel* doing it in a much more overt and purposeful way."

Perlman and LeFauve, at least, were being purposeful in thinking about how Carol Danvers would stand in for half of humanity. "I remember sending Nicole an article I had read about trying to teach girls coding and how they were having trouble and girls kept quitting," LeFauve said. "'Let's have a discussion about this. Why are girls taught that they can't make mistakes? Why are girls taught they can't embrace their own power?' There were many discussions—we used a lot of our own experiences."

Being married to a veteran helped Perlman with the parts of the Carol Danvers origin story that involved Carol being an Air Force pilot—and also influenced the portrayal of the Kree warrior "Vers" (whom Danvers appears to be before having her memory restored). "My husband was deployed right after 9/11," Perlman said, "and he was so sure that he was fighting for the good guys. He was a chemical weapons officer and obviously there were no chemical weapons in Iraq, so he had this moment of wondering, 'What if I'm not the good guy here?' That was a big influence for *Captain Marvel* too. She's been told that they're the good guys and she believes it. What happens when you crack that open? That was an important element to include."

Marvel needed the movie to be a period piece, predating the events of *Iron Man,* so it could avoid questions of how Captain Marvel would interact with S.H.I.E.L.D. and the various Avengers. But the established continuity of the MCU extended well into the past: How did someone like Howard Stark not know about Captain Marvel? Why would the world have been shocked by Tony Stark's admission that he was Iron Man if there had already been a superhero flying around? Given those complications, the writers had a hard time deciding on the ideal era for *Captain Marvel.*

"We didn't write a treatment or anything, but we discussed the idea of setting it in the sixties," Perlman said. "But then *Hidden Figures* was coming out, and we didn't want to set something in the same time period. We briefly talked about the eighties and then we were like, 'No, let's do it in the nineties.' So we did some drafts where Y2K was a thing, where that was an excuse for covering up some wackiness. But how do you keep it off the radar of everybody?"

The solution was to give Carol Danvers an origin story on Earth but then get her off the planet for a couple of decades. Perlman and LeFauve set the story of *Captain Marvel* in the 1990s. The movie would also work as an origin story for Nick Fury, showing where his interest in superheroes came from and explaining how he lost his eye: a significant chunk of the movie is Brie Larson and (a digitally de-aged) Samuel L. Jackson costarring in what is, essentially, a buddy road comedy. But the core of the story is Carol Danvers believing she is Vers and coming to Earth in pursuit of the shape-shifting Skrulls. In the comics, the Skrulls are longtime malevolent foes of Earth, but here, they prove to be the victims of the Kree. "It was really important that the Skrulls weren't actually the bad guys; they were refugees," Perlman said. She credits Larson for that crucial shift. "When Meg and I first met Brie, we were just so bowled over by her empathy. I think that was the first time we started talking about empathy as a superpower, just being impressed by how Brie Larson really gives a shit." The writers handed Marvel Studios the outline for their script in December 2016; now the studio needed to complete its search for a director.

✶

"**THIS WAS NOT OFFERED** to us, this was something that we, after really digging in, ran after," Anna Boden said of *Captain Marvel*. "Certainly, our agent had pitched us projects before that he thought we should go for, but we knew that we were gonna have to really care about it and love the character to dedicate ourselves to it." Boden and her directing partner, Ryan Fleck, had previously made well-regarded indie films such as *Half Nelson*, *Mississippi Grind*, and *Sugar*, which they knew didn't make them obvious candidates for a superhero movie. They had been in the mix to replace Edgar Wright on *Ant-Man*, so when they pursued the *Captain Marvel* job, they read stacks of comic books, absorbing everything they could from Carol Danvers' checkered print history. "Even though we liked the character and we liked the idea of Brie, we needed to make sure that we had our way in," Boden said. By their own admission, they are "terrible pitchers," but what they lacked in salesmanship they made up for with enthusiasm and their talent for presenting complex characters on screen.

Feige hired them, a decision he later described as based in the "belief that they wouldn't have lost the character amongst the spectacle and the fun and the effects." After sitting down with Larson to discuss the screenplay, Bowen and Fleck rewrote the script with *Tomb Raider* scribe Geneva Robertson-Dworet. "Brie is a writer and a director in her own right, so she thinks about the entire movie, and making sure that all the character journeys are telling one coherent story," Robertson-Dworet said. "But I will also say that if you've seen Anna and Ryan's movies, one of the things that's remarkable about them is that even the side characters feel incredibly truthful and have depth. It was very important to everyone that all of the female characters be nuanced and strong."

Larson prepared to play Captain Marvel by adopting a rigorous workout program that would let her get into superheroic shape—in some workouts, trainer Jason Walsh would have her push his Jeep uphill—and by researching the military background of the character. For the first time since Jon Favreau's *Iron Man* movies, Marvel Studios and the US military were working together: the production would get access to Edwards Air Force Base and its F-15C fighter planes, while the Pentagon would get script approval. That cooperation meant that Larson could visit with notable Air Force personnel. She went to Nellis Air Force Base in Nevada to meet with the commander of its 57th Wing, Major General Jeannie Leavitt—who had become, in 1993, the first female fighter pilot in the history of the Air Force.

Larson said that trip deepened her understanding of Carol Danvers. "In reading the comics, she has this interesting combo of being very sure of herself and humble, but also has this dry wit," Larson observed. "And then, once I was at the base, I realize that's how pilots are—that there's this certain level of camaraderie, and sense of humor that I could find everywhere—and that was the pilot in her."

Boden and Fleck shot most of *Captain Marvel* in California, thanks to a tax credit from the California Film Commission that refunded $20 million of the budget, provided that the studio spent at least $100 million on the movie in the state. Although the directors had limited experience with effects shots, filming in California gave them easy access to the Marvel Studios visual apparatus, from keyframe development to pre-viz to Victoria Alonso's postproduction department. "There is a camaraderie in the Marvel Studios sandbox that is encouraged, and that happens daily," Feige declared. "Anna and Ryan are working on *Captain Marvel*, talking to Taika who's just finished *Ragnarok*, talking with Ryan Coogler who's in the midst of postproduction."

Marvel heralded the arrival of Captain Marvel with the final postcredits scene in *Avengers: Infinity War*—before crumbling into black ashes, Nick Fury pulls out a pager emblazoned with Captain Marvel's logo, summoning her. The *Captain Marvel* trailer dramatically turned the word "Her" into "A Hero." While the MCU had long given short shrift to its female and minority heroes, Marvel Studios was now actively marketing to potential viewers it had neglected. The studio trumpeted the pioneering status of movies like *Black Panther* and *Captain Marvel* and hoped that nobody would point out that the movies were groundbreaking only because Marvel had previously refused to make them. *Captain Marvel* was more obviously late, owing to the existence and success of *Wonder Woman*, a hit for Warner Bros. two years earlier, in 2017. Feige praised *Wonder Woman* when it was released, but said, "*Captain Marvel* is a very different type of movie. I think they [Warner Bros.] have taken the brunt of the, 'Are people going to go see a female superhero movie?'" He admitted, "It's always fun to be first with most things, but I think it will have worked out by the time we've gotten our next few movies out."

In the age of Peak Superhero, DC Films wasn't as successful as

Marvel Studios, but had created a distinctive style—brutal, self-serious, and largely joyless when compared to the antic and bright MCU movies. *Wonder Woman* aside, DC seemed to be constantly two steps behind Marvel. After the MCU took off, Feige's friend and coworker from back in the Donner Company days, Geoff Johns, became the chief creative officer of DC Films from 2010 through 2018 and pushed for the DC superheroes (Superman, Batman, Wonder Woman, among others) to exist in a shared space dubbed the DCEU (or "DC Extended Universe").

Richard Donner was the source of one other unexpected connection between DC and Marvel, via the 1978 film he had directed that launched the modern era of superhero blockbusters. "*Superman: The Movie* is still to this day the archetype of the perfect superhero film origin story," Feige said. "We watch it before we make any one of our films."

When Larson went to see *Wonder Woman*, she broke down in tears, for reasons she couldn't articulate. Later, she realized it was because it was the fulfillment of dreams she had as a little girl but had long forgotten. "As a kid, I wanted to be an adventurer," she said. "I wanted to be a smart-ass. I wanted to get my hands dirty."

Now she hoped that her performance would inspire others. "The very nature of this film means that I'm having conversations that I'd like to have about what it means to be a woman," Larson said. "What strength looks like, the complexities of the female experience, female representation. It's surprising and cool that my first giant movie I get to be having those kinds of conversations. But that's also why I've waited and been particular about what jobs I do."

Alonso had spent years toiling in the dark for Marvel Studios (literally, given the dimmed rooms where much of postproduction happened), but when *Captain Marvel* was released, she had a moment in the spotlight. She told reporters about her journey, and how when she had first arrived in Los Angeles, one of her three jobs was cleaning the cabins of Alaska Airlines airplanes. As a promotional tie-in for the movie, Alaska Airlines repainted a couple of its jets with images of Captain Marvel—when Alonso first saw the results in a marketing meeting, she started weeping.

While Alonso loved the Marvel movies, she conceded that they weren't exactly to her personal taste. "If you have a movie that is out there and if it's *La La Land* or *Juno* or *12 Years a Slave* or *Moonlight*," she said, "I would rather go see those movies than a superhero movie. I do see our movies because I think they have a heart and they have a message. And they have more than one message, and it's really up to you see it. You know, you can peel our movies like an onion and find it, and eventually, you might cry."

During crunch time in Marvel postproduction—which seemed to be all the time, given that the studio now regularly released three movies a year—workdays could last twenty hours, a punishing schedule particularly hard for legions of anonymous CGI artists. Alonso did what she could to ameliorate the pain, ordering stacks of pizzas and walking around the offices with an oversized inflatable baseball bat covered with smiley faces that she dubbed the "Happy Stick." She wielded it as she made her rounds, making sure that "everyone is still remembering that we're supposed to be having fun, too."

Trinh Tran had spent a decade at Marvel Studios, beginning as an assistant on *Iron Man* and working her way up through a series of positions, eventually becoming a major creative producer; she's credited as an executive producer on *Infinity War*, *Endgame*, and the TV show *Hawkeye*. She spent a year of that decade as Alonso's assistant. "Victoria especially, since day one, brought me over to be with her and really allow me to just grow," Tran said. "Films are stronger when ideas are generated and questioned by different perspectives."

"Why would we only want to be recognized by only one type of person?" Alonso asked. "Our audience is global, is diverse, is inclusive. If we don't do it that way for them, we will fail. If we don't put pedal to the metal on the diversity and the inclusivity, we will not have continued success." She knew that Marvel Studios still had a lot of work to do. "The truth is, when it comes down to inclusiveness," she said, "we have to work harder. And no one knows that better than I do."

✦

CAPTAIN MARVEL, released in March 2019, grossed $1.128 billion worldwide, only slightly behind the numbers for *Black Panther*. On the largest possible scale, Marvel Studios had proved that people wanted to see superheroes who weren't played by white guys named Chris. The success of *Captain Marvel* further buttressed its star's sense of purpose. "The movie was the biggest and best opportunity I could have ever asked for," Larson said. "It was, like, my superpower. This could be my form of activism: doing a film that can play all over the world and be in more places than I can be physically."

Lashana Lynch, the actress who played Carol Danvers's friend Maria Rambeau, was proud that *Captain Marvel* represented a broad spectrum of female heroism. "Single moms doing a million jobs at once and hardly complaining: superheroes," she said. "And then female fighter pilots who were, again, so underrepresented, man, it's ridiculous. They're completely superheroes. To have all of them in one movie, it feels like a moment, but really, I think it's the start of a movement." Lynch was thrilled when she saw young girls reacting to the movie. "It gives the younger generation the opportunity to just see that as normal. When they grow up, they won't have to use their brainpower to think how hard they need to work to prove themselves," she said.

The positive cultural impact of *Captain Marvel* was palpable—but so was the backlash. For the first time, an MCU project was "review bombed": in an organized campaign before the movie even opened, tens of thousands of users gave it the lowest possible rating on websites such as IMDb (the Internet Movie Database) and Rotten Tomatoes, with many reviews little more than misogynist complaints, including accusations that Larson didn't smile enough in the trailer. Without having seen the film, many anonymous commenters already hated it: "You could not pay me to see this SJW laden white male hating worthless POS movie," one Rotten Tomatoes user wrote, using acronyms for "social justice warrior" and "piece of shit."

"I am sick of this identity politics taking over pop culture. Brie Larson could get hit by a bus and I would not shed a tear." While any movie that dared to not center on the experiences or interests of young white men got accused of "identity politics," the anonymous anger toward women was notably more intense: *Captain Marvel* was attacked in a way that *Black Panther* hadn't been. There were so many prerelease pans on Rotten Tomatoes that the site shut down the user review section until the official release date. That slowed the torrent of abuse but didn't stop it.

The vitriol had been building for some time. The year before, Larson had made headlines when she advocated for more diversity among film critics, using Ava DuVernay's *A Wrinkle in Time*, which starred Black teenager Storm Reid as Meg Murray, as an example of a movie that most critics were unable to engage with. "I don't need a 40-year-old white dude to tell me what didn't work for him about *A Wrinkle in Time*. It wasn't made for him! I want to know what it meant to women of color, biracial women, to teen women of color," Larson said. "Am I saying I hate white dudes? No, I am not. What I am saying is if you make a movie that is a love letter to women of color, there is an insanely low chance a woman of color will have a chance to see your movie and review your movie." The internet mob was correct that Larson wanted to change the status quo, which only made its members more determined to shout her down with negative reviews, online abuse, and YouTube videos accusing the actress of ruining the MCU.

Even if they didn't know the vagaries of Marvel Entertainment's corporate politics, they were siding with Ike Perlmutter, and the defunct Creative Committee, who had lost the long war to keep Marvel Studios focused on male (and white) characters. Marvel Studios, under Feige and Alonso and other leaders, recognized that its audience was the hundreds of millions of people, almost half of them women (according to a 2021 poll by Morning Consult), who loved the MCU—not a small-but-vocal coterie of cranks and trolls who campaigned against MCU movies with prominent female characters, like *Eternals* and *Black Widow* (both released in 2021), as representing the decline of Marvel and the rise of the "M-SHE-U." The studio made movies starring women and people of color with increasing frequency, and in the 2022 TV show *She-Hulk: Attorney at Law*, Marvel even had the hero, Jen Walters, battle her male online critics.

Larson seemed like an ideal spokesperson for a more diverse MCU. "I don't have time for it," she said when asked about the attacks. "The things that I have extra time to really look at are, like, Am I eating healthy food? Am I drinking water? Am I meditating? Have I called my mom today?" But relentless online abuse could wear down even the sunniest disposition. Asked three years later if she'd want to return as Captain Marvel after the 2023 movie *The Marvels*, Larson answered, "I don't know, does anyone want me to do it again?" Marvel had expected that Black Panther, Captain Marvel, and Spider-Man would be the trio of star characters leading the MCU into a new millennium, but that was no longer a future it could rely on.

CHAPTER TWENTY-FIVE

Snap

Everybody wants a happy ending,
right?

Avengers: Endgame

A SURPRISING LESSON FROM THE MCU WAS THAT THE defining characteristics of superheroes weren't what most people expected. Costumes, catchphrases, character names—Marvel Studios routinely dispensed with the trappings that seemed to define particular heroes and found other ways to represent the cores of their characters. Outfits that looked vivid on a comics page printed with the four-color process could look goofy on the movie screen, and so, for instance, Hawkeye didn't don a mask with a giant H on his forehead. Comics readers thrilled to the inevitability of the Hulk bellowing "HULK SMASH!" when he wreaked destruction, but in *The Avengers*, his trademark line was assigned to Captain America and cleverly inverted as a command: "Hulk, smash." Wanda Maximoff appeared in five movies before anyone called her the Scarlet Witch.

The Marvel superheroes, as Marvel Studios demonstrated, were defined by their actions and their attitudes, not the aspects that made them familiar to readers (and that made them toyetic). But those trademarks could still be doled out to thrill viewers in carefully allocated fan service. And Marvel Studios could patiently wait for the right moment. Six years after debuting in a muted costume, the Vision finally appeared in his traditional outfit of bright green and yellow, for a Halloween episode of the television series *WandaVision*. A fight scene in an *Avengers* comic book almost always included the rallying cry "Avengers assemble!"—but when Chris Evans's Captain America started to say that phrase, director Joss Whedon coyly cut him off midsentence as the credits rolled on *Avengers: Age of Ultron*. Nobody in the Marvel Cinematic Universe would say it onscreen until *Avengers: Endgame*, the twenty-second MCU film.

While Phase Three of the MCU had been powered by the cultural significance of *Black Panther* and *Captain Marvel*, the challenge of concluding it was thematically simpler but logistically much more complex. *Avengers: Infinity War* and *Avengers: Endgame* would offer a two-part capstone to an impossibly ambitious cinematic project that had begun with *Iron Man* in 2008 and earned $12 billion. While the MCU would continue after those two movies, Marvel Studios understood it had to present a world-shaking climax to the dramatic arcs of its most iconic heroes. The studio wanted to wrap it all up in a way that paid honor to the earliest moments of the saga and that made the work of thousands of creative people feel like an organic whole. The problem was that Marvel Studios didn't know how it was going to do that.

Kevin Feige described the grueling effort that went into planning those two movies: "We spent, it's no exaggeration, years in a room."

✳

AT THE THIRD Palm Springs creative retreat for Marvel Studios producers, in 2014, the conversation turned to resolving some of the MCU's longest-running plotlines, including the menace of Thanos and the studio's favorite MacGuffins, the Infinity Stones. The best suggestion anyone made that weekend: the conclusion was big enough that the studio could make it into two movies.

The advantages and disadvantages of that idea were basically the same. A superheroic diptych that resolved the saga of Thanos was a gargantuan task—but done right, it could be a huge payoff, narratively and financially. *Captain America: Civil War*, with two teams of six heroes battling against each other, had effectively been *Avengers 2.5*; Feige had watched with pleasure as Joe and Anthony Russo smoothly guided the film through production without the agita Joss Whedon had brought to *Avengers: Age of Ultron*. To make the valedictory movies, the studio signed up the Russo brothers in May 2015, along with their screenwriting partners on the *Captain America* franchise, Christopher Markus and Stephen McFeely. (A burned-out Whedon wasn't available, even if the studio had wanted him; he described his personal plan for wrapping up the Thanos saga as "get through *Ultron*, nap for four years, and then I'll come to the premiere.")

The writers began by creating a "blue sky" document that contained everything the Marvel Cinematic Universe could possibly deliver to fans. Early on, they realized that Tony Stark would have to sacrifice himself. The Russos and the Marvel Studios executives agreed that the logical endpoint for Stark's narrative arc was a noble death that saved the world, showing how far he had come since the first *Avengers* movie, when Steve Rogers told him that he wasn't the type "to make the sacrifice play."

The Russo brothers went to Robert Downey Jr. to get his approval for Tony's grand finale. "We did pitch Robert his arc, because he kicked off the entire MCU," said Anthony Russo. "We went over to meet with him, and we pitched it out to him. A lot of the actors are not opinionated about what we do. They like the fact that we are sort of in control of these stories and we are driving where they should go and we have a vision for where they should go and they trust in that." Downey and "not opinionated," however, have rarely appeared together in the same sentence. The actor was uncertain about killing off the character he had become so closely identified with, but ultimately he accepted the narrative logic of the ending the Russos proposed.

"Some of the greatest story development in the history of cinema has happened in the last five years at Marvel," Downey said on the set of *Endgame*. "I feel great about everything being in good hands. You know, the beat goes on."

The creative team also knew they needed to make Thanos truly terrifying. Although he had been looming behind the action for many years, he had appeared only briefly in *Guardians of the Galaxy* and in the end-credits scenes of two other movies. One of the most beloved Thanos storylines in the comics was the 1991 miniseries *The Infinity Gauntlet* (written by Jim Starlin and drawn by George Perez and Ron Lim), where the galactic villain collected the Infinity Stones, with genocidal results. After teasing it for years, Marvel Studios would finally deliver its own version.

Markus and McFeely wrote some scenes establishing Thanos's background and beliefs—most of them were jettisoned, but one, featuring his daughter Gamora as a child, made it to the screen—and soon realized that Thanos should drive the plot of the first movie, as he careened around the galaxy acquiring Infinity Stones. They discovered that the narrative could naturally be broken in two. In the first movie, Thanos would defeat the Avengers and execute his master plan, while in the second, the heroes would reverse that plan and triumph. Stretching the structure over two movies meant that *Avengers: Infinity War* would end on a tragic note, a first for the MCU.

As in the comics, Thanos would eliminate fifty percent of all life in the universe in a Malthusian coup. The Avengers wouldn't just lose but would see half their members evaporate into dust. To determine who would get eliminated when Thanos snapped his fingers, Feige convened Markus, McFeely, Joe Russo, Anthony Russo, and executive producer Trinh Tran in a conference room strewn with cards, slightly larger than baseball cards, each with the name and photograph of one of the MCU characters available for the movie (that is, all of them). The back of each card showed the salary and contractual status of the actor who played the character. "We didn't know how much [money] each actor made, but it had either one dollar sign or up to five dollar signs," McFeely said. Were the actors already under contract, or would Marvel need to make a new deal to feature them in the movies? Sometimes the cards were shuffled around on a table and sometimes they were tacked up on a whiteboard, but they were used to play just one game, called Who Lives and Who Dies.

The group made its choices early and mostly stuck to them; despite the financial information on the cards, Feige said they decided based on what "would be the most heartbreaking." Among those who would evaporate according to that logic: T'Challa, because he was the new audience favorite; Bucky Barnes because it would devastate Steve Rogers; and, likewise, Peter Parker because it would be a gut punch for Tony Stark. The filmmakers kept the six original Avengers alive so that *Endgame* could wrap up their stories, and made sure to retain non-Avengers characters with a range of personalities. As Markus said, "If people are joking, Nebula can come in and just kill the laughs, which is very fun to do. If people are very serious, Rocket can come in and make fun of them."

They also knew that *Endgame* needed to conclude with the most ambitious battle in MCU history. That meant they needed to start work on it right away: the studio engaged Industrial Light and Magic to do CGI and the Third Floor to handle pre-viz and post-visualization (the process of adding new elements into an established shot). "In Kevin's mindset," said Trinh Tran, "the dream is that everybody appears at the end, and they're fighting against Thanos." Pulling in every superhero in the MCU was just the starting point. "From there, we built on in terms of 'OK, who disappeared from the previous movie so they can come back on? Who was interacting with who?' We obviously don't want it to be that they're fighting for the sake of fighting."

Marvel Studios had used images in its movies that played like "splash pages"—high-impact, full pages of art in a comic book—and the studio kept increasing the number of characters featured in such moments. Six Avengers in a circle at the Battle of New York in *The Avengers* became twelve superheroes battling one another at the Leipzig/Halle airport in *Captain America: Civil War*, which became dozens of heroes in *Endgame*'s ruins of Avengers Compound, in the ultimate MCU splash page.

Work on the final brawl began with pre-visualization in 2016 and continued until a couple of weeks before press screenings of the movie started in 2019. "We actually didn't photograph most of the end battle until 2018," explained Jeffrey Ford, who was an editor on both *Infinity War* and *Endgame*. "We shot most of that sequence in October of 2018 with three units in Atlanta. It was a crazy month of crazy mo-cap. One of the reasons we didn't shoot it during the initial production phase was the movie was evolving and *Infinity War* was evolving. We had two movies that were going to interact with each other and affect each other, but we didn't want to repeat ourselves or get in the same rhythms, and we wanted to make sure that we delivered a unique final battle."

The story remained in flux, with Markus and McFeely turning out new drafts as they responded to other MCU movies. *Thor: Ragnarok* was shot in 2016 in Australia, where director Taika Waititi and star Chris Hemsworth reinvented the thunder god as a self-absorbed and absurd yet still virtuous hero. Hemsworth wanted to make sure that this new comedic tone wasn't abandoned when Thor rejoined the Avengers, so Markus and McFeely rewrote sections of the script that previously had Thor playing the straight man.

Thor: Ragnarok also introduced a few continuity problems to the *Endgame* plot, especially with a proposed scene where Captain America wields Thor's hammer, finally revealing, after a tease in *Avengers: Age of Ultron*, that he is worthy enough to lift Mjölnir. That rousing scene, a key moment in the final battle, dated back to the earliest version of the story, pitched by the writers in 2015. Christopher Markus said, "There was certainly a debate at one point because particularly in *Ragnarok*, it establishes that Thor can summon the lightning without the hammer. I think Odin even says, 'It was never the hammer.' And yet Cap summons the lightning with the hammer. You get to those things and you're like, 'It's too awesome not to do it! We'll talk about it later.'"

That improvisatory approach was characteristic of the entire MCU. As C. Robert Cargill, screenwriter on the 2016 *Doctor Strange*, said, "The biggest misunderstanding of how Marvel works is that everybody assumes that afterthought is forethought. There are lots of things that get added late in the process, but when you do it right, it feels like it was there all along. And movies are reacting to movies—when I wrote the scene with the Ancient One and talked about her looking forward into the future and seeing probabilities, there was no talk about 'Hey, we're going to use this in *Infinity War*.' But having watched *Doctor Strange*, they could say, 'You know what would be cool and fix this problem we have? If we use this power that the Ancient One expresses in *Doctor Strange* and show that Doctor Strange has that ability from the Time Stone.' It's not a master plan—the master document is the body of work, and Kevin. It's a bunch of geniuses building a story up rather than building towards a story." While Marvel Studios had constantly refined its process for producing visual effects in the name of reliability and consistency, it took a free-wheeling, almost ad hoc approach to the story those visuals would bring to life.

The studio initially hoped it could shoot *Infinity War* and *Endgame* simultaneously, doing what producers call "crossboarding"—filming every scene from both movies that happened in a particular location (at Avengers Compound, or on the Guardians' ship), and then moving on to the next set. That would have been more efficient, and saved a lot of money, but a few months before shooting on *Infinity War* began, it became clear that the *Endgame* script was not going to be ready in time. The movies would need to be shot back-to-back, with a combined budget of around $700 million. A huge portion of the budget was in the salaries for the actors, many of whom had completed their original contracts and were now irreplaceable stars: $15 million per movie for Chris Evans, Chris Hemsworth, and Scarlett Johansson—and $20 million for Downey, plus a profit-sharing deal that meant he would ultimately make about $75 million for each of the movies. Those ballooning salary commitments were part of the reason Marvel Studios was comfortable with killing off some of its heroes and introducing a new generation after Phase Three.

✳

FILMING FOR *INFINITY WAR* began in January 2017, when Downey and Tom Holland were joined by Chris Pratt and the other Guardians of the Galaxy for their scenes on Titan. To keep the plot secret, only two actors, Downey and Chris Evans, were given the complete screenplay. All the other actors had to make do with only the pages that involved their characters.

For Josh Brolin, returning as Thanos, that meant he had most of the script: the Avengers' big purple nemesis was virtually the protagonist of a heist movie. Yet *Infinity War* built up Thanos so effectively that the filmmakers wrote themselves into a corner. *Avengers: Endgame* needed to focus on the core Avengers, not tell the continuing adventures of the cosmic villain with the corrugated chin. But since the first movie had left Thanos in control of the all-powerful Infinity Stones, the creative team had trouble figuring out how the heroes could beat him. McFeely described their struggles with a character who was essentially omnipotent and omniscient: "It is ridiculous how much power he has at the opening of the movie. So for a good solid three weeks, we are trying to figure out, what is movie two with a character with that much power? At one point, I think Trinh Tran, our executive producer, in frustration said, 'God, I really wish we could just kill him.' We all went, 'Slow down. What does that mean? That's interesting.' It's absolutely within his character. When we asked, 'Why would he let you?': because he did what he wanted to do. It's strong for him to do that. We've been at it a long time and that's the kind of thing I beat myself up for not thinking of earlier. If I'm being consistent to his character, this is on the table."

Pushed from the first movie into the second was the debut of "Smart Hulk," with Bruce Banner's intellect finally in control of the Hulk's green body. In early cuts of *Infinity War*, Banner and the Hulk merged during the movie's climactic battle in Wakanda, in a sequence that saw the hybrid Smart Hulk burst out of the Hulk-buster armor. But the Russos decided that giving Banner a "win" just seconds before half the cast became ash would induce emotional whiplash. It was too late to shoot new footage, so the production employed the solution that had rescued the ending of the original *Iron Man*: concocting a sequence entirely from digital elements. Banner uses a Hulkbuster gauntlet (a digital object) to shoot Cull Obsidian (a digital character) into the digital air, where he gets squashed against a digital energy shield.

When Markus and McFeely started working on the *Endgame* plot, they briefly considered giving the Avengers a time machine before rejecting that idea as a cheap cop-out. "Time travel pops up in your head early in almost any difficult situation," Markus said. But when they were stuck on how to crack the *Endgame* plot, Ant-Man saved the day. The writers had left the character out of *Infinity War* because *Ant-Man and the Wasp* was coming out less than three months later, and they didn't want the depressing conclusion of *Infinity War* to cast a pall over a lighthearted Paul Rudd movie. Then they learned that the conclusion of *Ant-Man and the Wasp* involved a visit into the subatomic Quantum Realm, where particles can exist at two places at the same time.

Markus remembered the breakthrough: it happened in the fall of 2015, on yet another day "in the conference room where we were trapped for months," he said. While everyone else was discussing another script issue, he was researching physics on his laptop. "I Googled 'Quantum Realm' and . . . time is different in there. I think I sort of raised my hand and went, 'We can do a time machine! Because we have an excuse to do a time machine.' And that is around when cooler heads prevailed and brought in an actual physicist to tell us either we were crazy, or we were right, or that we were crazy but it was okay to do it because, you know, we're not making a documentary. And all of those things happened."

With quantum mechanics on their side, they constructed an intricate plot: the Avengers could not only undo the triumph of Thanos by collecting the Infinity Stones before him, they could revisit settings from previous movies, ranging from the Battle of New York in *The Avengers* to the *20,000 Leagues Under the Sea*-in-drydock planet in *Guardians of the Galaxy*. Time travel also gave them an avenue to resolve the big emotional issues of the movie's two main heroes: Steve Rogers would return to his past and find domestic bliss with Peggy Carter, while Tony Stark would visit the 1970s and make peace with his father, Howard Stark.

In every draft of the script, the battle with Thanos's army ended with Tony Stark's sacrifice: with the Infinity Stones on his hand, he would snap his fingers and wish away Thanos and his army at the cost of his own life. But Tony won the day silently. As Anthony Russo remembered, "We were in the editing room going, 'He has to say something. This is a character who has lived and died by quips.' And we just couldn't, we tried a million different last lines. Thanos was saying 'I am inevitable.' And our editor Jeff Ford, who's been with us all four movies and is an amazing storyteller, said 'Why don't we just go full circle with it and say "I am Iron Man."'"

A couple of weeks before Downey was scheduled to film additional footage for *Endgame*—reshoots that would include him saying the final "I am Iron Man" line—Joe Russo had dinner with the actor and discovered that his star was reluctant to film Tony Stark's dying moment again: "He was like, 'I don't know. I don't really want to go back and get into that emotional state. It'll take . . . it's hard.' And crazily enough, Joel Silver, the producer, was at the dinner. He's an old buddy of Robert's. And Joel jumps in and he's like, 'Robert, what are you talking about? That's the greatest line I've ever heard! You gotta say this line! You have to do this!' So thank God that Joel Silver was at dinner, because he helped us talk Robert into doing that line."

That scene, with Tony's last words, ended up being the final shot of reshoots. It was filmed in a soundstage next door to the studio where, a decade earlier, Downey had auditioned to play Iron Man, gliding into the role like a kid on a bicycle going downhill. Kevin Feige watched the scene, thinking about how much his life, and Downey's life, had changed since that moment.

The death of the MCU's flagship character ended up creating one of the biggest scheduling headaches in cinema history: Tony Stark's funeral. Over the prior decade, Marvel Studios had become extremely serious about operational security, having learned that every hint and whisper of MCU developments would end up as blaring internet headlines. Unfortunately, some of the worst leakers were the studio's own actors. Tom Holland and Mark Ruffalo, in particular, had the bad habit of blurting out plot twists or even accidentally broadcasting MCU screenings through their phones. (Marvel Studios assigned Benedict Cumberbatch to be Holland's interview partner during press junkets, basically to babysit the young actor so he wouldn't reveal any spoilers.) So the funeral was referred to in all production notes, memos, and scheduling documents as "The Wedding."

The silent sequence included just about every significant hero in the history of the MCU: Rocket Raccoon, as ever, was represented on set by Sean Gunn kneeling on the ground. Demonstrating its clout, Marvel Studios induced two Oscar winners (William Hurt and Marisa Tomei) and three Oscar nominees (Angela Bassett, Samuel L. Jackson, and Michelle Pfeiffer) to show up just to look somber in a two-minute tracking shot. (William Hurt, it turned out, was making one of his final appearances in the MCU: the actor died in March 2022.) Joe Russo noted, "We used to joke—and I don't know if it's joking—it's probably the most expensive shot in movie history. That's a lot of salary on the screen there. At the very least, it's the most expensive day of extras in movie history, outside of *Cleopatra*."

The Russos filmed the scene at a cabin on the 8,000-acre Bouckaert Farm property in Georgia, which stood in for Tony Stark's lakeside cabin. The location was only thirty minutes away from the airport, so actors who weren't otherwise involved in *Endgame* could get in and out as quickly as possible, both for their own convenience and to keep the "wedding" news from leaking. (Marvel Studios also took a tenth-anniversary group photo the same week, which helped provide a cover story for everyone converging on Atlanta.) Joe Russo remembered, "The day they got there and we started to dress them in the black outfits, they said, 'This is a very strange wedding.' We said, 'It's because it's actually a funeral.'"

"An Academy Award should go to the producer, who had to get everybody on set and match up all their schedules," said casting director Sarah Halley Finn. She was also present, observing the fruits of her labor across twenty-two movies: thirty-five actors, some of whom had been successful before they joined the MCU, but most of whom were global stars now.

One of the less-recognizable faces on screen was that of Ty Simpkins, who had played the kid sidekick Harley Keener in *Iron Man 3* but was now a gangly teenager. While he was getting ready for baseball practice, he got a call from Louis D'Esposito, who brought him up to speed on the major plot points of *Infinity War* and *Endgame*, and casually mentioned that Tony Stark died in the movie, which meant that Keener knew about Tony's death well before some of the MCU's biggest stars. "Him feeling comfortable telling me one of the biggest secrets of their franchise, that's mind-boggling to me," Simpkins said. "They just told me that they figured that Tony's just stayed in Harley's life and supported him, so they thought that he should be there."

Actress Kerry Condon, who had voiced Tony Stark's digital assistant, F.R.I.D.A.Y., ever since Paul Bettany's J.A.R.V.I.S. was integrated into the Vision's personality in *Age of Ultron*, found out about Downey's departure the hard way. In the middle of a voice recording session for *Endgame*, she was fed a line that took her aback: "Life functions critical." She asked for context: Even if Tony Stark was in critical condition, surely he could be saved, right? "Then there was just this blank look from everybody," she remembered. They instructed her, "Say it like it's the saddest thing you've ever said." As she read the line, Condon thought, "There goes my gravy train"— the sorrow in her delivery was very real.

In addition to the funeral scene, most of the MCU's stars featured in the final battle, which was shot in two big chunks. Filming started in January 2018 but then stopped so the Russo brothers could turn their attention to the postproduction of *Infinity War*; they resumed work in September 2018 and spent two more months shooting the ending. "I'll be honest—it was probably the hardest thing we did in all these films," Joe Russo said. The digital pre-viz version of the epic fight had been gestating for two years, so the actual filming entailed the actors being shot in bits and pieces on bare-bones green-screen sets in Atlanta.

For some shots, the sets were dressed with debris and tree stumps—the battle happens on the site of Avengers Compound immediately after Thanos destroys it—but almost none of those practical elements made it into the final movie. "When it was all cut together and assembled in a rough cut with pre-viz, those tree stumps that they'd dressed the sets with became a bit more prevalent than they had anticipated," said Matt Aitken, Weta Digital's visual effects supervisor on *Endgame*. "Because it sort of read more like they were fighting in the ruins of a bombed-out forest rather than the ruins of a bombed-out Avengers Compound. So for a majority of the sequences, we actually ended up roto-ing [short for *rotoscoping*, an old animation technique used in modern times for cutting characters out of a filmed background so they can be placed in a different scene] the characters off the environment and replacing the environment with a fully CG bombed out crater."

Halfway through the clash, portals open up from all around the world, bringing Marvel's resurrected heroes back on screen and deploying them into the battle royale. The Russos experimented with the portals' pacing: At one point, they all opened simultaneously and disgorged dozens of characters, but the Russos reconceived the moment so that there was more of a crescendo, both visually and emotionally. McFeely said, "The first time, it was quicker. It was very powerful, and I would say exciting, like, 'Holy crap, they're back!' And the music was at a 10 early, and you zipped around. I liked it a lot, but Joe and Anthony were absolutely right to reshoot it, because everybody didn't get their hero shot."

The filmmakers tried to give every character a moment to shine, but had to cut a few sequences, including a face-off between Black Panther and Ebony Maw and a sequence where Ant-Man accidentally attracts the attention of Thanos's army by playing his favorite Partridge Family song. The sprawling battle didn't exactly become concise in the editing room—it lasts over 20 minutes onscreen—but it did focus more on the essentials. "Panther, Doctor Strange, Star-Lord—they have narrative demands," said editor Jeffrey Ford. Moments of connection, like Peter Quill seeing an alternate-timeline Gamora seemingly back from the dead or Tony Stark locking eyes with Doctor Strange and remembering there's only one way this can all end, were essential to the storytelling. "Scarlet Witch has to have that confrontation with Thanos because of what he did. . . . The fight with Scarlet Witch was also longer, but it got repetitive. They were doing the same things, and the emotion is what we kept."

Reshoots let the Russos amplify the emotion. One key moment they revisited was Peter Parker reuniting with Tony Stark on the battlefield, after having died in his arms in *Infinity War*. Originally the moment also involved Pepper Potts, but once they saw the public's response to Tom Holland's performance in *Infinity War*, they knew they needed to give audiences the catharsis of a reunion between the two characters, even if it was short-lived. "I'm going to start crying just thinking about it," Finn said, "because I think for both of those characters and for me personally, the journeys to cast them and watching them become these characters over the years has been so poignant." The appearance of an army of superheroes was filled with subtle nods to their earliest moments: Sam Wilson introduced himself by saying "On your left," which had been Steve Rogers's refrain as he kept lapping him in the jogging scene in *Captain America: The Winter Soldier*, while Pepper showed up in Iron Man armor the same shade of blue as the dress she wore on the roof of the Walt Disney Concert Hall on the night when Tony Stark almost kissed her in *Iron Man*.

Once all the Avengers were, ahem, in one place, Captain America finally uttered the six syllables that comic-book fans had been waiting for: "Avengers assemble." (Chris Evans wisely underplayed the moment, as he had with "Hulk, smash," knowing that the line was powerful enough without him bellowing it.) "I think that was Kevin's highlight of all time. To be able to finally put those two words together and have him actually say it," Tran said. She vividly remembered an army of actors standing in front of a green screen, Captain America holding Thor's hammer and saying the line, and then an electric pause before everyone surged forward. "*This is happening! We're going for it!*" she thought. The Marvel heroes, surrounded by the most crew members the studio had ever had on a single set, all went rushing into battle together.

✶

AS DAVID MAISEL OBSERVED back in 2003, "A branded studio that would allow every movie to be a sequel—that was a good business model." The ultimate proof of that proposition came when *Infinity War* grossed $2.048 billion worldwide in 2018, making it the fifth-most-lucrative movie of all time—until the following year, when *Endgame* grossed $2.798 billion, which put it at the top of the all-time box-office chart. (James Cameron, the self-proclaimed "King of the World," then cheekily rereleased *Avatar* in Chinese theaters and took the crown back.) Markus and McFeely ranked as the most successful screenwriters ever (as measured by the total box office of all their films), while the Russo brothers were suddenly in second place among directors, behind only Steven Spielberg.

Other studios repeatedly tried, and failed, to find an IP steward who could replicate Kevin Feige's accomplishments at Marvel Studios. The job appeared to be nearly impossible, requiring a precise balance between what was best for the brand and what was best for the characters. Feige was a lifelong movie obsessive, but so were plenty of other people in Hollywood. He would be the first to say that many talented people were required to make the MCU, but he had an inarguable talent for getting creative people to do their very best work. When the Russo brothers followed up *Infinity War* and *Endgame* without Feige's guiding hand, for example, the results— *Cherry* and *The Gray Man*—were underwhelming.

Feige went deeper into Marvel lore than most other producers would have, and in so doing decided that the core appeal of the comic books was their sprawling interconnectedness, which made them perfect IP for an open-ended world-conquering franchise in the new era where franchises were king. He noted that he'd worked on many superhero movies before the launch of Marvel Studios, "but all of them, in those movies, Spider-Man was the only hero in that world; the X-Men were the only heroes in that world; Daredevil; Fantastic Four. They inhabited a world where they were the single extraordinary element. And that really wasn't what the Marvel Universe was all about. It was about all of these characters, inhabiting the same world."

Beyond that foundational insight, however, Feige's genius was his innate understanding of the simplicity of his task, even amid an unending torrent of decisions regarding casting, storylines, release dates, and more. As Joe Russo put it, "Marvel's secret sauce is that Kevin likes the films to be entertaining, right?"

Another way of explaining Feige's insight came from *Doctor Strange* screenwriter C. Robert Cargill. *Avengers: Endgame* concluded with a flourish borrowed from one of Feige's favorite film franchises: The final credit sequence features the six original Avengers, each of whom appear to be autographing the screen, signing off from the franchise. It mimicked the credits of *Star Trek VI: The Undiscovered Country*, which similarly bid farewell to the beloved original cast of the *Enterprise*. But Feige's love for the *Star Trek* franchise shaped the MCU in more fundamental ways.

"Kevin made an assertion to me that melted my brain because I'd never heard it," said Cargill. "He made the argument that *Star Trek V* is better than *Star Trek: The Motion Picture*." (To say this is a hot take is an understatement. Neither movie is as beloved as *Star Trek II: The Wrath of Khan* or *Star Trek IV: The Voyage Home*, but the first *Star Trek* movie retains some residual goodwill for relaunching the franchise ten years after it left TV, while *Star Trek V: The Final Frontier*, a movie directed by William Shatner that sees the crew of the *Enterprise* confront a false god at the center of the universe, is widely regarded as the worst installment in the series.)

Cargill summarized Feige's thesis, which rested on a scene in *Star*

Trek V where Kirk, Spock, and McCoy eat beans by a campfire: "You cannot find a great character moment in *The Motion Picture* that comes close to matching anything with the campfire scene, and the campfire scene gives us our three favorite characters from the show together, outside of the norm, and lets us experience who they are as people and not legends." Feige took pains, Cargill realized, to include "the DNA of that campfire scene in every Marvel movie. He wants to take your favorite characters and give you the campfire scene, and give you that sequence in which you just love these people for who they are as people, regardless of their powers, so that when the big stuff happens, you really care about it.'" (Sure enough, *Endgame* had campfire moments that gave human stakes to the cosmic battle to follow: Steve and Natasha having a heartfelt conversation about loss while sharing a peanut butter sandwich, for example, or Tony Stark splitting a juice pop with his daughter Morgan immediately after cracking the puzzle of time travel.)

"That's the job," Marvel producer Craig Kyle said. "How do we grab people out of the gate, and by the time we start pulling funny business on them, they're already too emotionally in to walk out? If you lean too much towards the explanations of the magic or the bullshit sci-fi, you just end up pushing people away."

Audiences undeniably responded to *Endgame*'s spectacle and to its emotional payoffs. On its way to becoming the top-grossing film ever, it had the top opening weekend in movie history. Many theaters showed nothing but *Endgame*; the entire world seemed to be watching it on repeat. Feige, D'Esposito, Markus, McFeely, and the Russos snuck into a Los Angeles movie house to see *Endgame* with a crowd that laughed and cheered and shouted. "To be in a movie theater that feels like a rock arena," Anthony Russo said, "I never imagined it."

Joe Russo added, "We had chills all around and were brought to tears once or twice, realizing you told a story that had such binding communal impact."

Endgame had no bonus scenes—Phase Four would roll out without a teaser—but it ended with one last reminder of the beginning.

In the final moments of the credits, the soundtrack was just a clanging noise: the sound of Tony Stark, trapped in a cave in Afghanistan, building the Iron Man armor. It also served as a representation of the immense labor that had gone into *Endgame*, and the MCU as a whole.

McFeely spent the rest of the opening weekend trying to grasp the scale of the movie he had spent years writing and rewriting, and how it even altered LA traffic patterns. "I just walked around like, 'I think everyone's at the movies this weekend, right? Crazy. The streets are empty. It's like the Super Bowl—or the Snap.'"

PHASE
FOUR

★

CHAPTER TWENTY-SIX

A Year Without Marvel

So . . . you got detention.

Spider-Man: Homecoming

THE PLAN WAS FOR MARVEL STUDIOS TO RELEASE *Guardians of the Galaxy Vol. 3* in May 2020 as the first movie in Phase Four of the MCU. While the global pandemic shut down the movie business and threw that release schedule into disarray, there was another reason the movie wasn't ready.

The immense success of the first *Guardians of the Galaxy* upended the lives of many people, not least writer-director James Gunn. "I was caught up in the adrenalized excitement of it all," he said, "and I crashed at a certain point. I came down to earth and I had to be like, 'Where am I as a human being?'" As he saw it, he had finally found his voice as an artist: "I've kinda danced around telling the truest story I can for many years of my life. I've been a little distracted by trying to be shocking or edgy or cool or whatever, and by letting go of that and telling the truest story I can—even if it's about aliens and talking raccoons—it works."

So *Guardians of the Galaxy Vol. 2* had Baby Groot and a giant alien octopus, but its emotional core was Chris Pratt's Star-Lord torn between his two father figures: Yondu (played by Michael

Rooker) and his actual biological daddy, Ego the Living Planet, portrayed in Marvel comics as a full-size sentient world with a bearded human face.

To play Ego, Gunn and Marvel wanted to cast a well-known actor who felt like a forerunner of Chris Pratt. They approached Matthew McConaughey, who turned them down. "I like *Guardians of the Galaxy*," he said, "but what I saw was 'It's successful, and now we've got room to make a colorful part for another big-name actor.' I'd feel like an amendment." The part went to another rakish star, one who got his big break with a ten-year Disney contract back in the 1960s: Kurt Russell.

The movie shot from February to June 2016, taking up all eighteen soundstages at Pinewood Atlanta Studios. Gunn played music from the second edition of the *Awesome Mix* to set the mood. When it came time to shoot the obligatory Stan Lee cameo—he played a spaceman talking to the omniscient Watcher—Marvel trusted Gunn to film Lee's cameos in two other movies to limit the number of times Lee, who was then ninety-three, would need to travel to Georgia. When Gunn introduced Lee to Tom Holland, the newest Peter Parker, Stan the Man ribbed the young actor: "Everyone says you're great! Personally, I don't see it."

The *Guardians* sequel was messier and less funny than the original but scored even bigger at the box office, grossing $863 million (the original made $772 million). Gunn and Marvel Studios quickly announced that he would be returning for *Vol. 3*. In the interim, Gunn was even allowed to rewrite the dialogue for the Guardians in the scripts for *Avengers: Infinity War* and *Avengers: Endgame* (and to nominate the song that heralded the group's entrance in *Infinity War*, choosing the Spinners' 1976 hit "The Rubberband Man"). By the end of 2017, Gunn had completed a draft of *Guardians of the Galaxy Vol. 3* and was expecting to film the movie in 2019 for a May 2020 release date.

Just as Joss Whedon had been the czar of Phase Two, Gunn believed he was on track to take greater control of a portion of the

MCU. His territory as he saw it: the far reaches of outer space, which he called the Marvel Cosmic Universe. Feige, having learned a lesson or two from the Whedon era, wasn't so sure. "With Joss it was more unique," Feige said in 2017. "What there is with James is that a lot of the great characters in *Guardians* could have potential as their own thing. Working with James to figure out where those could go and how that could work has certainly been part of our discussions." Either way, it seemed clear that intergalactic sagas would play an even larger role in Phase Four, and Marvel Studios believed it would have James Gunn on hand to weigh in.

"We're looking for completely different realms within Marvel," Disney chairman Bob Iger said of Marvel's post-*Endgame* plans. "*Guardians of the Galaxy* represented that initially, but now we're looking for worlds that are completely separate from the worlds that we've already visited. They can be separated not just in place, but in time."

On Twitter in January 2018, however, Gunn pledged $100,000 to the charity of Donald Trump's choice if the president would publicly get on a scale to prove that he weighed 239 pounds, as the White House physician claimed. Gunn hashtagged his tweet with "#GirtherMovement," mocking Trump's "birther" misinformation campaign against his predecessor, Barack Obama. That was enough to make Gunn a target of the right-wing agitator (and PizzaGate promoter) Mike Cernovich. In July 2018, Cernovich unearthed some of Gunn's old tweets from between 2009 and 2012, when he often made jokes that were deliberately offensive and sometimes included pedophilia and rape references, like "The Hardy Boys and the Mystery of What It Feels Like When Uncle Bernie Fists Me" or "Wondering which Disneyland character would be the worst to get raped by. I think it's Goofy. But Sleepy would suck too." (Gunn wasn't the only Trump critic to find his old jokes turned against him; others who received the same treatment included *The Daily Show* host Trevor Noah and *Rick and Morty* creator Dan Harmon.)

When screenshots of the tweets started trending, Gunn contacted

Kevin Feige. "I called Kevin the morning it was going on, and I said, 'Is this a big deal?' And he goes, 'I don't know.' That was a moment. I was like, 'You don't know?' I was surprised."

Late in the day on Thursday, July 19, Gunn issued a public statement on Twitter in which he apologized for the jokes. "I am very, very different than I was a few years ago; today I try to root my work in love and connection and less in anger. My days saying something just because it's shocking and trying to get a reaction are over," he wrote. "I used to make a lot of offensive jokes. I don't anymore. I don't blame my past self for this, but I like myself more and feel like a more full human being and creator today."

Gunn said that Feige soon let him know that his apology hadn't solved his problems: "Later he called me—he himself was in shock—and told me what the powers that be had decided."

Less than twenty-four hours later, on Friday, July 20, Gunn was publicly fired. "The offensive attitudes and statements discovered on James' Twitter feed are indefensible and inconsistent with our studio's values, and we have severed our business relationship with him," read a statement issued by Walt Disney CEO Alan Horn. Horn, a small-*c* conservative staple of the studio system who was famous for including tame dad jokes in his public presentations, had made his decision before Feige or anyone at Marvel Studios could act.

Ike Perlmutter was still close to Trump, and Perlmutter was one of Disney's largest shareholders, a man with a direct line to Iger. In a 2016 interview, Iger said, "He likes to call me at seven in the morning. Sometimes I'll say, 'Ike, I've just pushed the button on the coffee maker and I haven't had my first cup yet, so I need 10 minutes.'" Perlmutter or no, Disney prized its status as America's foremost family-friendly brand and didn't want to be in the position of defending jokes about pedophilia.

Although Gunn was shocked by how abruptly he had been jettisoned, he didn't publicly criticize Disney, accepting that the corporation had made what it felt was a necessary business decision. However, the cast of the *Guardians* franchise, including the director's own brother, Sean Gunn, released an open letter imploring Disney to reinstate Gunn as the director of *Vol. 3*, vouching for his character and saying, "Given the growing political divide in this country, it's safe to say instances like this will continue, although we hope Americans from across the political spectrum can ease up on the character assassinations and stop weaponizing mob mentality." Dave Bautista, the cast's most vocal supporter of Gunn, threatened to quit if another director was appointed to replace him.

Warner Bros. pounced, offering Gunn any DC superhero project he wanted. He gravitated toward another gang of misfits, pitching a sequel to *Suicide Squad*, the 2016 movie about a group of supervillains forced to go on missions for the US government. He was given free rein on *The Suicide Squad*, which came out in 2021 to strong reviews and middling box office (possibly suppressed by the pandemic), and followed it up with a successful spinoff TV series, *Peacemaker*, starring John Cena.

While he worked on those projects, Disney had time to reconsider its decision. Horn quietly met with the director and, deciding that Gunn had been unfairly targeted, or yielding to the pleas of the *Guardians* cast, announced in March 2019 (eight months after firing him) that Gunn would be directing *Guardians of the Galaxy Vol. 3* after he finished his work on *The Suicide Squad* and its TV spinoff. The movie was rescheduled for May 2023; Gunn also agreed to film a one-off TV program, *The Guardians of the Galaxy Holiday Special*. Gunn made it clear that he would soon be returning to DC; Warner Bros. had earned his loyalty. Marvel Studios not only lost one of the core creative voices it expected to have in the post-*Endgame* era but the anchor of the *Guardians* team. Some of Gunn's actors prepared to bid the MCU farewell.

"It's bittersweet," Zoe Saldaña said while *Vol. 3* was shooting, knowing that her days of playing Gamora were coming to an end. "After all those years of complaining about that green makeup, I find myself already nostalgic about it."

Although Gunn was chastened by the experience, he was buoyed by the support from his collaborators. Given the opportunity to inveigh against "cancel culture," he declined. "Cancel culture also is people like Harvey Weinstein, who should be canceled," he said. "It's painful. But some of it is accountability. And that part of it is good. It's just about finding that balance."

In 2022, Gunn and his former manager, producer Peter Safran, were named the co-CEOs of the rebranded DC Studios, overseeing DC's movies, TV shows, and animation projects. (In a vivid lesson on not burning bridges in Hollywood, Gunn was slated to work with Horn, who retired as Disney chairman in 2021 only to become a consultant at DC's parent company, Warner Bros., in 2022.) Safran was responsible for business issues, while Gunn was touted as the new creative mind of DC. Warner Bros. hoped that, finally, it had found its own Kevin Feige.

When Gunn and Safran announced an adventurous new slate of DC movies and shows in January 2023, it was clear that they were not trying to cut and paste the MCU blueprint for crossover success. Gunn had, however, paid close attention to a few of Feige's more important lessons. Foremost, in Feige's own words: "Don't worry about the universe. Worry about the movie."

Just as Marvel, by necessity, had to launch its studio on the back of lesser-known heroes, Gunn and Safran made sure to debut more esoteric characters, like Booster Gold or the Themysciran Amazonians *not* named Diana. "One of our strategies," Gunn said, "is to take our diamond characters—which is Batman, Superman, Wonder Woman—and we use them to prop up other characters that people don't know."

Safran added, "To build those lesser-known properties into the diamond properties of tomorrow."

Gunn had also learned from the low-risk rollout of the Guardians of the Galaxy: debuting far away from the Avengers on Earth had meant that if the franchise had been a failure, the studio could have amputated it without damaging the rest of the MCU. So Gunn and Safran branded certain stories, like the sequels to Matt Reeves's *The Batman* or Todd Phillips's *Joker*, as "DC Elseworlds" properties—a label borrowed from DC comic books that let readers know an adventure happened outside the main continuity.

Gunn hopping from Marvel to DC worked out better for him than it did for Whedon, who had finished the troubled *Justice League* movie in 2017, after director Zack Snyder dropped out following the death of his daughter. Whedon rewrote the script and oversaw additional photography, but his snarky tone fit awkwardly with the somber grandiloquence of Snyder's footage. Whedon infuriated just about everybody: stars of the movie like Gal Gadot and Ray Fisher, who complained that the director was abusive; Snyder's strident army of fans; and Snyder himself, who somehow convinced Warner Bros. to give him $70 million to finish his own cut of the movie, released as a streaming video four years later.

✶

IF KEVIN FEIGE FELT any sense of powerlessness about the James Gunn decision, he would soon be compensated with more control over Marvel than ever. In October 2019, shortly after the triumph of *Endgame*, Feige was promoted from head of Marvel Studios to chief creative officer of Marvel Entertainment, meaning that every branch of Marvel, including TV and publishing, would now report to him. Feige, in turn, would still report to Disney.

Feige could now take his place as the architect behind all Marvel storytelling, turning the fractured Marvel film and TV narratives into one cohesive saga. He had access to every single Marvel character. But that also meant that the man once in charge of shepherding a handful of movies a year was now responsible for an entire eco-system of superheroes. In addition, Disney announced that Feige would be applying his producing superpowers to a new project at Lucasfilm, bolstering the floundering studio. Feige would finally get to play in the world he'd named as of one of his earliest childhood "obsessions": Star Wars.

Feige had conquered the film world, but as Disney ventured into the streaming wars, he would need all the help he could get. This was, perhaps, the worst time for Feige to lose his most powerful ally in the Disney hierarchy. On February 25, 2020, Bob Iger announced that he was stepping down from his position as CEO of the Walt

Disney Company, having delayed his departure so he could oversee the launch of the streaming video service Disney Plus in November 2019. Disney planned to run the service at a loss while it built up its user base; its target number was sixty- to ninety-million subscribers in the first five years. It was also willing to sacrifice the short-term income of licensing out its properties to other streamers: before the launch, Disney pulled the MCU movies from Netflix and shut down *Daredevil* and the other Netflix shows starring street-level Marvel heroes.

Taking Iger's place was Bob Chapek, promoted from his job as chairman of Disney parks, experiences, and products, stepping up after a long career of crunching numbers for the company. Iger, widely respected throughout the industry for his talent-friendly relationships, his focus on creativity, and the IP empire he built during his fifty years at Disney, was also criticized for his inability to name a logical successor. The choice of Chapek raised eyebrows in the industry and, crucially, inside Disney itself, where the executive had few allies. Where, insiders wondered, was the visionary who could fill Iger's shoes?

That same day, the director of the Center for Disease Control's National Center for Immunization and Respiratory Diseases, Dr. Nancy Messonnier, warned that the new COVID-19 virus met two of the three criteria for a pandemic: sustained person-to-person spread and illness that could result in death. The third criterion was "worldwide spread." Three weeks later, the World Health Organization declared COVID-19 a pandemic. On March 15, the Walt Disney Company closed Disneyland in California, Disney World in Florida, and Disneyland Paris; its amusement parks in Shanghai, Hong Kong, and Tokyo had already been shuttered. That month, major movie studios stopped reporting weekly box-office numbers because there were so many theater closures.

The offices and productions of Marvel Studios also shut down in March 2020. On March 12, *Shang-Chi and the Legend of the Ten Rings* suspended filming, sending out this message to its cast and crew:

As many of you know, Destin [Daniel Cretton], our director, has a newborn baby. He wanted to exercise additional caution given the current environment and decided to get tested for Covid-19 today. He is currently self-isolating under the recommendation of his doctor. While he waits for the results of the test, we are suspending 1st unit production in an abundance of caution until he gets the results this coming week. Second unit and off production will continue as normal. . . . This is an unprecedented time. We appreciate everyone's understanding as we work through this.

The following day, Walt Disney halted production on most of its film shoots, including *Shang-Chi*. (Cretton ended up testing negative for COVID-19.)

The next Marvel theatrical release—the movie that had been bumped up to start Phase Four after the delay of *Guardians Vol. 3*—was the long-promised *Black Widow*. Since Scarlett Johansson's Black Widow had sacrificed herself for the Soul Stone in *Avengers: Endgame*, her solo movie needed to take place at a time when she was still alive. The result was a period film, in a sense, set directly after the events of *Captain America: Civil War*. Added bonus: it wouldn't have to grapple with the complicated geopolitical repercussions of Thanos's Snap.

Black Widow was slated for release on May 1, 2020, but would not make that date. As the pandemic raged, Disney and Marvel repeatedly shuffled release dates, attempting to predict when theaters might again be able to draw large enough crowds to make releasing movies profitable. The studio initially pushed each of its upcoming movies back one slot: *Black Widow* got pushed to November 2020, bumping *Eternals* to May 2021, which in turn bumped the third Spider-Man movie, which bumped the Doctor Strange sequel, and so on. When the persistence of the coronavirus triumphed over hopeful scheduling, Marvel pushed back each of its movies one more slot: *Black Widow* would come out in May 2021. For the first time since 2009— just as Feige was finally realizing his vision of a widely diverse and creatively challenging MCU—there were no Marvel Studios movies in a calendar year. The most visible new MCU content in 2020 would be appearances by the characters in the videogame *Fortnite*.

Investors were rattled by the COVID-generated tumult, which upended not only the film industry, but even bigger moneymakers for Disney such as parks and cruises. In order to assuage their fears, the company announced an event called Disney Investor Day in December 2020. Bob Chapek would lead a livestreamed hybrid of the quarterly earnings calls—a venue where, for years, anxious stockholders and curious journalists could dial in to hear Bob Iger soothingly sell them on his dreams of the future while reporting on the financial realities of today—and the splashy fan-friendly events like Comic-Con or D23.

Disney Investor Day was touted as Chapek's debut as the voice of a new Disney era. The resulting event, however, satisfied neither investors nor fans. A parade of Disney suits awkwardly rattled off business jargon. "We will increase the penetration," Disney CFO Christine McCarthy said of the company's plan to chip away at Netflix's stranglehold on the streaming market. Soon, the more fan-friendly figures of Kevin Feige and Lucasfilm chair Kathleen Kennedy appeared onscreen to announce a dizzying number of new projects that would launch on Disney Plus. Both Feige and Kennedy were pressured into announcing projects that were nowhere near ready, some of which have since been canceled (Patty Jenkins's *Rogue Squadron* movie, a *Rangers of the New Republic* series) or significantly overhauled and delayed (the *Armor Wars* TV series, a *Fantastic Four* film).

The event wrongfooted Marvel: The studio struggled to deliver on all the promises it made during that presentation. Furthermore, it had to reckon with a massive narrative complication it had established in the conclusion of its Infinity Saga.

The Blip—the five-year period when half the world's population was removed from existence by Thanos snapping his fingers—was an epochal event in the MCU. "I was wary of it becoming like the Battle of New York, which was the third act of *Avengers*, which ended up being referenced as an event kind of constantly," Feige said. Although he knew that temporarily erasing half of the MCU ensemble was dramatically interesting, he worried that as time went on, Marvel audiences wouldn't be able to connect emotionally to the pervasive sorrow from that event. But as the pandemic continued, he said, Marvel discovered that the Blip had accurately captured the mood of the age. "This experience that affected every human on Earth now has a direct parallel between what people who live in the MCU had encountered and what all of us in the real world have encountered."

Marvel Studios, like other Hollywood studios, set up testing and masking protocols that would make it possible to resume production. Sets were populated with COVID safety officers and broken up into "zones" designed to minimize exposure, so that actors could take off their masks when the cameras rolled. Every studio agonized over when audiences would want to return to movie theaters. No studio wanted a movie with a nine-digit budget to sit on the shelf, but no studio wanted to squander a valuable asset by releasing it into a hostile environment. Trying to kick-start the theatrical business, director Christopher Nolan insisted that Warner Bros. release his *Tenet* in September 2020; the results were respectable but mixed, giving more evidence to every side of the argument.

Warner Bros. then announced that it would be releasing its complete slate of 2021 films simultaneously in theaters and on its HBO Max service. Some filmmakers howled, either because they had conceived of their movies for the big screen and didn't want that experience diminished, or because they had financial bonuses that were triggered by box-office receipts, not streaming clicks.

Warner Bros. kicked off this strategy with the sequel *Wonder Woman 1984*, which appeared in theaters and on HBO Max on Christmas Day 2020. To compensate director Patty Jenkins and star Gal Gadot for the lost bonus money, the studio paid out an additional $10 million to each of them. In order not to upset other major talent with movies going straight to streaming, Warner Bros. reportedly paid about $200 million to make its stars and directors whole.

Disney's version of a simultaneous "day-and-date" release, which it used for movies including Pixar's *Soul* and the live-action remake of *Mulan*, was to charge anyone who wanted to watch one of those movies at home via Disney Plus an extra $30 (on the newly concocted "Premier Access" tier). Chapek, living up to his reputation as someone who prioritized the bottom line over creative decisions, regarded this as an elegant solution to a difficult situation, hoping that it would provide a new income stream and drive more subscribers to Disney Plus. Feige lobbied against releasing *Black Widow* under the hybrid scheme, wanting to preserve the luster of big-screen exclusivity and worrying about alienating his talent.

Nevertheless, Chapek proceeded, overruling Feige and not bothering to contact Johansson. *Black Widow* arrived in theaters and on Disney Plus on July 9, 2021. After waiting twelve years since her debut in *Iron Man 2* to headline her own Marvel movie, Scarlett Johansson became collateral damage in the streaming wars. When Disney trumpeted the first-week revenue of $60 million from Premier Access—an announcement that pleased investors but antagonized the actress—Johansson's team filed a lawsuit alleging that Disney had violated its commitment to give the movie a theatrical-only release and seeking $50 million in damages. "Why would Disney forgo hundreds of millions of dollars in box office receipts by releasing the Picture in theatres at a time when it knew the theatrical market was 'weak,' rather than waiting a few months for that market to recover?" her lawyers asked. "On information and belief, the decision to do so was made at least in part because Disney saw the opportunity to promote its flagship subscription service using the Picture and Ms. Johansson." According to the lawsuit, Johansson's representatives had contacted Disney seeking to work out a new arrangement but had been ignored.

Feige contacted Disney and urged them to "make things right" with Johansson, the kind of request that had been historically handled deftly during the Iger administration. But in the Chapek era, the official Disney statement did the opposite. It made the situation personal by revealing that Johansson had already been paid $20 million for the movie (unsubtly implying that she was greedy for wanting more) and by stating, "The lawsuit is especially sad and distressing in its callous disregard for the horrific and prolonged global effects of the COVID-19 pandemic." For insiders used to Iger's strict policy of not letting internal Disney conflict become public knowledge, this sniping seemed an alarming sign of what to expect under Chapek's leadership—and an indication that he might not be the successor that Iger had hoped for.

Losing the PR battle, Disney settled the suit two months later; the studio and Johansson each issued a conciliatory press release and pledged that they would be working together soon on a movie adaptation of the Tower of Terror ride. From a PR perspective, the main loser in the whole episode was Kevin Feige. He hadn't made the decision to fire or rehire James Gunn, and the *Black Widow* contretemps reminded everybody that although Feige had virtually unlimited creative control over the MCU with both movies and TV, his new Disney boss could and would overrule him at will.

CHAPTER TWENTY-SEVEN

Department of Yes

If we can't accept limitations,
then we're no better than the bad guys.

Captain America: Civil War

IN 2007, WHEN JON FAVREAU AND KEVIN FEIGE SCRAM-
bled to remake the final battle of *Iron Man* after principal
filming had stopped, they unintentionally established three
fundamental tenets of Marvel Studios. One was that a long-planned
element of a movie could be discarded without hesitation if a better solution presented itself at any point before the movie's release.
Another was that special effects worked best when they were manifestations of character, not just spectacle. And the third was that the
best method for fixing serious problems with a deadline looming was
to use a CGI solution. Combined, these principles would increase
the pressure on the VFX houses that contributed more and more of
the texture of the rapidly growing Marvel Cinematic Universe (and
on Victoria Alonso, who supervised them)—especially as Marvel
entered its effects-heavy cosmic age.

Marc Chu, a visual effects producer who worked on five MCU
projects with ILM (and two more with Method Studios), said,

"I always think that if you can finish a Marvel film two weeks before release, you're doing pretty good. But yeah, it's stressful."

When Feige began his career as a junior producer on the X-Men movies, computer graphics were reserved for extraordinary moments. Looking back, he thought that was a secret advantage. "The budgets were relatively limited and therefore you couldn't do everything we do nowadays," he said. "You had to drill down on the characters—and with Marvel comics, there's a great luxury in being able to do that, because the depth of character is amazing in the comics."

In the fifteen years after *Iron Man*, Marvel and other studios came to rely more and more on CGI. While *Iron Man* included roughly nine hundred effects shots, *Avengers: Endgame* had almost three times as many. During the editing of *Endgame*, Dan DeLeeuw, the movie's visual effects supervisor, would come in with his team on weekends to check what work remained to be done on the current cut, indulging in a brief celebration whenever there was a shot with no effects. "We got to cheer, like, 80 times," he said. "Eighty out of . . . well, there's 2,623 visual effects shots in the film."

A tentpole action movie was once typically made with only a few effects houses (or even just one); in the twenty-first century, they became so CGI-heavy that producers needed to hire a dozen or more different vendors for each movie. The rapid expansion of Marvel Studios after *Iron Man* meant that Victoria Alonso was responsible for integrating an ever-changing roster of vendors. Unlike most Hollywood studios, Marvel was willing to keep dozens of non-VFX designers and craftsmen on full-time salaries, including Ryan Meinerding's visual-development team. But it didn't want to hire hundreds of computer-graphics specialists, so it, too, relied on outside contractors to do the visual effects work.

None of the effects houses working with Marvel Studios were subsidiaries of Disney; each was an independent business that could rise or fall based on an estimated profit of 3 to 5 percent, a slim margin that did not factor in the costs of the company's potential responsibility to deliver entirely new sequences shortly before an immovable release date. Most VFX companies flirted with financial insolvency; the industry grew accustomed to a certain level of churn. Rhythm & Hues, for example, had been a key contributor of CGI to Marvel's *The Incredible Hulk* in 2008, but it was driven into bankruptcy by a pair of 2012 films: *Snow White and the Huntsman* and a movie for which it won an Academy Award, Ang Lee's *Life of Pi*.

That movie largely took place on a lifeboat holding a teenage boy and an adult Bengal tiger; the tiger was entirely digital, created by Rhythm & Hues. The VFX house got the job for the tiger with a fixed-rate bid, meaning that it committed to a price tag before work began. When the movie was delayed and Lee wanted to change the design of the tiger in postproduction, Rhythm & Hues had to swallow the costs of overages. "Twenty months of delays at $1.2 million to $1.6 million per month is anywhere from $24 million to $30 million of additional costs," said Rhythm & Hues founder James Hughes. At the Oscars ceremony in early 2013, the visual team accepting the award declared that Rhythm & Hues was going bankrupt because of its work on that movie—and then was played offstage by the *Jaws* theme. The company shuttered completely in 2020.

North American effects houses had adopted fixed-rate bids to remain competitive against foreign companies that benefited from cheaper labor and more abundant tax credits. But in an era when filmmakers and studios assumed that last-minute changes were part of the gig, the practice of fixed-rate work was untenable—it meant that effects houses bore the costs, financial and human, for directors who changed their minds, whether the reason was narrative necessity, an experimental spirit, or just pure whim. "We understand that if you have a vision, you are moving towards that vision," Hughes said. "But what we see often is that they'll be headed towards a vision, and you might be heading towards that vision for six months and then all of a sudden they turn around and are heading off in an entirely different direction!"

*

SOME COMPANIES that Marvel hired achieved greater cost certainty by developing specialties within the studio's visual-effects pipeline. The Third Floor handled pre-viz for all the Marvel projects, even expanding its preproduction 3D renders to something called "tech-viz." Its technology could capture data that would be fed to camera rigs. On a real set, the real camera would duplicate the movement of a virtual camera from preproduction.

Lola Visual Effects, founded in 2004, specialized in digital "cosmetic enhancements" to actors, which could entail anything from correcting problems with makeup to "digital plastic surgery," giving stars a tummy tuck or more defined muscles. On the 2006 movie *X-Men: The Last Stand* (aka *X3*), it was asked to do something new: de-age Patrick Stewart and Ian McKellen for a flashback scene set twenty years in the past.

Director Brett Ratner was insistent that he didn't want to cast younger lookalikes. Instead, he wanted his stars to look how they had in the 1980s. The *X3* producers solicited pitches for various methods, from prosthetics to digital doubles. The solution that impressed them came from Lola. The effects house said it could de-age the actors without affecting the filming at all. Its method didn't require tracking dots, motion capture, or MOVA dust.

Lola got the job, the first time the effect was attempted in a major motion picture. It started by compiling a massive amount of research, collecting as many images as possible of the younger Stewart and McKellen from multiple angles. Luckily, with two prolific actors, Lola had an abundance of footage. To smooth out wrinkles and tighten up the skin, its technicians then employed "digital skin grafts": sections of digital epidermis, modeled after how the actors had looked decades earlier. They were virtually attached to each actor's face and followed their movements. The grafts could be reshaped and relit for every frame, allowing digital artists to match the lighting and nuances of the original performance.

The Lola team also consulted with Hollywood plastic surgeons on how they could make men look younger without the benefit of computers. The physicians pointed out that there were two areas where cosmetic surgery couldn't do much: the nose and the ears, which continue growing over the human lifetime (because of gravity's effect on cartilage). Lola deleted the noses and ears from the footage of Stewart and McKellen, scaled them down by 10 percent, and then added the appendages back onto the actors, as if each of them were Mr. Potato Head (or Sir Potato Head).

When *X3* was released in 2006, the flashback scene was widely maligned by moviegoers for looking fake. But a barrier had been breached: older actors could play younger versions of themselves, if a production was willing to pay for it. Ideally, effects work is invisible, drawing viewers into the movie rather than showing off the technique of the artisans behind it, but Lola garnered considerable attention from *X3* and became the first-choice house for de-aging. The process had improved noticeably by the time Lola youthened Patrick Stewart again, in 2009's *X-Men Origins: Wolverine*, although it still didn't look fully naturalistic.

Marvel Studios had employed Lola since the studio's earliest days, when the rushed postproduction schedule on *Iron Man* hit a snag. "We came in after the fact on the first *Iron Man*," said Trent Claus, a visual effects supervisor at Lola. "The work that we got hired to do had already been tasked to another vendor, but it just wasn't working out. So they came to us to see if we could come up with something better in a very short amount of time. If I remember correctly, we had two weeks to do the effect. The previous vendor had several months. It was a 9-1-1 sort of thing."

Lola impressed Marvel with the quality and speed of its work, and picked up more assignments on *The Incredible Hulk* and *Iron Man 2* (mostly cosmetic work, like removing Mickey Rourke's confusing "Loki" tattoo). On *Captain America: the First Avenger*, director Joe Johnston was an effects pro himself, having spent years at ILM. He worked with Lola on "Skinny Steve": in the scenes before Steve Rogers takes the Super Soldier formula, the muscular Chris Evans needed to look like a ninety-eight-pound weakling. "We knew that the movie wouldn't work if you didn't buy Skinny Steve at the top," Feige said. "We're going to spend the whole first act with a scrawny version of Steve Rogers before he gets chosen for the program and undergoes the procedure that turns him into Captain America." Feige believed it was worth spending millions of dollars to establish that the protagonist had a pure heart before gaining superhuman muscles. If the movie got the look of Skinny Steve wrong, it would lose the trust of the audience.

Some shots were achieved by face replacement. Evans's slender body double, Leander Deeny, would mimic Evans's movements, and Evans's face would later be digitally superimposed on his body. In other scenes, Lola digitally reconstructed Evans's body frame by frame, using photographs of actual men under 100 pounds for anatomical reference. "Things that people don't think about are the way his shirt fit on him when he filmed. He's a big muscly guy, so the fabric stretches against him, and you see stretch marks in the fabric. It pulls tight against different areas. None of that works if you're trying to sell the idea that he's scrawny," said Claus. "You have to completely replace parts of the shirt and the fabric and then animate those by hand to make it look like they're airy and loose and falling off of him."

For *Captain America: The Winter Soldier*, Lola aged the actress Hayley Atwell, making her character Peggy Carter look like a woman in her nineties. Because it was actually Atwell giving the performance, her reunion with Steve Rogers was that much more heartbreaking, especially when he tells her, "I couldn't leave my best girl. Not when she owes me a dance." The emotional scene gave him human dimensions, especially important given the scale of the final act's battle royale, during which Captain America knocks giant surveillance airships out of the sky.

Avengers: Age of Ultron presented a greater challenge. Lola needed to make the Vision look more like an android and less like an actor (Paul Bettany) in maroon makeup. "We left only his face and his body," said Claus. "The remainder of his head—his ears, his neck, all of that—gets completely removed, frame by frame. So all you get is this floating face. Then around that, we built the CG head and then all of those little cybernetic details that are on his face. In the end, his head is CG except for his face, which is a blend. About fifty-fifty of live-action Paul and CG elements, which is a unique thing. I don't know of any other character that's ever gone through that process."

On *Ant-Man*, Marvel asked Lola for another de-aging job for a flashback sequence, returning Michael Douglas to the era of '80s movies like *Wall Street*. "We took thirty years off," Claus said. "That was the first time that we had done de-aging to that extent." When director Peyton Reed filmed Douglas in the flashback scenes, he made sure that for each camera setup, he shot an additional take with a younger actor substituting for Douglas and replicating his movements. "Then you have a built-in comparison of what younger skin looks like in that lighting and that environment, which was very helpful. It takes a lot of the guesswork out," Claus explained.

De-aging for MCU flashbacks became a frequent request for Lola. Robert Downey Jr. in *Captain America: Civil War*, Kurt Russell in *Guardians of the Galaxy Vol. 2*, Michelle Pfeiffer in *Ant-Man and the Wasp*: all were digitally made younger. As with McKellen and Stewart, each had decades of reference footage. Russell, however, insisted that his youthful appearance had been achieved almost entirely with hair and makeup. According to Russell, a VFX artist told him, "We touched it up here and there"—a polite understatement, since his entire face had been digitally altered.

Marvel was pleased enough with the results in those movies that it asked Lola to take on a more daunting job: de-aging Samuel L. Jackson for his entire costarring performance in *Captain Marvel*, roughly an hour of screen time. Although the technology had advanced in the four years between *Ant-Man* and *Captain Marvel*, Claus said that Lola relied on its artists, not software. "For us, it's not so much that the technology is evolving, because, for the most part, we use the same tools that we have for years and years. Software always updates, but the vast majority of the work is done by artists—it's their skills that improve year to year. With every project, we learn a bit more and get a little more experience under our belts. Unlike a lot of the effects houses, most of our de-aging artists have been with us for eight, ten, twelve years, so they've really gotten good at this." Indeed, the younger Nick Fury looked entirely plausible, except for the moment when Jackson had to engage in his least favorite activity, running in front of a camera.

Motion-capture performances that formed the basis of CGI characters such as the Hulk had long been shot in green-screen environments, with multiple cameras capturing the reference marks on an actor. But for 2011's *Rise of the Planet of the Apes*, Weta Digital, the New Zealand effects house founded by director Peter Jackson, made a breakthrough. Its new technology could capture performances on ordinary sets, indoor and outdoor, allowing actors playing CGI characters to work in the same environment as their non-digital colleagues. ILM soon adapted its motion-capture technology to do the same thing, so on *The Avengers*, Mark Ruffalo wore a gray motion-capture suit when he portrayed the Hulk, as did the actors playing Chitauri warriors. "The latest version of the suit has this triangle pattern all over it," explained Kevin Wooley, the lead engineer in ILM research and development. "Our new patented suit design works with a tracking system that likes the corner features of all the triangles. So if you see them in the really silly suit, we're trying to get it so it's as easy to do on-set capture as it is to do capture on the stage."

ILM handled the visual-effects shots of the Hulk from *The Avengers* through *Avengers: Endgame*. The character's look evolved slightly in each appearance, but ILM always strived to show audiences a version of Mark Ruffalo, not just a huge green monster. Marvel valued the continuity of working with ILM almost as much as it valued the continuity of working with Ruffalo. ILM's Marc Chu said that effects houses tried to keep groups of coworkers together. "You will always see groups of people going from one show to the next, because they understand each other. I'm always going to have a preference to use an animator that I've already worked with, if I know he or she fits the bill and can do the work—I don't have to overexplain anything. I want to have people take an idea and run with it. If they have something better, come back to me and pitch it. That's the same feeling that I get from all the creatives at Marvel."

As Marvel Studios increased its output to three movies a year, its CGI needs grew dramatically. The airport fight in *Captain America: Civil War* showed off a multitude of digital tricks that required a wide range of artistic skills, most of which went unnoticed by most moviegoers. During filming, Robert Downey Jr. and Don Cheadle could wear faceless helmets with tracking dots on them because their suits of armor would be added later. The Falcon's wings were digital, as were Hawkeye's arrows. Wanda Maximoff made objects float with CGI help, and the Vision was a blend of effects work and Paul Bettany's face. Black Widow and the Winter Soldier received some face-replacement work in fight scenes handled by their stunt doubles. And although the Black Panther and Spider-Man stuntmen showed up in face-covering costumes, their outfits were digitally painted over.

"When I saw the film, it broke my heart a little that they had CG'd over the suit," said Gui DaSilva-Greene, the stunt double for Chadwick Boseman as Black Panther. "Because then it makes certain things that I actually did look like I didn't do it—the chase sequence or the triple kick to Captain America's shield, I did all that."

Marvel Studios regularly conducted computer scans of the actors featured in its movies, getting detailed measurements of their physiques and features. According to Downey, the technology became more efficient with every MCU movie he made, and the studio used it more frequently. "Maybe you did one scan per movie at the beginning, because that's what they could swing. Now you might do three scans a week, and it takes no time."

Marvel could use the scans to make toys and other merchandise with uncanny accuracy. It also kept them on file for the future, in the event the studio wanted to be able to render digital versions of its stars in the prime of their youth. (Possessing the scans didn't give Marvel the rights to animate a performer's likeness in a movie—but that could always be negotiated later.)

DaSilva-Greene said that when he was scanned during the *Civil War* shoot, the process took about two hours. "It's like a science-fiction film. You walk into a dark room and there's a whole bunch of cameras," he said. A technician would instruct him: "Stand right there on that X. Cool, stay there. Look straight. Drop your chin a little bit. Your arms are not far apart enough." After the technician had the data he needed, he'd tell DaSilva-Greene to rotate 15 degrees to the right. "Or they put you on a little plate and they spin you themselves, because they don't trust that you understand '15 degrees.' I was like, 'Hey guys, I got an A in geometry, thanks.'"

By the time it made *Avengers: Infinity War* and *Avengers: Endgame*, Marvel Studios could feature fully realized digital characters that wouldn't have been possible ten years earlier, including Mark Ruffalo's Banner/Hulk hybrid "Smart Hulk" and Josh Brolin's Thanos. The sea change was the arrival of machine-learning software that picked up the nuances of an actor's face. AI software called Masquerade, developed by Digital Domain, took the low-resolution data captured from Brolin's face—adorned with the familiar white tracking dots—and then used artificial intelligence to comb through multiple scans of the actor to pick the best full-texture final render. Brolin was worried about how Thanos would come across onscreen, as was Marvel Studios VFX supervisor Dan Deleeuw, until the day they tested the new system. "We were just going to get two or three lines and then apply the technology to it," Deleeuw said. "It was Josh's first time in the motion-capture outfit and the helmet cam and working with the Russos."

Brolin delivered his villainous dialogue broadly, figuring that was the only way he would be able to get across the digital divide. But after he shouted his lines, he sat down with the script, thinking out loud about the emotional beats for Thanos and giving casual, subdued line readings that weren't meant for an audience. "We kept the motion-capture running while Josh was playing with the character," Deleeuw said. "The lines we did our first test on were Josh figuring out the character, and so we got this very introspective performance." That test helped refine the character's design: "We knew that the more of Josh's features we included in the sculpt of Thanos, the more successful we would be. The more detail you put into the mouth, even though it's this giant oversized mouth, the better you're able to carry his performance." Seeing the results convinced Brolin that he could play the role in a quiet, thoughtful mode.

"Our real ace in the hole is Brolin," Downey said. "To me, it's not Thanos, it's Brolin. Because he's the one who is making this avatar be scary. And he's a sweet guy, but he's a formidable guy."

When Brolin wasn't available, Karen Gillan, who played Nebula, filmed her Thanos scenes with director Joe Russo standing in for him, which she found to be a fascinating dynamic. But she relished Brolin's performance. "It's so easy to play an over-the-top villain, but he's soft-spoken and it's so much creepier that way. You're like, *Who are you? What are you capable of?*"

Jonathan Harb of Whiskeytree, who didn't work on *Infinity War*, believed Thanos was the pinnacle of Marvel Studios VFX. "What they've done with visual effects has given us all the ability to see things that none of us ever thought could even be possible. Not just the industry, but anyone that watches movies," Harb said. "You watch Josh Brolin's performance of Thanos, and you're moved by this giant purple thing talking."

"We knew he would have to carry the film. He has more screen time than the Avengers," Deleeuw said. "The audience had to believe and sympathize with him—until he did the horrible thing that made you hate him forever when all your heroes disappear at the end."

✱

BY THE TIME *Avengers: Infinity War* arrived in theaters, development on the Marvel Studios shows streaming on the Disney Plus service had already begun. Marvel, already one of the biggest players in the VFX world, was planning on three to five series every year on top of its schedule of three movies, roughly doubling the number of effects shots it needed, and accelerating some of the most punishing industry trends. The MCU's expansion into cosmic realms in Phases Four and Five would only make matters worse: films like *Doctor Strange in the Multiverse of Madness*, *Thor: Love and Thunder*, and *Ant-Man and the Wasp: Quantumania* relied, increasingly, on wholly digital characters and locations.

For each project, Marvel Studios circulated a sheet of shots it needed, and visual effects companies could bid to be vendors on each shot. The more complicated jobs, like the Hulk or a de-aging process, would be offered first to the biggest VFX vendors or to the effects houses with relevant expertise. But that left plenty of work for smaller firms. Companies bidding on the workaday jobs had to estimate how much time and labor would be required to create a shot of two heroes fighting a robot with tentacles, or a spaceship crash-landing on a trash planet. Marvel would probably take the lowest bid, so houses that wanted to stay busy had to determine just how small they could afford to make their margins. Soon enough, Marvel would be back with another project and another round of bidding, expecting a similar price, even if the previous project forced VFX staffers to work long hours with no weekends off just to make sure that the effects house that employed them didn't go bankrupt.

The visual effects in Marvel's Disney Plus shows were as high resolution as those in the feature films, and involved just as much work—but with a lower budget. In the case of *She-Hulk: Attorney at Law*, the main character of the show was a walking visual effect. (The strong reactions to the CGI superhero demonstrated that people had intense opinions about computer special effects. Kat Coiro, the series director, believed that there was a misogynist undertone to the commentary: "In terms of the CGI being critiqued, I think that has to do with our culture's belief in its ownership of women's bodies.") Once the COVID-19 pandemic took hold, most of the VFX industry switched to remote work, requiring close coordination between Marvel Studios, the effects houses, and hundreds of visual artists sending shots and edits back and forth. Homebound artists sent their work to the office, where high-powered computers with processing power measured in petabytes (1,000 terabytes) churned out final shots for Marvel's approval. Marvel Studios told visual effects houses that remote work was acceptable, but that home offices needed to be secure so that plot twists wouldn't leak.

Marvel Studios' in-house art department coordinated with pre-viz companies like the Third Floor, which helped streamline the process for its vendors, but not enough to compensate for the studio's habit of changing large portions of its films late in the process. Victoria Alonso believed that whenever she and her postproduction crew were asked any question that began with the words "Can you . . ." there was only one correct answer.

"It's the 'Yes' department," she stated flatly. "The answer is 'Yes, we can do it.'"

The principle of never saying no to potential improvements boosted the quality of Marvel Studios' productions, but it became increasingly burdensome for the visual effects houses and artists asked to bear the brunt of the resulting work.

"You see all these timelines for films and just think . . . It won't ever stop," one VFX artist said. "The workload becomes agonizing at times . . . These studios keep feeding from the same trough because the work is so abundant, and [Marvel] needs so many people, and artists need jobs. Where do you think these studios are going to go?" Even anonymously, it was rare for anybody to complain about Marvel as an employer—airing those grievances publicly was part of an effort to motivate VFX workers to join a nascent union. The studio kept many jobs in-house instead of relying on freelancers and had particularly aggressive NDAs (nondisclosure agreements), but even the anonymous complaints pointed toward some cracks in the Marvel method.

"It is noticeable that there were shortcuts," a Marvel VFX technician who worked on *Quantumania* said after the film was pummeled by critics and fans alike for its shoddy digital effects. "Certain things were used to cover up incomplete work. Certain editorial cuts were made to not show as much action or effects as there could have been—likely because there just wasn't enough time to render everything. . . . It really did feel like certain scenes were trimmed or otherwise altered to either save money, save time, or cover up the inability to get it done. . . . I think the movie is getting the reviews it's been getting because Marvel is doubling down as much as possible on constricting quality. They're squeezing blood out of stones. And we're out of blood."

While Marvel Studios was a particularly large and problematic client, it wasn't solely responsible for the endemic problems facing visual effects houses and the abusive work environments that exploited thousands of digital artists around the world. But how best to fix a broken part of the film industry?

One answer would be to get rid of the fixed-bid system and allow effects companies to participate in profit-sharing. However, given that Hollywood accounting departments have spent decades perfecting the art of hiding profits, that would require a total overhaul of studios' business practices. Another solution would be the creation of a visual effects artists' union that would negotiate pay standards and overtime rates for artists. And yet another option—one that Marvel was rumored to be considering—would be to bring the visual artists under a studio's corporate roof, either by establishing a large in-house VFX department or purchasing an existing effects house.

Tatiana Maslany, the star of *She-Hulk: Attorney at Law*, recognized that conditions weren't ideal for the digital artists who created her big green alter ego. "I feel incredibly deferential to how talented these artists are and how quickly they have to work," Maslany said while promoting her show on a Television Critics Association press-tour panel. "I do think we have to be super-conscious of how work conditions aren't always optimal."

Series creator Jessica Gao was more pointed: "It's just a massive undertaking to have a show of this scale where the main character is CG. It's a very overwhelming and ginormous thing to take on and it's terrible that a lot of artists feel rushed and feel the workload is too massive. I think everybody on this panel stands in solidarity with all workers and is very pro good working conditions."

Several years into its television venture, Marvel Studios acknowledged that the rapid pace of TV production and lower budgets didn't mix well with the demands of VFX-heavy stories. In 2022, *Armor Wars*—a project that was slated for the small screen—graduated to film status thanks, largely, to VFX concerns. "There were some great ideas coming out for that series that, to be quite honest, were too big for that show," Marvel producer Nate Moore said. "Our Disney Plus shows are awesome, and we love them, but the budgets are not the same as the features—that's no secret."

Making the world's biggest blockbusters and buzziest TV shows came with extra scrutiny. Marvel Studios had become the symbol of industry-wide problems, including the precarious position of digital-effects houses. While Alonso was silent on the looming VFX crisis, she was outspoken elsewhere.

In April 2022, when Alonso accepted a prize from the LGBTQ media watchdog group GLAAD for *Eternals*, she chastised Disney CEO Bob Chapek for not taking a stronger stance against Florida's "Parental Rights in Education" legislation, nicknamed the "Don't Say Gay" law. (After siding with Disney's gay employees, Chapek then softened his position under criticism from Florida governor Ron DeSantis, to no avail—Florida revoked Disney's special tax status in the state anyway.) Alonso had broken one of Feige's cardinal rules: don't speak out publicly against the company. A source close to the matter said that later that year Feige suggested to Alonso that she had outgrown her role at Marvel. He reportedly cautioned her to "keep her head down" and "do the work."

In early 2023, Alonso refused to act on Marvel Studios' request to remove LGBTQ pride symbols from *Quantumania* for foreign markets. The atmosphere at the studio was tense: the department of "yes" had said "no." D'Esposito outsourced the VFX work anyway, an act Alonso regarded as a betrayal.

In an unexpected move, Disney fired Victoria Alonso on March 17, 2023. After the news leaked, Disney claimed Alonso had violated her contract by producing and promoting *Argentina, 1985*, an Amazon Studios movie that was nominated for an Oscar for Best International Feature Film. Which, technically, she had. Nobody from Marvel intervened to defend her; a month later, Disney and Alonso reached a settlement (reportedly for millions of dollars). This messy and public rupture of the team of three—Alonso, D'Esposito, and Feige—who had shepherded Marvel through a decade-plus of success was a clear sign that the pressure for more hit content had shaken the bedrock of the company.

CHAPTER TWENTY-EIGHT

K.E.V.I.N.

He's a friend from work!

Thor: Ragnarok

FURTHER EVIDENCE THAT KEVIN FEIGE WASN'T LIKE other teenagers: "One of my hobbies was to be disappointed with the sequel to a movie, and then make the next version of the movie in my head."

Like many kids, Feige used Star Wars figurines to tell his own stories, but as he got older, he focused his storytelling impulses. "After *Robocop 2*, I was like, 'I got to fix it. I gotta come up with a better *Robocop 3*.' After *Superman IV: The Quest for Peace*, 'I gotta do a better *Superman V*, I gotta come up with a better *Superman V*.' After *Star Trek V*, 'I got a better idea for *Star Trek VI*.'" He insisted, "I did have better ideas for all of them—but nobody was interested."

That "I got to fix it" attitude became a philosophical touchstone of Feige's filmmaking career, and one that he acted on: he spent his adult life building a cinematic empire out of neglected IP and reviving characters that had gotten lost in the crowd.

"One of the great things about Marvel is they've got thousands of characters," Bob Iger observed. "In fact, when we bought the company, in due diligence we discovered that we were buying not only the name Marvel, but seven thousand characters."

The first time Feige applied his "I got to fix it" ethos to a troubled part of the MCU was in *Captain America: Civil War*, when he brought back William Hurt as General Thaddeus Ross, a character who hadn't been seen since *The Incredible Hulk*, eight years earlier. "I loved playing Ross the first time because I was able to try and create an ego as big as the monster he was chasing," Hurt said. "This is a much newer Ross. A much different Ross. And I liked that a lot. I haven't had a lot of time to understand it, but I'm doing the best I can. And they haven't fired me yet." *The Incredible Hulk* was long considered one of the least essential MCU films—nothing in it seemed to be relevant once Mark Ruffalo appeared as Bruce Banner in *The Avengers*—but Feige was determined to elevate it into the canon retroactively, or, at the very least, to strip-mine it and extract every useful element.

More importantly, Feige needed to jump-start Thor. Despite having starred in four hit movies (two solo outings and two Avengers pictures), the character appeared to be dwindling into irrelevance, a self-important thunder god who didn't have much to offer beyond muscles and earnest heroism. The character's second solo movie, *Thor: The Dark World*, was an ill-formed mess; in *Avengers: Age of Ultron*, he had been relegated to a dull side quest searching for more Infinity Stones; in *Captain America: Civil War*, he wasn't even invited to the party. Nobody was more aware of the problems than the actor who played Thor, Chris Hemsworth, although it took an outsider to spur him to action. When he heard the comic-book-obsessed writer/director Kevin Smith bashing the *Thor* franchise on a podcast, Hemsworth realized that his movies were losing the hardcore fans, and he approached Feige.

"I'm dying here. I feel like I have handcuffs on," Hemsworth pleaded. "Tonally, we've just got to wipe the table," he said. "It has to be funnier; it has to be unpredictable." The actor advocated for getting rid of some of Thor's trademarks, especially the hair and the hammer. Feige agreed to act on Hemsworth's suggestions in the third Thor movie, already titled *Thor: Ragnarok*. He realized that a reinvention could rely on audiences' familiarity with Thor, given all the hours Hemsworth had already spent on screen in the MCU.

"When we started Hemsworth on Thor," Feige said, "he has blond hair, he has a hammer, he has a cape. These are the things that make Thor. He has now appeared as that character so many times [that] Chris Hemsworth is Thor. So we cut his hair, we got rid of his hammer, and it's still him." Another defining feature of Thor—his grave mien—couldn't be removed so easily, but it could be subverted.

To oversee that reinvention, Feige drafted director Taika Waititi, a superstar in New Zealand for three eclectic movies that blended eccentric comedy with stories of heartbreak, parenthood, and vampirism: *Boy*, *Hunt for the Wilderpeople*, and *What We Do in the Shadows*. The budget for *Thor: Ragnarok* would be seventy times larger than anything Waititi had done as an independent filmmaker. But the director approached the opportunity fearlessly, describing his interview process with Marvel as saying "yes to everything" and then figuring out how to execute whatever he had agreed to.

What landed Waititi the job, though, was a sizzle reel for his version of *Thor*. Feige said, "Filmmakers sometimes will say, using clips of other movies, 'Here's what I have in mind.' And sometimes they're not good. Most of the times, they're okay. His was amazing and was scored to that Led Zeppelin song." ("Immigrant Song," by Led Zeppelin, was a shrewd choice for Thor: it's written from the perspective of aggressive Norsemen, even making reference to "the hammer of the gods.") "From the beginning, that song kind of defined what Taika was going to do with this. That it's in the trailer, that it's in the film—all from that first meeting, and from one of his first instincts of this movie, is very impressive."

After Waititi was hired, he, Feige, and producer Brad Winderbaum interviewed writers to update the screenplay for a third Thor movie. The existing draft, by franchise veterans Christopher Yost and Craig Kyle, didn't have the tone they wanted, but it finally featured the Norse death goddess Hela, a villain who previously had been vetoed by the Creative Committee solely because she was female.

Writer Stephany Folsom pitched her idea to take Thor down a notch. "My whole thing coming in was just like, *Let's put Thor in his place*," says Folsom, "They really dug that, and Taika and I hit it off well. I actually got hired in the room. Feige was like, 'This all sounds great, we'll bring you on board.' I called my agents, and I was like, 'I think I just got hired to do *Thor: Ragnarok*.' And they're like, 'I don't know, Stephany, I'm not so sure about that.' Then like an hour later business affairs called and they were like, 'Oh my God, you were right! You *did* get hired in the room!' "

Folsom developed the new script with Waititi and the producers, but ultimately lost a WGA credit arbitration to Eric Pearson, who did the final pass on the screenplay. (WGA arbitrators often favor a movie's first and last writers, at the expense of anyone who contributed in between.) "Kevin just wanted to reboot it all," recalls Folsom. "Taika would pitch something crazy, and he'd be like, 'That's possible.' I'd pitch something crazy, and he'd be like, 'That's possible.' It became a game: How far can we push it?"

The movie, which features Hela destroying Mjölnir and Asgard, also sends Thor to a planet where he is gang-pressed into gladiator combat, including a memorable battle against the Hulk. Thor's line when he recognizes his opponent—"We know each other! He's a friend from work!"—wasn't actually contributed by any of the screenwriters (or any of the actors, whom Waititi encouraged to improvise). In perhaps the ultimate example of Marvel's "best idea wins" philosophy, the movie's best line was suggested by a child with cerebral palsy who spent the day on the set courtesy of the Make-A-Wish Foundation.

The gladiator planet Sakaar in *Ragnarok* was borrowed from the *Planet Hulk* run of comics, written by Greg Pak and drawn by Carlo Pagulayan and Aaron Lopresti; Feige said that the filmmakers jokingly renamed it "Planet Thor." Marvel had finally figured out something about the Hulk: even putting aside the contractual entanglements with Universal Studios that made it expensive to do a solo Hulk movie, the character worked best when he could play off other superheroes. "It's hard to do this character in a stand-alone movie," Ruffalo explained, "because you're watching somebody who, for two hours, refuses to do the exact thing that you always want him to do: turn into the Hulk."

Thor: Ragnarok was a stunning success, bringing in $853.9 million worldwide and showcasing Hemsworth as an unlikely cut-up. The franchise went from being one of the weakest aspects of the MCU, both in box office and in critical terms, to being one of the strongest. Feige had reversed its fortunes—by reversing his own choices from a few years earlier. "We don't have to force a tone from movie to movie," Ruffalo said. "All we have to do is carry those characters forward with some semblance of the last story in mind."

"I was like, 'Holy shit, the craziness worked,'" Folsom said. "It went to insane places, but Taika never lost the emotional throughline."

✳

FEIGE'S RECLAMATION PROJECTS continued. For instance, *Avengers: Infinity War* found a place for the Red Skull, Captain America's perpetual foe in the comic books, who had been eliminated by the Tesseract in *Captain America: The First Avenger* and largely forgotten. Despite being disintegrated in the earlier movie, he showed up as the guardian of the Soul Stone and hardly anybody noticed that the character was now a CGI creation, voiced by Ross Marquand instead of the previous Skull, Hugo Weaving.

That was a warmup for *Avengers: Endgame*. Even as Feige wrapped up a twenty-two-movie sequence, he embraced some of the least-loved aspects of the Marvel Cinematic Universe, ensuring that in retrospect they felt essential. Hawkeye's family, featured in the farmhouse scenes in *Age of Ultron* that Joss Whedon had fought for so bitterly, now gave emotional weight to the global devastation of the Snap. James D'Arcy appeared as the butler Edwin Jarvis, reprising his role from the short-lived *Agent Carter* created by *Endgame* screenwriters Christopher Markus and Stephen McFeely. "I basically became a Trivial Pursuit–type question," D'Arcy noted. "I'm the only character who's gone from the television show to a film." (As Feige gained control over Marvel's film and TV enterprises, more actors joined D'Arcy in that exclusive club, including Charlie Cox and Anson Mount.)

The most surprising callback Feige engineered in *Endgame* was a scene set inside the action of *Thor: The Dark World*, arguably the least memorable entry in the MCU lineup. In that movie, Natalie Portman had suffered through a confusing subplot that saw Jane Foster infused with the Reality Stone (aka the Aether). Having sworn off Marvel because of how it handled Patty Jenkins during the production of *The Dark World*, Portman was reluctant to return to the MCU: she did some brief voiceover work, but her appearance onscreen was from a deleted scene from *The Dark World* that Marvel repurposed. Feige was simultaneously recycling a character, a plot point, and footage, all of which had previously been discarded.

Christopher Yost, one of the writers of *The Dark World* screenplay, was all too aware of the movie's reputation. "Every time a Marvel movie comes out, they put together a list of the worst Marvel movies and it's in the bottom two, and you're like, 'Ah, damn, that sucks,'" he said. "*Thor 2* was what it was. But it mattered. Important things happened to Thor in that movie. Instead of ignoring it, celebrate it. Make it meaningful. I certainly appreciated its inclusion [in *Endgame*], and I thought it was genius how they handled it."

In 2006, before Marvel Studios had shot a single frame of film, the studio had promised fans that the Mandarin would appear as a villain. Fifteen years after Jon Favreau made that pledge at the San Diego Comic-Con, Feige finally made good on it: in *Shang-Chi and the Legend of the Ten Rings*, Tony Leung played Shang-Chi's father Wenwu, whose identity as "The Mandarin" was stolen by Aldrich Killian (Guy Pearce) and assigned to the hapless actor Trevor Slattery (Ben Kingsley). While the Mandarin was rooted in racist stereotypes, the role was at least not literally Fu Manchu, the archetype of Yellow Peril menace, who was Shang-Chi's father in the comics. Leung was given a short monologue mocking how the white man appropriated a powerful Asian name—perhaps the only way Marvel could use the offensive character was to acknowledge that its original iteration, much like the use of Tilda Swinton as the Ancient One in

Doctor Strange, was a cop-out. "After a thirty-nine-year acting career, I really wanted to do something different," Leung said. "I wanted to play a villain."

In *Shang-Chi*, Marvel also unexpectedly revived the Abomination, the scaly monster played by Tim Roth in *The Incredible Hulk* in 2008. It seemed that Feige was determined to employ the entire cast of *The Incredible Hulk*: Tim Blake Nelson and Liv Tyler both agreed to revive their characters in *Captain America: Brave New World*, slated for 2024, joining Harrison Ford, who took over for the late William Hurt in the role of General "Thunderbolt" Ross.

"Originally I did the film that we did all those years ago for my children," Roth said. "I just thought it would make them laugh that Dad's a monster—that kind of monster—and also slightly embarrass them, which is always good. And it did, so it succeeded on both levels. And so years pass and then they asked me if I would come in to do some voice work on *Shang-Chi*."

Marvel Studios, though, hoped the Abomination could do more than make a brief appearance at an underground fight club in Macau. Kevin Feige also wanted Roth to play a substantial guest role in the *She-Hulk: Attorney at Law* TV series. "I went in and there's Kevin, who I hadn't seen in years," Roth remembered. "He told me what they had in mind. It appealed to the sort of anarchy in me, I suppose, in the sense that I love my career being chaos."

The biggest test of Feige's "I got to fix it" attitude would come when Disney Plus launched in November 2019. Programming for the streaming service, Feige needed to draw from every strand of Marvel's history, both in print and on screen, and he couldn't afford to leave characters behind just because they had been mishandled in the past.

Fortunately, a new acquisition by Disney had restocked the Marvel cupboard. Judging that Fox Entertainment wouldn't survive the transition to streaming, Rupert Murdoch sold his studio (and assets such as its film library) in 2018. After a bidding war with the cable company Comcast, Disney acquired 20th Century Fox for $71 billion—a crucial acquisition that bolstered its content just before it launched Disney Plus. The Fox acquisition came with some significant assets, notably the rights to the X-Men and the Fantastic Four, which had been held by Fox for many years. The teams would finally return to Marvel Studios, giving Feige the opportunity to reboot both properties.

Since Feige's days as Lauren Shuler Donner's representative on the set of *X-Men*, Fox had turned the mutant team into an empire, making a total of thirteen movies set in their world, including three Wolverine solo movies starring Hugh Jackman, four prequel movies with a new cast, and two R-rated action comedies starring Ryan Reynolds as Deadpool, a foul-mouthed mercenary mutant with a superhuman healing ability and a habit of breaking the fourth wall. Over the course of two decades, that empire had risen and fallen. The last X-Men movie Fox had in the can was *The New Mutants*, an unsuccessful spinoff released after the Disney merger.

When Feige rolled out Phase Four at the 2019 Comic-Con, he had a lot of other projects to announce, including *Eternals*, *Doctor Strange in the Multiverse of Madness*, a Fantastic Four movie, a Blade movie, and *Thor: Love and Thunder*, which would reunite Hemsworth and Waititi, and also bring Portman back as Jane Foster in a significant role—she would get to wield the hammer Mjölnir as Thor herself. "No time for mutants," Feige told the crowd.

The plan was to keep the X-Men dormant for a few years, building anticipation and making it easier to introduce the MCU version without viewers feeling like the characters were being perpetually rebooted. There would be some X-Men programming to tide over fans—just not in the form they expected. Although Hugh Jackman had concluded the saga of Wolverine in the elegiac 2017 film *Logan*—a John Ford Western in the guise of a superhero movie—Ryan Reynolds lured him back to play the character again in *Deadpool 3*. (That gave Kevin Feige one last chance to mess with Hugh Jackman's hair.) And the X-Men would come to Disney Plus, in an animated show that continued Fox's after-school hit *X-Men: The Animated Series*, which had run from 1992 to 1997. The Disney revival would pick up where the series left off, with the majority of its original voice cast signing on and with the executive producer of the '90s series, Eric Lewald, advising the production. Lewald said that Feige understood the original theme song was key: "I think a secondary person had the rights to the music, so it was a negotiation for them. Obviously, you can't do the new show without that song. But the guy selling it knew the same thing, so I'm sure it was a heavy price."

That theme music appeared in *Doctor Strange and the Multiverse of Madness*, heralding the arrival of Professor Charles Xavier, played by Patrick Stewart from the live-action movies, but seated in the yellow hoverchair from the cartoon. Like Jackman, Stewart had claimed he was done with the role of Professor X in 2017, but changed his mind. "I was a little unsure at first if it was a wise thing to do," said Stewart, "given that *Logan* had been such a powerful movie and we watched him die in Hugh Jackman's arms."

Stewart appeared as one of the Illuminati, a cabal of variants of Marvel characters. Hayley Atwell was present as Captain Peggy Carter, Lashana Lynch as an alternate-universe Captain Marvel, Chiwetel Ejiofor as an alternate-universe Mordo (from the first *Doctor Strange*), and in a piece of casting that fans had lobbied for, John Krasinski as Reed Richards, aka Mr. Fantastic, the attenuated leader of the Fantastic Four. This version of Mr. Fantastic, like the rest of the Illuminati, would not survive his encounter with Wanda Maximoff—but he did, nevertheless, represent the first appearance by a member of "Marvel's First Family" in the MCU. Perhaps the most unexpected figure, however, was Anson Mount as Black Bolt, reprising his role from the *Inhumans* series on ABC, the most reviled MCU project ever. He didn't have any lines—Black Bolt doesn't speak because of the raw destructive power of his voice—but his traditional comic-book outfit, which had been deemed unsuitable for the TV series, was restored.

If the Inhumans could be rehabilitated, apparently everyone in MCU history was on Feige's call list—except Edward Norton, the franchise's first Bruce Banner, and Joss Whedon, whose *Agents of S.H.I.E.L.D.* characters remained in limbo.

Mount, who said he was surprised to be invited onto an MCU motion picture, noted how few actors were actually present when he filmed the scene. "That was a very interesting shoot," he said. "As you can imagine, several of the actors were quite busy. Patrick was not there. Chiwetel was not there. Krasinski's contract wasn't even done. He wasn't there. We had actors playing those roles, knowing that they were going to either be substituting their shots or transplanting faces. I've never done anything quite like that, and I was in disbelief of how well it cut together."

"You could hear the audience knew exactly what the actors' characters were referring to," said Patrick Stewart after the premiere. "An actor would just mutter some line, and the audience would laugh, because they knew what the context was and they knew what the history of that expression was. And I found that delightful, when an audience become part of the film experience."

"It's so funny that Kevin cast John because the fans had a dream of who the perfect Reed Richards would be," director Sam Raimi said, referring to Krasinski. "And because this is an alternate universe, I think Kevin said, 'Let's make that dream come true.'" As the demands of the Disney Plus era loomed, Feige spent more and more of his days in alternate universes. He had one foot in the worlds that people had already seen on-screen, and the other one in the better versions that he was always imagining.

CHAPTER TWENTY-NINE

The Clone Saga

I don't know how to work as a team.

Spider-Man: No Way Home

MARVEL STUDIOS KEPT POACHING TALENTED PEOPLE from Dan Harmon's shows—maybe because Kevin Feige was a fan of *Community* and *Rick and Morty*, or maybe because Harmon was expert at blending science fiction, pathos, and goofy comedy in a way that made working for him a good MCU apprenticeship. Joe and Anthony Russo were the best-known names who left for Marvel, but the studio also hired writers such as Jessica Gao and Jeff Loveness, and even Harmon himself on an uncredited rewrite of *Doctor Strange*. (Not to mention the cameos for *Community* cast members, including Jim Rash, Yvette Nicole Brown, and Donald Glover.) Through Marvel's interest in his people, Harmon grew expert on the mores of Marvel.

As Harmon put it, "There's such a powerful culture at Marvel of teamwork that, literally, the janitor in the hallway outside the meeting about the Spider-Man sequel is allowed to say, 'You know what I like about Spider-Man?' and it will be taken seriously. If you can handle that, if your ego is simultaneously powerful but flexible enough to fit through that pipe, you are rewarded and you have a home there forever. There's a tremendous mandate at Marvel about all for one and respecting the franchise. Their leader, Kevin Feige, leads by example in that mode. He's like, 'I don't care if I have to cooperate with Sony on Spider-Man. I will do anything in the service of Marvel.'"

By the end of the Infinity Saga, working in that mode had elevated Feige to the ranks of the most successful movie producers ever: He had made twenty-three movies in twelve years, and each one was a hit. Feige produced three of the five top-grossing films of 2019: *Captain Marvel*, *Avengers: Endgame*, and *Spider-Man: Far from Home*. Per the Sony/Marvel deal, the box-office receipts of *Far from Home* went to Sony, while Marvel benefited indirectly, by selling Spidey merchandise. Financial analysts estimated that the Spider-Man movies had generated over $8 billion in profit by the end of 2022.

Everyone working on the Tom Holland Spider-Man franchise recognized that the cooperation between Marvel and Sony that made the movies possible was unusual and fragile. As Amy Pascal emphasized, having Peter Parker in the MCU opened up a wide range of stories that would otherwise have been impossible to tell. "This is something that we would never [have] been able to do in any other way," she said. "It was a very selfless thing that was very smart on the part of all the companies."

Sony was also doing well with Spider-Man IP outside the MCU. After *Venom* grossed $856 million worldwide and *Spider-Man: Into the Spider-Verse* won an Oscar for best animated film, Sony commissioned sequels to both movies and green-lit another villain spinoff, *Morbius*, starring Jared Leto. Sony also moved forward on a movie centered on Kraven the Hunter, yet another member of the Spider-Man rogues' gallery, and revived the Sinister Six movie written by Drew Goddard. Both Sony and Marvel believed, reasonably enough, that they were succeeding as joint stewards of Spider-Man.

However, Disney wanted a larger slice of the Spider-money: as *Spider-Man: Far from Home* went into production in 2018, the studio offered to cofinance the films it was producing for Sony, putting up half the budget and, in return, collecting half the profits. The top executives at Sony Pictures, Tom Rothman and Tony Vinciquerra, had no interest in the proposal. They had more than enough money to finance the movies and didn't want to surrender any of the profits, which were as close to a sure thing as existed in Hollywood. Sony made a series of counteroffers, which Disney batted away. (Reportedly, one proposed deal would have involved Kevin Feige producing not just Spider-Man movies for Sony, but additional films based on the other Spider-Man characters Sony held the rights to.) But it soon became clear that Sony would rather eject Spider-Man from the MCU than give up half of the franchise's box office.

Negotiations broke down in August 2019, and with the completion of *Far from Home*, the original deal expired. It seemed Marvel would lose Spider-Man, and Sony would lose Feige. After the news of the impending split leaked to the press, both sides were polite if slightly passive-aggressive.

"We are disappointed, but respect Disney's decision not to have him continue as a lead producer of our next live action Spider-Man film," a Sony spokesperson said of Feige. "We hope this might change in the future, but understand that the many new responsibilities that Disney has given him—including all their newly added Marvel properties—do not allow time for him to work on IP they do not own."

Feige responded, "It was never meant to last forever. We knew there was a finite amount of time that we'd be able to do this, and we told the story we wanted to tell, and I'll always be thankful for that."

In his public statement, Sony's Vinciquerra was blunter. "The Marvel people are terrific people, we have great respect for them, but on the other hand we have some pretty terrific people of our own. [Feige] didn't do all the work. . . . We're pretty capable of doing what we have to do here."

If it was an uncertain time to be a Spider-Man fan, it was even more confusing to be the actor playing Spider-Man. Amy Pascal and a squad of Sony creative executives pitched Tom Holland on their grand plans for the Spider-Man franchise, which would no longer involve appearances in the MCU. For once, Holland said all the right things publicly, sounding like a star athlete who just got traded to a new team: "I'm just so grateful that Marvel changed my life and allowed my dreams to come true and to Sony [for] allowing me to continue living my dream."

The same day however, Holland obtained the email address of Disney CEO Bob Iger and sent him a message thanking him for the opportunity that Marvel Studios had given him. Iger responded by calling Holland, who was taking some time off with his family in the UK. "My family and I went to the pub quiz in our local town," Holland said, "and I'm like three pints in, haven't eaten much, and I get a phone call from an unknown number and I have a feeling, I'm like, 'I think this is Bob Iger . . . but I'm drunk.' So my dad's like, 'Just take the call, you'll do fine!' " The conversation was unexpectedly emotional for Holland. He bore Sony no malice, but he told Iger how sad he was to be leaving the MCU.

In the kind of talent-friendly, big-picture move that he built his legacy on, Iger informed Holland that his MCU tenure wasn't necessarily over: "There is a world in which we can make this work."

Public sentiment had once again changed the tenor of a Disney/ Sony negotiation over Spider-Man. A few years earlier, fans yearning to see Spider-Man in the MCU had induced Sony to close a deal; now the pressure was on Disney, which reconsidered its hard line on a fifty-fifty split.

It was a custody battle unlike any other in Hollywood history. Crossover events like *Alien vs. Predator* and *Freddy vs. Jason* typically happened only when the rights to both franchises were controlled by a single studio; even cameos, like the Looney Tunes characters appearing in the 1988 Disney movie *Who Framed Roger Rabbit*, proved tense and complicated when more than one studio was involved. On September 26, 2019, however, the two megacorporations came to terms—one of the last great deals of the Iger administration before Bob Chapek took over at Disney. Holland would make one more Feige-produced solo Spider-Man movie and one more guest appearance in another MCU movie. For the former, Marvel would put up 25 percent of the production costs and receive 25 percent of the box-office profits. Though Amy Pascal was no longer a Sony employee, she still produced the Spider-Man movies through her company, Pascal Pictures. "Peter Parker's story took a dramatic turn in *Far from Home* and I could not be happier we will all be working together as we see where his journey goes," she said of the deal, which continued an alliance she had worked hard to secure in the first place.

To write the script for that third Tom Holland movie, Sony had already rehired the *Far from Home* team of Chris McKenna (another *Community* alum) and Erik Sommers. They pitched Kraven as the villain but were informed that he was unavailable until Sony had established him in a solo movie. The writers turned their attention to the end of *Far from Home*, when J. Jonah Jameson publicly reveals that Peter Parker is Spider-Man.

"That led us down different story roads," McKenna said. They played with an updated version of *It's a Wonderful Life*, where Peter Parker and Doctor Strange try to undo the fact of the world knowing his identity. That narrative echoed a 2007 comic-book story called *One More Day*, which was controversial among comics fans because it erased the twenty-year marriage of Peter Parker and Mary Jane Watson from history and even from their own memories.

Then somebody—McKenna thought it might have been Feige—suggested that the movie could have a post-credits scene with multiple villains that would set up Sony's Sinister Six project. "We were coming up with different storylines that would just sort of write towards a tag like that," McKenna explained.

They wrestled with how it would work until the day when Feige asked, "Remember that idea with all the villains that we were talking about for a tag? That Sinister Six idea? Why don't we just do it in the movie?"

"That just sort of blew everything open," McKenna said.

The plan was for the Spider-Man movie to follow *Doctor Strange and the Multiverse of Madness* on the release schedule, allowing the writers to take advantage of the multiverse established in the earlier movie and providing a justification to import major characters from past Sony Spider-Man movies. Sony had inadvertently done Marvel a favor with *Spider-Man: Into the Spider-Verse*, which served as a wildly entertaining primer on the very concept of the multiverse—the idea that there are an infinite number of alternate worlds paralleling our own but differing in some key details—that helped movie fans who hadn't spent time poring over metaphysical comic-book lore.

The prospect of bringing the ghosts of Spider-Men past into the Holland era was enticing but daunting: it gave the writers a lot of plot elements to juggle and the producers a lot of stars to persuade. The essential villains were the Green Goblin, played by Willem Dafoe, and Doctor Octopus, played by Alfred Molina. Even more import-ant were the two actors who had previously portrayed Peter Parker, Tobey Maguire and Andrew Garfield. Sommers and McKenna at various points wrote versions of the story that incorporated Emma Stone's Gwen Stacy, Kirsten Dunst's Mary Jane Watson, and Sally Field's Aunt May, but ultimately cut all those women when they decided the story was already overstuffed; the only female char-acters with significant screen time would be Marisa Tomei's Aunt May and Zendaya's MJ. Because the screenplay was constantly in flux, none of the actors could read a locked script, and they joined the project based on their faith in Feige, Pascal, and director Jon Watts.

"I really didn't want to do a cameo," Dafoe said. "I wanted to make sure there was something substantial enough to do that wasn't just a tip of the hat." Pascal persuaded Dafoe and the other actors to sign up by reminding them of their history together and promis-ing that they wouldn't be making cash-grab cameos. "These are the longest options that a studio has ever exercised on actors," Molina joked. The movie ended up with five villains—leaving out candi-dates such as Tom Hardy's Venom and Paul Giamatti's Rhino—deliberately falling one short of the canonical Sinister Six, reserving that possibility for a future Sony film. (Unlike Dafoe, Hardy didn't mind doing a cameo; he appeared in the film's post-credits stinger.)

Spider-Man: No Way Home was scheduled to begin produc-tion in June 2020, but COVID-19 continued to disrupt Marvel's post-*Endgame* plans and pushed filming back to late October. Sony also moved the release date back due to the pandemic—from July

2021 to November 2021, and then to December 2021. Because Marvel had pushed its own release schedule back even further, that meant *No Way Home* would come out before *Multiverse of Madness*, not after. Sony wasn't interested in delaying its blockbuster any longer, even if it scrambled the planned storylines of the MCU. But that decision required more rewriting, so filming began without a completed script. Throughout the shoot, Sommers and McKenna kept fabricating new pages as more actors signed their contracts and joined the cast.

On October 25, Tom Holland finished his work on another Sony movie, *Uncharted*, and went straight to the Atlanta production of *Spider-Man: No Way Home*, filming under the code name *Serenity Now* (a *Seinfeld* reference). The shoot had elaborate coronavirus protocols. Masking was governed by a system of colored lights: if the blue light was on, actors could take off their masks and perform. When the yellow light came on, the cast had to mask up and leave the set so crew members could do their jobs. "No, the Spider-Man mask does not count as PPE [personal protective equipment]," Holland quipped. The original cinematographer, Seamus McGarvey, contracted COVID shortly before production started and Mauro Fiore (*Training Day*) stepped in on short notice, but otherwise the production successfully avoided delays caused by the virus.

Benedict Cumberbatch shot his scenes in November before decamping to London for principal photography on *Doctor Strange and the Multiverse of Madness*. Sommers and McKenna kept furiously rewriting, working in a mode that was reminiscent of the frantic pace of *Iron Man*'s scripting process, but in a vastly more complicated scenario. The expanding yet interconnected Marvel web, incorporating Disney Plus shows, MCU films, and Sony coproductions, was an increasingly sticky thing to mess with—pull one string and the whole enterprise might come unraveled.

America Chavez (played by Xochitl Gomez), who has the power to punch holes between universes, was removed from the *No Way Home* script because her character was slated to debut in *Multiverse of Madness*. Her role, confusingly, went to Peter Parker's previously unpowered best friend Ned Leeds. Doctor Octopus was added when Alfred Molina finally signed his deal. Crucially, Maguire and Garfield weren't confirmed until December 2020, two months into filming. Sommers and McKenna had to write the third act of the movie, which sees all three Spider-Men team up, during the production's break for the holidays.

Rumors swirled around the movie, and the filmmakers did everything they could to keep the identities of its cast secret. To foil telephoto lenses, actors covered themselves in large, hooded robes when they moved from one soundstage to another. People in masks who looked like they might be Kirsten Dunst were spotted in Georgia. (They were not Kirsten Dunst.) The whole cloak-and-dagger operation was compromised when a food delivery driver in Atlanta bragged on Reddit about bringing dinner to Andrew Garfield. Later, Garfield recounted the secrecy-busting encounter as if it were a horror story. Soon he and Maguire were photographed *together* on the streets of Atlanta, and Garfield despaired. He told the filmmakers that it was impossible to keep a secret of this magnitude: "I worked so hard to keep it secret that I was in Atlanta shooting. All these leaks were happening, and I was like, 'Oh, my God, guys, what the hell is going on? I'm working so hard here to stay secret, and then here's an image of me with Tobey!' And they're like, 'No, no, we're gonna keep it quiet.' 'OK, I'll keep denying it.'"

Jamie Foxx went to Atlanta to reprise his work as Electro, but Thomas Haden Church's return as Sandman was a voice performance, as was Rhys Ifans's reprisal of the Lizard: their characters were now CGI. Alfred Molina discovered that playing Doctor Octopus no longer required him to use physical puppet arms—on *Spider-Man 2*, which was released in 2004, he had dubbed his team of puppeteers the "Octourage"—although he did need to be strapped into a device that would float him through sets so that that Doc Ock's arms could be added by computer artists in post-production. (The visual effects team at Lola shaved a couple of decades away from Molina and Dafoe so they would look the same age as they were when their characters originally appeared. Dafoe, sixty-five years old during the *No Way Home* shoot, insisted on doing as much of his fight scenes as he could. "Because that's really fun for me," he explained. "It's the only way to root the character. Otherwise it just becomes a series of memes.")

"We all believe so much in these characters and we give it 110%," Holland said. "I know in my fight scene with the Goblin, I bust my hand up. My knuckles were bloodied and we were really going for it. We were putting everything into it. I remember on the last day of shooting that fight scene when Jon [Watts] said cut, Willem and I both just collapsed to the floor because we were exhausted and we just had given him everything." Holland's survival technique: "chugging Red Bulls to try and keep my energy going."

By February 2021, people were already asking Holland about the rumors that Maguire and Garfield were in the film. "It would be a miracle if they could have kept that from me," Holland told Jimmy Fallon on *The Tonight Show* (via Zoom), the first in a long litany of deflections and denials. While the semiretired Maguire was able to avoid most press, Andrew Garfield had to lie his way through endless interviews during the awards campaign for one of his other 2021 films, *Tick, Tick . . . Boom!*

★

DESPITE A CONSTANT STREAM of leaks, audiences were uncertain exactly what they would get in *No Way Home* when it opened on December 15, 2021, and were largely delighted by three different Spider-Men and five villains from earlier movies (two of them, remarkably, from *The Amazing Spider-Man* series). Some of those characters were better-loved than others, but Feige had taken on a cross-studio fix-it job, retroactively giving them all the sheen of the Marvel Cinematic Universe (or maybe the Marvel Cinematic Multiverse). The most moving appearance belonged to Garfield, who had loved playing Spider-Man but whose franchise had been cut short, ending abruptly with the tragic death of Emma Stone's Gwen Stacy. The new movie provided closure for both the actor and his version of Peter Parker.

Sommers and McKenna had not only skillfully juggled a huge cast of characters but had come up with an ending that would set up Spider-Man's future either with Marvel Studios or with Sony Pictures. Believing that he has only had one way to save the multiverse, Peter Parker asks Doctor Strange to erase the knowledge that he is Spider-Man from everyone's memory. He ends the film alone and penniless in Manhattan, with his friends and fellow Avengers having no clue as to his identity. If Marvel stopped producing Spider-Man films starring Tom Holland, Sony Pictures could pick up this new life for Peter Parker without causing any continuity issues with the MCU.

Undeterred by the pandemic's omicron wave, fans couldn't get enough of *No Way Home* and went back for repeat viewings. The movie earned $1.9 billion at the box office, by far the highest-grossing Sony motion picture ever, and second only to *Avengers: Endgame* in MCU history. That box-office haul almost guaranteed that Sony and Disney were headed for another negotiation, but it also provided strong motivation for both parties to keep Peter Parker in the Marvel Cinematic Universe. Although the sequel *Venom: Let There Be Carnage* was generally considered a misstep and *Morbius* was a widely ridiculed flop, Sony kept pushing ahead with its own Spider-Verse movies, including *Kraven the Hunter*, *El Muerto*, and *Madame Web*. Pascal insisted that there would be more MCU Spider-Man movies, but almost immediately had to walk that promise back, saying "We're producers, so we always believe everything will work out."

Feige served as the steady hand, the producer who had learned not to make promises to Marvel's audience that he couldn't fulfill. "We're actively beginning to develop where the story heads next," he announced publicly, "which I only say outright because I don't want fans to go through any separation trauma like what happened after *Far from Home*. That will not be occurring this time." The future of Peter Parker in the MCU felt likely but wasn't a sure thing that Feige could build his post-*Endgame* strategy around.

While Avi Arad was an executive producer on *No Way Home*, his role was largely ceremonial. He was still active as a producer on Sony

Spider-projects like *Venom* and *Morbius*, though, and on the Tom Holland movie *Uncharted*; if Spider-Man had actually left the MCU, Arad likely would have been a key creative producer on a Tom Holland Spider-Man movie for Sony. Once again, Marvel Studios had pushed Arad aside. After decades of success on a bigger scale than even Arad had ever imagined, however, Marvel could afford to be magnanimous to the man whose outsize personality had once defined its presence in Hollywood. The credits of *No Way Home* included the following sentence, in capital letters: "THE FILMMAKERS WOULD LIKE TO GRATEFULLY ACKNOWLEDGE THE ORIGINAL TRUE BELIEVER, AVI ARAD, WHOSE VISION LED THE WAY TO BRINGING THESE ICONIC CHARACTERS TO THE SCREEN."

The credit baffled some fans who had been following the story of Marvel since its inception, especially the designation of "true believer"—a moniker Stan Lee gave his fans. Lee himself got a memorable and touching dedication after his death in 2018 with a sketch of his signature glasses appearing in the closing credits on *Into the Spider-Verse* beside his quote "That person who helps others simply because it should or must be done, and because it is the right thing to do, is indeed without a doubt, a real superhero."

Arad's all-caps dedication certainly eclipsed the demure "Special Thanks to Marvel Studios Founding Chairman" credit earned by his usurper and rival, David Maisel, in the *Avengers: Age of Ultron* closing credits. (Still, that "Founding Chairman" designation ran counter to the legend Arad had created for himself.) But a new title card started popping up in the MCU, starting with the Disney Plus show *Hawkeye*, that left no doubt as to who was calling the shots: "A Kevin Feige Production."

CHAPTER THIRTY

Into the Multiverse

Well, it's a big mess and thematically inconsistent,
to be honest.

She-Hulk: Attorney at Law

THE STARS OF THE TV SERIES *WANDAVISION* HAD TO adjust to many challenges during filming, perhaps none greater than strapping into a harness so they could act high above the ground. "I don't know, what do you look like when you fly?" series star Kathryn Hahn asked. "There are so many things happening off camera that are just bananas, you can't imagine what's going on with all that ruckus. As if I didn't have enough mad respect for Elizabeth Olsen and Paul Bettany before this."

"We both really relish the idea of doing a sitcom mom-and-pop fight, but with superheroes, but play it really real," Bettany said. "But there did seem to be a lot of time in a harness. And time goes really slowly when you're in a harness. There are lots of differences between Lizzie and I, and one of them's very obvious and makes being in a harness a little more *complicated* for me." Bettany guffawed. A role that had started as a few days of voiceover work playing Tony Stark's artificial intelligence assistant J.A.R.V.I.S. on *Iron Man* had become a fifteen-year job that somehow now required a mélange of emotional truth, retro comedy, and genital restriction. Such was life in the ever-expanding and unpredictable MCU in 2020.

For years, Marvel had been making TV series featuring its characters, some notable for their high points (*Daredevil*, *Legion*), some notable for their low points (*Inhumans*, *Iron Fist*). But whenever any of those shows aired—on ABC, Fox, FX, or Netflix—if Kevin Feige had any objections, he could only quietly grit his teeth, because Marvel Studios didn't control the results. That changed in 2019, when Feige's role as the dominant creative voice at Marvel was formalized with his promotion to chief creative officer of Marvel Entertainment. Animation, television, comic-book publishing: suddenly they all came under Feige's aegis.

Disney CEO Bob Iger and his successor, Bob Chapek, were happy to expand Feige's remit. (Chapek had a family connection to Marvel Studios—his son, Brian Chapek, had been working there since 2013.) But in return, they expected Feige to increase the studio's output dramatically, providing a steady flow of content for the Disney Plus streaming service. In the era of Peak TV, Disney Plus needed Marvel shows fast and, to stay competitive, it wanted a lot of them. Feige essentially had a blank check for television programming, so long as he could deliver volume.

Producer Nate Moore laid out the upside of making Disney Plus programs: "They've never said, 'You should do this' or 'You shouldn't do that.' When we're pitching the shows, they say, 'Great. If you guys are excited, let's go make those shows.'"

The downside was that while Feige was prolific and relentless, he had his limits. Producing three movies a year had been a full-time job; adding the oversight of multiple Marvel divisions and a streaming TV channel's full slate of programming to his responsibilities stretched even him too thin. "The amount of work that we're going to have going forward, you can get overwhelmed, because success is expected," D'Esposito admitted. The studio's top executives coordinated their schedules, with mornings devoted to development and preproduction, afternoons to postproduction. To distribute the workload further, Feige convened a group dubbed the "Marvel Parliament," composed of trusted long-term, in-house creative producers: Stephen Broussard, Eric Carroll, Nate Moore, Jonathan Schwartz, Trinh Tran, and Brad Winderbaum. The Marvel Parliament essentially revived the highly contentious and disbanded Creative Committee, with the key differences that it was within Marvel Studios and devoted to making the MCU work, not maximizing the toyetic elements of its movies.

The Parliament would decide which characters from the vast MCU ensemble could work on television, beyond the category of "heroes who aren't quite popular enough to merit their own movies." Schwartz said, "What's cool about Disney Plus is it gives us the opportunity to tell stories that are maybe outside of the norm of what we would be able to do in movies that want a different canvas, that want a different structure, that are maybe a little weirder and wilder."

Or as Moore put it, "Television is so much more about characters than it is about plot."

✳

IN THE FINEST TRADITION of Marvel's "best idea wins" philosophy, one of the first TV show ideas had its earliest roots in a 2016 press conference for *Captain America: Civil War*, when a journalist asked, "When are we going to get our Falcon/Bucky road-trip movie?" Feige's face lit up: "That's a good idea!" Anthony Mackie (who played Sam Wilson, aka the Falcon) and Sebastian Stan (who played James Buchanan "Bucky" Barnes, aka the Winter Soldier) had a crackling, antagonistic energy every time they were paired for press junket interviews. "Mackie and Sebastian brought out different colors in each other that weren't necessarily expected," Moore said, "both as people and performers. So we knew there was something special there."

Although Olsen and Bettany had only fleeting moments together in *Captain America: Civil War* and *Avengers: Infinity War*, they had also displayed an easy chemistry. (The Vision–Scarlet Witch pairing is one of the most cherished love stories in Marvel comics, so fans had long expected the MCU to head in the same direction.) Bettany's character, the Vision, had died at the hands of Thanos, but what is a superhero's death if not an opportunity for a resurrection persevering?

And Tom Hiddleston, whose Loki had died several times over, had an immediate connection with just about anyone and anything. "If you've ever been to a Comic-Con where Tom Hiddleston makes an appearance, you see what sort of magic that is," Moore said. Disney, eager for streaming content, cheerfully signed off on Marvel's top three ideas for TV shows: the first three MCU programs on Disney Plus would be *The Falcon and the Winter Soldier*, *WandaVision*, and *Loki*.

While the lines between TV and film have blurred with the advent of streaming and binge culture, they are not interchangeable, no matter how frequently TV executives describe a season of television as a ten-hour movie. Feige, who had spent his life studying and making films, now considered how comic-book storytelling might work in a different medium: "By the nature of the shorter run times and the multiple episodes, you could look at TV as issue by issue. That's what's so exciting about TV, having beginnings and ends every thirty minutes or so, all inspired by filmmaking rhythms, which also happen to track comic rhythms."

"Showrunner" was a relatively recent term, but the job wasn't. Almost all American television series had long been managed by a single person who acted as head writer, producer, and decision-maker. Completely relinquishing control to a single person from outside the company, however, was not the Marvel way. Feige and the Parliament approached each of its first three TV projects in the same manner they set up a film: with a concept in place, Marvel interviewed and hired a head writer for each show. That person would lead a writers' room, but rather than act as a traditional showrunner, they would serve, essentially, the same role as the screenwriter on a movie. Their work would usually get rewritten, and while they might end up sitting in a canvas-back chair on the set, the director would take over when filming started (a key difference from most TV shows, where directors are the hired guns and the head writer makes the final call).

Feige said he came up with the initial idea for *WandaVision* during the high-pressure production of *Infinity War* and *Endgame*: "While we were in Atlanta shooting those two films together, there was a cable channel in the hotel where I was staying that every morning had *Leave It to Beaver* and *My Three Sons*. Rather than watching the news in the morning, I just had that on. I found great comfort in old sitcoms. I found it so soothing. The way those people had a problem and got to figure it out, man, you think 'everything will be okay today' as we head to whatever production issue we were having. I also started showing my kids *The Brady Bunch*. So I started to become fascinated with the idea of being able to play with that genre in a way that could both subvert what we do at Marvel and subvert what those shows were." According to Feige, when he learned that Disney wanted Marvel to start making streaming TV, he thought, "I have an opportunity to not just have this stuff rattle around in my head. We could actually turn this into something."

Marvel Studios asked *WandaVision* head writer Jac Schaeffer to pitch a show about Wanda Maximoff's grief over losing Vision, told as a tour through the tropes and visual language of eight decades of family sitcom history, with an undercurrent of modern dread. "They had been internally noodling on it," she said. "I think I brought a structure to it." Wanda and the Vision live in laugh-track bliss with their two young children—until the cracks start to show and reality (which includes the Vision being dead) intrudes. "In the writers' room, we had intense conversations about grief and loss," Schaeffer said. Those discussions led to the show's best-known line, "What is grief, if not love persevering?"

*

THERE WERE OTHER significant creative minds behind *WandaVision* beyond Feige and Schaeffer, although their names were harder to find in the show's credits. Wanda's grief-induced break with reality was significantly inspired by the influential comic-book series *House of M* (2005) by writer (and former Creative Committee member) Brian Michael Bendis and artist Olivier Coipel. Meanwhile, its nightmare rot at the center of an unsettling suburbia comes from the award-winning book *The Vision* (2015–2016) by writer Tom King and artist Gabriel Hernandez Walta. Bendis, Coipel, King, and Walta all got "special thanks" acknowledgments deep in the closing credits, alongside a number of other Marvel luminaries including Joss Whedon (who introduced Wanda and Vision to the MCU), John Byrne (who invented the "White Vision" character), and Bill Mantlo (writer of the 1982 miniseries *Vision and the Scarlet Witch*).

If you create an original character that gets folded into the larger Marvel narrative, the corporation owns most of the rights connected to it—but how much are you owed for its continued use? For decades, Marvel Comics answered that question with "nothing" and bitterly fought any creators looking for additional compensation. Starting in the late 2000s, however, Marvel's publishing contracts included bonuses for original characters that appear in movies or TV through a "Special Characters Contract," although they're riddled with complicated loopholes. If a character appears for less than 15 percent of screen time, for example, that's considered "just" a cameo, meaning a creator is owed significantly less. By those metrics, for example, cameos include Sebastian Stan's Winter Soldier in *Captain America: Civil War*. Despite being the linchpin of the plot, he appears in twenty-two minutes (just under 15 percent) of its two-hour, twenty-eight-minute running time. Ditto Chris Evans as Captain America, who appeared for less than eight minutes in *Avengers: Infinity War*.

This rankled comic book legends like Jim Starlin, creator of Thanos and some of the Guardians of the Galaxy, who was aggrieved by Marvel's paltry payments. "Just received a very big check from D.C. Entertainment for my participation in *Batman v Superman, Dawn of Justice*," Starlin wrote on Facebook of the money he made off a laughably minor Batman antagonist known as KGBeast. "Much bigger than anything I've gotten for Thanos, Gamora and Drax showing up in any of the various Marvel movies they appeared in, combined."

Starlin's complaints around the terms he negotiated for Thanos, specifically, prompted Disney to renegotiate with him, resulting in what Starlin referred to as "a fairly fair deal." Ever since Bucky Barnes made his metallic-armed return in *Captain America: The Winter Soldier* in 2014, artist Steve Epting and writer Ed Brubaker, creators of the *Winter Soldier* storyline, had to be satisfied with little more than their "special thanks" credit.

When word reached Brubaker that Bucky would now be starring in a Disney Plus show, he wrote in his newsletter: "Everyone at Marvel Studios that I've ever met (all the way up to Kevin Feige) have been nothing but kind to me. . . . Work-for-hire work is what it is. . . . I have a great life as a writer and much of it is because of Cap and the Winter Soldier bringing so many readers to my other work. But I also can't deny feeling a bit sick to my stomach sometimes when my inbox fills up with people wanting comments on the show."

Brubaker later appeared on Kevin Smith's *Fatman Beyond* podcast to say, more pointedly: "There's nothing preventing anyone at Marvel from looking over how much the Winter Soldier has been used in all this stuff and calling me and Steve Epting and saying, 'You know what, we're going to try to adjust the standard thing so you guys feel good about this.'" Epting and Brubaker received another "special thanks" credit on *The Falcon and the Winter Soldier*, alongside Robert Morales and Kyle Baker, creators of the incendiary 2003 comic *Truth: Red, White, and Black*. That series inspired Malcolm Spellman, head writer of *The Falcon and the Winter Soldier*, to include a Black Super Soldier named Isaiah Bradley (created by Morales, Baker, and editor Axel Alonso) to tell the story of the racist underpinnings behind the Captain America shield. "When you start to see the direct impact that a Black superhero had on my nephew, that's branded on my brain," Spellman said.

While Marvel's movies were often loose adaptations of comic-book storylines, once Marvel got into the TV business, the studio hewed closer to specific issues and graphic novels, which made it harder to wave away the original comic-book creators. While Marvel had long observed a church-and-state separation between the comic-book publisher on the East Coast and Marvel Studios on the West Coast, those boundaries seemed blurrier now that Feige oversaw both divisions. A later Disney series, *Hawkeye*, drew so heavily from writer Matt Fraction and artist David Aja's award-winning 2012–2015 run on the comic that Fraction, at least, landed a consulting producer credit and a more significant payday.

✴

EVEN WITH THE ABILITY to draw from decades of popular superhero stories, the powers that be at Marvel Studios were learning on the job as they made the rapid adjustment from movie producers to TV power players. Nate Moore, the Marvel producer who helped develop *The Falcon and the Winter Soldier*, described his role as "pretty similar" to the one he would play on a film set. He credited Spellman (who had previously worked on *Empire*) for helping him acclimate to the medium: "He was so versed in how television was built from the ground up. I understood the story in the broader sense of what we wanted to tell and how it could fit into the other things in the MCU and even the legacy of the characters, but I didn't know how to make a television show. And so it was an education to sit with Malcolm and his team, because my lizard brain just goes to, 'Oh, it's just a long movie.' But Malcolm's like, 'There's no six-hour movies for a reason. You have to figure out the rhythms of the episode.' I like to think I was a sounding board and creative partner for Malcolm, but it was definitely me learning more than I was teaching."

To find a head writer for *Loki*, Feige went with his tried-and-true method of poaching from a Dan Harmon show. Michael Waldron was a staff writer on Harmon's sci-fi cartoon *Rick and Morty* and had written a spec screenplay for a time-travel action-comedy-romance that impressed Feige. Asked if he minded how often Feige dipped into the *Rick and Morty* talent pool, Harmon said: "Well, you can't fight Kevin Feige in the street. He'll just say, 'Oh, I love that you're fighting me. This is so wonderful,' and everyone will start booing you for being a bully. It does suck a little bit, but the part of you that thinks it sucks is the part of you that thinks you own people or something. It just means I have to turn my motor on harder to suck more talent towards me, and I am honored and validated by the idea that if people leave me, they leave me for Marvel."

Since Waldron was already steeped in time travel and multiverses, he was perfectly suited for a show in which Loki works with (and against) the Time Variance Authority, an organization that polices the various timelines of the multiverse. Waldron and his writers were mostly unburdened with the MCU continuity issues that often beset his colleagues. Loki was a man out of time *and* space.

Marvel Studios was represented on each show by a designated junior executive, each of whom had acted as production managers on previous MCU films. Zoie Nagelhout, who worked on *Black Panther*, stepped in for Moore on *The Falcon and the Winter Soldier*; Mary Livanos, who started on *Guardians of the Galaxy 2*, took the lead on *WandaVision*; and Kevin Wright, who worked on *Doctor Strange*, was assigned to *Loki*. Having those rising producers as liaisons meant that Schaeffer, Spellman, and Waldron didn't have to pester Kevin Feige and the Parliament with every single creative decision. But it also eliminated a key step in the Marvel method: close scrutiny by Feige.

Although the TV head writers were helping define the future of Marvel Studios, they were kept largely unaware of the bigger picture of the MCU and how their shows might fit into it. Filling out their casts, they were allowed to pick from the vast array of preexisting Marvel characters. Feige described the process on *WandaVision*: "We wanted a scientist, or we needed a federal officer, and because we have so many amazing cast members over the years, well, this could be [*Ant-Man* character] Jimmy Woo. Do you think Randall Park would wanna come back and do it?" Feige also cited Kat Dennings, who played fan favorite Darcy Lewis in the *Thor* franchise, as someone who could slot into that scientist role, saying of both, "It is a privilege that they agreed to come in and continue to play in our sandbox."

But the sands were always shifting. "They give you this menu of characters that they're excited about," Spellman said. "They don't make you pick any of them. As you start to play with that menu, certain characters may disappear and new characters who you might have asked about—they said, 'No, no, you can't use them'—are now available. They don't hide that you are joining something that's bigger than you and is already happening. It's a moving train. You get to decorate your car on this train however you want—except, wait a minute, one of the cars behind you changes." He had a very different attitude than Edgar Wright did when he zealously defended his *Ant-Man* script; since that debacle, writers had learned to work within Marvel's constraints, and the studio had learned to make its expectations clear.

Schaeffer, Spellman, and Waldron (and their teams of writers) were able to decide the initial shape of their shows but then each passed control of the project off to an assigned series director. Matt Shakman, experienced with sitcoms and spectacle from *It's Always Sunny in Philadelphia* and *Game of Thrones*, took over on *WandaVision*. Kari Skogland, with decades of film and television work under her belt, signed on for *The Falcon and the Winter Soldier*. The young Brit Kate Herron (*Sex Education*) directed *Loki*. The degree of collaboration varied; some characters and concepts got complete overhauls. *The Falcon and the Winter Soldier*, for example, still addressed issues of race in the finished series, but the theme was no longer as central as it had been in Spellman's scripts.

All three series were still filming when the pandemic hit, shutting down production. *WandaVision* was the furthest along, although it still had some outdoor shots and special-effects shots to complete. *The Falcon and the Winter Soldier* had already canceled location work in Puerto Rico after a devastating earthquake in January 2020. The pandemic not only forced the show to abort a shoot in Prague but made a planned plotline about the heroes rushing to stop a fast-spreading disease feel a bit too close to reality. (Spellman acknowledged that the series had removed the side story, although he said that it wasn't because of the coronavirus.)

During the COVID pause, Herron reworked a number of *Loki* episodes entirely. "Michael had done his writers' room and then I joined the project, and we did, I guess you could call it a mini-room," Herron said. The rewrite strike force, which included *Loki*'s designated Marvel executive, Kevin Wright, focused on practical questions of how the series' outlandish ideas could actually be executed onscreen.

All three series completed shooting and postproduction under the difficult circumstances of 2020; in each case, a collaborative effort abruptly fragmented into individual jobs. "You finish your scene and you get whisked away into these hermetically sealed bubbles," Paul Bettany said of shooting under the pandemic protocols. Though *WandaVision* was not originally meant to premiere first, it launched Marvel on Disney Plus in early 2021, and was perhaps the best debut Marvel could have hoped for. The show, overflowing with TV history and effervescent banter between Bettany and Olsen, was a bona fide phenomenon that reached an audience well beyond devoted MCU fans. The critically acclaimed show received twenty-three Emmy nominations, winning three, for costumes, production design, and composers Kristen Anderson-Lopez and Robert Lopez (for their iTunes chart-topper "Agatha All Along").

The Falcon and the Winter Soldier didn't draw the same reaction, from fans or critics, in part because it seemed caught halfway between TV and movie formats, as evidenced by the large cinematic climaxes unevenly paced throughout its run of episodes. The show also shouldered the burden of detailing the aftermath of the Snap and wound up bogged down in a sociopolitical thought experiment of what the world might look like if half its population were erased. Future MCU installments would largely opt to sidestep this narrative sinkhole.

The mixed response, however, did nothing to diminish Marvel's enthusiasm for Anthony Mackie as Sam Wilson. At the end of the series, the former Falcon assumed the title of Captain America; a solo film, *Captain America: Brave New World*, was promptly announced, with Spellman serving as screenwriter. *Loki*, the fan favorite of the three series, was the first green-lit for a second season.

✳

EMBOLDENED BY its success in transplanting established characters onto Disney Plus, Marvel Studios started using the streaming service to debut heroes from the comics who had long languished in Feige's filing cabinet, introducing Ms. Marvel and Moon Knight and She-Hulk into the MCU, with varying results. Marvel's experiment with disrupting the industry's long-established methods of TV production had caused more problems than it solved: a television series shot by a single director was prone to feeling like a cinematic experience cut into arbitrary slices, and effects-heavy characters ballooned the limited budgets of streaming shows. The studio settled into a more traditional model with its new series, each one employing rotating directors and a head writer who, working in partnership with a designated Marvel babysitter, more closely resembled a traditional showrunner.

The episode counts were flexible and could expand or contract depending on how much story Marvel felt it had to tell. "We decided to move *Hawkeye* from the feature side over to the Disney Plus side," Marvel Parliament member Trinh Tran said. "We have an Avenger whose backstory we haven't quite had time to explore yet. We also have to introduce a new character [Hailee Steinfeld's Kate Bishop], as well as allow enough time for them to bond and create that special dynamic that everybody finds so appealing in the comics. So, in moving it over, it allowed us six hours, three times as much time, which really gave us the creative flexibility we needed to tell the story."

Marvel Studios was introducing a new generation of characters, many of them direct analogues to its original Avengers. In addition to Sam Wilson as Captain America, the archer Kate Bishop was also known as Hawkeye in the comic books; Florence Pugh played Yelena Bolova who, like Natasha Romanoff, was a graduate of the Black Widow program; Ironheart was an updated version of Iron Man; and She-Hulk could step in for the He-Hulk. Their existence set up the possibility of an MCU version of a popular team from the comic books known as the Young Avengers—and adding teen heroes to the mix after the cancellation of *Runaways* and *Power Pack* was a long-delayed victory for Feige.

One luxury Marvel found it didn't have with TV was the built-in reshoot window that helped the studio polish its films (and created problems for visual effects houses). Gone were the days when Feige could send a filmmaker off to Atlanta or Australia and ask them to bring the "pieces" home so he could help assemble them and carefully spackle over the narrative gaps. TV production couldn't work on that schedule, certainly not at the rate Chapek demanded in order to keep investors happy. And as the Marvel Universe spread ever larger, Feige was juggling more and more active film and TV sets. Feige was largely a hands-off executive, but in this new era, he was occasionally required to show up on set to soothe ruffled feathers and settle "creative differences" spats.

As a result, most Marvel shows were sturdier at the beginning than at the end. Writers were hamstrung in their efforts to build up to a satisfying conclusion because they had to leave room to maneuver at the end of every storyline, knowing that the studio might abruptly change its future plans for a given character. "The finale was just this ongoing question," *WandaVision*'s Schaeffer said. "Which is pretty typical for Marvel projects—the climax of a Marvel movie is just iterated and iterated until the very end."

Nevertheless, the barriers between the big and small screen were more permeable than ever, with characters moving back and forth. "It's all intertwined, and it all stands alone," said Waldron.

Before *WandaVision*, Feige had teased that the events of the show would lead "directly" into the *Doctor Strange* sequel, *Doctor Strange in the Multiverse of Madness*. That plan fell apart when director Scott Derrickson abruptly departed the MCU to direct *The Black Phone*, cowritten with his *Doctor Strange* screenwriter, C. Robert Cargill, saying that he was leaving to protect his own mental health. "He wanted to do one movie, and Marvel wanted to do another movie," Cargill said. "So he sat there and said, 'Well, shit, I've got this great script [*The Black Phone*] that I wrote with Cargill.'"

Feige fixed it, bringing in Sam Raimi, who was almost overqualified to direct a horror-flavored version of a superhero movie, having helmed the *Evil Dead* series and the original *Spider-Man* trilogy. Feige had long credited Raimi for teaching him much of what he knew about moviemaking, on those *Spider-Man* movies; now, yet again, Feige was able to reach back into his past to solve a problem.

The project still required a complete overhaul. So, pleased with Michael Waldron's work on *Loki*, Feige plucked him out of production on that show to go to work on *Strange*. Waldron's time and dimension-hopping season of *Loki* had culminated with the multiverse fracturing open across every reality. " 'Yeah, we'll leave that for the next writer,'" Waldron said of the implications of this massive event. "But you do that on *Loki* and you find yourself writing *Doctor Strange* and then you have to clean up your own mess."

The real-world logistical complications of the MCU were transformed into the multiverse onscreen. The multiverse had long been a subject of physics, philosophy, and stoned late-night dorm-room discussions. It had been a staple of comic books since 1961, for its narrative convenience as much as its mind-bending potential: it first appeared in a DC comic book uniting two different versions of the Flash that had been published decades apart. For Marvel Studios, it was an easy way to incorporate characters like the Spider-Man villains, who were adjacent to the MCU without being part of it.

In the Marvel comic books, each alternate reality had a number: Earth-2192 was ruled by the Red Skull, Earth-82432 was annihilated by a cosmic villain called Korvac, and Earth-616 was the main timeline where superheroes had their adventures. In the comic books, the Marvel Cinematic Universe had been officially designated as Earth-199999, but in *Multiverse of Madness*, it was also called, confusingly, Earth-616. Some Marvel fans objected; one of them was Iman Vellani, who played the title role in the MCU TV show *Ms. Marvel*. "I don't believe that the MCU is 616, as much as Kevin Feige can make us think that it's 616," she said to the press while walking the red carpet for the premiere of *Ms. Marvel*. She later wrote that after she aired her fangirl grievances, Feige caught her eye. "He just stared at me from a far [*sic*] and gestured *6-1-6* with his fingers and walked away. I think about that every night before bed."

Rick and Morty, which Waldron had worked on, proved to be

a blueprint for establishing a multiverse within the MCU. On the animated show, there are infinite numbers of Ricks and Mortys across multiple timelines; fans aren't even sure they're watching the same iterations of the characters from week to week. *Loki* not only destroyed the unified timeline of the MCU in its first season but made Loki's very identity malleable: the character was not defined by gender, age, or even species, as evidenced by Kid Loki, Alligator Loki, and especially Sylvie (Sophia Di Martino), a female version of Loki with whom Tom Hiddleston's Loki has an extremely complicated relationship.

The multiverse was also the basis of the animated anthology show *What If . . . ?* featuring Jeffrey Wright as an omniscient Watcher who could see into universes that branched off from the MCU at key points: one where a vengeful Hank Pym kills the Avengers, or another where the Quantum Realm spawns a zombie virus. Marvel Studios got many of their major actors to contribute voice performances to the series. One was Chadwick Boseman, who made his last MCU appearance in four episodes, including one that saw T'Challa become a Guardian of the Galaxy instead of Black Panther.

Waldron, in short, had a lot to play with in the *Doctor Strange* sequel. Perhaps too much. He knew that Elizabeth Olsen had been confirmed as a costar, and that Marvel was considering the possibility of Wanda Maximoff making a heel turn at the end of the movie. "I had a strong perspective on making her a villain from the get-go. It was always like, 'Well, that'll happen in an Avengers movie or something,'" Waldron said. He objected: "Why are we letting some other movie get the best villain ever?"

Waldron and *WandaVision* head writer Jac Schaeffer had become friends when they were working down the hall from each other on their respective Disney Plus series. Bending Marvel's rules about keeping projects separate, they discussed how best to hand off Wanda from her show to his movie. "I admired Jac so much," Waldron said. "I didn't want to come in and blow this thing. I just wanted to make sure I wasn't going to let my friend down." Unfortunately, after Wanda was portrayed with nuance by Elizabeth Olsen across hours of serial television, many fans were disappointed by her appearance as the *Multiverse of Madness* villain. She seemed to repeat her grief-stricken arc from *WandaVision*, only faster and louder.

The multiverse opened up new possibilities for storytelling, however, and new avenues for fan service: *Multiverse of Madness* featured not only the All-Star Illuminati, with John Krasinksi and Patrick Stewart, but four different versions of Benedict Cumberbatch as Doctor Strange. Marvel Studios believed that audiences could follow complicated contingency timelines without comic-book-style explanatory captions, and tried not to abuse that trust.

"There are people whose sole task is to keep it in their head and deliver it for us, and then we have interconnected meetings quite often about how things grow and evolve," said Feige. "The multiverse is something we geek out about." Some companies have seminars on how to file expense reports; Marvel Studios had meetings that Feige described as "the whole broad Marvel Studios team going through the multiverse and the rules of the multiverse."

Phases One, Two, and Three of the MCU had been collectively known as "the Infinity Saga"; Phases Four, Five, and Six were dubbed "the Multiverse Saga." The saga's antagonist, introduced in *Loki* as He Who Remains and then showcased in the movie *Ant-Man and the Wasp: Quantumania*, was the time-traveling Kang, a character who had so many different versions and iterations in Marvel comic books that writers and fans had long ago given up on keeping them all straight. According to one Marvel source, Kang was not originally intended to be the overarching villain of the Multiverse Saga; the decision to elevate him to a Thanos-level threat was based on the positive buzz actor Jonathan Majors generated in the role. Disney flexed its marketing muscles for Kang's cinematic debut, hoping to get as many eyes as possible on Majors's performance and to hype two post-credits sequences promoting his central role in both TV (*Loki*) and film (everything else?). In the closing moments, thousands of versions of Kang crowded an arena: all of them wore the face of Jonathan Majors. Not since Robert Downey Jr. had the studio placed so many chips on one actor.

Although the reviews for *Quantumania* were woeful, and its box office dropped by 69 percent in its second weekend of release—setting a dismal new record for Marvel Studios—Majors seemed immune to criticism. His performance was lauded as the highlight of the movie and the de facto future of the MCU. But on March 22, 2023—less than two months after the movie's release—Majors was arrested on charges of assault and harassment, stemming from a domestic dispute where he allegedly strangled a woman. Suddenly, Marvel's safest bet for its future became its latest dilemma.

Feige couldn't wish away the difficulties of streaming excess and legal troubles. Nevertheless, he had a master plan to keep MCU viewers engaged. "This is not a secret, because it's why the comics have been around so long," he said. "You do it through character. Give them a character to anchor onto, even if it's a raccoon, and they'll follow you through all the crazy stuff. Give them Benedict Cumberbatch to latch onto, and we'll go through this, what we call the Magical Mystery Tour sequence of that movie, with you."

The future of those Marvel icons was unclear. The departure of franchise anchors like Robert Downey Jr., Chris Evans, and Scarlett Johansson had already taken its toll, as had the shocking loss of Chadwick Boseman, but other MCU stalwarts were heading for the exits. The *Guardians of the Galaxy* cast went on a farewell tour, Brie Larson grew disillusioned, and Marvel tussled with Sony in a custody battle over Tom Holland. And Chris Hemsworth, one of the last remaining original Avengers, received alarming news in 2022: genetic testing revealed he has a predisposition for Alzheimer's disease, which forced him to contemplate the end of his time playing Thor. "We'd probably have to close the book if I ever did it again," he said. "It'd probably be the finale."

Although Marvel Studios kept teasing grand plans and exciting new characters played by celebrities, the payoffs seemed increasingly tenuous. MCU post-credits sequences once played as promises to viewers about carefully laid plans that were just over the horizon, but fans grew increasingly skeptical that they would ever see pop star Harry Styles featured as the Eternal named Eros or *Ted Lasso* star Brett Goldstein make more than a cameo as Hercules.

The Multiverse Saga of the MCU was scheduled to conclude with another pair of Avengers movies: *Avengers: The Kang Dynasty* in May 2025 and *Avengers: Secret Wars* in May 2026. The 2015 comic book series *Secret Wars* (written by Jonathan Hickman and drawn by Esad Ribić) was an epic tale that ended with the collapse of the Marvel multiverse back into a single universe. "*Secret Wars* is a great, giant crossover," Feige said. "There are a lot of great, giant crossovers that we could [adapt]—it's the ongoing embarrassment of riches of Marvel." The studio leaned even harder into the *Rick and Morty*–fication of the MCU, hiring a pair of Harmon alums, Jeff Loveness and Michael Waldron, to write *Kang Dynasty* and *Secret Wars*, respectively. Feige also hired Waldron to work on his Star Wars project for Lucasfilm before the movie got sidelined in 2023. After the poor reception of *Quantumania*, however, rumors swirled that its writer, Loveness, would no longer be involved with the MCU.

But even with the endless possibilities of the multiverse, Marvel faced massive scrutiny in the post-*Endgame* era. Some in Hollywood actively rooted for the studio's demise, largely the highbrow contingent who felt the proliferation of superheroes left no room for other stories in the film industry. Even in the COVID-19 era, the Marvel films were profitable—but with so many Marvel shows and films of varying quality, the brand was bruised.

Leaving the uneven Disney Plus track record aside, the film offerings in Phases Four and Five were a mixed bag. Feige finally had what he wanted: near-complete control to break open the definition of what made a superhero. *Black Widow*, *Eternals*, *Shang Chi and the Legend of the Ten Rings*, *Doctor Strange in the Multiverse of Madness*, *Thor: Love and Thunder*, and *Wakanda Forever* boasted a wider range of genders, ages, and ethnicities than Marvel had previously featured.

Unfortunately, in the immediate aftermath of Feige's *Endgame* victory lap, his hard-won creative freedom bumped up against multiple unforeseen obstacles. Because of the pandemic and the new leadership at Disney, with its demand for more content, while Feige had control, he didn't necessarily have quality control. Phase Four's most successful entry, *Wakanda Forever*, was able to grapple meaningfully with the loss of Chadwick Boseman, which became the emotional spine of the film: Angela Bassett's marquee performance as Queen Ramonda, fueled by grief and loss, earned her a Best Supporting Actress Academy Award nomination, the first Oscar acting nomination for Marvel Studios. But even the movie's loudest champions would admit that Ryan Coogler's sequel was burdened by all the added characters and storylines stuffed into the narrative in order to spin off into future Disney Plus shows like *Ironheart* and an untitled Wakanda series, both projects Coogler had signed on to produce.

Marvel Studios hadn't been built to scale up the way Disney was demanding—its greatest strength quickly became its weakness. When asked a few years earlier why no other studio had been able to match Marvel's track record, Joe Russo said, "Simple. They don't have a Kevin." In the Disney Plus era, Marvel didn't have enough Kevin to go around.

An early pair of Marvel Studios stumbles, *The Incredible Hulk* and *Thor: The Dark World*, had once been widely accepted as the weakest MCU movies. According to Rotten Tomatoes, however, Phase Four's *Eternals* and Phase Five's *Ant-Man and the Wasp: Quantumania* displaced them—the only two films to rank as "rotten" on the website. Phase Four's *Thor: Love and Thunder* also sat low on the list, a sharp fall from grace for director Taika Waititi after his wildly popular *Thor: Ragnarok*. This, surely, must have rankled Feige. In 2017, when the MCU still enjoyed an unblemished record of "fresh" reviews, he said, "We always want those Rotten Tomatoes 'Certified Fresh' plaques, right? We take great pride in them. They send this little Lucite 'Certified Fresh' thing with the name of the movie on it. We got them lined up."

In short, after a decade of nearly unrivaled success, the Marvel logo no longer ensured the level of quality that Feige had worked so hard to establish. This violated the ethos of his longtime ally Bob Iger. Back in 2017, when Marvel was still on top of the world, Iger was asked how the franchise was able to draw in so many viewers who had no history with comic books. "That's where the brand becomes important," he said. "That's why the movies we're making are: Pixar, Disney, Marvel, Star Wars. We're not making any movies other than those, because we believe it gives us a little bit more license to tell unique stories and introduce unique characters that maybe the audience isn't well aware of. But the brand has become of value. There are known attributes of the storytelling and the characters and that gives us a competitive advantage."

This ability, Iger recognized, went all the way back to the beginning. "When the Iron Man movie came out, Iron Man was not an ultra-primary Marvel character," he said. "Everybody knew Hulk, and everybody knew Spider-Man. Iron Man, not that much. The movie elevated him. When we bought Marvel, one of the things I wanted to do was put a spotlight on their brand and then use the brand as the main selling point to the consumer, globally. I feel like I've achieved that."

Soon after Iger retired, however, he watched his achievements crumble. The brands he had built and polished so lovingly felt mundane once you could simply stream, say, the latest Pixar offering at home. In 2022, Disney's stock price plummeted by 40 percent.

The blame couldn't be laid entirely at Chapek's feet. The pandemic affected every sector of the global economy, and Disney Plus, which was hemorrhaging money, was a project he had inherited from Iger. But Chapek never had the ability to weave a convincing story for anxious shareholders; that was Iger's gift. And so, in November 2022, the Disney board of directors showed Chapek the door, despite having just renewed his contract. Iger promised to return for at least two years to help right the ship.

Disney stock rebounded by 10 percent on the day after Iger announced his return. Disney creatives, too, were overjoyed to have their greatest ally back. Less sanguine was Ike Perlmutter, who battled with Iger for control of the Disney board—after Perlmutter lost, Iger eliminated his fiefdom of Marvel Entertainment and removed Perlmutter from Disney's org chart on March 29, 2023.

In the wake of Iger's return, Marvel was on track for a year of renewal. In 2023, *The Marvels*, a follow-up to *Captain Marvel*, was pushed back from July to November, giving the studio four extra months to reshoot and fine-tune. After churning out eight TV series and two specials for Disney Plus in the span of two years, Marvel Studios would be responsible for three streaming shows, at most: tentatively, *Secret Invasion*, *Echo*, and the second season of *Loki*.

After Disney Plus lost 4 million subscribers in early 2023, the company shifted its strategy from expanding the streaming service as quickly as possible to actually turning a profit with it. That spring, Disney also laid off thousands of employees.

Ever the diplomat, Feige spun this new era of restraint as a positive: "One of the powerful aspects of being at Marvel Studios is having these films and shows hit the zeitgeist. It is harder to hit the zeitgeist when there's so much product out there—and so much 'content,' as they say, which is a word that I hate. But we want Marvel Studios and the MCU projects to really stand out and stand above. So, people will see that as we get further into Phase Five and Six. The pace at which we're putting out the Disney Plus shows will change so they can each get a chance to shine."

That meant no new Marvel show or film would be released until it was ready: the studio could check for narrative gaps and spackle over any holes. Marvel Studios would need to be more nimble than ever; not only was Disney tightening its belt, but the strike by the Writers Guild of America that started in May 2023 delayed the production of movies such as *Blade* and *Thunderbolts*, throwing the entire interconnected MCU schedule into chaos.

With the abrupt departure of one of his greatest allies, Victoria Alonso, and one of his greatest obstacles, Ike Perlmutter, all eyes once again turned to Kevin Feige to fix it.

CHAPTER 31

Annus Horribilis

"Confusion is but the first step on the
journey to knowledge."

—*The Marvels*

QUENTIN TARANTINO GLEEFULLY REMEMBERED THE moment, circa 1970, when the "old studio Broadway musical based extravaganza (*The Sound of Music, My Fair Lady, Hello, Dolly!*) was *finally* at long last dead." In his 2022 book of film criticism, *Cinema Speculation*, the director continued snarkily that "many filmmakers today can't wait for the day they can say that about superhero movies."

Tarantino was correct: he wasn't alone in his contempt for the superhero genre. He joined a choir of prominent directors, including not only Martin Scorsese and Francis Ford Coppola, but also Terry Gilliam ("It's bullshit"), Roland Emmerich ("When I see Marvel movies, my eyes glaze over"), and Ridley Scott ("Their scripts are not any fucking good"). By 2023, that wasn't just background noise: some of Marvel Studios' biggest names were willing to sing along, at least for a verse or two.

Christian Bale, who played the ashen villain Gorr the God Butcher, complained about the *Thor: Love and Thunder* shoot, saying "the definition of it was monotony." He added, "Can you differentiate one day from the next? No. Absolutely not. You have no idea what to do. I couldn't even differentiate one stage from the next."

Anthony Hopkins, who appeared in three MCU movies as Odin, sniffed, "They put me in armor; they shoved a beard on me. Sit on the throne, shout a bit."

"It's a silly performance, and I want to do more dramatic stuff," said Dave Bautista—a former professional wrestler. "I just don't know if I want Drax to be my legacy."

This was more than the bubbling undercurrent of discontent that had long accompanied Marvel's success. People were no longer piously worrying that the MCU business model was pushing other types of movies out of cineplexes—they were emboldened to say that they thought Marvel movies sucked because, more and more often, the general public agreed with them.

Some of Marvel Studios' problems in 2023 were industry-wide issues, such as the labor actions that paralyzed Hollywood. Trying to make sure that their members could earn a living wage in the era of streaming services and artificial intelligence, the WGA (Writers Guild of America) and SAG-AFTRA (Screen Actors Guild–American Federation of Television and Radio Artists) both went on strike. The twin strikes shut down Hollywood production for months and hamstrung the promotion of completed projects.

Disney CEO Bob Iger unwisely made himself into the uncaring face of the conflict when he gave a cable-TV interview in which he said of the unions, "There's a level of expectation that they have that is just not realistic." Iger was getting paid $27 million in 2023, so that line might have come off as tone-deaf wherever he said it—but since the setting was a luxury resort in Sun Valley, Idaho, his sound-bite was near-parodic.

Before his "retirement" (more of a sabbatical, it turned out), Iger was renowned for his deft touch with public relations, which now seemed to abandon him. Disney had a bad year overall in 2023: flagship projects like *Indiana Jones and the Dial of Destiny* (from Lucasfilm) and *Wish* (from Disney Animation, celebrating the company's

100th anniversary) failed to live up to expectations. But no Disney division was in a deeper hole than Marvel Studios.

Software developers have a term that refers to the hidden costs of shortcuts taken early in a project: "tech debt." You can cut corners to ship kludgy code, but eventually the consequences of those inelegant decisions will add up, and years later it'll take a lot of hours from a lot of elite programmers to untangle the mess hiding underneath the shiny interface of your popular app. There will probably be some warning signs of tech debt, but you may be able to ignore them for a while: if you do, at some point you will reach a crisis point where it feels like everything goes wrong at once.

Fifteen years after the release of *Iron Man*, Marvel Studios had a bad case of narrative debt.

Too many MCU movies had ended with a predictable blowout fight with subpar CGI; too many MCU television series had lost the thread as they went along; too many MCU plot holes had been hand-waved away as manifestations of the multiverse. Fans had once excused weak outings like *Eternals*, rooting for the studio as if it was the Golden State Warriors and showing up for every single installment of the Marvel saga. But as the bummers-to-thrills ratio crept upward, the mood of some moviegoers became distinctly skeptical.

✳

THE MOMENT THE MARVEL brain trust realized their problems were bigger than they had realized: February 2023, when the studio released *Ant-Man and the Wasp: Quantumania*. The movie abandoned the small-scale charm of the previous Ant-Man movies—and Michael Peña as Luis, the fast-talking sidekick—for an inner-cosmos psychedelic trudge marked by muddy CGI. The movie did respectably at the box office, grossing $476 million worldwide, but audiences did not love it. The CinemaScore rating, measuring audience enthusiasm, was a B, the lowest for any MCU movie other than *Eternals*.

What distinguished *Quantumania* from other MCU misfires over the years? While top Marvel executives knew that *Thor: The Dark*

World (for example) didn't deliver the way they had hoped, this time, they didn't anticipate the lukewarm reaction: executives thought they had worked out any production problems and delivered yet another crowd-pleasing flick. The chasm between expectations and reality meant that the studio had lost touch with its audience, or the fans had lost interest in the movies, or maybe both.

The studio scrambled: years of zigzag planning suddenly looked dodgy. Marvel wasn't going to reboot the MCU in the middle of Phase Five, but for the rest of the year, almost everything they released was second-guessed, reedited, and covered in a veneer of flop sweat.

The low point was *Secret Invasion*, a six-part miniseries about the shapeshifting Skrulls trying to take over Earth. It starred some major talent—Samuel L. Jackson, Emilia Clarke, Olivia Colman—but was a dispiriting mess. It was no fun for anybody, but especially disappointing for fans of Jackson who had been waiting since 2008 to see Nick Fury at the center of an MCU project. One major twist incoherently followed another: Fury has a Skrull wife! Maria Hill dies! Rhodey was replaced by a Skrull at some point back!

Kyle Bradstreet, executive producer of the show *Mr. Robot*, had been writing episodes for *Secret Invasion* since October 2020, when it was still known as "Untitled Nick Fury Project." When the project was announced, Bradstreet was introduced as the head creative, while two directors, Ali Selim and Thomas Bezucha, were slated to direct three episodes each.

"When I first started, Ali was one of two directors," Jackson said. "I met with [Selim], and I met with [Bezucha], and the next day, [Bezucha] quit." In July 2022, actor Christopher McDonald said that the series was headed back for the usual Marvel reshoots, but with a new writer. When the series was finally released, Brian Tucker (who wrote the Mark Wahlberg movie *Broken City*) was listed as the first executive producer (above Bradstreet) and had a writing credit on all six episodes, while Bradstreet retained cowriting credit on only the first and last episodes.

"It was weeks of people not getting along, and it erupted," an anonymous Marvel source revealed. Chris Gary, the Marvel Studios producer who had been overseeing *Secret Invasion*, was ousted; Jonathan Schwartz of the Marvel Parliament flew to the *Secret Invasion* production offices in London to do damage control. Needing major rewrites and reshoots, *Secret Invasion* couldn't hit the pause button without losing some of its big-name actors to scheduling conflicts. So production hurtled onward: four months of reshoots concluded in the fall of 2022. By the end, the show's budget had ballooned to $211.6 million, making it the most expensive Marvel series ever (except for *She-Hulk: Attorney at Law*, where the main character was a digital effect much of the time).

All that money didn't buy much in the way of onscreen spectacle, and the narrative felt pasted together. As soon as the series ended, Marvel tried to pretend it had never happened: the next time Nick Fury showed up, in *The Marvels*, nobody alluded to any of the allegedly earth-shaking plot developments of *Secret Invasion*.

Stung by the *Secret Invasion* debacle, Kevin Feige took a hard look at another series in progress: *Daredevil: Born Again*, which marked the return of the popular Charlie Cox, who had starred in the Netflix *Daredevil* series. Announced in 2022 as the first eighteen-episode MCU series on Disney Plus, it filmed its first six episodes with Matt Corman and Chris Ord as executive producers and head writers. But the pacing was deemed too slow: blind lawyer Matt Murdock didn't even suit up as Daredevil until the fourth episode.

In September 2023, after the studios and the WGA settled the five-month strike, Marvel dismissed Corman and Ord and rebooted the show. The studio had previously avoided designating writers as showrunners: "TV is a writer-driven medium," one insider said. "Marvel is a Marvel-driven medium." But the new WGA contract mandated a showrunner position, fuller staffing of writers' rooms, and a staff writer on set at all times. Marvel adhered to it. Having previously discarded decades of TV-production systems—with mixed results—Marvel conceded that there were good reasons to produce the MCU series like actual TV shows.

The showrunner was now Dario Scardapane, who had previously

worked on the Netflix *Punisher* series; he wrote a new season-long arc, salvaging sequences from *Born Again*'s first shoot where he could. Marvel cut down the planned eighteen-episode season to something closer to the thirteen-episode orders for the Netflix *Daredevil* seasons. It also added some alumni from the Netflix series, with cast members Elden Henson, Deborah Ann Woll, Wilson Bethel, and Jon Bernthal reprising their roles of (respectively) Foggy Nelson, Karen Page, Benjamin Poindexter (aka Bullseye), and Frank Castle (aka The Punisher).

Feige had established a gift for identifying characters who got short shrift when they first appeared in the MCU and reviving them for an unexpected payoff. Now he inverted that signature move—drawing on the Netflix cast let him exploit the nostalgia for a show he hadn't produced. Either way, it appeared that the Netflix shows produced by Marvel Television would finally get acknowledged by the official MCU (not you, *Agents of S.H.I.E.L.D.*).

Marvel's lack of confidence in *Echo*, a *Hawkeye* spinoff starring Alaqua Cox as the deaf Native American title character, was obvious: the studio repeatedly delayed the series and ultimately decided to release it under the new "Marvel Spotlight" banner, designed to reassure viewers that you wouldn't have to know anything about the MCU to enjoy this show about Maya Lopez fleeing her criminal past in New York City and going home to her Choctaw people, only for trouble to follow her there. Marvel pared the series down to five episodes and completed it for $40 million, making it the cheapest season of Marvel streaming TV yet.

When *Echo* debuted in January 2024, it was the first MCU series to make all its episodes available simultaneously, allowing binge-watching; it topped the charts on Disney Plus and (more surprisingly) Hulu, giving Marvel Studios a minor but much-needed victory. Despite being a Marvel Spotlight show, *Echo*'s popularity provided a halo effect: according to insiders, its release spiked streaming rewatches of old seasons of *Daredevil*, *Hawkeye*, and *Punisher*. That unforeseen success spurred Marvel not only to continue the story of Maya Lopez, but to develop more street-level characters unencumbered by superpowers requiring expensive visual effects—a far cry from Marvel's previous intention to go cosmic and multiversal.

The second season of *Loki*, about the time-traveling adventures of the god of mischief and his cohorts in the Time Variance Authority, was extremely cosmic and exceptionally multiversal. It was also the most problematic show Marvel had in the works: it featured Jonathan Majors in a dual role, playing a young variant of Kang called Victor Timely and reprising his season-one role as the aged variant named He Who Remains. Both characters were integral to the plot of the second season of *Loki*, making it near-impossible to remove Majors from the series after he was arrested on domestic violence charges in March 2023.

According to head writer Eric Martin, excising Majors wasn't even considered. "This is maybe—not maybe—this is the first Marvel series to never have any additional photography," Martin insisted. "The story that is on screen is the story we set out to make. We went out there with a very specific idea of what we wanted this to be, and we found a way to tell it in that production period."

When Marvel was on the upswing, the studio got credit for every lucky accident and viewers were quick to explain away missteps. When the MCU appeared to have peaked, every misfortune seemed like poor planning and viewers tended to ignore the legitimate successes. The second season of *Loki* was a high-wire act masterfully executed: not only did the series elegantly wrap up a complicated time-travel plot with a conclusion that was both antic and emotional, it gave a reasonable in-universe explanation for Majors's future absence from the MCU despite him previously seeming omnipresent (the TVA isolated his branch of the multiverse).

Majors's two-week trial concluded in December 2023: a jury of six people found him guilty of reckless assault in the third degree and guilty of harassment. After the verdict came down, Marvel Studios severed all ties with the actor. According to Majors, Marvel's response was swift: "Same hour, same half hour, I think."

Even before the trial, Marvel had been preparing for a post-Majors world. Once again, Feige and the top Marvel executives traveled to

Palm Springs for the annual Marvel retreat to hash out the company's future. The questions they faced were suddenly urgent: How could they navigate through Phases Five and Six of the MCU if Kang was suddenly not a central villain? And how could they redirect the projects already in the MCU pipeline to emphasize quality over quantity?

After the Marvel brain trust returned from the desert, the studio started internally referring to *Avengers: Kang Dynasty* as just *Avengers 5*. With the movie in flux, director Destin Daniel Cretton jumped ship (although he remained attached to a *Wonder Man* series for Disney Plus and a so-far-hypothetical *Shang-Chi 2*). *Avengers 5* screenwriter Jeff Loveness was replaced by Michael Waldron, who would once again have to clean up his own multiversal mess.

Marvel ultimately conceded that the strikes made it impossible to stick to the studio's 2024 release schedule: *Thunderbolts* hadn't started physical production before the actors went on strike and *Blade* hadn't even finalized its script when the writers went on strike. *Captain America: New World Order* had been completed but was apparently in poor shape: according to industry scuttlebutt, the initial cut tested so poorly with audiences that the studio needed a five-to-six-month reshoot window to fix it, extraordinary even by Marvel's usual second-draft methods.

All three movies were pushed back to 2025, taking slots previously designated "Untitled Marvel Film." In January 2024, Ayo Edebiri and Steven Yeun, two buzzy actors—each of them had just scored a big win at the Emmys—both announced that they would no longer be part of the *Thunderbolts* cast. The stated reason for each of them was that the repeated delays had led to scheduling conflicts, which seemed plausible, but it was hard to avoid the sense that all the cool kids were abandoning the sinking franchise ship.

The only movie remaining on Marvel's 2024 schedule was *Deadpool & Wolverine*, featuring Ryan Reynolds as the mercenary breaking the fourth wall with his wisecracks, Hugh Jackman making one last appearance as Wolverine, and allegedly, a battalion of cameos from other Marvel characters. Deadpool, inherited from the Fox merger, was now officially part of the MCU.

With big movie stars and an avid following, the Deadpool franchise was as close to a sure thing as Marvel had. The public anticipation for it could almost mask that the Marvel schedule was once again in tatters: the only film carrying the studio through an entire calendar year would be an R-rated comedy that mocked the entire notion of superhero movies. The silver lining, for a studio that was suddenly grasping for any shred of optimism it could find, was that it had an extra year to repair the multiverse.

★

IF MARVEL WANTED evidence that a long gestation period could help a film, it needed only to look at *Guardians of the Galaxy Vol. 3.* Writer-director James Gunn had six years to polish the script after the release of *Vol. 2* (admittedly, not by his choice). "I worked on this screenplay, for a lot of reasons, way longer than I worked on the other screenplays," Gunn said. "The screenplay took me way longer to write than both the first two movies, so, it was pretty worked out by the time we got to soundstage."

That not only made for a smoother filming and editing process, but helped immensely with the visual effects: because not much changed between Gunn's script and the final edit, the VFX houses working on *Vol. 3* didn't have to paper over plot holes and last-minute fixes. Instead, Weta, Framestore, and ILM could focus on bringing Rocket Raccoon's childhood family of genetically altered animals to life in poignant flashback scenes. "We don't have this thing where we're constantly shifting everything around like happens in a lot of big movies because test screenings aren't going well," Gunn boasted.

The third *Guardians* installment, released in May 2023, slightly underperformed the second ($848 million versus $869 million), but after the disappointment of *Quantumania,* maintaining pre-pandemic levels of box office felt like a triumph. Critics and audiences lauded *Vol. 3* as a satisfying conclusion to the trilogy, achieving some of the narrative highs that had been lacking since *Avengers: Endgame.* Gunn didn't need to kill any of the Guardians to give his movie a sense of finality: he achieved closure by leaving his trilogy's heroes alive and well with their found families. At the end of the film, post-credits scenes show Rocket Raccoon leading a new Guardians lineup and Chris Pratt's Peter Quill finally returning home to Earth and eating cereal with his grandfather.

The movie's final title card promised "The Legendary Star-Lord Will Return"—but more to the point, James Gunn wouldn't. He was now a company man at the Warner Bros. studio, where he was relaunching the DC Studios division with Peter Safran and gearing up to write and direct the movie *Superman*. That meant that while the MCU received a short-term hit of goodwill from *Guardians of the Galaxy Vol. 3*, it was a harbinger of future success for DC more than it was for Marvel.

✳

IN 2019, during the long months between *Avengers: Infinity War* and *Avengers: Endgame*, the *Captain Marvel* movie grossed $1.131 billion. Marvel Studios didn't expect the sequel, *The Marvels*, to go higher, faster, or further—it would have happily settled for treading water in a vaguely heroic fashion.

The movie, starring Brie Larson as Captain Marvel, Iman Vellani as Kamala Khan (from the *Ms. Marvel* series), and Teyonah Parris as Monica Rambeau (from the *WandaVision* series), was set to debut in February 2023 until it swapped release dates with *Ant-Man and the Wasp: Quantumania*, which was deemed closer to being ready. (Also, Marvel was excited to roll out Jonathan Majors as Kang as quickly as possible.) Then the studio kept bumping the release back.

This was a problem for director Nia DaCosta (*Candyman*), the first Black woman to direct a Marvel movie—with two months left to go on *Marvels* postproduction, she raised eyebrows by moving to London. DaCosta was simultaneously deep into preproduction on her next project, *Hedda*, an adaptation of Henrik Ibsen's 1891 play *Hedda Gabler* that would star Tessa Thompson. "For me personally, it was that they moved the date of the film four different times," DaCosta said. "They knew the entire time that I had an obligation—a green-lit movie with people who were waiting for me. And I pushed that and then I pushed it again and then I pushed it again. Eventually, we all knew that if [*The Marvels*] pushes again, I'm not going to be in LA to do the rest of this in person."

DaCosta, who grew up on *Sailor Moon* cartoons and the animated *X-Men* series, loved how directing a Marvel movie let her do nerdy things like name alien planets, but was particularly proud of how she shaped the relationships among her movie's three female leads. She acknowledged, however, that she didn't have final cut of the film. "It is a Kevin Feige production, it's his movie," she said. "You live in that reality."

When *The Marvels* finally came out in November 2023, it was the MCU's shortest theatrical entry, a brisk 105 minutes: it had clearly been edited ruthlessly. Keeping only the strongest footage meant emphasizing Vellani, who lit up the big screen, and foregrounding Kamala Khan's bickering-but-loving relationship with her parents. While those choices seemed sensible, they had an unfortunate side effect: once again, people felt like they had to do homework (i.e., watching all six episodes of *Ms. Marvel*) before they were ready to go to the multiplex to see the latest MCU movie.

The final trailers for *The Marvels* attempted to boost excitement for the sequel by incorporating footage of Robert Downey Jr. as Tony Stark, Chris Evans as Captain America, and dialogue from Josh Brolin's Thanos, although none of those characters appeared in the film. The actual stars of the movie couldn't promote it because the SAG-AFTRA strike didn't end until late on November 9, the very night *The Marvels* had its red-carpet premiere in Las Vegas.

Larson and Vellani showed up at screenings that weekend to surprise fans and build some buzz for a charming if minor movie, but it soon became clear that their efforts were in vain. Audiences stayed away, even after word spread of the post-credits appearance of Kelsey Grammer as Beast (reprising his role from Fox's X-Men movies). After a few weeks, attendance was so bad that Disney took the unusual step of not reporting weekly box office numbers. *The Marvels* grossed just $199 million, less than 20 percent of the box office for *Captain Marvel* and the lowest yield for any MCU movie ever.

Vellani wasn't interested in discussing the movie's financial performance. "I don't want to focus on something that's not even in my control, because what's the point?" she said. "That's for Bob Iger. [The box office] has nothing to do with me."

For his part, Iger tried to shift blame away from himself and Feige, and to place responsibility for the failure of *The Marvels* on DaCosta and producer Mary Livanos in a condescending fashion. "*The Marvels* was shot during COVID," Iger said. "There wasn't as much supervision on the set, so to speak, where we have executives [that are] really looking over what's being done day after day after day."

Iger acknowledged that the best days of Disney (and Marvel) might be in the rearview mirror. He suggested that the box-office outlook had changed, maybe permanently, after the combination of the COVID pandemic and the rise of streaming services nudged people out of the habit of going to movie theaters. "I'm not sure another studio will ever achieve some of the numbers that we achieved. I mean, we got to the point where if a film didn't do a billion dollars in global box office, we were disappointed," he said. "That's an unbelievably high standard and I think we have to get more realistic."

"The more you do, the tougher it is to maintain quality," said Eric Handler, a Wall Street analyst who covered Disney. "With budgets as big as these, you need home runs."

Marvel began contemplating desperate moves. What if the studio reunited the original Avengers? It would mean resurrecting multiple dead characters and require lots of money, but that's what the multiverse and Disney's checking account were for, respectively. There were other shortcuts to box-office success, but Feige wasn't in a hurry to take them: more than six years passed after Disney announced its acquisition of Fox before Marvel cast the Fantastic Four for a 2025 movie (Pedro Pascal, Vanessa Kirby, Joseph Quinn, and Ebon Moss-Bachrach).

Marvel Studios wasn't going out of business anytime soon—the franchise was too valuable in too many ways to Disney. The longer it went without consistent hitmaking, however, the more likely major changes—lower budgets, or new leadership, or a reboot of the whole MCU—would become. With the studio he led facing its greatest crisis since the kite-factory days, Kevin Feige now had firsthand experience with one of the fundamental truths in the lives of Marvel superheroes: no matter how many times you saved the world, it soon needed saving all over again.

How Much We Have Left

Are you quoting a comic book right now?

She-Hulk: Attorney at Law

IN THE 2022 SEASON FINALE OF THE *SHE-HULK: ATTOR-ney at Law* series, frustrated with how her own show is turning out, the eponymous heroine played by Tatiana Maslany pries herself out of the MCU and walks into the Marvel Studios headquarters on the Disney studio lot in Burbank, California. There she confronts the big brain that is running Marvel Studios, a super-intelligent robot named K.E.V.I.N. (Knowledge Enhanced Visual Interactivity Nexus). Feige had no problem with series writer Jessica Gao replacing him with an AI. He only objected when she wanted to put a baseball cap on top of the robot. "Well, that doesn't make a lick of sense," he said. "Why would a robot wear a hat?"

A real-life pilgrimage to Marvel Studios in Burbank for one visitor was remarkably similar to She-Hulk's journey, down to the receptionist, Matt Wilkie (who played himself on the show), and the absurdly long NDA that visitors were required to sign. Marvel had upgraded its offices considerably since the days of the kite factory, the Mercedes-Benz dealership, and the mismatched chairs. Anyone stepping out of the elevator on the second floor of the Frank G. Wells building would see immense murals and a carefully tended display of studio props and costumes.

The office of the flesh-and-blood Kevin Feige was at the center of a warren of cubicles and offices. Most Marvel Studios offices had glass windows and open doorways, although Ryan Meinerding and Andy Park, the leaders of the visual-development team, had doors that could close because they were often working on top-secret character designs. Feige's spacious, sunny office was decorated with a rotating collection of Marvel memorabilia, including a replica of the Infinity Gauntlet and the chair that Thor was strapped into for a haircut in *Ragnarok*. Feige was wearing a baseball cap; behind his desk was a shelf with a collection of others.

Feige revisited one of his formative experiences as a producer, when he was working for Lauren Shuler Donner and she was developing the script for the first X-Men movie. "I started reading up on the X-Men," he said. "I knew most of it through cultural osmosis, but then started thinking, 'Well, these scripts have these problems. Let's look in the comics to see if you can solve the problems,' and they were all solved."

The studio head had long emphasized the brilliance of the original comics. "There have been immensely talented creative people creating new stories once a month, every month, every year for the last fifty to sixty years," he said. He saw that the characterization in comic books was deeper than many filmmakers realized, including some of the people in charge of other superhero franchises—and that cameos and team-ups were central to their appeal. The MCU became what it is because the person overseeing it understood that in many ways, it already existed.

As the MCU spilled over into streaming programs and the Multiverse Saga, Feige had to learn different lessons from the comics: how superheroes periodically needed to be rebooted, how to stop variants and spinoffs from spiraling out of control, how an annual megacrossover event could unify a disparate line of characters.

"I want to show you something," he said, abruptly standing up. Eagerly striding through the Marvel labyrinth, Feige led the way to an enormous framed poster, a copy of one that had been on display at Marvel Studios in its earliest days. Emblazoned "MARVEL UNIVERSE," it was a promotional item from 1988 that featured hundreds of Marvel characters drawn by Ed Hannigan and Joe Rubinstein, from the mighty to the monstrous, the cosmic to the craven, the famous to the forgotten. When Feige was a junior producer killing time in the Marvel Studios office, he spent hours looking at the poster, thinking about its heroes and wondering what stories he might tell about them. "There are a lot of characters we haven't brought to the screen yet," he confided.

He could make a movie about almost any of them work—"Maybe not Woodgod," Feige conceded, laughing about the most obscure character on the poster, almost impossible to pick out of the crowd. He thought for a moment, and smiled slyly. "Although now I'm going to go look him up again."

ACKNOWLEDGMENTS

WE STARTED THIS BOOK BEFORE THE CORONAVIRUS CRASHED into our lives like a plummeting Helicarrier: it's been a very strange four years, and we are full of gratitude to everyone in our lives who made it even a little better.

Our thanks to Dan Gerstle, our very patient editor at Liveright/Norton, who was the first person to believe in this book and whose counsel on matters large and small was invaluable.

We are also hugely in the debt of the superstar agent Danielle Svetcov, who was a guiding force every single step of the way, and who, in concert with the always-menschy Daniel Greenberg, brought the three of us together. (We'd also like to thank everyone at the Levine Greenberg Rostan Literary Agency, especially Tim Wojcik, Melissa Rowland, and Miek Coccia.)

Thank you to everyone who spoke to us for this book, pulling back the curtain and making sense of the multiverse.

Lots of people worked hard on this book without getting their names on the cover. Thank you to Henry Erdman for that gorgeous cover, by the way. Thank you to Chris Hewitt for diligently checking our facts. And thank you to all the superheroes working at (and with) Liveright/Norton who devoted their talents to *MCU*, especially Zeba Arora, Ashley Patrick, Brian Mulligan (Lovedog Studio), Henry Erdnan, Becky Homiski, Lauren Abbate, Peter Miller, Nick Curley, Clio Hamilton, Cordelia Calvert, Steve Attardo, Fanta Diallo, and the mighty Peter Simon.

To our very own Pepper Potts, Morgan Robinson, who wrangled countless interviews with sources bored in their homes during lockdown: you can rest now. Our fulsome thanks to Julian and Justin Mitchell (fostering journalism as fandom); Katey Rich, Matt Patches, David Ehrlich, Neil Miller, Anthony Breznican, Richard Lawson, Kristin Russo, Mallory Rubin, Van Lathan Jr., Charles Holmes, Steve Ahlman, Jomi Adeniran, Arjuna Ramgopal, and David Chen (podcast cohorts); the post production team at 11th Street Productions; John Gonzales, Jim Gonzales, and Wendell Eastling (who passed away while supporting this project); Kim Renfro and Diana Helmuth (for writerly sympathy, tequila, and cake in that order); Darrell Borquez for telling us yes when everybody else said no; Dash, Sora, and Jen Sudul Edwards; Steve Crystal; Robert Rossney; Jeff Jackson; the Slightly Difficult Reading Society; Douglas Wolk (for his generosity, for the book *All of the Marvels*, and for the 616 Society, the online comic-book community he's fostered); Matthew Klise; Marc Weidenbaum; Scott Hess; Sunrise of Tambopata in Puerto Maldonado, Posada Salas & Kari Peru in Mollendo, Casa Panqarani in Puno, and Uros Aruma Uro on the Uro floating islands of Lake Titicaca (an unexpectedly high percentage of this book was written in Peru); Caryn Ganz, Peter Keepnews, Amy Padnani, and Bill McDonald at the *New York Times*; and the incomparable Mike Hogan at *Vanity Fair* for starting this all.

The three of us would also all thank each other, except it would be too meta and self-congratulatory. Suffice to say that we finished the book liking each other even more than when we started.

Excelsior!

NOTES

To write this book, we stood on the shoulders of goliaths (and sometimes Goliaths). If you're interested in further reading about the MCU, or just want to know where any of the quotations in the book came from, then avail yourself of these endnotes.

Prologue: ORIGIN STORY

1 **"Do you know where I put it?"**: Avengers UK Premier Press Conference, Claridge's hotel in London, April 20, 2012.

2 **"I thought"**: Author interview with Chris Hemsworth, 2017.

3 **"I would like to take"**: Author interview with Mark Ruffalo, 2017.

3 **"I'm socially awkward"**: Author interview with Kevin Feige, 2017.

5 **"Someday"**: Author interview with anonymous source, 2022.

7 **"Honestly, the closest"**: Nick De Semlyen, "The Irishman Week: Empire's Martin Scorsese Interview," *Empire*, November 7, 2019, empireonline.com/movies/features/irishman-week-martin-scorsese-interview.

8 **"There used to be studio films"**: David Taylor, "Francis Ford Coppola: 'A Marvel Picture Is One Prototype Movie Made Over And Over Again To Look Different,'" *GQ* (UK edition), February 17, 2022, gq-magazine.co.uk/culture/article/francis-ford-coppola-godfather-marvel.

Chapter One: PHOENIX SAGA

14 **"I think comic books are on the ground floor"**: Rita Reif, "Holy Record Breaker! $55,000 for First Batman Comic," *New York Times*, December 19, 1991.

15 **"Too many comic stores"**: Neil Gaiman, *Gods and Tulips* #1, Westhampton House, January 1, 1999.

15 **"Like costume heroes?"**: Stan Lee, *Amazing Fantasy* #15, Marvel Comics,

August 1962. Note that Lee himself forgot to include the hyphen in Spider-Man's name here.

16 **"Bruce"**: Both Stan Lee and Lou Ferrigno insisted that Banner's name was changed because the network thought "Bruce" was too gay. Lee: "When I found out they were changing the name from 'Bruce Banner' to 'David Banner,' I asked the logical question: 'Why are you doing that? His name is supposed to be Bruce.' Some genius at the network said 'Oh no, Stan. Bruce makes him sound homosexual, and it sounds gay. I said, 'There's Bruce Jenner the athletic decathlon champ! There's Bruce . . . well, I don't think I knew Bruce Willis at the time. It didn't faze them. They didn't like the sound of Bruce." (Quote from *Comic Book Confidential*, directed by Ron Mann, Cinecom, 1988.) Ken Johnson, the executive producer of *The Incredible Hulk*, denied that this was the concern: he felt that the alliterative name "Bruce Banner" was too comic-booky.

16 **"When Marvel"**: Author interview with Sean Howe, 2020.

16 **"We are looking forward"**: Marvel Productions advertisement, *Variety*, June 19, 1980.

16 **"Those of you who were careless enough"**: "Stan Lee Speech 7/1/84 Charlotte, N.C. Heroes Con" (video recording), Box 157, Stan Lee Archives, University of Wyoming, American Heritage Center. Bob Gale did actually write a script for a Doctor Strange movie; the screenplay was rewritten by Larry Cohen, Charles Band, and Lee himself. Band would ultimately produce his version of the screenplay as *Doctor Mordrid* in 1992, having lost the rights to the Doctor Strange character.

17 **"Stan wasn't rude to people"**: Abraham Josephine Riesman, *True Believer: The Rise and Fall of Stan Lee* (Crown, 2020), 213. Lee saw the Japanese TV show *Super Sentai* in the late 1980s and had a brainstorm about how to make it work in the United States, dubbing some footage and shooting new scenes with American actors, but wasn't able to interest any American networks. In 1992, after Loesch left Marvel Productions to run Fox Kids, she was approached by Haim Saban, an Israeli TV producer, who had the same epiphany about how to customize *Super Sentai* for local markets—and had licensed the footage. Despite skepticism from her bosses, Loesch green-lit the show, which became the massive phenomenon called *Mighty Morphin Power Rangers*.

17 **"We were great producers"**: Interview with Margaret Loesch, The Television Academy Foundation, January 15, 2019.

18 **"Lipstick Guy"**: Sean Howe, *Marvel Comics: The Untold Story* (HarperCollins, 2012), 313.

18 **"Love Me, Love My Cigar"**: Dan Raviv, *Comic Wars: Marvel's Battle for Survival* (Levant Books, 2012), location 305, Kindle.

20 **$250 in his pocket**: Matthew Garrahan, "Man in the News: Ike Perlmutter," *Financial Times*, September 4, 2009. Ike Perlmutter, in keeping with his lifelong avoidance of the press, declined to answer any questions for this book.

21 **"Our business is other people's mistakes"**: Douglas Martin, "Sam Osman, 88, Founder of Job Lot Trading," *New York Times*, February 18, 2000.

22 **"Maybe I just wanted"**: Scott Bowles, "Marvel's Chief: A Force Outside, 'a Kid Inside,'" *USA Today*, June 5, 2003.

22 **"When you grow up in Israel"**: Carol Lawson, "A One-Man Thrill Factory for Children," *New York Times*, July 8, 1993.

22 **"In baseball"**: Ibid.

23 **"I don't believe in work hours"**: Author interview with Avi Arad, 2017.

23 **"It is a mini-Disney"**: Raviv, *Comic Wars*, loc. 305.

24 **"We realized he didn't know"**: Eric Lewald and Julia Lewald, *X-Men: The Art and Making of the Animated Series* (Abrams, 2020), 34.

24 **"a conventional kids' show"**: Ibid., 13.

24 **"But he would nod his head"**: Riesman, *True Believer*, 225.

24 **"I did the show"**: Geoff Boucher, "Avi Arad: From 'Blade' to 'Morbius,' Three Decades Of Mining Marvel," *Deadline*, March 20, 2019, deadline.com/2019/03/avi-arad-marvel-blade-spider-man-morbius-toys-1202576569.

24 **shorn**: Raviv, *Comic Wars*, loc. 2228.

25 **"What do *you* believe Spider-Man is worth?"**: Ibid., loc. 3201.

25 **"Ladies and gentlemen"**: Ibid., loc. 3228.

26 **"It was so much fun"**: Author interview with Avi Arad, 2017.

Chapter Two: GIFTED YOUNGSTERS

28 **"was never supposed to be seen"**: Robert Ito, "Fantastic Faux!," *Los Angeles*, March 2005.

29 **"Everybody liked the film"**: Ibid. Note that Corman's production company on *Fantastic Four*, New Horizons Pictures, is not the same entity as his New World Pictures, which he sold in 1983 (and which bought Marvel in 1986, after Corman sold it).

29 **"Avi's a very fine guy"**: Ibid.

29 **"I absolutely believe that the negative exists"**: Russ Burlingame, "DOOMED! Director Marty Langford Doesn't Believe Marvel Really Destroyed the Fantastic Four Negatives," ComicBook.com, September 9, 2016, comicbook.com/marvel/news/doomed-director-marty-langford-doesnt-believe-marvel-really-dest-2.

29 **"When you get into business"**: Nancy Hass, "Marvel Superheroes Take Aim at Hollywood," *New York Times*, July 28, 1996.

30 **"If the movies do great"**: Willow Green, "Avi Quits," *Empire*, June 1, 2006, empireonline.com/movies/news/avi-quits.

30 **"There wouldn't have been a movie"**: Interview with Margaret Loesch, The Television Academy Foundation, January 15, 2019.

31 **"Why waste money on anything else?"**: Howe, *Marvel Comics*, 399.

31 **"Marvel as a movie-making entity"**: Author interview with Peter Frankfurt, 2020.

32 ***Blade* was a weird oddity**: Ibid.

32 **"So we're chatting"**: "Columbia University Libraries: Comic New York—A Symposium: Chris Claremont, Day 1, Keynote," uploaded to YouTube by Columbia University, April 11, 2012, youtube.com/watch?v=WEpZrZNtgxE.

33 **"I tried to get Fox"**: Matt Singer, "James Cameron Calls His Spider-Man 'The Greatest Movie I Never Made,'" ScreenCrush.com, December 6, 2021, screencrush.com/james-cameron-spider-man-movie.

34 **"Nobody gives a shit"**: Ben Fritz, *The Big Picture: The Fight for the Future of Movies* (HarperCollins, 2019), 46.

35 **"Because Lauren is"**: Anthony Breznican, "The Man Behind the Movies," in *The Marvel Universe* (Meredith, 2021), 57.

35 **"I had the toys"**: Author interview with Kevin Feige, 2017.

35 **"It was all very nerdy"**: Brent Lang, "How Kevin Feige Super-Charged Marvel Studios into Hollywood's Biggest Hit Machine," *Variety*, April 16, 2019, variety.com/2019/film/features/kevin-feige-avengers-endgame-marvel-studios-1203188721.

35 **"I was always excited"**: Ibid.

36 **"My friends and my family"**: "Kevin Feige: USC School of Cinematic Arts Mary Pickford Alumni Award," uploaded to YouTube by USC, May 19, 2014, youtube.com/watch?v=dmvLLYoY35Y.

36 **"that the smart kids"**: "Kevin Feige," interview, *Produced By*, January 2017.

36 **"the most perfect superhero movie"**: Ibid.

36 **"I learned to enjoy the adrenaline rush of phones ringing"**: Ibid.

37 **"A word that I was never able to pronounce but always understood"**: "Tribute to Richard Donner—How 'Superman' Influenced Today's Biggest Superhero Movies," uploaded to YouTube by Oscars, June 8, 2017, youtube.com/watch?v=PrNwMXcKxWE.

37 **"The two of us washed cars together"**: Ibid.

37 **"when Dick wasn't working"**: "Kevin Feige," interview, *Produced By*, January 2017.

38 **"I had probably only learned"**: Erin Carlson, *I'll Have What She's Having: How Nora Ephron's Three Iconic Films Saved the Romantic Comedy* (Hachette, 2017), 232.

38 **"He saw Marvel"**: Author interview with Craig Kyle, 2020.

38 **"As a walking encyclopedia"**: Brooks Barnes, "With Fan at the Helm, Marvel Safely Steers Its Heroes to the Screen," *New York Times*, July 24, 2011.

38 **"I would hear people"**: Devin Leonard, "The Pow! Bang! Bam! Plan to Save Marvel, Starring B-List Heroes," *Bloomberg Businessweek*, April 3, 2014, bloomberg.com/news/articles/2014-04-03/kevin-feige-marvels-superhero-at-running-movie-franchises#xj4y7vzkg.

39 **"I can wear makeup"**: Tatiana Siegel, "Bryan Singer's Traumatic 'X-Men' Set: The Movie 'Created a Monster,'" *Hollywood Reporter*, July 31, 2020.

39 **"Kevin was someone who" et seq.**: Author interview with Craig Kyle, 2020.

39 **"eventually went, 'Fine!'"**: Author interview with Kevin Feige, 2017.

40 **"I had been in touch with Avi"**: Ibid.

40 **"DC guy"**: Adam B. Vary, "'Spider-Man' at 20: How Sam Raimi and Sony Pictures Rescued the Superhero Genre and Changed Hollywood Forever," *Variety*, May 2022.

40 **"Sam was unique"**: Ibid.

41 **"I had to leave everything behind"**: Stacey Wilson, "In Her Own Words," *Hollywood Reporter*, June 15, 2011.

41 **"There's a difference"**: Author interview with Lauren Shuler Donner, 2017.

41 **"He's an iceberg of an intellect"**: Author interview with Rick Heinrichs, 2020.

41 **"And when I say"**: Author interview with Kevin Feige, 2017.

42 **"That's it?"**: Vary, "'Spider-Man' at 20."

42 **"He was new"**: Ibid.

42 **"Wow"**: Ibid.

42 **"The toys sold"**: Ibid.

Chapter Three: ONCE UPON A TIME IN MAR-A-LAGO

44 **"At all times"**: Isaac Arnsdorf, "The Shadow Rules of the VA," *ProPublica*, August 7, 2018, propublica.org/article/ike-Perlmutter-bruce-moskowitz -marc-sherman-shadow-rulers-of-the-va.

44 **"My dad would take me"**: Author interview with David Maisel, 2020.

46 **"Sony made nine figures"**: Ibid.

46 **"It was so bad"**: Author interview with David Maisel, 2023.

47 **"We suggested but they didn't listen"**: Author interview with Kevin Feige, 2017.

47 **"From the moment"**: Author interview with Craig Kyle, 2020.

47 **"As a public company"**: Author interview with David Maisel, 2020.

48 **"I love *Daredevil*"**: Ken P., "An Interview with Avi Arad," IGN, February 10, 2004, ign.com/articles/2004/02/10/an-interview-with-avi-arad.

48 **"Really, the movie"**: Author interview with David Maisel, 2020.

49 **"It was the first time"**: Ibid.

50 **"Ike's scared of the film business"**: Ben Fritz, *The Big Picture: The Fight for the Future of Movies* (HarperCollins, 2019), 55. The alleged plan: a seventy-five-page proposal for "Marvel World," where a studio would be financed by outside investors who would receive 20 percent ownership for their investment. David Maisel's response (in an interview for this book): "I saw that in Ben Fritz's book, and I was like, 'Whoa. Shit. If there was a presentation to the board a few months before I joined, why didn't I see it?' That would have helped me because I had to put together a whole business plan. And I called John Turitzen and he said, 'No, of course that never existed.'"

50   **"Don't come back"**: Author interview with David Maisel, 2020.

50   **"in his own head"**: Author interview with John Turitzin, 2020.

51   **"I had to ask my board"**: Author interview with David Maisel, 2020.

51   **"It was a very frightening idea"**: Author interview with John Turitzin, 2020.

52   **"We were able to get the financing"**: Author interview with Kevin Feige, 2017.

52   **"We were guaranteed four at-bats"**: Author interview with David Maisel, 2020.

53   **"This has been a fun project"**: Author interview with John Turitzin, 2020.

53   **"I'm in the conference room"**: Author interview with David Maisel, 2020.

53   **"Be afraaaaaaid"**: Tara Bennett and Paul Terry, *The Story of Marvel Studios: The Making of the Marvel Cinematic Universe* (Abrams, 2021), vol. 1, 21.

Chapter Four: PLAUSIBILITY

57   **"I had not talked to Ike"**: Tara Bennett and Paul Terry, *The Story of Marvel Studios: The Making of the Marvel Cinematic Universe* (Abrams, 2021), vol. 1, 21.

58   **"After describing Iron Man"**: Author interview with John Turitzin, 2020.

58   **"Kevin! Kevin!"**: Bennett and Terry, *Story of Marvel Studios*, vol. 1, 22.

59   **"was only my choice"**: Geoff Boucher, "Avi Arad: From 'Blade' to 'Morbius,' Three Decades Of Mining Marvel," *Deadline*, March 20, 2019, deadline.com/2019/03/avi-arad-marvel-blade-spider-man-morbius-toys-1202576569/.

59   **"I needed the security"**: Ben Fritz and Pamela McClintock, "Exec Makes Marvel Move," *Variety*, November 1, 2005.

61   **"It's clear that the leaders"**: "Valenti and Rove Hold News Conference," CNN, transcript, November 11, 2001, transcripts.cnn.com/show/se/date/2001-11-11/segment/03.

61   **"It might have seemed an opportunist"**: Bernard Weinraub, "The Moods They Are A'Changing In Films; Terrorism Is Making Government Look Good," *New York Times*, October 10, 2001. Admittedly, by the end of the *Alias* pilot, Jennifer Garner's character Sydney Bristow has learned that the branch of the CIA she is working for, SD-6, is actually a terrorist organization hostile to the United States, but Abrams's shows were never famous for their internal consistency.

63   **"We're in two wars"**: Author interview with Matt Holloway, 2019.

63   **"I think I gave myself a dare"**: James White, "The Story Behind Iron Man from page to Tarantino to screen and now . . . sequel!," *Total Film*, May 5, 2009, gamesradar.com/the-story-behind-iron-man.

64   **"It wasn't even a question"**: Author interview with Matt Holloway, 2019.

64 **"*X-Men* was proving"**: Author interview with Art Marcum, 2019.

64 **"9/11 and terrorism essentially supplanted"**: Author interview with Mark Fergus, 2020.

65 **"Going back to my experience"**: Author interview with Kevin Feige, 2017.

65 **"That's why Jon Favreau"**: Author interview with David Maisel, 2020.

66 **"We were outsiders"**: Author interview with Jon Favreau, 2017.

66 **"People forget that *Iron Man* was an independent movie"**: Author interview with Kevin Feige, 2017.

66 **"Look, I'm going to lean"**: Author interview with Stephen Platt, 2020.

67 **"That was a huge get"**: Author interview with Art Marcum, 2019.

67 **"Hollywood likes them to be twenty-six and cut"**: Author interview with Avi Arad, 2017.

67 **"The big internet rumor"**: Author interview with Eric Vespe, 2021.

67 **"the one everyone was rooting for"**: Author interview with an anonymous source, 2020.

68 **"Jon, I know, felt in his bones"**: Author interview with Matt Holloway, 2019.

68 **"The missus says"**: Chris Heath, "RD3," *GQ*, May 2013.

69 **"very broken guy"**: *The Howard Stern Show*, SiriusXM, May 4, 2016.

69 **"There was a lot of conversation"**: Author interview with Stephen Platt, 2020.

69 **"We recommended Robert"**: Author interview with David Maisel, 2020.

69 **"Under no circumstances"**: Heath, "RD3."

69 **"great beacon"**: Clark Collis, "Forging *Iron Man:* How Director Jon Favreau Launched the Marvel Cinematic Universe," *Entertainment Weekly*, March 15, 2018, ew.com/movies/2018/03/15/iron-man-jon-favreau-marvel-cinematic-universe.

69 **"It's like a 1950s love story"**: Author interview with David Maisel, 2020.

70 **"There was a point where Mandarin"**: Author interview with Matt Holloway, 2019.

70 **"We thought we were making"**: Author interview with Art Marcum, 2019.

70 **"begging"**: Author interview with Mark Fergus, 2020.

70 **"It saved a ton of money"**: Author interview with David Maisel, 2020.

71 **"this character"**: Author interview with Dianne Chadwick, 2020.

72 **"There was no script"**: Author interview with Stephen Platt, 2020.

Chapter Five: PROOF OF CONCEPT

73 **"They had no script"**: Kris Tapley, "Interview with Crazy Heart's Jeff Bridges," InContention.com, December 1, 2009, incontention.com/2009/11/04/crazy-heart-has-the-goods.

73 **"I don't even know how"**: Author interview with Nina Paskowitz, 2020.

74 **"Martinis, beer"**: Author interview with Stephen Platt, 2020.

74 **"I remember Jeff Bridges"**: Author interview with Jamie Kelman, 2020.

74 **"It was crazy"**: Author interview with Art Marcum, 2019.

74 **"We looked at everything"**: Author interview with Mark Fergus, 2020.

74 **"We continued to rewrite"**: Author interview with Art Marcum, 2019.

75 **"Jeff loved to have a script"**: "American Cinematheque: Iron Man," in-theater commentary, September 6, 2008.

75 **"They had an outline"**: Tapley, "Jeff Bridges."

75 **"In the morning"**: Author interview with Loyd Catlett, 2020.

75 **"five seconds"**: Author interview with Nina Paskowitz, 2020.

75 **"The script changed so much"**: Author interview with Susan Wexler, 2020.

76 **"He wanted that to be"**: Author interview with Mark Fergus, 2020.

76 **"plopped down"**: Author interview with Lauri Gaffin, 2020.

77 **"When they were storyboarding"**: Author interview with L. J. Shannon, 2020.

77 **"Jon was really intense"**: Author interview with Lauri Gaffin, 2020.

77 **"This is one of those scenes"**: "American Cinematheque: Iron Man."

78 **"The US military has made it"**: Author interview with Siddhant Adlakha, 2020.

78 **"I figure that it would be a waste"**: Donna Miles, "Edwards team stars in 'Iron Man' superhero movie," American Forces Press Service, May 2, 2007, af.mil/News/Article-Display/Article/127002/edwards-team-stars-in-iron-man-superhero-movie.

78 **"This movie is going"**: Ibid.

79 **"It never got resolved"**: Samantha L. Quigley, "To Tap Into the Military's Arsenal, Hollywood Needs the Pentagon's Blessing," USO.org, December 18, 2015, uso.org/stories/105-to-tap-into-the-military-s-arsenal-hollywood-needs-the-pentagon-s-blessing.

79 **"Reagan, Clinton, Bush"**: "American Cinematheque: Iron Man."

80 **"[Stark] does get a firsthand look"**: Author interview with Siddhant Adlakha, 2020.

80 **"The emotional appeal"**: Matthew Alford, *Reel Power: Hollywood Cinema and American Supremacy* (Pluto Press, 2010), 111.

80 **"like a ladybug"**: Author interview with Robert Downey Jr., 2017.

81 **"looked like a Power Ranger"**: "American Cinematheque: Iron Man."

81 **"The depth of character"**: Author interview with Kevin Feige, 2017.

81 **"They shot a bunch of B-roll"**: Author interview with Marc Chu, 2020.

81 **"he was rolling his eyes"**: Jonathan Wilkins, ed., *Marvel Studios: The First 10 Years* (Titan, 2018), 14.

82 **"Act three was basically"**: Author interview with Jamie Kelman, 2020.

83 **"What if Iron Man's getting"**: Author interview with Matt Holloway, 2019.

83 **"Pitch it to Jon"**: Ibid.

83 **"Suddenly it was"**: Ibid.

83 **"It was a process of pitching"**: Author interview with Marc Chu, 2020.

84 **"Kevin is the one who probably"**: Author interview with Robert Downey Jr., 2017.

84 **"Everybody deals with stress"**: Author interview with Kevin Feige, 2017.

84 **"only potato chips"**: Kim Masters, "How Marvel Became the Envy (and Scourge) of Hollywood," *Hollywood Reporter*, July 23, 2014.

Chapter Six: POST-CREDITS SCENE

86 **"It was the greatest"**: Shirley Li, "Marvel chief Kevin Feige tells the origin story of the MCU's post-credits scenes," *Entertainment Weekly*, April 25, 2018.

87 **"Today, though"**: Drew McWeeny [Moriarty], "AICN EXCLUSIVE! Guess Who's Shooting His IRON MAN Role Today!!," *Ain't It Cool News*, June 21, 2007, legacy.aintitcool.com/node/33090.

88 **"I would also like to thank"**: Jon Favreau, Myspace.com, June 25, 2007, forum.myspace.com/index.cfm?fuseaction=messageboard.viewThread& entryID=37970867&groupID=102795074.

88 **"How do you know"**: Larry Carroll, "Confirmed: Hilary Swank Will Appear in 'Iron Man,'" MTV.com, July 23, 2007, mtv.com/news/wbebm5/ confirmed-hilary-swank-will-appear-in-iron-man.

89 **"I originally wrote"**: "The Art of Adapting Comics to the Screen: David S. Goyer Q&A," uploaded to YouTube by Comic-Con International, July 25, 2020, youtube.com/watch?v=Hg15UXVh72U.

90 **"At the time it did shoot"**: Jason Myers, "David Goyer: Stripped to the Bone," RevolutionSF.com, July 2000, revolutionsf.com/article.php? id=1082.

90 **"My Nick Fury"**: Jen Yamato, "David Hasselhoff: I Was the Ultimate Nick Fury," Movieline, May 25, 2012, movieline.com/2012/05/25/ david-hasselhoff-avengers-nick-fury-samuel-jackson.

90 **"I called Avi"**: Jeff Otto, "David S. Goyer Talks Batman, Iron Man, Comics and More," IGN, February 27, 2004, ign.com/articles/2004/02/27/ david-s-goyer-talks-batman-iron-man-comics-and-more.

91 **"I went to Harvard Law"**: Sean Howe, *Marvel Comics: The Untold Story* (HarperCollins, 2012), 404.

92 **"The movie was for 20-year-olds"**: Ibid., 405.

92 **"Look, the lunatics"**: Author interview with Bryan Hitch, 2020.

93 **"I wanted an African-American Nick Fury"**: Gus Lubin, "Samuel L. Jackson had the perfect response to the writer who made his 'Avengers' role possible," *Business Insider*, April 27, 2018.

93 **"with the eyepatch"**: Author interview with Bryan Hitch, 2020.

93 **"Sam's people got in touch"**: Ibid.

94 **"The idea that this might"**: Lubin, "Samuel L. Jackson."

94 **"We wanted Nick Fury"**: Li, "Post-Credits Scenes."

94 **"It was purely a love letter"**: Author interview with Jon Favreau, 2017.

94 **"We don't have X-Men"**: Li, "Post-Credits Scenes."

95 **"Kevin was definitely very involved with all of that"**: Author interview with Jon Favreau, 2017.

95 **"I thought it would just begin"**: Author interview with Kevin Feige, 2017.

Chapter Seven: EXTRAORDINARY LEVELS OF TOXICITY

96 **"We all love the Hulk because he smashes"**: Alex Spencer, "The Hulk mutated over 55 years to become Marvel's most multifaceted character," *Polygon*, July 11, 2018, polygon.com/comics/2018/7/11/17550926/the-hulk-history-writers-marvel-comics-thor-ragnarok.

97 **"Hulk was our second-biggest"**: Author interview with David Maisel, 2020.

97 **"We have a no-asshole policy"**: Author interview with Terry Notary, 2020.

97 **"It's a great policy"**: Author interview with Craig Kyle, 2020.

97 **"There'd already been"**: Author interview with David Maisel, 2020.

98 **"Frankly"**: Ibid.

98 **"I get the rights back"**: Ibid.

100 **"My greatest memory"**: Author interview with Kurt Williams, 2020.

100 **"To have him calm"**: Author interview with Aaron Sims, 2020.

101 **"generously given himself"**: Tony Kaye, "Losing It," *Guardian*, October 25, 2002.

102 **"If there's no way"**: *The Making of* The Incredible Hulk, bonus feature, *The Incredible Hulk* (Universal, 2008), Blu-ray.

102 **"He was always my favorite"**: Larry Carroll, "William Hurt Says New Hulk Is More Heroic, Reveals Iron Man Crossover Scene," MTV, January 19, 2008, mtv.com/news/rgyagm/william-hurt-says-new-hulk-is-more-heroic-reveals-iron-man-crossover-scene.

102 **"My agent called me"**: K. J. Matthews, "Liv Tyler: Swift 'Hulk' offer a big surprise," CNN, June 12, 2008, edition.cnn.com/2008/SHOWBIZ/Movies/06/12/people.tyler.

103 **"I liken the Abomination thing"**: Eric Vespe [Quint], "Quint's hilarious interview with Tim Roth and Louis Leterrier! HULK! INGLORIOUS BASTARDS! And . . . Johnny To?!?," *Ain't It Cool News*, June 13, 2008, legacy.aintitcool.com/node/37074.

103 **"Whatever you can come up with"**: Author interview with Terry Notary, 2020.

103 **"Edward Norton has very narrow features"**: Author interview with Aaron Sims, 2020.

104 **"It was kind of painful"**: Author interview with Zak Penn, 2019.

104 **"part one"**: "The Incredible Hulk Comic-Con Panel," uploaded to YouTube by Abel McBride, August 5, 2007, youtube.com/watch?v=_q3Ui91qbIA.

104 **"three different sizes"**: Ibid.

104 **"Well, I wrote the film"**: Ibid.

104 **"I had him walking east"**: Author interview with Zak Penn, 2019.

105 **"we did 'rehearsals' for three weeks"**: Vespe, "Tim Roth and Louis Leterrier."

105 **"When you're working with Louis"**: Author interview with Kurt Williams, 2020.

106 **"Hulk doesn't have"**: Barbara Robertson, "Heavy-Handed," *Computer Graphics World*, July 2008.

106 **"[Norton] wasn't really engaged"**: Author interview with Terry Notary, 2020.

106 **"Try this, mate!"**: Ibid.

106 **"one of those quintessential"**: Ibid.

107 **"you could really see"**: Author interview with Kurt Williams, 2020.

107 **"It was important to nail"**: Author interview with Aaron Sims, 2020.

109 **"It's as much Marvel's fault"**: Gregory Kirschling, "New 'Hulk': behind-the-scenes drama," *Entertainment Weekly*, April 17, 2008.

110 **"We have made the decision"**: Drew McWeeny, "EXCLUSIVE: Marvel confirms they will hire new 'Hulk' for 'The Avengers,'" HitFix, July 10, 2010, hitfix.com/blogs/motion-captured/posts/exclusive-marvel-confirms-they-will-hire-new-hulk-for-avengers. The actors getting a chummy name-check from Feige were Robert Downey Jr., Chris Hemsworth, Chris Evans, Samuel L. Jackson, and Scarlett Johansson.

110 **"Yeah, which was cheap"**: David Marchese, "The Disruptive World of Edward Norton," *New York Times Magazine*, October 7, 2019.

Chapter Eight: SOME ASSEMBLY REQUIRED

111 **"Kevin, Avi, and Ari"**: Tara Bennett and Paul Terry, *The Story of Marvel Studios: The Making of the Marvel Cinematic Universe* (Abrams, 2021), vol. 1, 24.

112 **"You're given your mantra"**: Matt Donnelly, "Meet the Executive Avengers Who Help Kevin Feige Make Marvel Magic," *Variety*, April 17, 2019.

112 **"Pain is temporary, film is forever"**: Author interview with Craig Kyle, 2020.

113 **"I'm a teenager of the military dictatorship"**: "Eva Longoria, Victoria Alonso & more—Academy Dialogues: The Erasure of Latinos in Hollywood," uploaded to YouTube by the Academy of Motion Picture Arts and Sciences, September 10, 2020, youtube.com/watch?v=vdAJ8pCnSvQ&t=18s.

113 **"My mother never remarried"**: Elayna Fernandez, "Motherhood Inspiration From Powerful Marvel Mom Victoria Alonso," *The Positive Mom*, April 30, 2018, thepositivemom.com/powerful-marvel-mom-victoria-alonso.

113 **"Because it was the only thing"**: Victoria Alonso, "Historias de super-héroes que merecen ser contadas," TEDxCordoba, uploaded to YouTube by TEDx Talks, November 15, 2019, youtube.com/watch?v=dfEL609-KKg. (Author translation from the original Spanish.)

114 **"Oh, I see you met" et seq.**: Bennett and Terry, *Story of Marvel Studios*, vol. 1, 24.

115 **"She's a treasure"**: Author interview with Craig Kyle, 2020.

115 **"She didn't want to say"**: Author interview with Jamie Kelman, 2020.

116 **"There was some sort of kismet"**: Bennett and Terry, *Story of Marvel Studios*, vol. 1, 65.

116 **"I'll be fielding"**: Donnelly, "Executive Avengers."

117 **"Suddenly, we were working"**: Bennett and Terry, *Story of Marvel Studios*, vol. 1, 23.

117 **"He would bring stacks"**: Author interview with Craig Kyle, 2020.

118 **"The movie-specific conversation"**: Bennett and Terry, *Story of Marvel Studios*, vol. 1, 68.

119 **"Once Kevin took charge"**: Author interview with Craig Kyle, 2020.

120 **"*Captain America* has a very"**: Jim Thacker, "Q&A: Victoria Alonso, Marvel's visual effects chief," CGchannel.com, September 15, 2011, https://www.cgchannel.com/2011/09/qa-victoria-alonso-marvels-visual-effects-chief/.

121 **"zero point"**: Bennett and Terry, *Story of Marvel Studios*, vol. 1, 70.

Chapter Nine: DEMON IN A BOTTLE

123 **"They both drove"**: Author interview with David Maisel, 2020.

123 **"Fortunately, I'd had the experience"**: Author interview with Jon Favreau, 2017.

123 **"I remember we got a lot"**: Author interview with David Maisel, 2020.

124 **"There was a feeling"**: *Ultimate Iron Man: The Making of Iron Man 2*, written by Adam Gallagher, bonus feature, *Iron Man 2* (Paramount, 2010), Blu-ray.

125 **"It was super-organic"**: Peter Sciretta, "Interview: Iron Man 2 Screenwriter Justin Theroux," *SlashFilm*, May 10, 2010, slashfilm.com/508942/interview-iron-man-2-screenwriter-justin-theroux.

125 **"There was no explanation"**: Scott Simon, "Terrence Howard Talks Tunes, Family, Science," *Weekend Edition Saturday*, NPR, October 18, 2008.

126 **"I'm at my kid's laser tag party"**: Will Harris, "Don Cheadle got the Avengers call in the middle of his kid's laser tag party," *AV Club*, February 6, 2022, avclub.com/don-cheadle-got-the-avengers-call-in-the-middle-of-his-1842692765.

126 **"You've never done"**: Ibid.

127 **"look the same"**: Matthew Garrahan, "Superheroes soar above Disney tensions," *Financial Times*, August 16, 2012.

127 **"Ike Perlmutter neither discriminates"**: Author interview with an anonymous source, 2017.

127 **"It's not that it's beneath me"**: *The Howard Stern Show*, SiriusXM, February 11, 2021.

128 **"I was totally out of my element"**: *Ultimate Iron Man: The Making of Iron Man 2*.

128 **"Herbal Essences moments"**: Ibid.

128 **"I hadn't done the human jungle-gym"**: Author interview with Heidi Moneymaker, 2020.

128 **"Kevin was laying out some larger plans"**: Author interview with Jon Favreau, 2017.

129 **"The average person goes to work"**: Hilary de Vries, "Samuel L. Jackson: My Character Is No Sex Machine," *Chicago Tribune*, June 20, 2000.

129 **"I wasn't sure where the character"**: CBR Staff, "Sam Rockwell Talks 'Iron Man 2,'" CBR, August 25, 2009, cbr.com/sam-rockwell-talks-iron-man-2.

130 **"Favreau just really wanted someone"**: *Ultimate Iron Man: The Making of Iron Man 2*.

130 **"You may see us"**: Ibid.

131 **"The cockatoo that he has"**: "Commentary," *Iron Man 2* (Paramount, 2010), two-disc special edition DVD.

131 **"He took it upon himself"**: *Ultimate Iron Man: The Making of Iron Man 2*.

132 **"I wanted to bring some other layers"**: William Bibbiani, "Mickey Rourke Talks 'Immortals,'" CraveOnline, November 7, 2011, craveonline .com/film/interviews/177591-mickey-rourke-talks-immortals.

132 **"Marvel just wanted a one-dimensional"**: "Mickey Rourke Laments Lack Of 'Depth' In Iron Man 2," MTV News, November 8, 2011, mtv.com/ video-clips/7wt215/mickey-rourke-laments-lack-of-depth-in-iron-man-2.

132 **"You could see the steam coming out of his ears"**: Author interview with Jim Rothwell, 2020.

132 **"I don't know where I fall"**: Hilary De Vries, "Robert Downey Jr.: The Album," *New York Times*, November 21, 2004.

133 **"We didn't want to be"**: Chris Lee, "Rewriting the Behind-the-Scenes Story of Iron Man 2," *Vulture*, April 28, 2022, vulture.com/2022/04/ rewriting-the-behind-the-scenes-story-of-iron-man-2.html.

133 **"There's too much convenience"**: *Ultimate Iron Man: The Making of Iron Man 2*.

134 **"Jon was a fan"**: Brandon Davis, "Genndy Tartakovsky Reveals Details of Iron Man 2 Work," ComicBook.com, September 30, 2020, comicbook. com/marvel/news/iron-man-2-genndy-tartakovsky-animation-fight-scene.

134 **"come to Jesus"**: Author interview with Marc Chu, 2020.

134 **"A lot of things"**: *Ultimate Iron Man: The Making of Iron Man 2*.

Chapter Ten: NO STRINGS ON ME

136 **"I went to Dubai"**: Author interview with David Maisel, 2020.

137 **"a shame"**: Ibid.

137 **"Disney's culture will destroy"**: Robert Iger, *The Ride of a Lifetime: Lessons Learned from 15 Years as CEO of the Walt Disney Company* (Random House, 2019), 136.

138 **"What I saw that day"**: Corey Stieg, "How Bob Iger convinced Steve Jobs

to sell Pixar to Disney: 'I've got a crazy idea,'" CNBC, December 2, 2020, cnbc.com/2020/12/02/bob-iger-on-how-he-convinced-steve-jobs-to-sell-pixar-to-disney.html.

138 **"*Iron Man?* I'm not scared"**: Author interview with David Maisel, 2023.

138 **"There didn't seem to be"**: Author interview with David Maisel, 2020.

139 **"Well, then, the next thing"**: Ibid.

140 **"There was an assumption"**: Iger, *Ride of a Lifetime*, 155.

141 **"He stood to make"**: Ibid., 154.

141 **"Here's what Tom and Kevin"**: Author interview with David Maisel, 2020.

142 **"who claimed to have never read"**: Iger, *Ride of a Lifetime*, 158.

142 **"Is this one important"**: Ibid., 157.

142 **"He said you were true"**: Ibid., 161.

142 **$1.5 billion**: Matthew Garrahan. "Man in the News: Ike Perlmutter," *Financial Times*, September 4, 2009, ft.com/content/4080d0de-997f-11de-ab8c-00144feabdc0.

142 **"I told Bob that"**: Author interview with David Maisel, 2020.

142 **"become so watered-down"**: Ryan Gilby, "Fans fear ker-pow after Disney's Marvel takeover," *Guardian*, September 1, 2009, theguardian.com/film/2009/sep/01/marvel-disney-spiderman.

143 **"completely inherent to the DNA of what Marvel is"**: Author interview with Kevin Feige, 2017.

143 **"Seemed brilliant"**: Iger, *Ride of a Lifetime*, 162.

144 **"screaming matches"**: Devin Leonard, "The Pow! Bang! Bam! Plan to Save Marvel, Starring B-List Heroes," *Bloomberg*, April 3, 2014, bloomberg.com/news/articles/2014-04-03/kevin-feige-marvels-superhero-at-running-movie-franchises#xj4y7vzkg.

145 **"what Pixar had"**: Author interview with Craig Kyle, 2020.

146 **"I never had any experiences"**: Author interview with Kevin Feige, 2017.

Chapter Eleven: OUR BRAND IS CHRISES

147 **"We're interested in what goes on"**: Christina Radish, "Director Kenneth Branagh and Kevin Feige Interview THOR," *Collider*, May 5, 2011, collider.com/kenneth-branagh-kevin-feige-interview-thor.

148 **"It's about fathers and sons"**: Author interview with Craig Kyle, 2020.

149 **"Marvel was looking for television writers"**: Author interview with Ashley Miller, 2019.

149 **"One of my most vivid memories"**: Author interview with Zack Stentz, 2019.

150 **"super weird"**: Josh Grossberg, "Natalie Portman's 'Weird' Reason for Hooking Up With Thor," E! News, November 23, 2009, eonline.com/news/155129/natalie_portmans_weird_reason_hooking.

150 **"We were casting Cap and Thor"**: Author interview with Sarah Halley Finn, 2021.

151 **"When you start to look at the comics"**: *Casting the MCU*, bonus feature, *Avengers: Endgame* (Buena Vista, 2019), Blu-ray.

151 **"an actor who could play Asgardian"**: Author interview with Sarah Halley Finn, 2021.

152 **"Don't let it be like Fabio"**: Ethan Alter, "How 'Thor' opened up the MCU: Kenneth Branagh on hiring Chris Hemsworth, going to space and the terror of Fabio," Yahoo!, May 10, 2019, yahoo.com/now/thor-chris-hemsworth-kenneth-branagh-tom-hiddleston-160246757.html.

152 **"Why aren't you in the mix here"**: Lynn Hirschberg, "Chris Hemsworth Admits He Almost Lost Out Thor To His Younger Brother Liam Hemsworth," *W*, September 13, 2017, https://www.wmagazine.com/story/chris-hemsworth-thor-audition-liam-hemsworth.

152 **"When he came in for a screen test"**: *Thor: From Asgard to Earth*, bonus feature, *Thor* (Paramount, 2001), Blu-ray.

153 **"The singular mandate"**: Author interview with Zack Stentz, 2019.

153 **"These will be the most important calls"**: Alter.

153 **"And we're all looking around"**: Author interview with Craig Kyle, 2020.

153 **"If you remember"**: Author interview with Zack Stentz, 2019.

154 **"I had read the comics"** et seq.: Amy Kaufman, " 'Thor': Chris Hemsworth got so muscular his costume wouldn't fit," *Los Angeles Times*, March 29, 2011, herocomplex.latimes.com/2011/03/29/thor-chris-hemsworth-got-so-muscular-his-costume-wouldnt-fit/?dlvrit=63378.

154 **"When I was casting Captain America"**: Author interview with Sarah Halley Finn, 2021.

154 **"We knew the central"**: *Casting the MCU*.

155 **"But we saw something there"**: Author interview with Sarah Halley Finn, 2021.

155 **"it wasn't quite a fit"**: Ibid.

155 **"Casting Captain America was super hard and it took a long time"**: Author interview with Kevin Feige, 2017.

156 **"My oldest two boys"**: Author interview with Sarah Halley Finn, 2021.

156 **"Bringing him in"**: Author interview with Kevin Feige, 2017.

156 **"Getting the offer"**: Alex Pappademas, "The Political Avenger: Chris Evans Takes on Trump, Tom Brady, Anxiety and Those Retirement Rumors," *Hollywood Reporter*, March 27, 2019.

156 **"I like my privacy"**: Sage Young, "Watch Chris Evans Explain Why He Originally Said No to Captain America," Yahoo!, January 14, 2021, yahoo.com/lifestyle/watch-chris-evans-explain-why-222639913.html.

157 **"maybe the thing you're most scared of"**: Matthew Evans, "How Chris Evans Copes With Anxiety and Depression," *Men's Health*, February 4, 2019, menshealth.com/uk/mental-strength/a758320/watch-why-chris-evans-still-gets-anxiety-about-captain-america.

157 **"This is it"**: Mike Ryan, "Chris Evans, 'The Iceman' Star: 'Am I A Good Person? I Think I'm A Good Person,' " *Huffington Post*, September 12, 2012, huffpost.com/entry/chris-evans-the-iceman_n_1875728.

157 **"Just eating all the time"**: "Chris Evans Workout for Captain America," uploaded to YouTube by Brent Manning, July 25, 2011, youtube.com/watch?v=lc7cAAyjBZc.

157 **"Fortunately, that is not my job"**: Author interview with Sarah Halley Finn, 2021.

159 **"I got a phone call"**: Tom Ward, "The 3-Move Workout That Transformed Chris Pratt From Slob to Superhero," *Esquire*, March 24, 2021.

159 **"I was peeing all day long"**: David Katz, "Chris Pratt: Ready to Go Galactic," *Men's Journal*, July/August 2014.

160 **"We realized we couldn't do it"**: Author interview with Michael Schur, 2015.

160 **"I was so insecure"**: Brett Williams, "Get Winter Soldier Arms Like Sebastian Stan With This Workout" Men's Health, December 19, 2019, menshealth.com/fitness/a30260124/sebastian-stan-arm-workout-don-saladino.

160 **"I feel like I got a five-to-seven-year window"**: *I Am Iron Man: The Making of* Iron Man, bonus feature, *Iron Man* (Paramount, 2008), Blu-ray.

161 **"Even if you change the regimen"**: Author interview with Chadwick Boseman, 2017.

161 **"It's probably changed"**: Author interview with Paul Rudd, 2017.

161 **"I will keep those opinions to myself"**: Author interview with anonymous source, 2020.

161 **"At least for the short term"**: Author interview with Dr. Todd Schroeder, 2022.

162 **"Actors are trying to get on camera"**: Alex Abad-Santos, "The open secret to looking like a superhero," *Vox*, November 5, 2021, vox.com/the-goods/22760163/steroids-hgh-hollywood-actors-peds-performance-enhancing-drugs.

162 **"There's long-term health concerns"**: Author interview with Dr. Todd Schroeder, 2022.

Chapter Twelve: THE RUNAWAYS

164 **"A few of the writers"**: Author interview with Christopher Yost, 2022.

165 **"they said 'We really want to make this'"**: Ashley Scott Meyers, "Writer Edward Ricourt Talks About Now You See Me and Breaking Into the Business," *SYS*, podcast, episode 145, October 9, 2016, sellingyourscreenplay.com/podcasts/sys-podcast-episode-145-writer-edward-ricourt-talks-about-now-you-see-me-and-breaking-into-the-business.

165 **"They said how much they liked"**: Author interview with Nicole Perlman, 2019.

166 **"It's important that we don't feel"**: Kyle Buchanan, "Kevin Feige is Ready to Move Beyond the 'Completely White' Casts of Comic Book Movies," *Vulture*, November 1, 2016, vulture.com/2016/10/kevin-feige-doctor-strange-marvel-casting-diversity.html.

166 **"The offices were always temporary"**: Author interview with Christopher Yost, 2022.

167 **"He brought out box after box"**: Author interview with Nicole Perlman, 2019.

168 **"I don't have the talent to write"**: Kelley L. Carter, "The man who put Marvel in the black," *Andscape* (formerly *The Undefeated*), May 17, 2016, andscape.com/features/marvel-nate-moore-black-panther.

170 **"It reached a crescendo"**: Author interview with Drew Pearce, 2020.

170 **"Heard you were still in town"**: Ibid.

171 **"from twenty to twelve"**: Ibid.

173 **"They'll throw some pages"**: Author interview with Christopher Yost, 2019.

173 **"Because I had this massive crush"**: Author interview with Nicole Perlman, 2019.

173 **"We were in a parking lot"**: Author interview with Christopher Yost, 2022.

Chapter Thirteen: EARTH'S MIGHTIEST HEROES

175 **"The essence of filmmaking"**: Author interview with Joss Whedon, 2005.

176 **"rediscovered television"**: *THR* staff, "Shonda Rhimes Reveals How 'Buffy' Helped Her Rediscover TV," *Hollywood Reporter*, October 8, 2014, hollywoodreporter.com/news/general-news/shonda-rhimes-reveals-how -buffy-739109.

176 **"*Buffy The Vampire Slayer* shows the whole world"**: Sarah Dobbs, "10 Ways Buffy The Vampire Slayer Changed the World," *Den of Geek*, March 10, 2017, denofgeek.com/tv/10-ways-buffy-the-vampire-slayer-changed-the-world.

176 **"If there's a bigger influence"**: Author interview with Joss Whedon, 2005.

177 **"Everything I write"**: Alex Pappademas, "The Geek Shall Inherit the Earth," *GQ*, May 2012.

177 **"We pitched him"**: Germain Lussier, "/Film Interview: Kevin Feige, Producer Of 'The Avengers,'" *SlashFilm*, April 26, 2012, slashfilm .com/520762/film-interview-kevin-feige-producer-the-avengers.

178 **"There was a script"**: Pappademas, "The Geek Shall Inherit the Earth."

178 **"All the other directors"**: Author interview with Zak Penn, 2019.

178 **"I started on square one"**: Matt Patches and Ian Failes, "The Battle of New York: An 'Avengers' Oral History" *Thrillist*. April 23, 2018, thrillist .com/entertainment/nation/the-avengers-battle-of-new-york-joss-whedon.

179 **"I'm an old-fashioned storyteller"**: Author interview with Joss Whedon, 2005.

180 **"Look out your window"**: "MARK RUFFALO Gets Hulk Role in The Avengers—By Mistake?! The Graham Norton Show on BBC AMERICA,"

uploaded to YouTube by BBC America, June 10, 2014, youtube.com/watch?v=bYe1-9oLdkI.

180 **"I have my animator"**: Author interview with Marc Chu, 2020.

181 **"Listen, I might not be here tomorrow"**: Adam White "Marvel boss Kevin Feige almost quit over lack of representation, says Mark Ruffalo," *Independent*, February 22, 2020, independent.co.uk/arts-entertainment/films/news/mark-ruffalo-kevin-feige-marvel-quit-representation-ike-Perlmutter-disney-a9350921.html.

181 **"I'm used to having people"**: Dave Itzkoff, "A Film's Superheroes Include the Director," *New York Times*, April 11, 2012.

182 **"Oh, that's easy"**: Ibid.

182 **"I would give him stuff"**: Ibid.

183 **"What's this say here?"**: Author interview with Eric Vespe, 2021.

184 **"It happened to be the worst time"**: Patches and Failes, "Battle of New York."

185 **"is why we all showed up"**: Ibid.

187 **"Don't worry about the universe"**: Author interview with Kevin Feige, 2017.

187 **"It's my favorite thing"**: Author interview with Joss Whedon, 2005.

Chapter Fourteen: HOUSE OF M

192 **"If you were lucky"**: Author interview with James Rothwell, 2020.

192 **"I wanted to do a believable"**: The Artists of Marvel Studios Visual Development with Troy Benjamin, *How to Paint Characters the Marvel Studios Way* (Marvel Worldwide, 2019), 57.

193 **"The fabrication of the first suit"**: Ibid., 58.

193 **"There aren't enough words"**: Author interview with Susan Wexler, 2020.

193 **"He has a way"**: Matt Patches and Ian Failes, "The Battle of New York: An 'Avengers' Oral History," *Thrillist*, April 23, 2018, thrillist.com/entertainment/nation/the-avengers-battle-of-new-york-joss-whedon.

194 **"I was sold when [Feige] spoke to me"**: Artists of Marvel and Benjamin, *How to Paint Characters*, 15.

195 **"The first pass"**: Artists of Marvel and Benjamin, *How to Paint Characters*, 66.

195 **"Joe seemed happiest"**: Author interview with Rich Heinrichs, 2020.

195 **"When Joe wanted to hide"**: Author interview with Andy Nicholson, 2020.

196 **"We formed"**: Author interview with Andy Park, 2020.

196 **"cape graveyard"**: *Thor* press notes, Paramount Pictures, 2011.

SMASH CUT TO—

CHAPTER THIRTY-TWO

It's Not Easy
Being Green

There's a shawarma joint about
two blocks from here.

The Avengers

THE BIGGEST SPECIAL EFFECT ON *THE AVENGERS* WAS
the Hulk: a member of the team who would appear onscreen
only as CGI. During the movie's 2011 shoot, a visual effects
team at Industrial Light and Magic worked with director Joss Whedon to get as much data as possible. Any scene involving the Hulk
was filmed an extra time without any actors so ILM could work with
a "clean plate" that captured all the lighting and spatial data.

A key point: Getting exactly the right shade of green. "The tone was
very important, so that he wasn't comically green," said Marc Chu,
animation supervisor at ILM. To make the Hulk look real, rather
than a cartoon plopped into a scene like MC Skat Kat, required a lot
of tinkering and experimentation. Chu's secret weapon: a guy called
"Green Steve." "He was a Chippendales dancer and we painted him
green," Chu explained. "At the end of every take, we would call out
Green Steve, and he would come out and start flexing and turning
around. We could see how his skin reacted to light."

Green Steve was Long Island native Steve Romm, an

ex-Chippendales dancer and part-time bouncer who stood 6'5" and weighed 270 well-defined pounds. Romm, who had auditioned to be an extra in *The Avengers*, initially landed a role as a soldier. But the casting department soon realized he could fill a specific need and asked him, "How would you feel about being painted green?"

Romm was game—and he even had a family connection to the niche job of being painted green for money. He said that his grandfather had worked at a sheet-metal factory with Lou Ferrigno before the bodybuilder was hired to play the Hulk in *The Incredible Hulk* (the TV series that aired on CBS from 1977 to 1982).

Every morning he was needed, it took hours to paint Romm green—and then almost as much time to wash every fleck of green off his body at the end of the day. Because of the secrecy surrounding the movie, Romm wasn't allowed to head home with even a green particle left on his skin.

"Green Steve was awesome," Chu said. "One, it's just crazy that he was a Chippendales dancer. Two, he was so into it. He had the greatest attitude. We would film him doing roughly what we needed the Hulk doing. If the Hulk was running through the belly of the Helicarrier, chasing Black Widow and screaming, we'd say, 'Green Steve, can you come through this way and stand here? Just let out some crazy scream. We can see how that works.' He would just give it his all, which was awesome. Green Steve was replaced on the second *Avengers* movie by some other guy, who we still called Green Steve, for some reason."

Though visual-effects techniques for developing photorealistic green skin for the Hulk have evolved, the tradition of Green Steve lives on. For *She-Hulk: Attorney at Law* on Disney Plus, six-foot-five actress Malia Arrayah donned the She-Hulk wardrobe and green face paint to provide reference for replacing five-foot-four Tatiana Maslany with her digital counterpart. "I had a muscle suit to wear, but I knew that the character of the She-Hulk would be somebody that's very physically strong," Arrayah said. "I had to walk confidently. For somebody like me, just in my personal life, some part of my story felt more like a metaphor. I had to learn how to love myself and work on self-acceptance and self-esteem for a long time."

196 **"We're designing"**: Author interview with Andy Park, 2020.

197 **"When working on the keyframe illustration"**: Giovanni Menicocci, "Interview with Rodney Fuentebella, concept artist for 'Avengers: Infinity War,'" *Dailybloid*, April 26, 2019, dailybloid.com/interview/interview-with-rodney-fuentebella--concept-artist-for-'avengers--infinity-war'.

198 **"Reinforcing corporate culture"**: Mike Winder, "Earth's Mightiest Artists," *Dot Magazine*, August 22, 2019, artcenter.edu/connect/dot-magazine/articles/earths-mightiest-artists.html.

199 **"We start by making a Saturday-morning-cartoon"**: Author interview with James Rothwell, 2020.

199 **"It was going to take off in the air"**: Ibid.

200 **"I've seen movies where"**: Matt Patches and Ian Failes, "The Battle of New York: An 'Avengers' Oral History," *Thrillist*, April 23, 2018, thrillist.com/entertainment/nation/the-avengers-battle-of-new-york-joss-whedon.

200 **"They also told me"**: "Was offered 'Black Widow' film by Marvel Studios, says Lucrecia Martel," *Pioneer*, October 30, 2018, dailypioneer.com/2018/entertainment/was-offered--black-widow--film-by-marvel-studios--says-lucrecia-martel.html.

200 **"My God, for a year and a half, three times a week"**: Eric Kohn, " 'Eternals': Chloé Zhao Disputes Claim That Marvel Directors Don't Have a Say in Action Scenes," *IndieWire*, October 26, 2021, indiewire.com/2021/10/eternals-chloe-zhao-marvel-directors-action-scenes-1234674422.

200 **"although some Marvel"**: James Gunn (@JamesGunn), Twitter, February 5, 2021. NB that he spelled the term "previs"; we've rendered it as "pre-viz" to avoid confusion.

200 **"Our creative process"**: Dan Sarto, "Victoria Alonso Talks VFX Production, Marvel and 'The Avengers,'" Animation World Network, April 9, 2012, awn.com/vfxworld/victoria-alonso-talks-vfx-production-marvel-and-avengers.

201 **"We're very lucky"**: Winder, "Earth's Mightiest Artists."

Chapter Fifteen: THE FORBIDDEN CITY

204 **"We will build your brand"**: Chris Fenton, *Feeding the Dragon: Inside the Trillion Dollar Dilemma Facing Hollywood, the NBA, & American Business* (Post Hill, 2020), 87.

204 **"In theory, *Iron Man 3*"**: Rick Marshall, " 'Iron Man 3' Will Be A Sequel To 'Thor,' 'Captain America' And 'The Avengers,' Says Jon Favreau," MTV, December 6, 2010, mtv.com/news/sb9s0y/iron-man-3-jon-favreau-avengers.

205 **"As far as I'm concerned"**: Dave Itzkoff. "A Film's Superheroes Include the Director," *New York Times*, April 11, 2012.

205 **"Marvel was very gracious"**: Adam Chitwood, "Shane Black on How Trailers Influence His Storytelling, 'Iron Man 3' and 'The Predator,'" *Collider*, October 26, 2016, collider.com/shane-black-interview-iron-man-3 -predator.

205 **"I don't know if"**: Author interview with Drew Pearce, 2020.

206 **"And my first instinct"**: Ibid.

206 **"Well, obviously"**: Ibid.

206 **"I'm a scrub"**: Ibid.

206 **"I didn't know Drew"**: "Commentary," *Iron Man 3* (Disney/Buena Vista, 2013), single-disc Blu-ray.

207 **"The cookie was for his dog"**: Author interview with Drew Pearce, 2020.

208 **"You've got to do the Mandarin"**: Larry Carroll, " 'Iron Man 2' Director Jon Favreau Wants The Mandarin For Third Movie," MTV, May 5, 2010, www.mtv.com/news/sc3uec/iron-man-2-director-jon-favreau-wants-the -mandarin-for-third-movie.

209 **"The Mandarin scares the shit"**: Fenton, *Feeding the Dragon*, 98.

209 **"I pitched the twist"**: Author interview with Drew Pearce, 2020.

209 **"We had a female character"**: Mike Ryan, "Shane Black On 'The Nice Guys,' Mel Gibson, And Why A Female 'Iron Man 3' Villain's Gender Changed," *Uproxx*, May 16, 2016.

209 **"She wasn't entirely the villain"**: Jessica Derschowitz, "Rebecca Hall: Iron Man 3 role was reduced," *Entertainment Weekly*, September 14, 2016.

210 **"Your Chinese-kid idea is not happening" et seq.**: Fenton, *Feeding the Dragon*, 1262.

211 **"We're setting aspects"**: Christina Radish, "Comic-Con: Robert Downey Jr., Don Cheadle, Shane Black and Kevin Feige Talk IRON MAN 3, How THE AVENGERS Impacts the Film, Iron Patriot and More," *Collider*, July 15, 2012, collider.com/robert-downey-jr-shane-black-iron-man-3-interview.

211 **"We'll figure out"**: Fenton, *Feeding the Dragon*, 146.

211 **"Robert reached out"**: Author interview with Ty Simpkins, 2020.

211 **"He had to do a stunt"**: "Guy Pearce Breaks Down His Most Iconic Characters" uploaded to YouTube by *GQ*, March 19, 2020, youtube.com/ watch?v=2tKQSp2sJ-g.

212 **"The Chinese version"**: Peter Ford, "Chinese roll their eyes at local footage added to 'Iron Man 3,' " *Christian Science Monitor*, May 10, 2013, csmonitor .com/World/Asia-Pacific/2013/0510/Chinese-roll-their-eyes-at-local -footage-added-to-Iron-Man-3.

212 **"People love Marvel precisely"**: Rebecca Davis, "How the Avengers Became Such a Marvel in China," *Variety*, April 25, 2019, variety.com/2019/film/ news/avengers-endgame-marvel-universe-china-box-office-1203197686.

213 **"third world"**: Nancy Tartaglione, " 'Shang-Chi' China Release Unlikely in Wake of Unearthed Comments By Star Simu Liu; 'Eternals' Hopes In Question," *Deadline*, September 10, 2021, deadline.com/2021/09/ shang-chi-china-release-simu-liu-marvel-1234830474.

213 **"a place where there are lies everywhere"**: Scott Macaulay, "25 New

Faces of Independent Film: Chloe Zhao," *Filmmaker*, July 21, 2013. One of the few Marvel movies to get specific feedback from Chinese censors in this era was *Spider-Man: No Way Home* (released in 2021, when Spider-Man had finally become a well-established character in the MCU). The censors wanted the scenes set at the Statue of Liberty to be relocated, but since the entire climactic battle took place there, Marvel declined.

Chapter Sixteen: REMOTE CONTROL

217 **"Jeepers, I'm not"**: Joss Whedon, comment on "The Avengers cast versus Marvel Studios," *Whedonesque*, May 8, 2013, whedonesque.com/comments/30943.

217 **"They had said"**: Adam B. Vary, "Joss Whedon's Astonishing, Spine-Tingling, Soul-Crushing Marvel Adventure!," *BuzzFeed News*, April 20, 2015, buzzfeednews.com/article/adambvary/joss-whedon-spine-tingling-soul-crushing-marvel-adventure.

218 **"[Marvel Studios] didn't actually want"**: Ibid.

219 **"There was a period"**: Ibid.

221 **"Marvel is a known and loved brand"**: David Lieberman and Nellie Andreeva, "Netflix Picks Up Four Marvel Live-Action Series & A Mini Featuring Daredevil, Jessica Jones, Iron Fist, Luke Cage For 2015 Launch." *Deadline*, November 7, 2013.

221 **"The thing about Matt Murdock"**: Leigh Singer, "Drew Goddard on How He Would've Made the Sinister Six Movie and Comparisons to Suicide Squad," IGN, September 29, 2015, ign.com/articles/2015/09/29/drew-goddard-on-how-he-wouldve-made-the-sinister-six-movie-and-comparisons-to-suicide-squad.

222 **"Been in meetings with Marvel"**: Drew Goddard, email to Amy Pascal, March 13, 2014.

222 **"I tried to help"**: Amy Pascal, email to Doug Belgrad, April 18, 2014. Email lightly edited for spelling and readability.

223 **"We don't ever want"**: Tim Baysinger, "Why 'Agents of S.H.I.E.L.D.' Will Avoid Any 'Avengers: Endgame' Tie-Ins," *The Wrap*, May 3, 2019, thewrap.com/agents-of-shield-season-6-avengers-endgame-marvel.

223 **"The future's a long time"**: Germain Lussier, "Kevin Feige Thinks That Eventually, Marvel TV and Movies Will Cross Over," *Gizmodo*, May 5, 2017, gizmodo.com/kevin-feige-thinks-that-eventually-marvel-tv-and-movie-1794974004.

224 **"I could not have predicted"**: Author interview with Cheo Hodari Coker, 2016.

224 **"It seemed like these were not"**: Akhil Arora, " 'Danny Rand Is No White Saviour,' Says Marvel's Iron Fist Showrunner," Gadgets 360, December 7, 2016, gadgets360.com/tv/features/danny-rand-is-no-white-saviour-says-marvels-iron-fist-showrunner-1634910.

225 **"I was learning the fight scenes"**: Adam Sarkey, "Marvel Iron Fist's Finn Jones on 'white saviour' controversy and teaming up with Luke Cage in The Defenders," *Metro*, March 16, 2017, metro.co.uk/2017/03/16/marvel-iron-fists-finn-jones-on-white-saviour-controversy-and-teaming-up-with-luke-cage-in-the-defenders-6513597.

225 **"You know"**: "Emmy Nominated Stunt Coordinator—Brett Chan" *JAM-Cast*, episode 129, uploaded to YouTube by JoiningAllMovement, July 23, 2021, youtube.com/watch?v=aBIIlckINw8.

225 **"One of the most troubling"**: Eric Deggans, "Netflix's 'Iron Fist' Stumbles in Depiction of Asian Culture," March 17, 2017, npr.org/2017/03/17/520576925/netflixs-iron-fist-stumbles-in-depiction-of-asian-culture.

226 **"It was crazy to talk"**: Shirley Li, "*Marvel's The Defenders*: Sigourney Weaver says her character is an 'adversary,' not a 'villain,'" *Entertainment Weekly*, July 14, 2017, ew.com/tv/2017/07/14/marvel-the-defenders-sigourney-weaver-alexandra-details.

227 **"That has everything"**: Rich Johnston, "'If Film Rights Were Owned By Marvel, The X-Men Would Probably Still Be The Paramount Book In The Canon'—Chris Claremont Talks Shop At NYCC," Bleeding Cool, November 4, 2016, bleedingcool.com/comics/film-rights-owned-marvel-x-men-probably-still-paramount-book-canon-chris-claremont-talks-shop-nycc.

228 **"At least I got"**: Author interview with anonymous source, 2017.

228 **"Different universes, different worlds"**: Frank Palmer, "Exclusive: Anthony Mackie Says Marvel TV and Movie Crossover Wouldn't Work At All," *ScreenGeek*, March 19, 2017, screengeek.net/2017/03/19/anthony-mackie-says-marvel-tv-movie-crossover-wouldnt-work.

Chapter Seventeen: ON YOUR LEFT

229 **"We try to be honest"**: Author interview with Stephen McFeely, 2019.

230 **"There's a certain comfort level"**: Author interview with Jon Favreau, 2017.

230 **"*Three Days of Captain America*"**: Scott Huver, "THE '70S CONSPIRACY THRILLER THAT INFLUENCED 'WINTER SOLDIER,'" Fandango, April 3, 2014, fandango.com/movie-news/the-70s-conspiracy-thriller-that-influenced-winter-soldier-747688.

231 **"I think we're ready"**: James Hunt, "Christopher Markus interview: writing Captain America 2 and 3," *Den of Geek*, August 13, 2014, denofgeek.com/movies/christopher-markus-interview-writing-captain-america-2-and-3.

231 **"because, honestly"**: Ibid.

231 **"We have to introduce" et seq.**: Kelley L. Carter, "The man who put Marvel in the black," *Andscape* (formerly *The Undefeated*), May 17, 2016, andscape.com/features/marvel-nate-moore-black-panther.

232 **"The guy with the wings?"**: Ryan Faughnder, "How 'Wakanda Forever' producer Nate Moore pushed for Black heroes in the MCU," *Los Angeles Times*, November 13, 2022.

232 **"Do people like the Falcon?"**: Carter, "The man who put Marvel in the black," *Andscape,* May 17, 2016.

232 **"*People love the Falcon*"**: Ibid.

232 **"He's a comic book fan"**: Ryan Faughnder, "How 'Wakanda Forever' producer Nate Moore pushed for Black heroes in the MCU," *Los Angeles Times,* November 11, 2022, latimes.com/entertainment-arts/business/story/2022-11-11/marvel-black-panther-nate-moore-wakanda-forever-disney-boseman.

232 **"When I heard I got the role"**: Jessica Herndon, " 'Captain America' role 'epic' for Anthony Mackie," *Statesman Journal,* April 2, 2014.

232 **"vibe guy"**: Claude Brodesser-Akner, "*Community* Directors Are in Running to Helm the *Captain America* Sequel," *Vulture,* March 30, 2012, vulture.com/2012/03/captain-america-sequel-director-community-russo-brothers.html.

233 **"We grew up in a big Italian family"**: Author interview with Anthony Russo, 2017.

234 **"We understand ensemble storytelling"**: Ibid.

234 **"Kevin is a big comedy lover"**: Author interview with Paul Rudd, 2017.

235 **"You've got to be a bit of a politician"**: Author interview with Dan Harmon, 2021.

235 **"But what Brubaker did"**: Simon Brew, "Joe & Anthony Russo interview: Captain America, Marvel," *Den of Geek,* March 26, 2014, denofgeek.com/comics/joe-anthony-russo-interview-captain-america-marvel.

236 **"It's hard to make a political film"**: Frank Lovece, "Soldier showdown: Joe and Anthony Russo take the helm of 'Captain America' franchise," *Film Journal International,* March 25, 2014, filmjournal.com/filmjournal/content_display/news-and-features/features/movies/e3ie3493397f4a48111 966630c800986a35.

237 **"The Russos, what they did"**: Kevin P. Sullivan, "Anthony Mackie On 'Captain America' Sequel And The Perils Of Slow-Mo Skydiving," MTV, August 13, 2013, mtv.com/news/9g2h65/anthony-mackie-captain-america-winter-soldier-skydiving.

237 **"We still haven't moved Nick Fury"**: Rick Marshall, "Exclusive: Sam Jackson Says Nick Fury Won't See Action In 'Iron Man 2,' " MTV, June 30, 2009, mtv.com/news/5l34fw/exclusive-sam-jackson-says-nick-fury-wont-see-action-in-iron-man-2.

238 **"moment of tension"**: "Commentary," *Captain America: The Winter Soldier* (Disney/Buena Vista, 2014), single-disc Blu-ray.

238 **"Essentially, he's a man"**: Peter Sciretta, "On Set Interview: Directors Joe And Anthony Russo Talk 'Captain America: The Winter Soldier,' " *SlashFilm,* March 6, 2014, www.slashfilm.com/530703/interview-joe-and-anthony-russo-captain-america.

239 **"They would take one or two"**: Author interview with Monty Granito, 2020.

239 **"He'd say"**: Author interview with Anthony Russo, 2017.

239   **"Joe and Anthony had the stamina"**: Tara Bennett and Paul Terry, *The Story of Marvel Studios: The Making of the Marvel Cinematic Universe* (Abrams, 2021), vol. 2, 10.

239   **"We talked about golf"**: Michael Lee, "Samuel L. Jackson And Sebastian Stan Talk 'Captain America: The Winter Soldier,' Working With Robert Redford, And More," *MovieViral*, March 27, 2014, movieviral.com/2014/03/27/samuel-l-jackson-and-sebastian-stan-talk-captain-america-the-winter-soldier-working-with-robert-redford-and-more.

240   **"Joe and Anthony, they were very clear"**: Jim Slotek, "Captain America: The Winter Soldier' a 'trust no one' epic," *Toronto Sun*, March 12, 2014.

240   **"If you are a comic book geek"**: Dave Trumbore, "Directors Anthony and Joe Russo Talk CAPTAIN AMERICA: THE WINTER SOLDIER, Landing the Job, Core Relationships, Easter Eggs, and the Talented Cast," *Collider*, March 6, 2014, collider.com/anthony-russo-joe-russo-captain-america-the-winter-soldier-interview.

Chapter Eighteen: WE ARE GROOT

241   **"*Guardians of the Galaxy* opened up"**: Author interview with Mark Ruffalo, 2017.

241   **"*Galaxy* in some ways"**: Bruce Kirkland, "Robert Downey Jr.: 'Guardians of the Galaxy' the best Marvel movie yet," *Toronto Sun*, August 27, 2014.

241   **"the best example of the audience"**: Author interview with Kevin Feige, 2017.

242   **"It seems so simple now"**: Author interview with an anonymous source, 2022.

242   **"For years, I told my parents"**: Author interview with Nicole Perlman, 2019.

242   **"No, no. Got to keep Rocket"**: Ibid.

242   **"They had these plywood boards"**: Ibid.

243   **"I always knew"**: Adam B. Vary, "Meet The Woman Who Made History With Marvel's 'Guardians Of The Galaxy,'" BuzzFeed, July 30, 2014, buzzfeed.com/adambvary/guardians-of-the-galaxy-nicole-perlman.

243   **"We would use tissue paper"**: Jarrett Medlin, "A Conversation with Director James Gunn," *St. Louis*, May 26, 2011. (The Gunns also have one sister, Beth, who has steered clear of moviemaking.)

244   **"We weren't the best at being married"**: Ibid.

244   **"I knew he liked"**: Author interview with James Gunn, 2017.

244   **"there were the basic Marvel comic books"**: Ibid.

245   **"I wrote him an email"**: Eric Eisenberg, "Joss Whedon's Behind The Scenes Role On Guardians Of The Galaxy Revealed," CinemaBlend, July 8, 2014, cinemablend.com/new/Joss-Whedon-Behind-Scenes-Role-Guardians-Galaxy-Revealed-43790.html.

245   **"You're fucking late"**: Ibid.

245   **"I don't think there's a huge difference"**: Medlin, "James Gunn."

245 **"definitely got the ball rolling"**: Vary, "Meet the Woman."

245 **"In Nicole's script"**: Charles Madison, "James Gunn on Guardians of the Galaxy 2—the promise of Nebula, Yondu and Peter Quill's father," *Film Divider*, July 26, 2014, filmdivider.com/4171/james-gunn-on-guardians-of-the-galaxy-2-promising-nebula-yondu-and-peter-quills-father.

245 **"I credit everybody on that movie"**: Author interview with Nicole Perlman, 2019.

245 **"Nicole had to knife-fight"**: Author interview with Zack Stentz, 2019.

246 **"I started the process"**: Alex Suskind, "Director James Gunn on How He Chose the Music in *Guardians of the Galaxy*," *Vulture*, August 4, 2014, vulture.com/2014/08/how-guardians-of-the-galaxy-music-soundtrack-was-chosen.html.

247 **"Joss sent me a memo"**: Tara Bennett and Paul Terry, *The Story of Marvel Studios: The Making of the Marvel Cinematic Universe* (Abrams, 2021), vol. 1, 172.

247 **"Joss was happy"**: Eisenberg, "Joss Whedon's Behind The Scenes Role."

247 **"I didn't get Drax"**: Steve Weintraub, "Dave Bautista Talks Fight Scenes and Finding The Humor in Drax on the Set of GUARDIANS OF THE GALAXY," *Collider*, July 8, 2014, collider.com/guardians-of-the-galaxy-interview-dave-bautista.

247 **"I didn't want to be part"**: Zack Sharf, "Amanda Seyfried Recalls Turning Down 'Guardians of the Galaxy' Over Fears It Was Box Office Bomb," *IndieWire*, December 8, 2020, indiewire.com/2020/12/amanda-seyfried-rejected-guardians-of-the-galaxy-box-office-bomb-1234603056.

248 **"I was not that excited"**: Christie Cronan, "Zoe Saldana Guardians Interview: Gamora Is More Than Green," raisingwhasians.com, July 31, 2014, raisingwhasians.com/zoe-saldana-guardians-interview-gamora-green-guardiansofthegalaxyevent.

248 **"the people who are making"**: Jack de Aguilar, "Karen Gillan Clears Up The Star Wars Wig Confusion," Contactmusic, July 25, 2014, contactmusic.com/karen-gillan/news/karen-gillen-shaved-head-star-wars-episode-vii-wig_4301551. Gillan initially spoke imprecisely about the wig, telling Christina Radish of *Collider* on April 10, 2014, "They made my hair into the most incredible well-made wig and they gave it to the *Star Wars* people. It's just so funny to think that my hair is made into a wig, next to all these *Star Wars* monster heads in a warehouse." That quote provoked rumors that the wig would make an appearance—without the actress—in *Star Wars Episode VII*, but Gillan later clarified, "It's not in *Star Wars*; it's in my bedroom."

248 **"It's a complete"**: Daniel Fienberg, "Interview: Lee Pace on 'Halt and Catch Fire' and 'Guardians of the Galaxy,'" HitFix.com, May 30, 2014, hitfix.com/the-fien-print/interview-lee-pace-on-halt-and-catch-fire-and-guardians-of-the-galaxy.

249 **"I would keep a pile"**: James Gunn [@jamesgunn], Instagram post, September 11, 2014, instagram.com/p/s0E2xQIzem/?hl=en.

249 **"There were so many things"**: Author interview with Nicole Perlman, 2019.

249 **"Baby Groot dancing"**: Kevin Polowy, "Exclusive: Here's That Clip of Dancing Baby Groot in All Its Galactic Glory," Yahoo!, August 14, 2014, yahoo.com/entertainment/dancing-baby-groot-clip-guardians-of-the-galaxy-94738291414.html.

250 **"We wanted to focus"**: Russ Fischer, "Kevin Feige Says Thanos Is To the Marvel Universe As The Emperor Is To Star Wars," *SlashFilm*, August 4, 2014, slashfilm.com/532782/thanos-like-emperor-palpatine.

250 **"What do you think"**: *Late Night with Seth Myers*, NBC, May 17, 2018.

251 **"Look, you're gonna feel"**: Ibid.

251 **"I will never forget it"**: Bennett and Terry, *Story of Marvel Studios*, vol. 1, 239.

251 **"The *Iron Man*s and the *Thors*"**: Kirkland, "Robert Downey Jr.."

252 **"We have a really great relationship"**: James Gunn, Facebook, March 7, 2015, facebook.com/jgunn/posts/10152539339056157.

Chapter Nineteen: WHERE'S NATASHA?

254 **"I didn't feel like I owned"**: Author interview with Scarlett Johansson, 2017.

254 **"Joss Whedon and I"**: Zorianna Kit, "A Minute With: Scarlett Johansson and the Black Widow," Reuters, May 2, 2012, reuters.com/article/uk-scarlettjohansson/a-minute-with-scarlett-johansson-and-the-black-widow-idUKBRE84111M20120502.

254 **"There's no definitive plans"**: Edward Davis, "Marvel Head Kevin Feige Says 'Hawkeye' & 'Black Widow' Could Be Their Own Solo Films," *IndieWire*, May 2, 2011, indiewire.com/2011/05/marvel-head-kevin-feige-says-hawkeye-black-widow-could-be-their-own-solo-films-118878.

254 **"I personally think"**: Alexis L. Loinaz, "*Iron Man 3*'s Black Widow Blackout: Scarlett Johansson Skipping Out on Flick?," E! News, April 26, 2012, eonline.com/news/311686/iron-man-3-s-black-widow-blackout-scarlett-johansson-skipping-out-on-flick.

254 **"Toymakers will tell you"**: Marlow Stern, "'Avengers: Age of Ultron's' Black Widow Disgrace," *Daily Beast*, May 5, 2015, thedailybeast.com/avengers-age-of-ultrons-black-widow-disgrace.

255 **"Unfortunately, as I was coming up"**: Kickpuncher, "What Could've Been: A Black Widow Solo Film," FemPop, November 14, 2011, fempop.com/2011/11/14/what-couldve-been-a-black-widow-solo-film.

255 **"When we were doing"**: Donna Freydkin, "Scarlett Johansson Says Goodbye to 'Black Widow,'" *Fatherly*, July 8, 2021, fatherly.com/play/scarlett-johansson-black-widow-interview.

255 **"Power Glow Storm"**: "Toy Biz X-Men 1991 Toy Line Launch Retrospec-

tive," *Toysplosion*, uploaded to YouTube by Pixel Dan, September 3, 2018, https://www.youtube.com/watch?v=Y6Q1QnPbl4c.

256 **"Very bad idea"**: Ike Perlmutter, email to Michael Lynton, August 7, 2014.

256 **"I very much believe"**: Scott Huver, "Feige Talks Taking a Risk On "Guardians," Targeting the Right Female Superhero Lead," CBR.com, August 1, 2014, cbr.com/feige-talks-taking-a-risk-on-guardians-targeting-the-right-female-superhero-lead.

257 **"We rely on advice"**: Isha Aran, "Gamora Not Included on *Guardians of the Galaxy* Tee Since It's for Boys," *Jezebel*, August 18, 2014, jezebel.com/gamora-not-included-on-guardians-of-the-galaxy-tee-sinc-1623411263.

257 **"Remember when *The Avengers*"**: Amy Ratcliffe, "A Sad Lack of Gamora," *Geek with Curves*, August 4, 2014, geekwithcurves.com/2014/08/a-sad-lack-of-gamora.html.

257 **"@Marvel we need more"**: Mark Ruffalo [@MarkRuffalo], Twitter, April 28, 2015, MarkRuffalo/status/593222325325209601.

258 **"Little girls need better messages"**: Patricia V. Davis, "Add Black Widow to the AVENGERS action figure pack," change.org, April 2015, change.org/p/hasbro-add-more-female-superhero-merc-add-black-widow-to-the-avengers-action-figure-pack.

258 **"It looked exactly like her face"**: Author interview with Heidi Moneymaker, 2020.

258 **"She's a slut"**: Justin Harp, "Avengers 2 stars Chris Evans and Jeremy Renner sorry for Black Widow "slut" joke," *Digital Spy*, April 23, 2015, digitalspy.com/movies/a643756/avengers-2-stars-chris-evans-and-jeremy-renner-sorry-for-black-widow-slut-joke.

258 **"She's a whore"**: Ibid.

258 **"in a very juvenile"**: Ibid.

259 **"*Age of Ultron* sees Black Widow"**: Jen Yamato, "The Avengers' Black Widow Problem: How Marvel Slut-Shamed Their Most Badass Superheroine," *Daily Beast*, April 28, 2015, thedailybeast.com/the-avengers-black-widow-problem-how-marvel-slut-shamed-their-most-badass-superheroine.

259 **"You know, I'm happy"**: Anthony Breznican, "Captain America: Civil War star Scarlett Johansson on the scrutiny of Black Widow," *Entertainment Weekly*, December 3, 2015, ew.com/article/2015/12/03/captain-america-civil-war-black-widow.

260 **"The board put"**: Author interview with John Turitzin, 2020.

260 **"I remember some conversations"**: Author interview with David Maisel, 2020.

Chapter Twenty: MARVEL STUDIOS VS. THE COMMITTEE

262 **"They were cheap"**: Author interview with James Gunn, 2017.

263 **"shithole-adjacent"**: Author interview with anonymous source, 2017.

263 **"unassuming and a bit disheveled"**: Chris Fenton, *Feeding the Dragon: Inside the Trillion Dollar Dilemma Facing Hollywood, the NBA, & American Business*, (Post Hill, 2020), 84.

263 **"You like our purple pens?"**: Author interview with Jodi Hildebrand, 2022.

263 **"Why do you need a new pencil?"**: Kim Masters, "How Marvel Became the Envy (and Scourge) of Hollywood," *Hollywood Reporter*, July 23, 2014.

263 **"He used to do this thing"**: Matthew Garrahan, "Man in the News: Ike Perlmutter" *Financial Times*, September 4, 2009.

264 **"The first two films"**: Author interview with anonymous source, 2020.

264 **surveillance cameras**: Brooks Barnes, "Disney Lays Off Ike Perlmutter, Chairman of Marvel Entertainment," *New York Times*, March 29, 2023.

265 **"That wasn't the whole Creative Committee"**: Author interview with anonymous source, 2019.

266 **"We were doing heroes"**: Author interview with Craig Kyle, 2020.

266 **"In our original film"**: Ibid.

266 **"Word got out"**: Marc Maron, "Patty Jenkins," *WTF with Marc Maron*, podcast, episode 1187, December 28, 2020.

266 **"I did not believe"**: Ibid.

267 **"Kevin is an all-powerful force"**: Author interview with Craig Kyle, 2020.

268 **"Every problem I had"**: Author interview with James Gunn, 2017.

269 **"Kevin always had to pick"**: Author interview with Craig Kyle, 2020.

270 **"I called Ike"**: Robert Iger, *The Ride of a Lifetime: Lessons Learned from 15 Years as CEO of the Walt Disney Company* (Random House, 2019), 164.

270 **"We were flying high"**: Author interview with anonymous source, 2022.

271 **"Absolutely nobody cared"**: Brent Andrew, comment on "Comic-Con 2006—Kevin Feige teases The Avengers," uploaded to YouTube by Danniel Roberts, October 2021, youtube.com/watch?v=x-iw7FN0t3E.

271 **"He'll still have"**: Author interview with Chris Hemsworth, 2017.

271 **"He gets why"**: Author interview with anonymous source, 2022.

271 **"Ten films, over seven billion dollars"**: "FULL Marvel Phase 3 announcement with clips, Robert Downey Jr, Chris Evans," uploaded to YouTube by Inside the Magic, October 29, 2014, youtube.com/watch?v=L2VoJuVfbjI.

273 **"The way we reveal Scarlet Witch"**: Devin Faraci, "Joss Whedon Shot FX Plates For Captain Marvel In AGE OF ULTRON," Birth.Movies.Death., April 14, 2015, birthmoviesdeath.com/2015/04/14/joss-whedon-shot-fx-plates-for-captain-marvel-in-age-of-ultron.

273 **"What I said was"**: Kyle Buchanan, "How *Avengers: Age of Ultron* Nearly Killed Joss Whedon," *Vulture*, April 13, 2015, vulture.com/2015/04/how-age-of-ultron-nearly-broke-joss-whedon.html.

273 **"The dreams were not"**: Chris Hewitt, James Dyer, and Helen O'Hara, "Avengers: Age of Ultron Spoiler Special," *Empire Film Podcast*, May 4, 2015.

274 **"They pointed a gun"**: Ibid.

274 **"Kevin says"**: Author interview with Craig Kyle, 2020.

274 **"I have been to the other side"**: Adam B. Vary "Joss Whedon's Astonishing, Spine-Tingling, Soul-Crushing Marvel Adventure!," *BuzzFeed News*, April 20, 2015, buzzfeednews.com/article/adambvary/joss-whedon-spine-tingling -soul-crushing-marvel-adventure.

275 **"With so much at stake"**: Buchanan, "How *Avengers: Age of Ultron* Nearly Killed Joss Whedon."

275 **"We were discussing"**: Author interview with Craig Kyle, 2020.

275 **"Kevin is one of the most"**: Iger, *Ride of a Lifetime,* 164. Brooks Barnes, however, claimed (in the *New York Times* article "Disney Lays Off Ike Perlmutter, Chairman of Marvel Entertainment," on March 29, 2023) the breaking point was the budget of the *Doctor Strange* movie, which was also in the planning stages at that time.

276 **"I thought that was a mistake"**: *Squawk on the Street,* CNBC, February 9, 2023, cnbc.com/2023/02/09/cnbc-exclusive-cnbc-transcript-disney-ceo-bob-iger-speaks-with-cnbcs-david-faber-on-squawk-on-the-street-today. html. Perlmutter was advocating for activist investor Nelson Peltz to get a seat on the Disney board. Peltz, who (like Perlmutter) often focused on making companies more profitable by cutting costs, wanted Disney to overhaul its streaming business, focus on profits over growth, reinstate its dividend, and make a clear plan for who Iger's successor would be. Iger kept Peltz off the board but announced a plan to revamp Disney that addressed all his issues and cut roughly seven thousand jobs. Asked by *Squawk on the Street* host David Faber if Perlmutter had supported Peltz because he resented having Marvel Studios removed from his control, Iger said, "What the link is between that and Nelson, his relationship, I think that's something that you can speculate about. I won't."

276 **"It was such a long time"**: Author interview with Craig Kyle, 2020.

276 **"The minute the Creative Committee"**: Author interview with anonymous source, 2019.

276 **"Holy hell, ding dong"**: Author interview with Craig Kyle, 2020.

277 **"[Kevin's] a rock"**: Ibid.

Chapter Twenty-One: WRIGHT MAN, WRONG TIME

279 **"I said that I always"**: Edward Douglas, "Exclusive: Edgar Wright Talks Ant-Man," SuperHeroHype.com, July 25, 2006, superherohype.com/ features/91587-exclusive-edgar-wright-talks-ant-man.

279 **"Weirdly enough"**: Ibid.

280 **"four at-bats"**: Author interview with David Maisel, 2020.

280 **"It's not like"**: Douglas, "Edgar Wright."

281 **"If you listen"**: Matt Fowler, "Watch Kevin Feige's Very First Tease in 2006 Revealing His Marvel Avengers Plan and the MCU," IGN, April 12,

2020, ign.com/articles/watch-the-first-ever-tease-of-the-avengers-and-the-marvel-cinematic-universe.

282 **"That changed everything"**: Mike Fleming Jr., "Comic-Con Q&A With Edgar Wright: How Working Title Partner Eric Fellner's Health Scare Put 'The World's End' Before Marvel's 'Ant-Man,'" *Deadline*, July 25, 2013, deadline.com/2013/07/comic-con-q-how-working-title-partner-eric-fellners-health-scare-put-the-worlds-end-before-marvels-ant-man-548997.

283 **"To Marvel's credit"**: Ibid.

283 **"the Terrence Malick approach"**: Roth Cornet, "Edgar Wright: Comic-Con Test Footage is a Good Indication of Ant-Man's Look," IGN, November 22, 2013, ign.com/articles/2013/11/22/edgar-wright-comic-con-test-footage-is-a-good-indication-of-ant-mans-look.

283 **"It is pretty standalone"**: Angie Han, "Edgar Wright Says 'Ant-Man' Is More Of A 'Standalone' Than Connected Marvel Film," *SlashFilm*, August 22, 2013, slashfilm.com/527726/edgar-wright-says-ant-man-is-more-of-a-standalone-than-connected-marvel-film.

284 **"Filmmakers we've worked with"**: Author interview with Kevin Feige, 2017.

285 **"I wish it wasn't as late"**: Helen O'Hara, "Kevin Feige On Ant-Man And Doctor Strange," *Empire*, July 18, 2014, empireonline.com/movies/news/kevin-feige-ant-man-doctor-strange.

285 **"I thought the script"**: Adam B. Vary, "Joss Whedon's Astonishing, Spine-Tingling, Soul-Crushing Marvel Adventure!," *BuzzFeed News*, April 20, 2015, buzzfeednews.com/article/adambvary/joss-whedon-spine-tingling-soul-crushing-marvel-adventure.

286 **"I wanted to make"**: Kristopher Tapley, "Playback: Edgar Wright on 'Baby Driver,' Music and Walking Away From 'Ant-Man,'" *Variety*, June 22, 2017.

286 **"[Rudd] called me"**: Adam Chitwood, "Adam McKay Talks Rewriting ANT-MAN with Paul Rudd; Reveals They Added 'a Giant Action Sequence,' Made the Film Bigger and 'a Little More Aggressive,'" *Collider*, October 17, 2014, collider.com/ant-man-script-changes-adam-mckay-paul-rudd.

287 **"It was like six to eight"**: Ibid.

287 **"I think everyone was"**: Author interview with Evangeline Lilly, 2017.

287 **"The idea, the trajectory"**: Clark Collis, "Edgar Wright and Joe Cornish receive 'Ant-Man' writing and 'story by' credits," *Entertainment Weekly*, April 24, 2015.

288 **"going to a music convention"**: Author interview with Paul Rudd, 2017.

288 **"I got a salty DM"**: Author interview with Eric Vespe, 2021.

289 **"The truth is"**: Germain Lussier, "Kevin Feige Explains 'Ant-Man's' MCU Significance; New Trailer Out Monday," *SlashFilm*, April 11, 2015, slashfilm.com/537213/kevin-feige-ant-man-marvel-cinematic-universe.

289 **"There seemed to be a period"**: Author interview with Eric Vespe, 2021.

Chapter Twenty-Two: TANGLED WEB

295 **"I don't want to make a movie"**: Kyle Buchanan, "Sam Raimi on Oz, The Avengers, and Two Huge Movies He Never Made," *Vulture*, March 5, 2013, vulture.com/2013/03/sam-raimi-on-oz-and-two-huge-films-he-never-made.html.

297 **"Even though we were"**: Amy Pascal, email to Brian Lourd, August 19, 2014.

297 **"I have only the Spider universe"**: Amy Pascal, email to Jeff Robinov, November 10, 2014. Email messages in this chapter have been lightly edited for spelling and readability.

298 **"We're distracted by the idea"**: Rachel O'Connor, email to Amy Pascal, November 20, 2013.

298 **"Uneven, schizo tone"**: Amy Pascal, email to Doug Belgrad, March 27, 2014.

298 **"billion dollar club"**: Rachel O'Connor, email to Amy Pascal, November 11, 2013.

298 **"This story is way too dark"**: Alan Fine, email to Tom Cohen, July 31, 2014.

299 **"I saw the spider bite"**: Kevin Feige, email to Alan Fine and Tom Cohen, September 18, 2012.

299 **"Okay for comic books"**: Alan Fine, email to Tom Cohen and Kevin Feige, September 18, 2012.

299 **"I really want you to help"**: Selome Hailu, "Kevin Feige and Amy Pascal Discuss Their Future 'Spider-Man' Plans: 'We Want to Top Ourselves in Quality and Emotion,'" *Variety*, December 18, 2021, variety.com/2021/film/news/kevin-feige-amy-pascal-spider-man-mcu-1235137818.

299 **"I'm not good at that"**: Ibid.

300 **"Get the fuck out of here"**: Ben Fritz, *The Big Picture: The Fight for the Future of Movies* (HarperCollins, 2019), 79.

300 **"Michael [Lynton] had no ego"**: Ibid., 80.

301 **"Which makes you love somebody"**: Bennett and Terry, *Story of Marvel Studios*, vol. 1, 230.

303 **"I knew that he had been dancing"**: Author interview with Sarah Halley Finn, 2021.

304 **"We wanted to depart"**: Author interview with Jonathan Goldstein, 2019.

305 **"In the past"**: The Artists of Marvel Studios Visual Development with Troy Benjamin, *How to Paint Characters the Marvel Studios Way* (Marvel Worldwide, 2019), 76.

307 **"Sony did a fantastic job with *Venom*"**: Erik Davis, "Tom Holland in 'Venom 2'? Producer Amy Pascal Offers Updates on the Future of the Spider-Verse," Fandango, June 20, 2019, fandango.com/movie-news/tom-holland-in-venom-2-producer-amy-pascal-offers-updates-on-the-future-of-the-spider-verse-753795.

307 **"Many kids of color"**: Ethan Sacks, "EXCLUSIVE: Spider-Man Miles Morales—popular biracial version of the hero—joins main Marvel comics universe this fall," *New York Daily News*, June 20, 2015.

Chapter Twenty-Three: LONG LIVE THE KING

310 **"It felt to me like a deal-breaker"**: Scott Feinberg, " 'Awards Chatter' Podcast—Chadwick Boseman ('Black Panther')," *Hollywood Reporter*, August 29, 2018, hollywoodreporter.com/movies/movie-news/awards-chatter-podcast-chadwick-boseman-black-panther-1138476.

310 **"I found a dialect coach"**: Author interview with Chadwick Boseman, 2016.

310 **"I was like, 'Oh my God"**: Author interview with Sebastian Stan, 2021.

310 **"The turn in the scene"**: Author interview with Chadwick Boseman, 2017.

311 **"As a kid I played"**: Lucy Rock, " 'This is the movie I wish I'd had to look up to': Joe Robert Cole on co-writing Black Panther," *Guardian*, February 13, 2018.

311 **"I really have a thing"**: Author interview with Ava DuVernay, 2014.

311 **"I'll just say we had different ideas"**: Yolanda Sangweni, "EXCLUSIVE: Ava DuVernay Won't Be Directing 'Black Panther' Movie," *Essence*, July 15, 2015, essence.com/entertainment/exclusive-ava-duvernay-not-directing-black-panther-movie.

312 **"One of his questions"**: Kelley L. Carter, "The man who put Marvel in the black," *Andscape*, May 17, 2016, andscape.com/features/marvel-nate-moore-black-panther.

312 **"The way he works"**: Author interview with Chadwick Boseman, 2016.

313 **"When I came back"**: Chris Giles, "A journey into Wakanda: How we made Black Panther," CNN, February 19, 2018, cnn.com/2018/02/16/africa/black-panther-behind-the-scenes-marvel/index.html.

313 **"It was such a challenge"**: Ibid.

313 **"You might say that"**: Jamil Smith, "The Revolutionary Power Of Black Panther," *Time*, February 19, 2019.

313 **"thatched roofing on skyscrapers"**: "Commentary," *Black Panther* (Marvel, 2018), DVD.

314 **"I would say the Afrofuturistic"**: Smith, "Revolutionary Power."

314 **"I think the thing that distinguishes"**: Author interview with Chadwick Boseman, 2016.

315 **"He did not look well"**: Clayton Davis, "Spike Lee on Chadwick Boseman, Donald Trump and How Black and Brown People Rescued New York," *Variety*, October 8, 2020.

315 **"We did ten-hour days"**: *The Late Show with Stephen Colbert*, CBS, March 13, 2018.

316 **"I remember Chadwick"**: "The Russo Brothers Break Down Scenes from 'Avengers: Endgame,' 'Captain America: Civil War' & More," uploaded to YouTube by *Vanity Fair*, July 28, 2022, youtube.com/watch?v=Tc4WIUCbPqk.

316 **"He would go off"**: Ibid.

316 **"He would take them through"**: Ibid.

316 **"He was the leader of Wakanda"**: Ibid.

316   **"[She] shook everybody's hand"**: "Commentary," *Black Panther*.

316   **"We worked on separate sections"**: Peter Caranicas, "Editing Duo Worked Together to Raise 'Black Panther' to Blockbuster Status," *Variety*, January 9, 2019.

316   **"When I was on the set"**: Ibid.

317   **"Thumbs up to Ryan"**: Author interview with Letitia Wright, 2018.

317   **"Because it's the first of its kind"**: Author interview with Chadwick Boseman, 2016

317   **"I saw Chad crying"**: "BLACK PANTHER: Daniel Kaluuya at Comic-Con 2017," uploaded to YouTube by MovieWeb, July 23, 2017, youtube.com/watch?v=eUwtwNngplQ.

318   **"I've been a massive Kendrick fan"**: Sidney Madden and Daoud Tyler-Ameen, "Here's How 'Black Panther: The Album' Came Together," NPR, February 6, 2018, npr.org/sections/therecord/2018/02/06/582841574/heres-how-black-panther-the-album-came-together.

318   **"It was a good look"**: Shaheem Reid, "Ghostface Killah's Iron Man Obsession Lands Him A Cameo In Upcoming Comic Book Flick," MTV, November 19, 2007, mtv.com/news/1vlom5/ghostface-killahs-iron-man-obsession-lands-him-a-cameo-in-upcoming-comic-book-flick.

319   **"Wakanda itself is a dream state"**: Carvell Wallace, "Why 'Black Panther' Is a Defining Moment for Black America," *New York Times Magazine*, February 12, 2018.

319   **"Do I think it merits"**: Glenn Whipp, " 'Black Panther' is on the hunt for a best picture Oscar, no matter what happens with the 'popular film' prize," *Los Angeles Times*, August 23, 2018.

320   **"I spent the last year"**: Sonaiya Kelley, "Read 'Black Panther' director Ryan Coogler's moving tribute to Chadwick Boseman," *Los Angeles Times*, August 30, 2020.

321   **"Hey, you're here"**: Author interview with Chadwick Boseman, 2017.

321   **"Tell 'em what we did"**: Kate Storey, " 'A Man With a Purpose': Chadwick Boseman's Life's Work Is Far From Over," *Esquire*, April 21, 2021.

Chapter Twenty-Four: HIGHER, FURTHER, FASTER

322   **"I always say that both"**: Christine Dinh, "Marvel's Voices: Victoria Alonso on Marvel Studios' Approach to Filmmaking, Stan Lee's Enduring Legacy, and Finding Your Inner Super Hero," Marvel, October 14, 2020, marvel.com/articles/culture-lifestyle/voices-victoria-alonso-marvel-studios-filmmaking.

323   **"My identity was tangled"**: Esther Zuckerman, "Shailene Woodley and Brie Larson Emerged from Within the Hollywood Machine Before Defying It," *Atlantic*, June 2, 2014.

323   **"They brought me back"**: Author interview with Nicole Perlman, 2019.

323   **"That process went on"**: Ibid.

325 **"If you look at the comics"**: Rebecca Keegan, " 'Captain Marvel's' Brie Larson Can't Save Womankind—But She's Doing Her Best," *Hollywood Reporter*, February 13, 2019.

325 **"I quit about a week"**: Author interview with Kelly Sue DeConnick, 2019.

235 **"I said, 'The thing about Carol'"**: Ibid.

326 **"We're trying to get a little more"**: Terri Schwartz, "Why Hiring a Female Director for Captain Marvel Is Important to Kevin Feige," IGN, October 12, 2016, ign.com/articles/2016/10/12/why-hiring-a-female-director-for-captain-marvel-is-important-to-kevin-feige.

326 **"The issue is"**: Gregg Kilday, "Paul Rudd and Marvel's Kevin Feige Reveal 'Ant-Man's' Saga, from Director Shuffle to Screenplay Surgery to Studio's 'Phase Three' Plans," *Hollywood Reporter*, June 24, 2015.

327 **"I remember sending Nicole"**: Author interview with Meg LaFauve, 2019.

327 **"My husband was deployed"**: Author interview with Nicole Perlman, 2019.

327 **"We didn't write a treatment"**: Ibid.

328 **"It was really important"**: Ibid.

328 **"This was not offered"**: Kate Erbland, " 'Captain Marvel': How a Beloved Filmmaking Duo Stayed True to Their Indie Roots and Made a Blockbuster," *IndieWire*, March 7, 2019, indiewire.com/2019/03/captain-marvel-directors-anna-boden-ryan-fleck-indie-1202048958.

329 **"belief that they wouldn't"**: " 'Captain Marvel' Press Conference Recap" *Geeks of Color*, March 5, 2019, geeksofcolor.co/2019/03/05/captain-marvel-press-conference-recap.

329 **"Brie is a writer and a director"**: Author interview with Geneva Robertson-Dworet, 2019.

329 **"In reading the comics"**: Clarisse Loughrey, "Captain Marvel exclusive: Brie Larson hopes new film will inspire more women to become pilots," *Independent* (UK edition), March 8, 2019.

330 **"There is a camaraderie"**: Author interview with Kevin Feige, 2017.

330 **"*Captain Marvel* is"**: *Variety* [@variety] on twitter.com, October 26, 2018, twitter.com/Variety/status/1056008763361046528?s=20.

331 **"*Superman: The Movie* is still"**: "Tribute to Richard Donner—How 'Superman' Influenced Today's Biggest Superhero Movies," uploaded to YouTube by Oscars, June 8, 2017, youtube.com/watch?v=PrNwMXcKxWE.

331 **"As a kid, I wanted to be an adventurer"**: Keegan, " 'Captain Marvel's' Brie Larson."

332 **"If you have a movie"**: Jana Seitzer, "Working Mother Marvel Studios' Victoria Alonso Tells All," *Whiskey + Sunshine*, April 30, 2018, whiskynsunshine.com/working-mother-marvel-studios-victoria-alonso-tells-all.

332 **"everyone is still remembering"**: Marjua Estevez, "A Glass-Shattering Woman Is Responsible For Marvel's Greatest Blockbusters," *Vibe*, December 6, 2016, vibe.com/features/viva/victoria-alonso-marvel-studios-producer-471994.

332 **"Victoria especially"**: Elayna Fernandez, "Supporting Diversity in the

Film Industry: Interview with AVENGERS: INFINITY WAR Executive Producer Trinh Tran," *The Positive Mom*, April 30, 2018, www.thepositivemom.com/supporting-diversity-in-the-film-industry.

332 **"Why would we only want"**: Marc Malkin, "Top Marvel Executive: 'The World Is Ready' for a Gay Superhero in the MCU," *Variety*, March 7, 2019.

333 **"The movie was the biggest"**: Sana Amanat, "Brie Larson Is Ready to Kick Some Ass," *InStyle*, February 5, 2019, instyle.com/celebrity/brie-larson-march-cover.

333 **"Single moms doing a million jobs"**: Author interview with Lashana Lynch, 2019.

333 **"You could not pay me"**: Eric Francisco, " 'Captain Marvel' Review Bombing: Rotten Tomatoes Removes Toxic 'Reviews,' " *Inverse*, February 22, 2019, inverse.com/article/53523-captain-marvel-rotten-tomatoes-review-bombing-explained.

334 **"I don't need a 40-year-old"**: "Brie Larson's speech at Crystal Award for Excellence in Film 2018," uploaded to YouTube by SorrelGum, February 27, 2019, youtube.com/watch?v=9e852S8RvlU.

335 **"I don't have time"**: Kate Aurthur, "Brie Larson on Creating a Symbol With 'Captain Marvel' " *Variety*, October 8, 2019.

335 **"I don't know"**: Jessica Wang, "Brie Larson gives a wry response when asked if she'd play Captain Marvel again," *Entertainment Weekly*, September 11, 2022, https://ew.com/movies/brie-larson-wry-response-play-captain-marvel-again/.

Chapter Twenty-Five: SNAP

337 **"We spent, it's no exaggeration"**: "Kevin Feige on Planning the 'Infinity War' Ending, 'Captain Marvel,' And Honoring Stan Lee," uploaded to YouTube by Rotten Tomatoes, March 4, 2019, youtube.com/watch?v=ljrdxgsfdug.

338 **"get through *Ultron*"**: Joshua Yehl, "Joss Whedon Pleased With How Avengers: Infinity War Diverted From His Thanos Setup—Comic-Con 2018," IGN, July 21, 2018, ign.com/articles/2018/07/21/joss-whedon-pleased-with-how-avengers-infinity-war-diverted-from-his-thanos-setup-comic-con-2018.

338 **"We did pitch Robert"**: Aaron Couch, " 'Avengers: Endgame' Directors on Seeking Robert Downey Jr.'s Blessing and Marvel's First Gay Character," *Hollywood Reporter*, May 1, 2019.

338 **"Some of the greatest story development"**: Author interview with Robert Downey Jr., 2017.

339 **"We didn't know"**: Anthony Breznican, "How the Avengers: Endgame Writers made Life-and-Death Decisions," *Vanity Fair*, November 20, 2019, vanityfair.com/hollywood/2019/11/avengers-endgame-writers-alternate-storylines.

340 **"would be the most heartbreaking"**: "Kevin Feige On Planning the 'Infinity War' Ending, 'Captain Marvel,' And Honoring Stan Lee" uploaded to YouTube by Rotten Tomatoes, March 4, 2019, youtube.com/watch?v=ljrdxgsfdug.

340 **"If people are joking"**: Author interview with Christopher Markus, 2019.

340 **"In Kevin's mindset"**: Ben Pearson, " 'Avengers: Endgame' Final Battle Oral History: How The Biggest Scene In Comic Book Movie History Came Together," *SlashFilm*, November 1, 2019, slashfilm.com/570137/avengers-endgame-final-battle-oral-history.

341 **"We actually didn't photograph"**: Ibid.

341 **"There was certainly a debate"**: Ibid.

342 **"The biggest misunderstanding"**: Author interview with C. Robert Cargill, 2019.

343 **"It is ridiculous"**: Aaron Couch, "Avengers: Endgame' Writers Share Ideas Abandoned along the Way," *Hollywood Reporter*, May 11, 2019.

344 **"Time travel pops up"**: Ibid.

344 **"in the conference room"**: David Pountain, "Avengers: Endgame Writers Say The Time Travel Was Accidental," *We Got This Covered*, August 18, 2019, wegotthiscovered.com/movies/avengers-endgame-time-travel-plot-happened-accident.

345 **"We were in the editing room"**: Ethan Anderton, "Robert Downey Jr.'s Finest Moment in 'Avengers: Endgame' Was A Last Minute Addition," *SlashFilm*, May 1, 2019, slashfilm.com/566106/tony-starks-final-scene-in-avengers-endgame.

345 **"He was like, 'I don't know.' "**: Sean O'Connell, "Apparently Robert Downey Jr. Didn't Want To Do Tony Stark's Last Big Line In Avengers: Endgame," CinemaBlend, May 6, 2019, cinemablend.com/news/2471343/apparently-robert-downey-jr-didnt-want-to-do-tony-starks-last-big-line-in-avengers-endgame.

346 **"We used to joke"**: Josh Wilding, "AVENGERS: ENDGAME Directors Reveal The Marvel Studios Movie's Single Most Expensive Shot," ComicBookMovie, July 29, 2019, comicbookmovie.com/avengers/avengers_endgame/avengers-endgame-directors-reveal-the-marvel-studios-movies-single-most-expensive-shot-a169783#gs.oj9t5o.

346 **"The day they got there"**: "Endgame Writers, Russo Bros & Anthony Mackie Reveal Deleted Scene, Surprises & Decapitated Cap Idea," uploaded to YouTube by IMDb, July 22, 2019, youtube.com/watch?v=QREOp3p5NkI.

347 **"An Academy Award"**: Pearson, " 'Avengers: Endgame.' "

347 **"Him feeling comfortable"**: Author interview with Ty Simpkins, 2020.

347 **"Then there was just this blank look"**: Author interview with Kerry Condon, 2020. Things worked out fine for Condon; in 2022, she costarred in the movie *The Banshees of Inisherin*, a performance that earned her an Oscar nomination for Best Supporting Actress.

348 **"I'll be honest"**: Ethan Anderton, "How The 'Avengers: Endgame' Directors

Assembled The Most Star-Filled Shot In Marvel History," *SlashFilm*, May 1, 2019, slashfilm.com/566102/avengers-endgame-final-battle-and-funeral.

348 **"When it was all cut together"**: Pearson, " 'Avengers: Endgame.' "

348 **"The first time, it was quicker"**: Ibid.

349 **"Panther, Doctor Strange, Star-Lord"**: Ibid.

349 **"I'm going to start crying"**: Ibid.

349 **"I think that was Kevin's highlight"**: Nick Evans, "Captain America's 'Avengers Assemble' Moment Was Kevin Feige's 'Highlight Of All Time,' " CinemaBlend, November 18, 2019, cinemablend.com/news/2485027/captain-americas-avengers-assemble-moment-was-kevin-feiges-highlight-of-all-time.

350 **"A branded studio"**: Author interview with David Maisel, 2020.

351 **"but all of them, in those movies"**: Mandalit del Barco, "Marvel Studios' Kevin Feige On The Future Of Marvel Movies," NPR, April 26, 2018, npr.org/2018/04/26/605648453/marvel-studios-kevin-feige-on-the-future-of-marvel-movies.

351 **"Marvel's secret sauce"**: Mike Fleming Jr., "From Slamdance Walkouts To 'Avengers: Endgame' & Choosing Which Marvel Superheroes To Kill Off: A Conversation With Joe Russo At Sands International Film Festival," *Deadline*, March 30, 2022, deadline.com/video/joe-russo-avengers-endgame-sands-international-film-festival-st-andrews-scotland.

351 **"Kevin made an assertion"**: Author interview with C. Robert Cargill, 2019.

352 **"You cannot find"**: Ibid.

352 **"That's the job"**: Author interview with Craig Kyle, 2020.

352 **"To be in a movie theater"**: Mike Fleming Jr.,"Year After Record 'Avengers: Endgame' B.O. Launch, AGBO's Joe & Anthony Russo Open 'Extraction' On Netflix," *Deadline*, April 24, 2020, deadline.com/2020/04/avengers-endgame-anniversary-joe-russo-anthony-russo-extraction-netflix-chris-hemsworth-1202917408.

352 **"We had chills"**: Ibid.

353 **"I just walked around"**: Joe Deckelmeier, "Christopher Markus & Stephen McFeely Interview: MCU," *Screen Rant*, November 5, 2019, screenrant.com/marvel-cinematic-universe-christopher-markus-stephen-mcfeely-interview.

Chapter Twenty-Six: A YEAR WITHOUT MARVEL

357 **"I was caught up"**: Kyle Buchanan, "*Guardians of the Galaxy* Is Huge—and That's Not Always Easy for James Gunn," *Vulture*, May 3, 2017, vulture.com/2017/05/james-gunn-loves-and-hates-the-boost-he-got-from-guardians.html.

358 **"I like *Guardians of the Galaxy*"**: Stephen Rebello, "Matthew McConaughey Talks 'Gold,' Unbranding and New Twists in a Singular Career," *Playboy*, December 2016.

358 **"Everyone says you're great!"**: James Gunn, Facebook, October 29, 2016, facebook.com/jgunn/posts/10153721692566157.

359 **"With Joss it was more unique"**: Author interview with Kevin Feige, 2017.

359 **"#GirtherMovement"**: James Gunn [@jamesgunn], Twitter (tweet since deleted), January 17, 2018, twitter.com/JamesGunn/status/9534330941 02556672.

359 **"The Hardy Boys"**: Bryan Bishop, "Writer-director James Gunn fired from Guardians of the Galaxy Vol. 3 over offensive tweets," *The Verge*, July 20, 2018, theverge.com/2018/7/20/17596452/guardians-of-the-galaxy-marvel-james-gunn-fired-pedophile-tweets-mike-cernovich.

359 **"Wondering which Disneyland character"**: Ibid.

360 **"I called Kevin"**: Dave Itzkoff, "James Gunn Nearly Blew Up His Career. Now He's Back with 'The Suicide Squad,'" *New York Times*, July 14, 2021.

360 **"The offensive attitudes"**: Brent Lang, "James Gunn Fired From 'Guardians of the Galaxy Vol. 3,'" *Variety*, July 20, 2018.

360 **"He likes to call me at seven in the morning"**: Matthew Belloni, "In-Depth With Disney CEO Bob Iger on China Growth, 'Star Wars' Reshoots and Political Plans: 'A Lot of People Have Urged Me to [Run],'" *Hollywood Reporter*, June 22, 2016, hollywoodreporter.com/movies/movie-features/bob-iger-interview-star-wars-905320.

361 **"Given the growing political divide"**: Devon Ivie, "Chris Pratt, Zoe Saldana, *Guardians of the Galaxy* Cast Write Open Letter to 'Fully Support' James Gunn," *Vulture*, July 30, 2018, vulture.com/2018/07/guardians-of-the-galaxy-cast-fully-support-james-gunn.html.

361 **"It's bittersweet"**: Debopriyaa Dutta, "Zoe Saldana Says Playing Gamora In Guardians Of The Galaxy Vol. 3 Was 'Bittersweet,'" *SlashFilm*, February 15, 2022, slashfilm.com/767048/zoe-saldana-says-playing-gamora-in-guardians-of-the-galaxy-vol-3-was-bittersweet.

361 **"Cancel culture also is"**: Itzkoff, "James Gunn."

362 **"Don't worry about the universe"**: Author interview with Kevin Feige, 2020.

362 **"One of our strategies"**: Borys Kit, "DC Slate Unveiled: New Batman, Supergirl Movies, a Green Lantern TV Show, and More From James Gunn, Peter Safran," *Hollywood Reporter*, January 31, 2023, hollywood reporter.com/movies/movie-features/james-gunn-unveils-dc-slate-batman-superman-1235314176.

362 **"To build those lesser-known properties"**: Ibid.

363 **"obsessions"**: Author interview with Kevin Feige, 2017.

364 **"worldwide spread"**: Benjamin Haynes, "Transcript for the CDC Tele-briefing Update on COVID-19," February 26, 2020, cdc.gov/media/releases/2020/t0225-cdc-telebriefing-covid-19.html.

365 **"As many of you know"**: Borys Kit, "Marvel's 'Shang-Chi' Temporarily Suspends Production as Director Self-Isolates (Exclusive)," *Hollywood Reporter*, March 12, 2020.

366 **"We will increase"**: "Disney Investor Day 2020—Full Presentation,"

uploaded to YouTube by TV Clips, December 15, 2020, https://www.youtube.com/watch?v=CRdYiquh8Bg.

366 **"I was wary of it becoming"**: Adam B. Vary, "Marvel's Kevin Feige on 'WandaVision,' 'Star Wars' and How the Pandemic Is Like Thanos' Blip," *Variety*, January 11, 2021.

368 **"Why would Disney forgo"**: Pamela McClintock and Eriq Gardner, "Scarlett Johansson Files Lawsuit Against Disney Over 'Black Widow' Release," *Hollywood Reporter*, July 29, 2021.

368 **"make things right"**: Matthew Belloni, *What I'm Hearing*, newsletter, July 30, 2021.

369 **"The lawsuit is especially sad"**: Danny Cevallos, "Disney Co.'s Covid excuse in Scarlett Johansson lawsuit is darkly comical and clearly flawed," NBC News, August 10, 2021, nbcnews.com/think/opinion/disney-co-s-covid-excuse-scarlett-johansson-lawsuit-darkly-comical-ncna1275840.

Chapter Twenty-Seven: DEPARTMENT OF YES

371 **"I always think that"**: Author interview with Marc Chu, 2020.

371 **"The budgets were relatively limited"**: Author interview with Kevin Feige, 2017.

371 **"We got to cheer"**: Eric Eisenberg, "Avengers: Infinity War Has A Crazy Small Number Of Shots Without Visual Effects," CinemaBlend, February 7, 2019, cinemablend.com/news/2466549/avengers-infinity-war-has-a-crazy-small-number-of-shots-without-visual-effects.

372 **"Twenty months of delays"**: *Life After Pi*, directed by Scott Leberecht (Hollywood Ending, 2014), uploaded to YouTube by Hollywood Ending Movie, February 26, 2014, youtu.be/9lcB9u-9mVE.

372 **"We understand that"**: Ibid.

374 **"We came in after the fact"**: Author interview with Trent Claus, 2020.

375 **"We knew that the movie"**: "The Transformation," featurette, *Captain America: The First Avenger* (Paramount, 2011), Blu-ray.

375 **"Things that people don't think"**: Author interview with Trent Claus, 2020.

375 **"We left only his face"**: Ibid.

376 **"We took thirty years off"**: Ibid.

376 **"we touched it up"**: Ben Pearson, "10 Things We Learned At The 'Guardians Of The Galaxy Vol. 2' Press Junket," *SlashFilm*, April 25, 2017, slashfilm.com/550527/10-things-we-learned-at-the-guardians-of-the-galaxy-vol-2-press-junket.

376 **"For us, it's not so much"**: Author interview with Trent Claus, 2020.

377 **"The latest version of the suit"**: "ILM: Behind the Magic of the Hulk in Marvel Studios' The Avengers (Part 1)," uploaded to YouTube by Industrial Light & Magic, January 14, 2013, youtube.com/watch?v=fB_3r4b-CAU.

377 **"You will always see groups"**: Author interview with Marc Chu, 2020.

378 **"When I saw the film"**: Author interview with Gui DaSilva-Greene, 2020.

378 **"Maybe you did one scan"**: Author interview with Robert Downey Jr., 2017.

378 **"It's like a science-fiction film"**: Author interview with Gui DaSilva-Greene, 2020.

379 **"We were just going"**: Author interview with Dan Deleeuw, 2019.

379 **"We kept the motion-capture running"**: Ibid.

380 **"Our real ace in the hole"**: Author interview with Robert Downey Jr., 2017.

380 **"It's so easy to play"**: Author interview with Karen Gillan, 2019.

380 **"What they've done with visual effects"**: Author interview with Jonathan Harb, 2020.

380 **"We knew he would have"**: Author interview with Dan Deleeuw, 2019.

381 **"In terms of the CGI"**: James Hibberd, " 'She-Hulk' Producers Respond to CGI Criticisms," *Hollywood Reporter*, August 2, 2022.

382 **"It's the 'Yes' department"**: "Victoria Alonso, Executive Producer/EVP, Marvel," *The Close-Up*, episode 2, uploaded to YouTube by Advanced Imaging Society, September 16, 2105, youtube.com/watch?v=xZuOxj5IWXc.

382 **"You see all these timelines"**: Linda Codega, "Abuse of VFX Artists Is Ruining the Movies," *Gizmodo*, August 9, 2022, gizmodo.com/disney-marvel-movies-vfx-industry-nightmare-1849385834.

382 **"It is noticeable"**: Chris Lee, " 'Honestly, I Equate It to Human Greed,' " *Vulture*, February 22, 2023, https://www.vulture.com/2023/02/marvel-vfx-workers-on-ant-man-and-the-wasp-quantumania.html.

383 **"I feel incredibly deferential"**: Natasha Jokic, "The 'She-Hulk' Creators Discussed The Show's Questionable CGI, And They Made A Good Point," BuzzFeed, August 4, 2022, buzzfeed.com/natashajokic1/the-she-hulk-team-addressed-criticism-of-the-shows-cgi.

383 **"It's just a massive undertaking"**: Hibberd, " 'She-Hulk.' "

384 **"There were some great ideas"**: Matthew Belloni, "The Secret of Marvel's Magic," *The Town with Matthew Belloni*, podcast, November 16, 2022.

384 **"keep her head down"**: Author interview with anonymous source, 2023.

Chapter Twenty-Eight: K.E.V.I.N.

385 **"One of my hobbies was to be disappointed"**: Author interview with Kevin Feige, 2017.

385 **"After *Robocop 2*"**: Ibid.

385 **"One of the great things"**: Author interview with Bob Iger, 2017. For years, the Marvel Studios production logo that ran at the beginning of its movies featured the riffling panels of comic-book pages (but with no identifiable heroes, said Peter Frankfurt, cofounder of Imaginary Forces, the firm that designed the logo, in a 2020 interview for this book: "They are the idea of Marvel Comics without any specificity to character"). Beginning with *Doc-*

tor Strange in 2016, however, the logo was updated to include screenplay pages and starred a host of MCU actors, with glimpses of action scenes like Chris Evans throwing Captain America's shield—an acknowledgement that more people were watching the movies than reading the comics that served as source material. The logo was originally silent, but in 2013 it got a fanfare by composer Brian Tyler. "Like all great studio logos, you need a fanfare, and we'd never had that before," Kevin Feige said to Marvel.com. In 2016, Michael Giacchino wrote a new fanfare; Marvel Studios has regularly rotated the footage contained in its logo, so that new heroes, like Hailee Stanfield as Kate Bishop, can appear next to Robert Downey Jr. as Tony Stark.

386 **"I loved playing Ross"**: Matt Fowler, "William Hurt Teases a 'Much Different' General Ross for Captain America: Civil War," IGN, June 24, 2015, ign.com/articles/2015/06/24/william-hurt-talks-a-much-different-general-ross-for-captain-america-civil-war.

386 **"I'm dying here"**: Author interview with Chris Hemsworth, 2017.

387 **"When we started Hemsworth"**: Author interview with Kevin Feige, 2017.

387 **"yes to everything"**: *The Late Late Show with James Corden*, CBS, March 1, 2022.

387 **"Filmmakers sometimes will say"**: Vanessa Diaz, "Chatting with the Cast & Filmmakers of Thor Ragnarok!," *Brite & Bubbly*, November 1, 2017, briteandbubbly.com/chatting-cast-filmmakers-thor-ragnarok.

388 **"My whole thing"**: Author interview with Stephany Folsom, 2019.

388 **"Kevin just wanted to reboot"**: Ibid.

388 **"It's hard to do this character"**: Author interview with Mark Ruffalo, 2017.

389 **"We don't have to force"**: Ibid.

389 **"I was like, 'Holy shit'"**: Author interview with Stephany Folsom, 2019.

389 **"I basically became a Trivial Pursuit–type question"**: Janet A. Leigh, "Marvel's James D'Arcy teases possible return after Avengers: Endgame," *Digital Spy*, April 7, 2022, digitalspy.com/tv/ustv/a39662624/marvel-james-darcy-possible-return-avengers-endgame.

390 **"Every time a Marvel movie"**: Author interview with Christopher Yost, 2019.

391 **"After a thirty-nine-year acting career"**: Author interview with Tony Leung, 2021.

391 **"Originally I did the film"**: Sydney Bucksbaum, "Tim Roth talks returning to Marvel as Abomination for *She-Hulk*: 'I love my career being chaos,'" *Entertainment Weekly*, September 1, 2022, ew.com/tv/tim-roth-talks-returning-to-marvel-as-abomination-for-she-hulk-attorney-at-law.

391 **"I went in and there's Kevin"**: Ibid.

392 **"No time for mutants"**: "Full Marvel Cinematic Universe Phase 4 Panel at Hall H," San Diego Comic-Con 2019," uploaded to YouTube by Beyond Fandom, July 26, 2019, youtube.com/watch?v=it9ObhXBZiE.

393 **"I think a secondary person"**: Jeremy Blum, "Marvel Paid a 'Heavy Price' to Use X-Men: TAS' Iconic Theme Song for the Reboot," CBR, September 2, 2022, cbr.com/marvel-paid-heavy-price-x-men-tas-theme-song.

393 **"I was a little unsure"**: Adam B. Vary, "Patrick Stewart on Playing Charles Xavier Again in 'Doctor Strange 2': 'I Was a Little Unsure at First,'" *Variety*, May 6, 2022.

394 **"That was a very interesting shoot"**: Ryan Britt, "Anson Mount Sets a High Bar," *Esquire*, July 7, 2022.

394 **"You could hear the audience knew"**: Vary, "Patrick Stewart."

394 **"It's so funny that Kevin cast John"**: "Commentary," *Doctor Strange in the Multiverse of Madness*, Disney Plus digital release, June 22, 2022.

Chapter Twenty-Nine: THE CLONE SAGA

395 **"There's such a powerful culture"**: Author interview with Dan Harmon, 2021.

396 **"This is something"**: Matt Pressberg, "'Spider-Man: Homecoming' Producer Hints at End of Sony-Marvel Collaboration After Next Movie," *The Wrap*, March 28, 2017, thewrap.com/sony-marvel-collaboration-after-spider-man-homecoming.

397 **"We are disappointed"**: Yohana Desta, "Sony Responds to Spider-Man Fallout: 'We Are Disappointed, but Respect Disney's Decision,'" *Vanity Fair*, August 21, 2019, vanityfair.com/hollywood/2019/08/sony-pictures-spider-man-marvel-kevin-feige-response.

397 **"It was never meant"**: Devan Coggan, "Tom Holland opens up about Spider-Man's future in wake of Disney-Sony rift," *Entertainment Weekly*, August 24, 2019, ew.com/movies/2019/08/24/tom-holland-spider-man-future-disney-sony.

397 **"The Marvel people are terrific people"**: Will Thorne, "Sony Pictures Chief on Spider-Man Split: 'For the Moment the Door Is Closed,'" *Variety*, September 5, 2019.

398 **"I'm just so grateful"**: Jamie Lovett, "Tom Holland Says Next Spider-Man Movie Will Be Very Different After Marvel Split," ComicBook.com, August 25, 2019, comicbook.com/marvel/news/spider-man-3-tom-holland-different-special-marvel-sony.

398 **"My family and I"**: *Jimmy Kimmel Live*, ABC, December 4, 2019.

398 **"There is a world"**: Ibid.

399 **"Peter Parker's story"**: Mike Fleming Jr., "Kevin Feige Back in 'Spider-Man Homecoming' for One More Film," *Deadline*, September 27, 2019, deadline.com/2019/09/spider-man-kevin-feige-back-sony-pictures-1202746503.

399 **"That led us down different story roads"**: Adam Chitwood and Drew Taylor, "Kevin Feige Suggested Turning a Fun Tag Scene into the Main Plot of 'Spider-Man: No Way Home,'" *The Wrap*, January 3, 2022, thewrap.com/spider-man-no-way-home-villains-plot-kevin-feige.

399 **"We were coming up"**: Ibid.

399 **"Remember that idea"**: Ibid.

399 **"That just sort of blew"**: Ibid.

400 **"I really didn't want"**: Dave Itzkoff, "The Devils You Know: Three 'Spider-Man' Villains Return in 'No Way Home,'" *New York Times*, January 5, 2022.

400 **"These are the longest options"**: "SPIDER-MAN: NO WAY HOME—Villains Panel," uploaded to YouTube by Spider-Man, December 4, 2021, youtube.com/watch?v=oKzWmAehB0c.

401 **"No, the Spider-Man mask"**: "Tom Holland on 'Cherry,' COVID protocols, if Spider-Man's mask counts as PPE (FULL)," *Entertain This*, uploaded to YouTube by *USA Today* Entertainment, March 12, 2021, youtube.com/watch?v=zFMRFB5Z5KU.

402 **"I worked so hard"**: Steve Pond, "Andrew Garfield Says Lying about 'Spider-Man' Role Was 'Weirdly Enjoyable,'" *The Wrap*, January 9, 2022, thewrap.com/andrew-garfield-spider-man-no-way-home-lying.

403 **"Because that's really fun"**: Itzkoff, "Devils You Know."

403 **"We all believe so much"**: "Tom Holland, Zendaya and Jacob Batalon on Spider-Man: No Way Home and Fight Scene With Green Goblin," uploaded to YouTube by *Collider* Interviews, December 9, 2021, youtube.com/watch?v=Z5ag0hn1-bQ.

403 **"It would be a miracle"**: *The Tonight Show Starring Jimmy Fallon*, NBC, February 23, 2021.

404 **"We're producers"**: Brooks Barnes, "Kevin Feige and Amy Pascal on the Future of 'Spider-Man' and the M.C.U.," *New York Times*, December 17, 2021.

404 **"We're actively beginning"**: Ibid.

Chapter Thirty: INTO THE MULTIVERSE

406 **"I don't know, what do you look like when you fly?"**: Author interview with Kathryn Hahn, 2021.

406 **"We both really relish"**: Author interview with Paul Bettany, 2021.

407 **"They've never said"**: Author interview with Nate Moore, 2021.

407 **"The amount of work"**: Matt Donnelly, "Meet the Executive Avengers Who Help Kevin Feige Make Marvel Magic," *Variety*, April 17, 2019.

408 **"What's cool about Disney Plus"**: Scott Campbell, "Marvel Producer Reveals How The Studio Decides On Disney Plus Projects," *We Got This Covered*, September 7, 2021, wegotthiscovered.com/tv/marvel-producer-reveals-how-the-studio-decides-on-disney-plus-projects.

408 **"Television is so much"**: Author interview with Nate Moore, 2021.

408 **"When are we going to get"**: "Captain America: Civil War—European Press Conference in Full," uploaded to YouTube by *Digital Spy*, April 26, 2016, youtube.com/watch?v=yc9AYSKWTkk.

408 **"That's a good idea!"**: Ibid.

408 **"Mackie and Sebastian"**: Author interview with Nate Moore, 2021.

409 **"If you've ever been"**: Ibid.

409 **"By the nature of"**: Author interview with Kevin Feige, 2021.

410 **"While we were in Atlanta"**: Brian Hiatt, "The Oral History of 'Wanda-Vision,'" *Rolling Stone*, June 1, 2021.

410 **"They had been internally noodling"**: Author interview with Jac Schaeffer, 2021.

411 **"Special Characters Contract"**: Aaron Couch, "Marvel's Movie Math: Comic Creators Claim It's 'Bait and Switch' on Payments," *Hollywood Reporter*, July 20, 2022, hollywoodreporter.com/movies/movie-features/marvel-movie-math-comic-creators-1235183158.

411 **"Just received"**: Jim Starlin, Facebook, January 24, 2017, facebook.com/396963960387829/posts/1232284023522481.

411 **"a fairly fair deal"**: Abraham Josephine Riesman, "The Creator of Avengers: Endgame Villain Thanos Has Beef With Marvel," *Vulture*, April 24, 2019, vulture.com/2019/04/jim-starlin-creator-of-infinity-war-thanos-hates-marvel.html.

412 **"Everyone at Marvel Studios"**: Ed Brubaker, *From the Desk of Ed Brubaker*, "And now the full cover reveal . . . ," email newsletter, March 19, 2021.

412 **"There's nothing preventing"**: "Falcon and Winter Soldier Episode 4 Review! *SPOILERS* FMB Live for 4/12/2021!," uploaded to YouTube by Kevin Smith, April 12, 2021, youtube.com/watch?v=uG7VFaatjEE.

412 **"When you start to see"**: Keisha Hatchett, "*The Falcon and the Winter Soldier*'s Malcolm Spellman Is Ready to Deliver an Undeniably Black Superhero Story," TVLine, February 16, 2021, tvline.com/2021/02/16/falcon-and-the-winter-soldier-malcolm-spellman-black-history-month.

413 **"pretty similar"**: Author interview with Nate Moore, 2021.

413 **"He was so versed"**: Ibid.

413 **"Well, you can't fight Kevin Feige"**: Author interview with Dan Harmon, 2021.

414 **"We wanted a scientist"**: Author interview with Kevin Feige, 2021.

414 **"They give you this menu"**: Author interview with Malcolm Spellman, 2021.

415 **"Michael had done his writers' room"**: Author interview with Kate Herron, 2021.

416 **"You finish your scene"**: Dave Itzkoff, "Marvel's Latest Frontier? In 'WandaVision,' It's the Suburbs," *New York Times*, January 8, 2021.

417 **"We decided to move"**: Brian Davids, " 'Hawkeye' EP Trinh Tran on Casting Hailee Steinfeld and the Influence of 'Better Call Saul,'" *Hollywood Reporter*, November 19, 2021.

418 **"The finale was just"**: Author interview with Jac Schaeffer, 2021.

418 **"It's all intertwined"**: Author interview with Michael Waldron, 2021.

418 **"He wanted to"**: Mike Reyes, "Doctor Strange 2: Why Scott Derrickson And C. Robert Cargill Left The Marvel Sequel," Cinemablend, May 25, 2021, https://www.cinemablend.com/news/2568025/doctor-strange-2-why-scott-derrickson-and-c-robert-cargill-left-marvel-sequel-mcu.

419 **"Yeah, we'll leave that"**: Author interview with Michael Waldron, 2021.

419 **"I don't believe that the MCU is 616"**: "Iman Vellani on mcu 616 Ms. Marvel," uploaded to YouTube by Marvel Entanglement, June 3, 2022.

419 **"He just stared at me"**: Iman Vellani, "What's up r/marvelstudios, I'm Iman Vellani—AKA the one and only Kamala Khan, AKA Ms. Marvel! AMA!," Reddit, July 14, 2022, reddit.com/r/marvelstudios/comments/vz1hfa/whats_up_rmarvelstudios_im_iman_vellaniaka_the.

420 **"I had a strong perspective"**: *Assembled: The Making of Doctor Strange in the Multiverse of Madness*, Disney Plus, July 8, 2022.

420 **"I admired Jac"**: Author interview with Michael Waldron, 2021.

421 **"There are people whose sole task"**: "Kevin Feige on 'Black Widow,'" *D23 Inside Disney Podcast*, episode 96, July 15, 2021.

422 **"This is not a secret"**: Author interview with Kevin Feige, 2017.

422 **"We'd probably have to"**: Anthony Breznican, "Chris Hemsworth Changed His Life After an Ominous Health Warning," *Vanity Fair*, November 17, 2022, vanityfair.com/hollywood/2022/11/chris-hemsworth-exclusive-interview-alzheimers-limitless.

423 **"*Secret Wars* is a great, giant crossover"**: Cameron Bonomolo, "Marvel's Kevin Feige on Rumors Secret Wars Is the Next Major MCU Crossover (Exclusive)," ComicBook.com, November 8, 2021, comicbook.com/movies/news/marvel-studios-kevin-feige-secret-wars-movie-rumors-exclusive-interview-shang-chi.

424 **"Simple. They don't have a Kevin"**: Author interview with Joe Russo, 2017.

424 **"We always want"**: Author interview with Kevin Feige, 2017.

425 **"That's where the brand becomes important"**: Author interview with Bob Iger, 2017.

426 **"One of the powerful aspects"**: Devan Coggan, "Kevin Feige opens up about Phase 5, Kang, and the future of the MCU," *Entertainment Weekly*, February 14, 2023, ew.com/movies/kevin-feige-marvel-phase-5-exclusive-interview.

Chapter 31: ANNUS HORRIBLIS

427 **"old studio Broadway musical"**: Quentin Tarantino, *Cinema Speculation* (HarperCollins, 2022), 160.

427 **"It's bullshit"**: Ryan Lattanzio, "Terry Gilliam on Marvel Movies' Dangerous Lie and the 'Don Quixote' Producer He Compares to Trump," *IndieWire*, December 20, 2019.

427 **"When I see Marvel movies"**: Tom Murray, "The Director of 'Independence Day' Says He Watches Marvel Movies to Fall Asleep on Planes," *Business Insider*, November 4, 2019.

427 **"Their scripts are not"**: Zack Sharf, "Ridley Scott Slams Superhero Movies: 'Boring as Sh*t' with Scripts That 'Aren't Any F*cking Good'," *IndieWire*, November 15, 2021.

428 **"the definition of it was monotony"**: Ellie Harrison, "Christian Bale Says

Green-screen Movies Like Thor Are 'Monotony' to Film," *Independent* (UK edition), October 6, 2022.

428 **"They put me in armor"**: Michael Schulman, "How the Marvel Cinematic Universe Swallowed Hollywood," *The New Yorker*, June 5, 2023.

428 **"It's a silly performance"**: Yang-Yi Goh, "The Dave Bautista Method," gq.com, January 4, 2023.

428 **"There's a level of expectation"**: David Faber, "CNBC Exclusive: CNBC Transcript: Disney CEO Bob Iger Speaks with CNBC's David Faber on 'Squawk Box' Today," cnbc.com, July 13, 2023.

430 **"When I first started, Ali was one of two directors"**: "Samuel L. Jackson & Olivia Colman Interview: Marvel's Secret Invasion," uploaded to YouTube by Collider Interviews, June 16, 2023, youtube.com/watch?v=au5FFuEM_jA.

430 **"It was weeks of people not getting along"**: Borys Kit, "'Daredevil' Hits Reset Button as Marvel Overhauls Its TV Business," *Hollywood Reporter*, October 11, 2023.

431 **"TV is a writer-driven medium"**: Ibid.

433 **"This is maybe"**: Adam B. Vary, "'Loki' EP Explains Why Jonathan Majors' Arrest Didn't Affect the Series, Casting Ke Huy Quan and Tom Hiddleston's MCU Future," *Variety*, October 2, 2023.

433 **"Same hour, same half hour"**: Interview by Linsey Davis, "Jonathan Majors Speaks Out Against Misdemeanor Assault Verdict in Exclusive Interview," *Impact x Nightline*, January 11, 2024.

435 **"I worked on this screenplay"**: Steve Weintraub, "James Gunn Says Guardians of the Galaxy Vol. 3 'Isn't About Saving the Universe'," *Collider*, April 28, 2023.

435 **"We don't have this thing"**: Ibid.

436 **"For me personally"**: "THE MARVELS Director Talks X-MEN Tease and Her Dream Cyclops / Storm Movie | Nia DaCosta Interview," uploaded to YouTube by Jake's Takes, November 6, 2023, youtube.com/watch?v=uU2K0Jq7iEo.

437 **"It is a Kevin Feige production"**: Rebecca Ford, "Nia DaCosta, Barrier-Breaking Director of The Marvels, on Navigating the Blockbuster Machine," *Vanity Fair*, September 2023.

438 **"I don't want to focus"**: Ethan Alter, "'Marvels' Star Iman Vellani Isn't Concerned with the Focus on the Movie's Box Office: 'That's for Bob Iger'," Yahoo.com, November 20, 2023.

438 **"*The Marvels* was shot"**: Sarah Whitten, "Bob Iger Says 'The Marvels' Had Little 'Supervision' and Disney Has Made Too Many Sequels," cnbc.com, November 29, 2023.

438 **"I'm not sure another studio"**: Ibid.

438 **"The more you do"**: Tatiana Siegel, "Crisis at Marvel: Jonathan Majors Back-Up Plans, 'The Marvels' Reshoots, Reviving Original Avengers and More Issues Revealed," *Variety*, November 1, 2023.

Epilogue: HOW MUCH WE HAVE LEFT

441 **"Well, that doesn't make"**: Rachel Paige, " 'She-Hulk': Introducing Marvel Studios' K.E.V.I.N.," Marvel, October 13, 2022, marvel.com/articles/tv-shows/she-hulk-finale-kevin.

442 **"I started reading up"**: Author interview with Kevin Feige, 2017.

442 **"I want to show you something"**: Ibid.

443 **"Maybe not Woodgod"**: Ibid.

Chapter Thirty-Two: IT'S NOT EASY BEING GREEN

465 **"clean plate"**: An industry term for a shot with certain unwanted objects removed—such as wires, stunt men in motion capture suits, or additional actors—so that when CGI is added into the scene (in this case, the Hulk) by visual-effects artists, they are using a shot that matches the rest of the footage captured on set.

465 **"The tone was very important"**: Author interview with Marc Chu, 2020.

465 **"He was a Chippendales dancer"**: Ibid.

466 **"How would you feel"**: Emily Smith, "LI bouncer and male stripper did CGI work as the Hulk in 'The Avengers,'" *New York Post*, May 4, 2012, nypost.com/2012/05/04/li-bouncer-and-male-stripper-did-cgi-work-as-the-hulk-in-the-avengers.

466 **"Green Steve was awesome"**: Author interview with Marc Chu, 2020.

466 **"I had a muscle suit"**: Joe Deckelmeier, "She-Hulk On-Set Reference Malia Arrayah Shares MCU Secrets," *Screen Rant*, October 20, 2022, screenrant.com/she-hulk-finale-interview-malia-arrayah.

INDEX

3D version, 183
VFX, 377, 465–66
visual development, 197, 198

Avengers: Age of Ultron (2015)
  Ant-Man and, 282
  character reclamation and, 389
  characters in, 272–73
  Creative Committee and, 268–69, 275
  locations, 268
  Maisel credits dedication in, 405
  Marvel Studios timeline and, xii
  merchandise and, 257–59
  Mjölnir in, 341
  success of, 276–77
  Thor in, 273, 274, 386
  VFX, 375–76

Avengers: Endgame (2019)
  Boseman in, 321
  CGI in, 341, 371
  character reclamation and, 389–90
  Chinese market and, 213
  final credit sequence, 351, 352–53
  Iron Man cave scene and, 75
  Marvel Studios timeline and, xiii
  Phase Three and, 337
  pre-visualization, 340, 341
  script, 340, 341
  Spider-Man in, 306
  splash-page battle in, 340–41
  success of, 7
  visual development, 198
  See also MCU Phase Three conclusion

Avengers 5 (Avengers: The Kang Dynasty), 423, 434

Avengers: Infinity War (2018)
  Black Panther and, 315–16
  Captain Marvel and, 330
  character deaths in, 339–40

character reclamation and, 389
  Marvel Studios timeline and, xiii
  Phase Three conclusion and, 337
  script, 340, 341
  Spider-Man in, 306, 340
  visual development, 198
  See also MCU Phase Three conclusion

Avengers: Secret Wars, 423

Babe, 100
Baby Groot (character), 249
Back to the Future, 16–17
Bagley, Mark, 92
Baker, Kyle, 412
Bale, Christian, 427–28
Bana, Eric, 97, 101
Band, Charles, 448n
Barham, Amy, 170
Baron Zemo (character), 310
Bassett, Angela, 314, 315, 346, 424
Batman (character), 14, 21, 62, 84–85, 90
Batman (1989), 14
Batman: Year One (comic book), 14
Batman & Robin, 62
Batman Begins, 90
Batman v Superman, Dawn of Justice, 411
Batman vs. Superman, 62
Batroc the Leaper (character), 236
Battle at Lake Changjin, The, 214
Bautista, Dave, 158, 247, 361, 428
Bay, Michael, 78
Beachler, Hannah, 312, 313, 319
Beast (character), 437
Belgrad, Doug, 222
Bendis, Brian Michael, 91, 94, 144, 216, 265, 307, 410, 411
Berman, Debbie, 316–17
Bernthal, Jon, 432
Berry, Halle, 38, 62
Besson, Luc, 99
Bethel, Wilson, 432

Bettany, Paul, 347, 375–76, 378, 406, 408–9, 416
  See also Vision, the/ J.A.R.V.I.S.
Betty Ross (character), 102
Bezucha, Thomas, 430
Bibb, Leslie, 75
Billingsley, Peter, 113
Bird, Brad, 63
Bixby, Bill, 15–16, 96
Black, Jack, 127
Black, Shane, 144, 172, 204–5, 206–8, 209, 211–12
Black Bolt (character), 393
Black Cat/Felicia Hardy (character), 294
Black characters
  Creative Committee and, 270
  Disney Plus and, 412
  Feige's advocacy for, 272
  hip-hop and, 318–19
  Marvel Television and, 224
  merchandise and, 266
  Nate Moore's advocacy for, 232, 311
  Perlmutter's racism and, 126–27
  Ultimate character versions and, 93
  Writer's Program and, 165
  See also specific characters
Black Lives Matter, 224
Black Panther (2018)
  Alonso and, 322
  Boseman's cancer diagnosis and, 314–15
  Captain Marvel and, 330
  casting, 158, 166
  costume design, 319
  Creative Committee and, 270
  creativity and, 7
  dialogue in, 314
  director choice, 311–12
  female characters in, 318
  Kevin-Con announcement of, 272
  locations, 316
  Marvel Studios timeline and, xiii

ABOUT THE AUTHORS

JOANNA ROBINSON is a podcaster and cultural critic for the Ringer appearing on several shows including *The Ringer-Verse*, *Trial By Content*, *The Prestige TV* feed, and more. A senior writer at *Vanity Fair* from 2014 to 2021, she was also the founder and cohost of the independent podcasts *A Storm of Spoilers* and *A Cast of Kings*. Joanna has been profiled in the *San Francisco Chronicle*, *IndieWire*, and *Recode Media* for her work on pop culture. In 2019, Syfy dubbed her the "Queen of *Game of Thrones*" for her exhaustive (and exhausting) coverage of the biggest TV event of the young century. She fell in love with Marvel Comics with *The Unbeatable Squirrel Girl* #1 and has been kicking butts and eating nuts ever since. Robinson enjoys listening to the rhythmic waves of the Pacific Ocean and watching Chris Evans hold onto the landing skid of a helicopter. She can be found on most social media platforms @jowrotethis, and at her own website, jowrotethis.com.

DAVE GONZALES is a writer, producer, and podcast host living in Denver, Colorado. He has written about movies and pop culture for the *New York Times*, the *Guardian*, Forbes.com, TVGuide.com, VanityFair.com, Thrillist.com, Polygon.com, and Geek.com, including a weekly column about Marvel at LatinoReview.com from 2013 to 2017. While attending New York University, he cofounded the independent podcast *Fighting In The War Room*, one of *Time* magazine's top ten podcasts of 2021. After returning to Colorado, Dave expanded his podcast work, hosting *The Storm: A Lost Rewatch Podcast* and *Trial By Content* for The Ringer network. He bought *Spectacular Spider-Man* #226 in 1995 and believes Ben Reilly was the real Peter Parker. He has been an animation producer for the *Teen Mom* franchise on MTV since 2009. He's on Twitter (@da7e) and Instagram (@grumpyda7e).

GAVIN EDWARDS is the *New York Times* best-selling author of thirteen books, ranging from *Kindness and Wonder: Why Mister Rogers Matters Now More Than Ever* to *Bad Motherfucker: The Life and Movies of Samuel L. Jackson, the Coolest Man in Hollywood*, and including *The Beautiful Book of Exquisite Corpses* and *The Tao of Bill Murray: Real-Life Stories of Joy, Enlightenment, and Party Crashing*. He has also written for numerous magazines and newspapers— most frequently, the *New York Times, Rolling Stone*, and *Details*. He is currently working on a book about the card game Magic: The Gathering, titled *Chaos Orb*. The first Marvel comic book he ever read was *X-Men* Annual #4, where the mutants visit Dante's Inferno. Formerly a resident of New York, London, and Los Angeles, he now lives with his family in Charlotte, North Carolina. He can be found online as @mrgavinedwards on Twitter and Instagram, and at his own website, rulefortytwo.com.